Growing Wisdom

AN INVITATION TO WESTERN PHILOSOPHY

Charles E. Cardwell
Pellissippi State Community College

E. Frank Mashburn
Pellissippi State Community College

D0067228

Kendall Hunt
publishing company

Cover image © Shutterstock, Inc.

Kendall Hunt
publishing company

www.kendallhunt.com
Send all inquiries to:
4050 Westmark Drive
Dubuque, IA 52004-1840

Revised Printing 2016

ISBN 978-1-4652-9248-3

Printed in the United States of America

CONTENTS

Philosophy?

1. What is Enlightenment?   3
Kant

2. The Value of Philosophy   9
Russell

3. The Ethics of Belief   15
Clifford

4. Euthyphro   23
Plato

5. Apology   39
Plato

Society and Politics

6. Crito   61
Plato

7. Human Flourishing and The Ideal State   73
Aristotle

8. The State of Nature and Natural Law   79
Hobbes

9. Limits on Government   87
Locke

10. Liberty   99
J.S.Mill

11. Class Struggle   109
Marx

Knowledge and Reality

12. Allegory of the Cave   117
Plato

13. Knowledge is Recollection   123
Plato

14. Meditations I and II   131
       Descartes

15. Ideas in the Understanding   145
       Locke

16. To Be is To Be Perceived   153
       Berkeley

17. Causation   175
       Hume

18. A Copernican Revolution for Knowledge   181
       Kant

God

19. An Ontological Proof of God's Existence   191
       Anselm

20. Demonstrations that God Exists   201
       Aquinas

21. Analogy and the Argument from Design   211
       Hume

22. The Wager   223
       Pascal

23. The Will to Believe   229
       James

24. Why God Allows Evil   249
       Swinburne

Human Nature and Personal Identity

25. The Ring of Gyges   263
       Plato

26. The Madman   269
       Nietzsche

27. Existentialism is a Humanism   273
       Sartre

28. The Myth of Sisyphus   285
       Camus

29. Where Am I?   289
   Dennett

30. Do We Survive Death?   303
   Russell

31. A Defense of Life After Death   307
   Hick

32. Free Will and Determinism   315
   Stace

33. Are we Really Free?   325
   Hospers

PHILOSOPHY?

WHAT IS ENLIGHTENMENT? (1784)

Immanuel Kant

Immanuel Kant (1724–1804), the most influential philosopher of the Enlightenment era, has profoundly influenced contemporary thinking about epistemology (study of knowledge) and ethics. (He also made important contributions to the science of his day.) Kant was born in Königsburg, East Prussia, where he lived his entire life. (East Prussia was an important province in the German Empire. Königsburg is now called Kaliningrad and is the administrative center of Kaliningrad Oblast, the Russian exclave between Poland and Lithuania on the Baltic Sea.) At age 8, Kant enrolled in a Latin Pietist school, where he became interested in the classics. At 16, he entered the University of Königsburg. There he studied mathematics and developed an interest in philosophy. When Kant was 22, financial concerns following the death of his father forced him to leave the University so that he could help support his younger siblings by working as a tutor for three influential families. At 31, Kant returned to the University and received his doctorate, staying on as a lecturer, earning the fees paid by students to attend his classes. At 47, he became a professor and taught metaphysics and logic until the age of 73. At 57, he published his greatest work, the <u>Critique of Pure Reason</u>. Only 5 feet tall, Kant's small physical stature and fragile health contrast sharply with his intellectual legacy. He attributed his longevity to his strict routine of living: up at 5 a.m. for an hour of tea and meditation followed by an hour of preparation for the two hours of lecture that he gave at home, four hours of study, three hours of dining with friends, a one-hour walk followed by reading and writing until bedtime. It was said that the citizens of Königsburg set their watches by Kant's daily walk. Wholly dedicated to his work, Kant never married.

What to look for: Understanding philosophical writing is best done by imagining yourself in a conversation with the author. Ask the author questions and examine his or her answers. In this case, your first question is likely to be that given in the title. Notice how Kant defines <u>enlightenment</u> in terms of <u>immaturity</u>. What is immaturity? (Be sure that you understand these concepts well enough to state them in your own words.) As you

> *read on, other questions naturally arise: Why would anyone self-impose*
> *immaturity? What is necessary and/or sufficient for enlightenment? When*
> *should freedom be restricted? What exactly is the <u>public</u> use of reason?*
> *What is <u>private</u> use? Is enlightenment really desirable? Why (not)?*

Enlightenment is man's emergence from his self-imposed immaturity. Immaturity is the inability to use one's understanding without guidance from another. This immaturity is self-imposed when its cause lies not in lack of understanding, but in lack of resolve and courage to use it without guidance from another. *Sapere Aude*! [Dare to know!] "Have courage to use your own understanding!"–that is the motto of enlightenment.

Laziness and cowardice are the reasons why so great a proportion of men, long after nature has released them from alien guidance…nonetheless gladly remain in lifelong immaturity, and why it is so easy for others to establish themselves as their guardians. It is so easy to be immature. If I have a book to serve as my understanding, a pastor to serve as my conscience, a physician to determine my diet for me, and so on, I need not exert myself at all. I need not think, if only I can pay: others will readily undertake the irksome work for me. The guardians who have so benevolently taken over the supervision of men have carefully seen to it that the far greatest part of them (including the entire fair sex) regard taking the step to maturity as very dangerous, not to mention difficult. Having first made their domestic livestock dumb, and having carefully made sure that these docile creatures will not take a single step without the go-cart to which they are harnessed, these guardians then show them the danger that threatens them, should they attempt to walk alone. Now this danger is not actually so great, for after falling a few times they would in the end certainly learn to walk; but an example of this kind makes men timid and usually frightens them out of all further attempts.

Thus, it is difficult for any individual man to work himself out of the immaturity that has all but become his nature. He has even become fond of this state and for the time being is actually incapable of using his own understanding, for no one has ever allowed him to attempt it. Rules and formulas, those mechanical aids to the rational use, or rather misuse, of his natural gifts, are the shackles of a permanent immaturity. Whoever threw them off would still make only an uncertain leap over the smallest ditch, since he is unaccustomed to this kind of free movement. Consequently, only a few have succeeded, by cultivating their own minds, in freeing themselves from immaturity and pursuing a secure course.

But that the public should enlighten itself is more likely; indeed, if it is only allowed freedom, enlightenment is almost inevitable. For even among the entrenched guardians of the great masses a few will always think for themselves, a few who, after having themselves thrown off the yoke of immaturity, will spread the spirit of a rational appreciation for both their own worth and for each person's calling to think for himself. But it should be particularly noted that if a public that was first placed in this yoke by the guardians is suitably aroused by some of those who are altogether incapable of enlightenment, it may force the guardians themselves to remain under the yoke–so pernicious is it to instill prejudices, for they finally take revenge upon their originators, or on their descendants. Thus a public can only attain enlightenment slowly. Perhaps a revolution can overthrow autocratic despotism and profiteering or power-grabbing oppression, but it can never truly reform a manner of thinking; instead, new prejudices, just like the old ones they replace, will serve as a leash for the great unthinking mass.

Nothing is required for this enlightenment, however, except *freedom*; and the freedom in question is the least harmful of all, namely, the freedom to use reason *publicly* in all matters. But on all sides I hear: "*Do not argue!*" The officer says, "Do not argue, drill!" The tax man says, "Do not argue, pay!" The pastor says, "Do not argue, believe!" (Only one ruler in the World says, "*Argue* as much as you want and about what you want, but obey!") In this we have examples of pervasive restrictions on freedom. But which restriction hinders enlightenment and which does not, but instead actually advances it? I reply: The *public use* of one's reason must always be free, and it alone can bring about enlightenment among mankind; the *private use* of reason may, however, often be very narrowly restricted, without otherwise hindering the progress of enlightenment. By the public use of one's own reason I understand the use that anyone as a *scholar* makes of reason before the entire *literate world*. I call the private use of reason that which a person may make in a *civic post* or office that has been entrusted to him. Now in many affairs conducted in the interests of a community, a certain mechanism is required by means of which some of its members must conduct themselves in an entirely passive manner so that through an artificial unanimity the government may guide them toward public ends, or at least prevent them from destroying such ends. Here one certainly must not argue, instead one must obey. However, insofar as this part of the machine also regards himself as a member of the community as a whole, or even of the world community, and as a consequence addresses the public in the role of a scholar, in the proper sense of that term, he can most certainly argue, without thereby harming the affairs for which as a passive member he is partly responsible. Thus it would be disastrous if an officer on duty who was given a command by his superior were to question the appropriateness or utility of the order. He must obey.

But as a scholar he cannot be justly constrained from making comments about errors in military service, or from placing them before the public for its judgment. The citizen cannot refuse to pay the taxes imposed on him; indeed, impertinent criticism of such levies, when they should be paid by him, can be punished as a scandal (since it can lead to widespread insubordination). But the same person does not act contrary to civic duty when, as a scholar, he publicly expresses his thoughts regarding the impropriety or even injustice of such taxes. Likewise a pastor is bound to instruct his catechumens and congregation in accordance with the symbol of the church he serves, for he was appointed on that condition. But as a scholar he has complete freedom, indeed even the calling, to impart to the public all of his carefully considered and well-intentioned thoughts concerning mistaken aspects of that symbol, as well as his suggestions for the better arrangement of religious and church matters. Nothing in this can weigh on his conscience. What he teaches in consequence of his office as a servant of the church he sets out as something with regard to which he has no discretion to teach in accord with his own lights; rather, he offers it under the direction and in the name of another. He will say, "Our church teaches this or that and these are the demonstrations it uses." He thereby extracts for his congregation all practical uses from precepts to which he would not himself subscribe with complete conviction, but whose presentation he can nonetheless undertake, since it is not entirely impossible that truth lies hidden in them, and, in any case, nothing contrary to the very nature of religion is to be found in them. If he believed he could find anything of the latter sort in them, he could not in good conscience serve in his position; he would have to resign. Thus an appointed teacher's use of his reason for the sake of his congregation is merely *private*, because, however large the congregation is, this use is always only domestic; in this regard, as a priest, he is not free and cannot be such because he is acting under instructions from someone else. By contrast, the cleric–as a scholar who speaks through his writings to the public as such, i.e., the world–enjoys in this of reason an unrestricted freedom to use his own rational capacities and to speak his own mind. For that the (spiritual) guardians of a people should themselves be immature is an absurdity that would insure the perpetuation of absurdities.

But would a society of pastors, perhaps a church assembly or venerable presbytery (as those among the Dutch call themselves), not be justified in binding itself by oath to a certain unalterable symbol in order to secure a constant guardianship over each of its members and through them over the people, and this for all time: I say that this is wholly impossible. Such a contract, whose intention is to preclude forever all further enlightenment of the human race, is absolutely null and void, even if it should be ratified by the supreme power, by parliaments, and by the most solemn peace treaties. One age cannot bind itself, and thus conspire, to place a succeeding one in a condition whereby it would be impossible for the later age to expand its knowledge (particularly where it is so very important), to rid itself of errors, and generally to increase its enlightenment. That would be a crime against human nature, whose essential destiny lies precisely in such progress; subsequent generations are thus completely justified in dismissing such agreements as unauthorized and criminal.

The criterion of everything that can be agreed upon as a law by a people lies in this question: Can a people impose such a law on itself? Now it might be possible, in anticipation of a better state of affairs, to introduce a provisional order for a specific, short time, all the while giving all citizens, especially clergy, in their role as scholars, the freedom to comment publicly, i.e., in writing, on the present institution's shortcomings. The provisional order might last until insight into the nature of these matters had become so widespread and obvious that the combined (if not unanimous) voices of the populace could propose to the crown that it take under its protection those congregations that, in accord with their newly gained insight, had organized themselves under altered religious institutions, but without interfering with those wishing to allow matters to remain as before. However, it is absolutely forbidden that they unite into a religious organization that nobody may for the duration of a man's lifetime publicly question, for so doing would deny, render fruitless, and make detrimental to succeeding generations an era in man's progress toward improvement. A man may put off enlightenment with regard to what he ought to know, though only for a short time and for his own person; but to renounce it for himself, or, even more, for subsequent generations, is to violate and trample man's divine rights underfoot. And what a people may not decree for itself may still less be imposed on it by a monarch, for his lawgiving authority rests on his unification of the people's collective will in his own. If he only sees to it that all genuine or purported improvement is consonant with civil order, he can allow his subjects to do what they find necessary to their spiritual well-being, which is not his affair. However, he must prevent anyone from forcibly interfering with another's working as best he can to determine and promote his well-being. It detracts from his own majesty when he interferes in these matters, since the writings in which his subjects attempt to clarify their insights lend value to his conception of governance. This holds whether he acts from his own highest insight–whereby he calls upon himself the reproach, "*Caesar non est supra grammaticos.*" [Caesar is not above grammarians]—as well as, indeed even more, when he despoils his highest authority by supporting the spiritual despotism of some tyrants in his state over his other subjects.

If it is now asked, "Do we presently live in an *enlightened* age?" the answer is, "No, but we do live in an age of *enlightenment*." As matters now stand, a great deal is still lacking in order for men as a whole to be, or even to put themselves into a position to be able without external guidance to apply understanding confidently to religious issues. But we do have clear indications that the way is now being opened for men to proceed freely in this direction and that the obstacles to general enlightenment–to their release from their self-imposed immaturity–are gradually diminishing. In this regard, this age is the age of enlightenment, the century of Frederick.

A prince who does not find it beneath him to say that he takes it to be his *duty* to prescribe nothing, but rather to allow men complete freedom in religious matters–who thereby renounces the arrogant title of *tolerance*–is himself enlightened and deserves to be praised by a grateful present and by posterity as the first, at least where the government is concerned, to release the human race from immaturity and to leave everyone free to use his own reason in all matters of conscience. Under his rule, venerable pastors, in their role as scholars and without prejudice to their official duties, may freely and openly set out for the world's scrutiny their judgments and views, even where these occasionally differ from the accepted symbol. Still greater freedom is afforded to those who are not restricted by an official post. This spirit of freedom is expanding even where it must struggle against the external obstacles of governments that misunderstand their own function. Such governments are illuminated by the example that the existence of freedom need not give cause for the least concern regarding public order and harmony in the commonwealth. If only they refrain from inventing artifices to keep themselves in it, men will gradually raise themselves from barbarism.

I have focused on religious matters in setting out my main point concerning enlightenment, i.e., man's emergence from self-imposed immaturity, first because our rulers have no interest in assuming the role of their subjects' guardians with respect to the arts and sciences, and secondly because that form of immaturity is both the most pernicious and disgraceful of all. But the manner of thinking of a head of state who favors religious enlightenment goes even further, for he realizes that there is no danger to his *legislation* in allowing his subjects to use reason *publicly* and to set before the world their thoughts concerning better formulations of his laws, even if this involves frank criticism of legislation currently in effect. We have before us a shining example, with respect to which no monarch surpasses the one whom we honor.

But only a ruler who is himself enlightened and has no dread of shadows, yet who likewise has a well-disciplined, numerous army to guarantee public peace, can say what no republic may dare, namely: "*Argue as much as you want and about what you want, but obey!*" Here as elsewhere, when things are considered in broad perspective, a strange, unexpected pattern in human affairs reveals itself, one in which almost everything is paradoxical. A greater degree of civil freedom seems advantageous to a people's *spiritual* freedom; yet the former established impassable boundaries for the latter; conversely, a lesser degree of civil freedom provides enough room for all fully to expand their abilities. Thus, once nature has removed the hard shell from this kernel for which she has most fondly cared, namely, the inclination to and vocation for free *thinking*, the kernel gradually reacts on a people's mentality (whereby they become increasingly able to *act freely*), and it finally even influences the principles of *government*, which finds that it can profit by treating men, *who are now more than machines*, in accord with their dignity.

Konigsberg in Prussia, 30 September 1784
I. Kant

THE VALUE OF PHILOSOPHY (1912)

Bertrand Russell

Bertrand Russell (1872–1970) ranks high among the most important philosophers of the twentieth century. Grandson of a Prime Minister (Lord John Russell), godson of John Stuart Mill, Russell was orphaned at age 4 and subsequently reared by his grandmother. At Trinity College, Cambridge, he excelled in his studies of mathematics and the moral sciences. In 1902 (at age 30), he discovered the paradox that showed serious problems with the foundations of set theory and which now bears his name: Some sets are elements of themselves (the set of all sets is itself a set); others are not (the set of all donkeys is not itself a donkey). Is the set of all sets that are not elements of themselves an element of itself? If it is, it isn't; but if it isn't, it is! This paradox set Russell onto his most important philosophical work, beginning with <u>Principles of Mathematics</u> (1903), in which he argued that mathematics could be derived from logic. In 1908, he was elected to the Royal Academy. From 1907 through 1910, he collaborated with Alfred North Whitehead (1861–1947) to develop this idea. The resulting three-volume <u>Principia Mathematica</u> (1910–1913) revolutionized the study of logic. During these years, Russell also grounded his life as a pro-suffrage, antiwar, political activist. His political views cost him academic appointments (both in the UK and in the USA) and twice landed him in jail. He knew or worked with many prominent contemporaries in philosophy, mathematics, science, literature, and politics. He wrote more than 70 books, authored thousands of essays, and received the Nobel Prize for Literature (1950). Russell married four times and had three children. He remained active as a social and political gadfly until his death.

What to look for: *Consider how Russell addresses some basic questions: Who benefits from the study of science? Who benefits from the study of philosophy? Is the idea that philosophy does not provide answers completely correct? If the benefit of philosophy is not found in answers, where is it found? What is the not-Self? How does philosophy change the Self? What is the highest good?*

Having now come to the end of our brief and very incomplete review of the problems of philosophy, it will be well to consider, in conclusion, what is the value of philosophy and why it ought to be studied. It is the more necessary to consider this question, in view of the fact that many men, under the influence of science or of practical affairs, are inclined to doubt whether philosophy is anything better than innocent but useless trifling, hair-splitting distinctions, and controversies on matters concerning which knowledge is impossible.

This view of philosophy appears to result, partly from a wrong conception of the ends of life, partly from a wrong conception of the kind of goods which philosophy strives to [238] achieve. Physical science, through the medium of inventions, is useful to innumerable people who are wholly ignorant of it; thus the study of physical science is to be recommended, not only, or primarily, because of the effect on the student, but rather because of the effect on mankind in general. This utility does not belong to philosophy. If the study of philosophy has any value at all for others than students of philosophy, it must be only indirectly, through its effects upon the lives of those who study it. It is in these effects, therefore, if anywhere, that the value of philosophy must be primarily sought.

But further, if we are not to fail in our endeavour to determine the value of philosophy, we must first free our minds from the prejudices of what are wrongly called "practical" men. The "practical" man, as this word is often used, is one who recognizes only material needs, who realizes that men must have food for the body, but is oblivious of the necessity of providing food for the mind. If all men were well off, if poverty and disease had been reduced to their lowest possible point, there [239] would still remain much to be done to produce a valuable society; and even in the existing world the goods of the mind are at least as important as the goods of the body. It is exclusively among the goods of the mind that the value of philosophy is to be found; and only those who are not indifferent to these goods can be persuaded that the study of philosophy is not a waste of time.

Philosophy, like all other studies, aims primarily at knowledge. The knowledge it aims at is the kind of knowledge which gives unity and system to the body of the sciences, and the kind which results from a critical examination of the grounds of our convictions, prejudices, and beliefs. But it cannot be maintained that philosophy has had any very great measure of success in its attempts to provide definite answers to its questions. If you ask a mathematician, a mineralogist, a historian, or any other man of learning, what definite body of truths has been ascertained by his science, his answer will last as long as you are willing to listen. But if you put the same question to a philosopher, he will, if he is [240] candid, have to confess that his study has not achieved

"The Value of Philosophy," by Bertrand Russell, from *The Problems of Philosophy*. (New York: Henry Holt and Company, 1912), *Home University Library of Modern Knowledge*, ser. 35.

positive results such as have been achieved by other sciences. It is true that this is partly accounted for by the fact that, as soon as definite knowledge concerning any subject becomes possible, this subject ceases to be called philosophy, and becomes a separate science. The whole study of the heavens, which now belongs to astronomy, was once included in philosophy; Newton's great work was called "the mathematical principles of natural philosophy." Similarly, the study of the human mind, which was, until very lately, a part of philosophy, has now been separated from philosophy and has become the science of psychology. Thus, to a great extent, the uncertainty of philosophy is more apparent than real: those questions which are already capable of definite answers are placed in the sciences, while those only to which, at present, no definite answer can be given, remain to form the residue which is called philosophy.

This is, however, only a part of the truth concerning the uncertainty of philosophy. There are many questions—and among them [241] those that are of the profoundest interest to our spiritual life—which, so far as we can see, must remain insoluble to the human intellect unless its powers become of quite a different order from what they are now. Has the universe any unity of plan or purpose, or is it a fortuitous concourse of atoms? Is consciousness a permanent part of the universe, giving hope of indefinite growth in wisdom, or is it a transitory accident on a small planet on which life must ultimately become impossible? Are good and evil of importance to the universe or only to man? Such questions are asked by philosophy, and variously answered by various philosophers. But it would seem that, whether answers be otherwise discoverable or not, the answers suggested by philosophy are none of them demonstrably true. Yet, however slight may be the hope of discovering an answer, it is part of the business of philosophy to continue the consideration of such questions, to make us aware of their importance, to examine all the approaches to them, and to keep alive that speculative interest in the universe which is [242] apt to be killed by confining ourselves to definitely ascertainable knowledge.

Many philosophers, it is true, have held that philosophy could establish the truth of certain answers to such fundamental questions. They have supposed that what is of most importance in religious beliefs could be proved by strict demonstration to be true. In order to judge of such attempts, it is necessary to take a survey of human knowledge, and to form an opinion as to its methods and its limitations. On such a subject it would be unwise to pronounce dogmatically; but if the investigations of our previous chapters have not led us astray, we shall be compelled to renounce the hope of finding philosophical proofs of religious beliefs. We cannot, therefore, include as part of the value of philosophy any definite set of answers to such questions. Hence, once more, the value of philosophy must not depend upon any supposed body of definitely ascertainable knowledge to be acquired by those who study it.

The value of philosophy is, in fact, to be sought largely in its very uncertainty. The [243] man who has no tincture of philosophy goes through life imprisoned in the prejudices derived from common sense, from the habitual beliefs of his age or his nation, and from convictions which have grown up in his mind without the co-operation or consent of his deliberate reason. To such a man the world tends to become definite, finite, obvious; common objects rouse no questions, and unfamiliar possibilities are contemptuously rejected. As soon as we begin to philosophize, on the contrary, we find, as we saw in our opening chapters, that even the most everyday things lead to problems to which only very incomplete answers can be given. Philosophy, though unable to tell us with certainty what is the true answer to the doubts which it raises, is able to suggest many possibilities which enlarge our thoughts and free them from the tyranny of custom. Thus, while diminishing our feeling of certainty as to what things are, it greatly increases our knowledge as to what they may be; it removes the somewhat arrogant dogmatism of those who have never travelled into the region of liberating [244] doubt, and it keeps alive our sense of wonder by showing familiar things in an unfamiliar aspect.

Apart from its utility in showing unsuspected possibilities, philosophy has a value— perhaps its chief value—through the greatness of the objects which it contemplates, and the freedom from narrow and personal aims resulting from this contemplation. The life of the instinctive man is shut up within the circle of his private interests: family and friends may be included, but the outer world is not regarded except as it may help or hinder what comes within the circle of instinctive wishes. In such a life there is something feverish and confined, in comparison with which the philosophic life is calm and free. The private world of instinctive interests is a small one, set in the midst of a great and powerful world which must, sooner or later, lay our private world in ruins. Unless we can so enlarge our interests as to include the whole outer world, we remain like a garrison in a beleaguered fortress, knowing that the enemy prevents escape and that ultimate surrender [245] is inevitable. In such a life there is no peace, but a constant strife between the insistence of desire and the powerlessness of will. In one way or another, if our life is to be great and free, we must escape this prison and this strife.

One way of escape is by philosophic contemplation. Philosophic contemplation does not, in its widest survey, divide the universe into two hostile camps—friends and foes, helpful and hostile, good and bad—it views the whole impartially. Philosophic contemplation, when it is unalloyed, does not aim at proving that the rest of the universe is akin to man. All acquisition of knowledge is an enlargement of the Self, but this enlargement is best attained when it is not directly sought. It is obtained when the desire for knowledge is alone operative, by a study which does not wish in advance that its objects should have this or that character, but adapts the Self to the characters which it finds in its objects. This enlargement of Self is not obtained when, taking the Self as it is, we try to show that the world is so similar [246] to this Self that knowledge of it is possible without any admission of what seems alien. The desire to prove this is a form of self-assertion, and like all self-assertion, it is an obstacle to the growth of Self which it desires, and of which the Self knows that it is capable. Self-assertion, in philosophic speculation as elsewhere, views the world as a means to its own ends; thus it makes the world of less account than Self, and the Self sets bounds to the greatness of its goods. In contemplation, on the contrary, we start from the not-Self, and through its greatness the boundaries of Self are enlarged; through the infinity of the universe the mind which contemplates it achieves some share in infinity.

For this reason greatness of soul is not fostered by those philosophies which assimilate the universe to Man. Knowledge is a form of union of Self and not-Self; like all union, it is impaired by dominion, and therefore by any attempt to force the universe into conformity with what we find in ourselves. There is a widespread philosophical tendency towards the view which tells [247] us that man is the measure of all things, that truth is man-made, that space and time and the world of universals are properties of the mind, and that, if there be anything not created by the mind, it is unknowable and of no account for us. This view, if our previous discussions were correct, is untrue; but in addition to being untrue, it has the effect of robbing philosophic contemplation of all that gives it value, since it fetters contemplation to Self. What it calls knowledge is not a union with the not-Self, but a set of prejudices, habits, and desires, making an impenetrable veil between us and the world beyond. The man who finds pleasure in such a theory of knowledge is like the man who never leaves the domestic circle for fear his word might not be law.

The true philosophic contemplation, on the contrary, finds its satisfaction in every enlargement of the not-Self, in everything that magnifies the objects contemplated, and thereby the subject contemplating. Everything, in contemplation, that is personal or private, everything that depends upon habit, [248] self-interest, or desire, distorts the object, and hence impairs the union which the intellect seeks. By thus making a barrier between subject and object, such personal and private things become a prison to the intellect. The free intellect will see as God might see, without a here and now, without hopes and fears, without the trammels of customary beliefs and traditional prejudices, calmly, dispassionately, in the sole and exclusive desire of knowledge—knowledge as impersonal, as purely contemplative, as it is possible for man to attain. Hence also the free intellect will value more the abstract and universal knowledge into which the accidents of private history do not enter, than the knowledge brought by the senses, and dependent, as such knowledge must be, upon an exclusive and personal point of view and a body whose sense-organs distort as much as they reveal.

The mind which has become accustomed to the freedom and impartiality of philosophic contemplation will preserve something of the same freedom and impartiality in the world of action and emotion. It will view its purposes [249] and desires as parts of the whole, with the absence of insistence that results from seeing them as infinitesimal fragments in a world of which all

the rest is unaffected by any one man's deeds. The impartiality which, in contemplation, is the unalloyed desire for truth, is the very same quality of mind
which, in action, is justice, and in emotion is that universal love which can
be given to all, and not only to those who are judged useful or admirable.
Thus contemplation enlarges not only the objects of our thoughts, but also the
objects of our actions and our affections: it makes us citizens of the universe,
not only of one walled city at war with all the rest. In this citizenship of the
universe consists man's true freedom, and his liberation from the thraldom of
narrow hopes and fears.

Thus, to sum up our discussion of the value of philosophy: Philosophy is
to be studied, not for the sake of any definite answers to its questions, since no
definite answers can, as a rule, be known to be true, but rather for the sake of
the questions themselves; because these questions enlarge our conception of
what [250] is possible, enrich our intellectual imagination, and diminish the
dogmatic assurance which closes the mind against speculation; but above all
because, through the greatness of the universe which philosophy contemplates,
the mind also is rendered great, and becomes capable of that union with the
universe which constitutes its highest good.

THE ETHICS OF BELIEF (1877)

William Kingdon Clifford

William Kingdon Clifford (1845–1879) has left a mark both as mathematician and as philosopher. At age 15, he entered King's College, London, where he excelled in mathematics, classics, English literature, and gymnastics. At 18, he began studies at Trinity College, Cambridge, where, at 23, he was elected to a fellowship. After surviving a shipwreck off the coast of Sicily during an expedition to gather data from an eclipse, Clifford was (at 26) appointed chair of Mathematics and Mechanics at University College London. At 29, he was elected a fellow of the Royal Society. Known for fulfilling his teaching and administrative duties in the day and then working all night on research, at 31, Clifford suffered physical collapse. He never fully recovered and died (of tuberculosis) three years later. Most of his work was published posthumously. As a mathematician, Clifford is remembered for his work in topology and non-Euclidean geometries. He foreshadowed Einstein's general relativity in suggesting that matter and energy are different types of curvature of space. As a philosopher, Clifford coined the term "mind stuff" (denoting the simple elements of which consciousness is composed) and "the tribal self." He contended that conscience and moral law arise with the development of a "self" that prescribes conduct that is conducive to the welfare of the "tribe."

*What to look for: Good philosophical writing presents (1) a clear thesis, (2) a solid defense of the thesis, supported by clear reasoning, (3) an acknowledgement of possible objections to the thesis, and (4) a response to any objections. Look for all of these in this selection. Clifford's thesis is easy to spot: he restates it in italics several times. His support of the thesis turns on a pair of thought experiments. Thought experiments are often used in philosophy as a way of pointing out something that may not have been noticed, but is evident once it is pointed out. It is for the reader to decide whether the examples make the case. Clifford recognizes that some may agree that something is wrong in the cases, but say that the problem is not what Clifford says it is. What do they think is the problem? What is Clifford's response? Clifford wraps up his paper by going beyond the minimum of arguing for his position; he also attempts to explain **why***

15

it is true, using a comparison between a certain sort of believing and thievery. How well does this comparison explain the truth of Clifford's thesis? Finally, Clifford considers a different sort of objection—what is it?—and responds.

I. THE DUTY OF INQUIRY

A shipowner was about to send to sea an emigrant-ship. He knew that she was old, and not over-well built at the first; that she had seen many seas and climes, and often had needed repairs. Doubts had been suggested to him that possibly she was not seaworthy. These doubts preyed upon his mind, and made him unhappy; he thought that perhaps he ought to have her thoroughly overhauled and refitted, even though this should put him at great expense. Before the ship sailed, however, he succeeded in overcoming these melancholy reflections. He said to himself that she had gone safely through so many voyages and weathered so many storms that it was idle to suppose she would not come safely home from this trip also. He would put his trust in Providence, which could hardly fail to protect all these unhappy families that were leaving their fatherland to seek for better times elsewhere. He would dismiss from his mind all ungenerous suspicions about the honesty of builders and contractors. In such ways he acquired a sincere and comfortable conviction that his vessel was thoroughly safe and seaworthy; he watched her departure with a light heart, and benevolent wishes for the success of the exiles in their strange new home that was to be; and he got his insurance-money when she went down in mid-ocean and told no tales.

What shall we say of him? Surely this, that he was verily guilty of the death of those men. It is admitted that he did sincerely believe in the soundness of his ship; but the sincerity [290] of his conviction can in no wise help him, because *he had no right to believe on such evidence as was before him.* He had acquired his belief not by honestly earning it in patient investigation, but by stifling his doubts. And although in the end he may have felt so sure about it that he could not think otherwise, yet inasmuch as he had knowingly and willingly worked himself into that frame of mind, he must be held responsible for it.

Let us alter the case a little, and suppose that the ship was not unsound after all; that she made her voyage safely, and many others after it. Will that diminish the guilt of her owner? Not one jot. When an action is once done, it is right or wrong for ever; no accidental failure of its good or evil fruits can possibly alter that. The man would not have been innocent, he would only have been not found out. The question of right or wrong has to do with the origin of

"The Ethics of Belief," by William Kingdon Clifford, from *Contemporary Review*, 29 (Dec. 1876 – May 1877). (Reprinted in Clifford, William K. *Lectures and Essays*. Ed. Leslie Stephen and Frederick Pollock. London: Macmillan and Co., 1886.)

his belief, not the matter of it; not what it was, but how he got it; not whether it turned out to be true or false, but whether he had a right to believe on such evidence as was before him.

There was once an island in which some of the inhabitants professed a religion teaching neither the doctrine of original sin nor that of eternal punishment. A suspicion got abroad that the professors of this religion had made use of unfair means to get their doctrines taught to children. They were accused of wresting the laws of their country in such a way as to remove children from the care of their natural and legal guardians; and even of stealing them away and keeping them concealed from their friends and relations. A certain number of men formed themselves into a society for the purpose of agitating the public about this matter. They published grave accusations against individual citizens of the highest position and character, and did all in their power to injure these citizens in their exercise of their professions. So great was the noise they made, that a Commission was appointed to investigate the facts; but after the Commission had carefully inquired into all the evidence that could be got, it appeared that the accused were innocent. Not only had they been accused on insufficient evidence, but the evidence of their innocence was such as the agitators might easily have obtained, if they had attempted a fair inquiry. After these disclosures the inhabitants of that country looked upon the members of the agitating society, not only as persons whose judgment was to be distrusted, but also as no longer to be counted honourable men. For although they had sincerely and conscientiously believed in the charges they had made, *yet they had no right to believe on such evidence as was before them.* Their sincere convictions, instead of being honestly earned by patient inquiring, were stolen by listening to the voice of prejudice and passion. [291]

Let us vary this case also, and suppose, other things remaining as before, that a still more accurate investigation proved the accused to have been really guilty. Would this make any difference in the guilt of the accusers? Clearly not; the question is not whether their belief was true or false, but whether they entertained it on wrong grounds. They would no doubt say, "Now you see that we were right after all; next time perhaps you will believe us." And they might be believed, but they would not thereby become honourable men. They would not be innocent, they would only be not found out. Every one of them, if he chose to examine himself *in foro conscientiae*, would know that he had acquired and nourished a belief, when he had no right to believe on such evidence as was before him; and therein he would know that he had done a wrong thing.

It may be said, however, that in both these supposed cases it is not the belief which is judged to be wrong, but the action following upon it. The shipowner might say, "I am perfectly certain that my ship is sound, but still I feel it my duty to have her examined, before trusting the lives of so many people to her." And it might be said to the agitator, "However convinced you were of the justice of your cause and the truth of your convictions, you ought not to have made a public attack upon any man's character until you had examined the evidence on both sides with the utmost patience and care."

In the first place, let us admit that, so far as it goes, this view of the case is right and necessary; right, because even when a man's belief is so fixed that he cannot think otherwise, he still has a choice in the action suggested by it, and so cannot escape the duty of investigating on the ground of the strength of his convictions; and necessary, because those who are not yet capable of controlling their feelings and thoughts must have a plain rule dealing with overt acts."

But this being premised as necessary, it becomes clear that it is not sufficient, and that our previous judgment is required to supplement it. For it is not possible so to sever the belief from the action it suggests as to condemn the one without condemning the other. No man holding a strong belief on one side of a question, or even wishing to hold a belief on one side, can investigate it with such fairness and completeness as if he were really in doubt and unbiased; so that the existence of a belief not founded on fair inquiry unfits a man for the performance of this necessary duty.

Nor is it that truly a belief at all which has not some influence upon the actions of him who holds it. He who truly believes that which prompts him to an action has looked upon the action to lust after it, he has committed it already in his heart. If a belief is not [292] realized immediately in open deeds, it is stored up for the guidance of the future. It goes to make a part of that aggregate of beliefs which is the link between sensation and action at every moment of all our lives, and which is so organized and compacted together that no part of it can be isolated from the rest, but every new addition modifies the structure of the whole. No real belief, however trifling and fragmentary it may seem, is ever truly insignificant; it prepares us to receive more of its like, confirms those which resembled it before, and weakens others; and so gradually it lays a stealthy train in our inmost thoughts, which may someday explode into overt action, and leave its stamp upon our character for ever.

And no one man's belief is in any case a private matter which concerns himself alone. Our lives are guided by that general conception of the course of things which has been created by society for social purposes. Our words, our phrases, our forms and processes and modes of thought, are common property, fashioned and perfected from age to age; an heirloom which every succeeding generation inherits as a precious deposit and a sacred trust to be handled on to the next one, not unchanged but enlarged and purified, with some clear marks of its proper handiwork. Into this, for good or ill, is woven every belief of every man who has speech of his fellows. A awful privilege, and an awful responsibility, that we should help to create the world in which posterity will live.

In the two supposed cases which have been considered, it has been judged wrong to believe on insufficient evidence, or to nourish belief by suppressing doubts and avoiding investigation. The reason of this judgment is not far to seek: it is that in both these cases the belief held by one man was of great importance to other men. But forasmuch as no belief held by one man, however seemingly trivial the belief, and however obscure the believer, is ever actually insignificant or without its effect on the fate of mankind, we have no choice but to extend our judgment to all cases of belief whatever. Belief, that sacred faculty which prompts the decisions of our will, and knits into harmonious working all the compacted energies of our being, is ours not for ourselves but for humanity. It is rightly used on truths which have been established by long experience and waiting toil, and which have stood in the fierce light of free and fearless questioning. Then it helps to bind men together, and to strengthen and direct their common action. It is desecrated when given to unproved and unquestioned statements, for the solace and private pleasure of the believer; to add a tinsel splendour to the plain straight road of our life and display a bright mirage beyond it; or even to drown the common sorrows of our kind by a self-deception which [293] allows them not only to cast down, but also to degrade us. Whoso would deserve well of his fellows in this matter will guard the purity of his beliefs with a very fanaticism of jealous care, lest at any time it should rest on an unworthy object, and catch a stain which can never be wiped away.

It is not only the leader of men, statesmen, philosopher, or poet, that owes this bounden duty to mankind. Every rustic who delivers in the village alehouse his slow, infrequent sentences, may help to kill or keep alive the fatal superstitions which clog his race. Every hard-worked wife of an artisan may transmit to her children beliefs which shall knit society together, or rend it in pieces. No simplicity of mind, no obscurity of station, can escape the universal duty of questioning all that we believe.

It is true that this duty is a hard one, and the doubt which comes out of it is often a very bitter thing. It leaves us bare and powerless where we thought that we were safe and strong. To know all about anything is to know how to deal with it under all circumstances. We feel much happier and more secure when we think we know precisely what to do, no matter what happens, then when we have lost our way and do not know where to turn. And if we have supposed ourselves to know all about anything, and to be capable of doing what is fit in regard to it, we naturally do not like to find that we are really ignorant and powerless, that we have to begin again at the beginning, and try to learn what the thing is and how it is to be dealt with—if indeed anything can be learnt about it. It is the sense of power attached to a sense of knowledge that makes men desirous of believing, and afraid of doubting.

This sense of power is the highest and best of pleasures when the belief on which it is founded is a true belief, and has been fairly earned by investigation. For then we may justly feel that it is common property, and hold good for others as well as for ourselves. Then we may be glad, not that *I* have learned secrets by which I am safer and stronger, but that *we men* have got mastery over more of the world; and we shall be strong, not for ourselves but in the

name of Man and his strength. But if the belief has been accepted on insufficient evidence, the pleasure is a stolen one. Not only does it deceive ourselves
by giving us a sense of power which we do not really possess, but it is sinful,
because it is stolen in defiance of our duty to mankind. That duty is to guard
ourselves from such beliefs as from pestilence, which may shortly master our
own body and then spread to the rest of the town. What would be thought of
one who, for the sake of a sweet fruit, should deliberately run the risk of deliv-
ering a plague upon his family and his neighbours?

And, as in other such cases, it is not the risk only which has to be [294]
considered; for a bad action is always bad at the time when it is done, no matter what happens afterwards. Every time we let ourselves believe for unworthy
reasons, we weaken our powers of self-control, of doubting, of judicially and
fairly weighing evidence. We all suffer severely enough from the maintenance
and support of false beliefs and the fatally wrong actions which they lead to,
and the evil born when one such belief is entertained is great and wide. But
a greater and wider evil arises when the credulous character is maintained
and supported, when a habit of believing for unworthy reasons is fostered and
made permanent. If I steal money from any person, there may be no harm
done from the mere transfer of possession; he may not feel the loss, or it may
prevent him from using the money badly. But I cannot help doing this great
wrong towards Man, that I make myself dishonest. What hurts society is not
that it should lose its property, but that it should become a den of thieves, for
then it must cease to be society. This is why we ought not to do evil, that good
may come; for at any rate this great evil has come, that we have done evil and
are made wicked thereby. In like manner, if I let myself believe anything on
insufficient evidence, there may be no great harm done by the mere belief; it
may be true after all, or I may never have occasion to exhibit it in outward acts.
But I cannot help doing this great wrong towards Man, that I make myself
credulous. The danger to society is not merely that it should believe wrong
things, though that is great enough; but that it should become credulous, and
lose the habit of testing things and inquiring into them; for then it must sink
back into savagery.

The harm which is done by credulity in a man is not confined to the foster-
ing of a credulous character in others, and consequent support of false beliefs.
Habitual want of care about what I believe leads to habitual want of care in
others about the truth of what is told to me. Men speak the truth of one another
when each reveres the truth in his own mind and in the other's mind; but how
shall my friend revere the truth in my mind when I myself am careless about
it, when I believe thing because I want to believe them, and because they are
comforting and pleasant? Will he not learn to cry, "Peace," to me, when there
is no peace? By such a course I shall surround myself with a thick atmosphere
of falsehood and fraud, and in that I must live. It may matter little to me, in
my cloud-castle of sweet illusions and darling lies; but it matters much to Man

that I have made my neighbours ready to deceive. The credulous man is father to the liar and the cheat; he lives in the bosom of this his family, and it is no marvel if he should become even as they are. So closely are our duties knit together, that whoso shall keep the whole law, and yet offend in one point, he is guilty of all. [295]

To sum up: it is wrong always, everywhere, and for anyone, to believe anything upon insufficient evidence.

If a man, holding a belief which he was taught in childhood or persuaded of afterwards, keeps down and pushes away any doubts which arise about it in his mind, purposely avoids the reading of books and the company of men that call into question or discuss it, and regards as impious those questions which cannot easily be asked without disturbing it—the life of that man is one long sin against mankind.

If this judgment seems harsh when applied to those simple souls who have never known better, who have been brought up from the cradle with a horror of doubt, and taught that their eternal welfare depends on *what* they believe, then it leads to the very serious question, *Who hath made Israel to sin?*

It may be permitted me to fortify this judgment with the sentence of Milton—

"A man may be a heretic in the truth; and if he believe things only because his pastor says so, or the assembly so determine, without knowing other reason, though his belief be true, yet the very truth he holds becomes his heresy." [Areopagitica]

And with this famous aphorism of Coleridge—

"He who begins by loving Christianity better than Truth, will proceed by loving his own sect or Church better than Christianity, and end loving himself better than all." [Aids to Reflection]

Inquiry into the evidence of a doctrine is not to be made once for all, and then taken as finally settled. It is never lawful to stifle a doubt; for either it can be honestly answered by means of the inquiry already made, or else it proves that the inquiry was not complete.

"But," says one, "I am a busy man; I have no time for the long course of study which would be necessary to make me in any degree a competent judge of certain questions, or even able to understand the nature of the arguments."

Then he should have no time to believe.

EUTHYPHRO (399–380? BC)

Plato

Plato (428?–348? BC) is so highly regarded as to inspire A.N. White-head to write that the Western philosophical tradition "consists of a series of footnotes to Plato" (Process and Reality, 1929). Surprisingly, little is known about Plato's life. He was born into Athenian aristoc-racy. His father's ancestry traced to the last Kings of Athens; his mother descended from the family of Solon. "Plato" (meaning "broad shoul-ders") is a nickname—his given name was Aristocles. His early educa-tion was appropriate to his social class. From age 20 to 28 (the time Socrates was executed), Plato was part of the Socratic circle. At 41, he founded the Academy, where (except for two largely unsuccessful efforts in Sicily to educate and advise Dionysius the Younger) he taught until his death at age 80. More than twenty five of Plato's works have survived. Most are dialogues notable for their literary as well as philosophical quality. His early writings are thought to give us a realistic, though ideal-ized, picture of Socrates' character, thought, and method. Plato's middle and later works develop his own views.

What to look for: Socrates' (469–399 BC) father was an Athenian stone cutter; his mother was a midwife. He learned his father's trade but devoted his life to a sort of "midwifery," engaging in discussion with per-sons he chanced to meet in public places and thereby assisted in "birth-ing" his interlocutor's ideas. This led to his being charged with impiety and corrupting the youth. At the entrance to the chief magistrate's office, Socrates encounters Euthyphro and enters into conversation. That dis-cussion gives us a nice picture of Socrates at work as he seeks to extract a clear notion of piety from Euthyphro. Follow carefully Socrates' reason-ing as he examines and evaluates Euthyphro's proposals.

"Euthyphro," by Plato, from *The Dialogues of Plato: Translated into English with Analyses and Introductions.* Trans. B. Jowett. 3rd ed. Vol. 2. (Oxford: Oxford University Press, 1892).

PERSONS OF THE DIALOGUE: Socrates, Euthyphro.
SCENE: The Porch of the King Archon [Chief Magistrate]

Euthyphro: [2]¹ Why have you left the Lyceum, Socrates? and what are you
              doing in the Porch of the King Archon? Surely you cannot be
              concerned in a suit before the King, like myself?
Socrates: Not in a suit, Euthyphro; impeachment is the word which the
              Athenians use.
E: What! I suppose that some one has been prosecuting you, for I cannot
      believe that you are the prosecutor of another.
S: Certainly not.
E: Then some one else has been prosecuting you?
S: Yes.
E: And who is he?
S: A young man who is little known, Euthyphro; and I hardly know him:
      his name is Meletus, and he is of the deme of Pitthis. Perhaps you may
      remember his appearance; he has a beak, and long straight hair, and a
      beard which is ill grown.
E: No, I do not remember him, Socrates. But what is the charge which he
      brings against you?
S: What is the charge? Well, a very serious charge, which shows a good deal
      of character in the young man, and for which he is certainly not to be
      despised. He says he knows how the youth are corrupted and who are
      their corruptors. I fancy that he must be a wise man, and seeing that I am
      the reverse of a wise man, he has found me out, and is going to accuse me
      of corrupting his young friends. And of this our mother the state is to be
      the judge. Of all our political men he is the only one who seems to me to
      begin in the right way, with the cultivation of virtue in youth; like a good
      husbandman, he makes the young [3] care, and clears away us who are the
      destroyers of them. This is only the first step; he will afterwards attend to
      the elder branches; and if he goes on as he has begun, he will be a very
      great public benefactor.
E: I hope that he may; but I rather fear, Socrates, that the opposite will turn
      out to be the truth. My opinion is that in attacking you he is simply aiming
      a blow at the foundation of the state. But in what way does he say that you
      corrupt the young?

---

¹ Plato's works are normally referenced to the pages in a three-volume edition of his works published in Geneva in 1578 by Henri Estienne ["Stephanus."] (1528–1598). A full reference cites
the work title (plus the book number for *Republic* and *Laws*) and the Stephanus page number
(plus a letter – "a" through "e" – indicating in which fifth of the page the first word of the quotation appears). Here, bracketed numbers indicate the Stephanus page.

S: He brings a wonderful accusation against me, which at first hearing excites surprise: he says that I am a poet or maker of gods, and that I invent new gods and deny the existence of old ones; this is the ground of his indictment.

E: I understand, Socrates; he means to attack you about the familiar sign which occasionally, as you say, comes to you. He thinks that you are a neologian, and he is going to have you up before the court for this. He knows that such a charge is readily received by the world, as I myself know too well; for when I speak in the assembly about divine things, and foretell the future to them, they laugh at me and think me a madman. Yet every word that I say is true. But they are jealous of us all; and we must be brave and go at them.

S: Their laughter, friend Euthyphro, is not a matter of much consequence. For a man may be thought wise; but the Athenians, I suspect, do not much trouble themselves about him until he begins to impart his wisdom to others; and then for some reason or other, perhaps, as you say, from jealousy, they are angry.

E: I am never likely to try their temper in this way.

S: I dare say not, for you are reserved in your behaviour, and seldom impart your wisdom. But I have a benevolent habit of pouring out myself to everybody, and would even pay for a listener, and I am afraid that the Athenians may think me too talkative. Now if, as I was saying, they would only laugh at me, as you say that they laugh at you, the time might pass gaily enough in the court; but perhaps they may be in earnest, and then what the end will be you soothsayers only can predict.

E: I dare say that the affair will end in nothing, Socrates, and that you will win your cause; and I think that I shall win my own.

S: And what is your suit, Euthyphro? are you the pursuer or the defendant?

E: I am the pursuer.

S: Of whom? [4]

E: You will think me mad when I tell you.

S: Why, has the fugitive wings?

E: Nay, he is not very volatile at his time of life.

S: Who is he?

E: My father.

S: Your father! my good man?

E: Yes.

S: And of what is he accused?

E: Of murder, Socrates.

S: By the powers, Euthyphro! how little does the common herd know of the nature of right and truth. A man must be an extraordinary man, and have made great strides in wisdom, before he could have seen his way to bring such an action.

E: Indeed, Socrates, he must.

S: I suppose that the man whom your father murdered was one of your relatives—clearly he was; for if he had been a stranger you would never have thought of prosecuting him.

E: I am amused, Socrates, at your making a distinction between one who is a relation and one who is not a relation; for surely the pollution is the same in either case, if you knowingly associate with the murderer when you ought to clear yourself and him by proceeding against him. The real question is whether the murdered man has been justly slain. If justly, then your duty is to let the matter alone; but if unjustly, then even if the murderer lives under the same roof with you and eats at the same table, proceed against him. Now the man who is dead was a poor dependent of mine who worked for us as a field labourer on our farm in Naxos, and one day in a fit of drunken passion he got into a quarrel with one of our domestic servants and slew him. My father bound him hand and foot and threw him into a ditch, and then sent to Athens to ask of a diviner what he should do with him. Meanwhile he never attended to him and took no care about him, for he regarded him as a murderer; and thought that no great harm would be done even if he did die. Now this was just what happened. For such was the effect of cold and hunger and chains upon him, that before the messenger returned from the diviner, he was dead. And my father and family are angry with me for taking the part of the murderer and prosecuting my father. They say that he did not kill him, and that if he did, the dead man was but a murderer, and I ought not to take any notice, for that a son is impious who prosecutes a father. Which shows, Socrates, how little they know what the gods think about piety and impiety.

S: Good heavens, Euthyphro! and is your knowledge of religion and of things pious and impious so very exact, that, supposing the circumstances to be as you state them, you are not afraid lest you too may be doing an impious thing in bringing an action against your father?

E: The best of Euthyphro, and that which distinguishes him, Socrates, from other men, is his exact knowledge of all [5] such matters. What should I be good for without it?

S: Rare friend! I think that I cannot do better than be your disciple. Then before the trial with Meletus comes on I shall challenge him, and say that I have always had a great interest in religious questions, and now, as he charges me with rash imaginations and innovations in religion, I have become your disciple. You, Meletus, as I shall say to him, acknowledge Euthyphro to be a great theologian, and sound in his opinions; and if you approve of him you ought to approve of me, and not have me into court; but if you disapprove, you should begin by indicting him who is my teacher, and who will be the ruin, not of the young, but of the old; that is to say, of myself whom he instructs, and of his old father whom he admonishes and chastises. And if Meletus refuses to listen to me, but will go on, and will not shift the indictment from me to you, I cannot do better than repeat this challenge in the court.

E: Yes, indeed, Socrates; and if he attempts to indict me I am mistaken if I do not find a flaw in him; the court shall have a great deal more to say to him than to me.

S: And I, my dear friend, knowing this, am desirous of becoming your disciple. For I observe that no one appears to notice you—not even this Meletus; but his sharp eyes have found me out at once, and he has indicted me for impiety. And therefore, I adjure you to tell me the nature of piety and impiety, which you said that you knew so well, and of murder, and of other offences against the gods. What are they? Is not piety in every action always the same? and impiety, again—is it not always the opposite of piety, and also the same with itself, having, as impiety, one notion which includes whatever is impious?

E: To be sure, Socrates.

S: And what is piety, and what is impiety?

E: Piety is doing as I am doing; that is to say, prosecuting anyone who is guilty of murder, sacrilege, or of any similar crime—whether he be your father or mother, or whoever he may be—that makes no difference; and not to prosecute them is impiety. And please to consider, Socrates, what a notable proof I will give you of the truth of my words, a proof which I have already given to others:—of the principle, I mean, that the impious, whoever he may be, ought not to go unpunished. For do not men regard [6] Zeus as the best and most righteous of the gods?—and yet they admit that he bound his father (Cronos) because he wickedly devoured his sons, and that he too had punished his own father (Uranus) for a similar reason, in a nameless manner. And yet when I proceed against my father, they are angry with me. So inconsistent are they in their way of talking when the gods are concerned, and when I am concerned.

S: Does Euthyphro believe these amazing stories about the gods? May not this be the reason, Euthyphro, why I am charged with impiety—that I cannot away with these stories about the gods? and therefore I suppose that people think me wrong. But, as you who are well informed about them approve of them, I cannot do better than assent to your superior wisdom. What else can I say, confessing as I do, that I know nothing about them? Tell me, for the love of Zeus, whether you really believe that they are true.

E: Yes, Socrates; and things more wonderful still, of which the world is in ignorance.

S: And do you really believe that the gods fought with one another, and had dire quarrels, battles, and the like, as the poets say, and as you may see represented in the works of great artists? The temples are full of them; and notably the robe of Athene, which is carried up to the Acropolis at the great Panathenaea, is embroidered with them. Are all these tales of the gods true, Euthyphro?

E: Yes, Socrates; and, as I was saying, I can tell you, if you would like to hear them, many other things about the gods which would quite amaze you.

S: I dare say; and you shall tell me them at some other time when I have leisure. But just at present I would rather hear from you a more precise answer, which you have not as yet given, my friend, to the question, What is 'piety'? When asked, you only replied, Doing as you do, charging your father with murder.

E: And what I said was true, Socrates.

S: No doubt, Euthyphro; but you would admit that there are many other pious acts?

E: There are.

S: Remember that I did not ask you to give me two or three examples of piety, but to explain the general idea which makes all pious things to be pious. Do you not recollect that there was one idea which made the impious impious, and the pious pious?

E: I remember.

S: Tell me what is the nature of this idea, and then I shall have a standard to which I may look, and by which I may measure actions, whether yours or those of any one else, and then I shall be able to say that such and such an action is pious, such another impious.

E: I will tell you, if you like.

S: I should very much like.

E: Piety, then, is that which is dear to the gods, and impiety is that which is not dear to them.

S: Very good, Euthyphro; you have now given me the [7] sort of answer which I wanted. But whether what you say is true or not I cannot as yet tell, although I make no doubt that you will prove the truth of your words.

E: Of course.

S: Come, then, and let us examine what we are saying. That thing or person which is dear to the gods is pious, and that thing or person which is hateful to the gods is impious, these two being the extreme opposites of one another. Was not that said?

E: It was.

S: And well said?

E: Yes, Socrates, I thought so; it was certainly said.

S: And further, Euthyphro, the gods were admitted to have enmities and hatreds and differences?

E: Yes, that was also said.

S: And what sort of difference creates enmity and anger? Suppose for example that you and I, my good friend, differ about a number; do differences of this sort make us enemies and set us at variance with one another? Do we not go at once to arithmetic, and put an end to them by a sum?

E: True.

S: Or suppose that we differ about magnitudes, do we not quickly end the difference by measuring?

E: Very true.

S: And we end a controversy about heavy and light by resorting to a weighing machine?

E: To be sure.

S: But what differences are there which cannot be thus decided, and which therefore make us angry and set us at enmity with one another? I dare say the answer does not occur to you at the moment, and therefore I will suggest that these enmities arise when the matters of difference are the just and unjust, good and evil, honourable and dishonourable. Are not these the points about which men differ, and about which when we are unable satisfactorily to decide our differences, you and I and all of us quarrel, when we do quarrel?

E: Yes, Socrates, the nature of the differences about which we quarrel is such as you describe.

S: And the quarrels of the gods, noble Euthyphro, when they occur, are of a like nature?

E: Certainly they are.

S: They have differences of opinion, as you say, about good and evil, just and unjust, honourable and dishonourable: there would have been no quarrels among them, if there had been no such differences—would there now?

E: You are quite right.

S: Does not every man love that which he deems noble and just and good, and hate the opposite of them?

E: Very true.

S: But, as you say, people regard the same things, some as just and others as unjust,—about these they dispute; and so there arise wars and fightings among them. [8]

E: Very true.

S: Then the same things are hated by the gods and loved by the gods, and are both hateful and dear to them?

E: True.

S: And upon this view the same things, Euthyphro, will be pious and also impious?

E: So I should suppose.

S: Then, my friend, I remark with surprise that you have not answered the question which I asked. For I certainly did not ask you to tell me what action is both pious and impious: but now it would seem that what is loved by the gods is also hated by them. And therefore, Euthyphro, in thus chastising your father you may very likely be doing what is agreeable to Zeus but disagreeable to Cronos or Uranus, and what is acceptable to

Hephaestus but unacceptable to Herè, and there may be other gods who
have similar differences of opinion.

E: But I believe, Socrates, that all the gods would be agreed as to the propriety
of punishing a murderer: there would be no difference of opinion about that.

S: Well, but speaking of men, Euthyphro, did you ever hear any one arguing
that a murderer or any sort of evil-doer ought to be let off?

E: I should rather say that these are the questions which they are always arguing, especially in courts of law: they commit all sorts of crimes, and there
is nothing which they will not do or say in their own defence.

S: But do they admit their guilt, Euthyphro, and yet say that they ought not to
be punished?

E: No; they do not.

S: Then there are some things which they do not venture to say and do: for
they do not venture to argue that the guilty are to be unpunished, but they
deny their guilt, do they not?

E: Yes.

S: Then they do not argue that the evil-doer should not be punished, but they
argue about the fact of who the evil-doer is, and what he did and when?

E: True.

S: And the gods are in the same case, if as you assert they quarrel about just
and unjust, and some of them say while others deny that injustice is done
among them. For surely neither God nor man will ever venture to say that
the doer of injustice is not to be punished?

E: That is true, Socrates, in the main.

S: But they join issue about the particulars—gods and men alike; and, if
they dispute at all, they dispute about some act which is called in question,
and which by some is affirmed to be just, by others to be unjust. Is not
that true?

E: Quite true. [9]

S: Well then, my dear friend Euthyphro, do tell me, for my better instruction
and information, what proof have you that in the opinion of all the gods a
servant who is guilty of murder, and is put in chains by the master of the
dead man, and dies because he is put in chains before he who bound him
can learn from the interpreters of the gods what he ought to do with him,
dies unjustly; and that on behalf of such an one a son ought to proceed
against his father and accuse him of murder. How would you show that all
the gods absolutely agree in approving of his act? Prove to me that they do,
and I will applaud your wisdom as long as I live.

E: It will be a difficult task; but I could make the matter very clear indeed
to you.

S: I understand; you mean to say that I am not so quick of apprehension as
the judges: for to them you will be sure to prove that the act is unjust, and
hateful to the gods.

E: Yes indeed, Socrates; at least if they will listen to me.

S: But they will be sure to listen if they find that you are a good speaker. There was a notion that came into my mind while you were speaking; I said to myself: 'Well, and what if Euthyphro does prove to me that all the gods regarded the death of the serf as unjust, how do I know anything more of the nature of piety and impiety? for granting that this action may be hateful to the gods, still piety and impiety are not adequately defined by these distinctions, for that which is hateful to the gods has been shown to be also pleasing and dear to them.' And therefore, Euthyphro, I do not ask you to prove this; I will suppose, if you like, that all the gods condemn and abominate such an action. But I will amend the definition so far as to say that what all the gods hate is impious, and what they love pious or holy; and what some of them love and others hate is both or neither. Shall this be our definition of piety and impiety?

E: Why not, Socrates?

S: Why not! certainly, as far as I am concerned, Euthyphro, there is no reason why not. But whether this admission will greatly assist you in the task of instructing me as you promised, is a matter for you to consider.

E: Yes, I should say that what all the gods love is pious and holy, and the opposite which they all hate, impious.

S: Ought we to enquire into the truth of this, Euthyphro, or simply to accept the mere statement on our own authority and that of others? What do you say?

E: We should enquire; and I believe that the statement will stand the test of enquiry.

S: We shall know better, my good friend, in a little while. The point which I should first wish to understand is whether the pious or holy is beloved by the gods because it [10] is holy, or holy because it is beloved of the gods.

E: I do not understand your meaning, Socrates.

S: I will endeavour to explain: . . . my meaning is, that any state of action or passion implies previous action or passion. It does not become because it is becoming, but it is in a state of becoming because it becomes; neither does it suffer because it is in a state of suffering, but it is in a state of suffering because it suffers. Do you not agree?

E: Yes.

S: Is not that which is loved in some state either of becoming or suffering?

E: Yes.

S: And the same holds as in the previous instances; the state of being loved follows the act of being loved, and not the act the state.

E: Certainly.

S: And what do you say of piety, Euthyphro: is not piety, according to your definition, loved by all the gods?

E: Yes.

S: Because it is pious or holy, or for some other reason?

E: No, that is the reason.

S: It is loved because it is holy, not holy because it is loved?

E: Yes.

S: And that which is dear to the gods is loved by them, and is in a state to be loved of them because it is loved of them?

E: Certainly.

S: Then that which is dear to the gods, Euthyphro, is not holy, nor is that which is holy loved of God, as you affirm; but they are two different things.

E: How do you mean, Socrates?

S: I mean to say that the holy has been acknowledged by us to be loved of God because it is holy, not to be holy because it is loved.

E: Yes.

S: But that which is dear to the gods is dear to them because it is loved by them, not loved by them because it is dear to them.

E: True.

S: But, friend Euthyphro, if that which is holy is the same with that which is dear to God, and is loved because it is holy, then that which is dear to God would have been [11] loved as being dear to God; but if that which is dear to God is dear to him because loved by him, then that which is holy would have been holy because loved by him. But now you see that the reverse is the case, and that they are quite different from one another. For one (θεοφιλὲς) is of a kind to be loved because it is loved, and the other (ὅσιον) is loved because it is of a kind to be loved. Thus you appear to me, Euthyphro,when I ask you what is the essence of holiness, to offer an attribute only, and not the essence—the attribute of being loved by all the gods. But you still refuse to explain to me the nature of holiness. And therefore, if you please, I will ask you not to hide your treasure, but to tell me once more what holiness or piety really is, whether dear to the gods or not (for that is a matter about which we will not quarrel); and what is impiety?

E: I really do not know, Socrates, how to express what I mean. For somehow or other our arguments, on whatever ground we rest them, seem to turn round and walk away from us.

S: Your words, Euthyphro, are like the handiwork of my ancestor Daedalus; and if I were the sayer or propounder of them, you might say that my arguments walk away and will not remain fixed where they are placed because I am a descendant of his. But now, since these notions are your own, you must find some other gibe, for they certainly, as you yourself allow, show an inclination to be on the move.

E: Nay, Socrates, I shall still say that you are the Daedalus who sets arguments in motion; not I, certainly, but you make them move or go round, for they would never have stirred, as far as I am concerned.

S: Then I must be a greater than Daedalus: for whereas he only made his own inventions to move, I move those of other people as well. And the beauty of it is, that I would rather not. For I would give the wisdom of Daedalus, and the wealth of Tantalus, to be able to detain them and keep them fixed. But enough of this. As I perceive that you are lazy, I will myself endeavour to show you how you might instruct me in the nature of piety; and I hope that you will not grudge your labour. Tell me, then,—Is not that which is pious necessarily just?

E: Yes.

S: And is, then, all which is just pious? or, is that which [12] is pious all just, but that which is just, only in part and not all, pious?

E: I do not understand you, Socrates.

S: And yet I know that you are as much wiser than I am, as you are younger. But, as I was saying, revered friend, the abundance of your wisdom makes you lazy. Please to exert yourself, for there is no real difficulty in understanding me. What I mean I may explain by an illustration of what I do not mean. The poet (Stasinus) sings—

'Of Zeus, the author and creator of all these things,
You will not tell: for where there is fear there is also reverence.'

Now I disagree with this poet. Shall I tell you in what respect?

E: By all means.

S: I should not say that where there is fear there is also reverence; for I am sure that many persons fear poverty and disease, and the like evils, but I do not perceive that they reverence the objects of their fear.

E: Very true.

S: But where reverence is, there is fear; for he who has a feeling of reverence and shame about the commission of any action, fears and is afraid of an ill reputation.

E: No doubt.

S: Then we are wrong in saying that where there is fear there is also reverence; and we should say, where there is reverence there is also fear. But there is not always reverence where there is fear; for fear is a more extended notion, and reverence is a part of fear, just as the odd is a part of number, and number is a more extended notion than the odd. I suppose that you follow me now?

E: Quite well.

S: That was the sort of question which I meant to raise when I asked whether the just is always the pious, or the pious always the just; and whether there may not be justice where there is not piety; for justice is the more extended notion of which piety is only a part. Do you dissent?

E: No, I think that you are quite right.

S: Then, if piety is a part of justice, I suppose that we should enquire what part? If you had pursued the enquiry in the previous cases; for instance, if you had asked me what is an even number, and what part of number the even is, I should have had no difficulty in replying, a number which represents a figure having two equal sides. Do you not agree?

E: Yes, I quite agree.

S: In like manner, I want you to tell me what part of justice is piety or holiness, that I may be able to tell Meletus not to do me injustice, or indict me for impiety, as I am now adequately instructed by you in the nature of piety or holiness, and their opposites.

E: Piety or holiness, Socrates, appears to me to be that part of justice which attends to the gods, as there is the other part of justice which attends to men.

S: That is good, Euthyphro; yet still there is a little [13] point about which I should like to have further information, What is the meaning of 'attention'? For attention can hardly be used in the same sense when applied to the gods as when applied to other things. For instance, horses are said to require attention, and not every person is able to attend to them, but only a person skilled in horsemanship. Is it not so?

E: Certainly.

S: I should suppose that the art of horsemanship is the art of attending to horses?

E: Yes.

S: Nor is every one qualified to attend to dogs, but only the huntsman?

E: True.

S: And I should also conceive that the art of the huntsman is the art of attending to dogs?

E: Yes.

S: As the art of the oxherd is the art of attending to oxen?

E: Very true.

S: In like manner holiness or piety is the art of attending to the gods?—that would be your meaning, Euthyphro?

E: Yes.

S: And is not attention always designed for the good or benefit of that to which the attention is given? As in the case of horses, you may observe that when attended to by the horseman's art they are benefited and improved, are they not?

E: True.

S: As the dogs are benefited by the huntsman's art, and the oxen by the art of the oxherd, and all other things are tended or attended for their good and not for their hurt?

E: Certainly, not for their hurt.

S: But for their good?

E: Of course.

S: And does piety or holiness, which has been defined to be the art of attending to the gods, benefit or improve them? Would you say that when you do a holy act you make any of the gods better?

E: No, no; that was certainly not what I meant.

S: And I, Euthyphro, never supposed that you did. I asked you the question about the nature of the attention, because I thought that you did not.

E: You do me justice, Socrates; that is not the sort of attention which I mean.

S: Good: but I must still ask what is this attention to the gods which is called piety?

E: It is such, Socrates, as servants show to their masters.

S: I understand—a sort of ministration to the gods.

E: Exactly.

S: Medicine is also a sort of ministration or service, having in view the attainment of some object—would you not say of health?

E: I should.

S: Again, there is an art which ministers to the ship-builder with a view to the attainment of some result?

E: Yes, Socrates, with a view to the building of a ship.

S: As there is an art which ministers to the house-builder with a view to the building of a house?

E: Yes.

S: And now tell me, my good friend, about the art which ministers to the gods: what work does that help to accomplish? For you must surely know if, as you say, you are of all men living the one who is best instructed in religion.

E: And I speak the truth, Socrates.

S: Tell me then, oh tell me—what is that fair work which the gods do by the help of our ministrations?

E: Many and fair, Socrates, are the works which they do.

S: Why, my friend, and so are those of a general. But [14] the chief of them is easily told. Would you not say that victory in war is the chief of them?

E: Certainly.

S: Many and fair, too, are the works of the husbandman, if I am not mistaken; but his chief work is the production of food from the earth?

E: Exactly.

S: And of the many and fair things done by the gods, which is the chief or principal one?

E: I have told you already, Socrates, that to learn all these things accurately will be very tiresome. Let me simply say that piety or holiness is learning how to please the gods in word and deed, by prayers and sacrifices. Such piety is the salvation of families and states, just as the impious, which is unpleasing to the gods, is their ruin and destruction.

S: I think that you could have answered in much fewer words the chief question which I asked, Euthyphro, if you had chosen. But I see plainly that you are not disposed to instruct me—clearly not: else why, when we reached the point, did you turn aside? Had you only answered me I should have truly learned of you by this time the nature of piety. Now, as the asker of a question is necessarily dependent on the answerer, whither he leads I must follow; and can only ask again, what is the pious, and what is piety? Do you mean that they are a sort of science of praying and sacrificing?

E: Yes, I do.

S: And sacrificing is giving to the gods, and prayer is asking of the gods?

E: Yes, Socrates.

S: Upon this view, then, piety is a science of asking and giving?

E: You understand me capitally, Socrates.

S: Yes, my friend; the reason is that I am a votary of your science, and give my mind to it, and therefore nothing which you say will be thrown away upon me. Please then to tell me, what is the nature of this service to the gods? Do you mean that we prefer requests and give gifts to them?

E: Yes, I do.

S: Is not the right way of asking to ask of them what we want?

E: Certainly.

S: And the right way of giving is to give to them in return what they want of us. There would be no meaning in an art which gives to any one that which he does not want.

E: Very true, Socrates.

S: Then piety, Euthyphro, is an art which gods and men have of doing business with one another?

E: That is an expression which you may use, if you like.

S: But I have no particular liking for anything but the truth. I wish, however, that you would tell me what benefit accrues to the gods from our gifts. There is no doubt about [15] what they give to us; for there is no good thing which they do not give; but how we can give any good thing to them in return is far from being equally clear. If they give everything and we give nothing, that must be an affair of business in which we have very greatly the advantage of them.

E: And do you imagine, Socrates, that any benefit accrues to the gods from our gifts?

S: But if not, Euthyphro, what is the meaning of gifts which are conferred by us upon the gods?

E: What else, but tributes of honour; and, as I was just now saying, what pleases them?

S: Piety, then, is pleasing to the gods, but not beneficial or dear to them?

E: I should say that nothing could be dearer.

S: Then once more the assertion is repeated that piety is dear to the gods?

E: Certainly.

S: And when you say this, can you wonder at your words not standing firm, but walking away? Will you accuse me of being the Daedalus who makes them walk away, not perceiving that there is another and far greater artist than Daedalus who makes them go round in a circle, and he is yourself; for the argument, as you will perceive, comes round to the same point. Were we not saying that the holy or pious was not the same with that which is loved of the gods? Have you forgotten?

E: I quite remember.

S: And are you not saying that what is loved of the gods is holy; and is not this the same as what is dear to them—do you see?

E: True.

S: Then either we were wrong in our former assertion; or, if we were right then, we are wrong now.

E: One of the two must be true.

S: Then we must begin again and ask, What is piety? That is an enquiry which I shall never be weary of pursuing as far as in me lies; and I entreat you not to scorn me, but to apply your mind to the utmost, and tell me the truth. For, if any man knows, you are he; and therefore I must detain you, like Proteus, until you tell. If you had not certainly known the nature of piety and impiety, I am confident that you would never, on behalf of a serf, have charged your aged father with murder. You would not have run such a risk of doing wrong in the sight of the gods, and you would have had too much respect for the opinions of men. I am sure, therefore, that you know the nature of piety and impiety. Speak out then, my dear Euthyphro, and do not hide your knowledge.

E: Another time, Socrates; for I am in a hurry, and must go now.

S: Alas! my companion, and will you leave me in despair? I was hoping that you would instruct me in the nature of piety and impiety; and then I might have cleared myself of Meletus and his indictment. I would have told [16] him that I had been enlightened by Euthyphro, and had given up rash innovations and speculations, in which I indulged only through ignorance, and that now I am about to lead a better life.

APOLOGY (399–380? BC)

Plato

Plato—*see p. 23.*

What to look for: *In* Euthyphro, *we learned that Socrates has been charged with impiety (a capital crime) and corrupting the youth. The prosecutors have presented their case to a Jury of 500 Athenians.* Apology *is Socrates' defense. Here are some questions to ponder as you witness the trial: What contrasts between his presentation and that of the orators who have prosecuted him does Socrates draw? What are the accusations that he fears most? What are the "old" charges? How did they arise? Who or what started Socrates on the path that led to this trial? What does Socrates gain (or lose) in his cross-examination of Miletus? What does Socrates say about avoiding death? Who will be the real loser if Socrates is executed? Why? If Socrates in fact corrupts the youth, why are parents not among the accusers?*

How [Stephanus 17] you, O Athenians, have been affected by my accusers, I cannot tell; but I know that they almost made me forget who I was—so persuasively did they speak; and yet they have hardly uttered a word of truth. But of the many falsehoods told by them, there was one which quite amazed me; —I mean when they said that you should be upon your guard and not allow yourselves to be deceived by the force of my eloquence. To say this, when they were certain to be detected as soon as I opened my lips and proved myself to be anything but a great speaker, did indeed appear to me most shameless—unless by the force of eloquence they mean the force of truth; for if such is their meaning, I admit that I am eloquent. But in how different a way from theirs! Well, as I was saying, they have scarcely spoken the truth at all; but from me you shall hear the whole truth: not, however, delivered after their manner in a set oration duly ornamented with words and phrases. No, by heaven! but I shall use the

"Apology," by Plato, from *The Dialogues of Plato: Translated into English with Analyses and Introductions.* Trans. B. Jowett. 3rd ed. Vol. 2. (Oxford: Oxford University Press, 1892).

words and arguments which occur to me at the moment; for I am confident in the justice of my cause: at my time of life I ought not to be appearing before you, O men of Athens, in the character of a juvenile orator—let no one expect it of me. And I must beg of you to grant me a favour:—If I defend myself in my accustomed manner, and you hear me using the words which I have been in the habit of using in the agora, at the tables of the money-changers, or any-where else, I would ask you not to be surprised, and not to interrupt me on this account. For I am more than seventy years of age, and appearing now for the first time in a court of law, I am quite a stranger to the language of the place; and therefore I would have you regard me as if I were really a stranger, whom you would excuse if [18] he spoke in his native tongue, and after the fashion of his country:—Am I making an unfair request of you? Never mind the manner, which may or may not be good; but think only of the truth of my words, and give heed to that: let the speaker speak truly and the judge decide justly.

And first, I have to reply to the older charges and to my first accusers, and then I will go on to the later ones. For of old I have had many accusers, who have accused me falsely to you during many years; and I am more afraid of them than of Anytus and his associates, who are dangerous, too, in their own way. But far more dangerous are the others, who began when you were chil-dren, and took possession of your minds with their falsehoods, telling of one Socrates, a wise man, who speculated about the heaven above, and searched into the earth beneath, and made the worse appear the better cause. The dis-seminators of this tale are the accusers whom I dread; for their hearers are apt to fancy that such enquirers do not believe in the existence of the gods. And they are many, and their charges against me are of ancient date, and they were made by them in the days when you were more impressible than you are now—in childhood, or it may have been in youth—and the cause when heard went by default, for there was none to answer. And hardest of all, I do not know and cannot tell the names of my accusers; unless in the chance case of a Comic poet. All who from envy and malice have persuaded you—some of them hav-ing first convinced themselves—all this class of men are most difficult to deal with; for I cannot have them up here, and cross-examine them, and therefore I must simply fight with shadows in my own defence, and argue when there is no one who answers. I will ask you then to assume with me, as I was saying, that my opponents are of two kinds; one recent, the other ancient: and I hope that you will see the propriety of my answering the latter first, for these accusations you heard long before the others, and much oftener.

Well, then, I must make my defence, and endeavour to clear [19] away in a short time, a slander which has lasted a long time. May I succeed, if to succeed be for my good and yours, or likely to avail me in my cause! The task is not an easy one; I quite understand the nature of it. And so leaving the event with God, in obedience to the law I will now make my defence.

I will begin at the beginning, and ask what is the accusation which has given rise to the slander of me, and in fact has encouraged Meletus to prefer this charge against me. Well, what do the slanderers say? They shall be my prosecutors, and I will sum up their words in an affidavit: 'Socrates is an evil-doer, and a curious person, who searches into things under the earth and in heaven, and he makes the worse appear the better cause; and he teaches the aforesaid doctrines to others.' Such is the nature of the accusation: it is just what you have yourselves seen in the comedy of Aristophanes, who has intro-duced a man whom he calls Socrates, going about and saying that he walks in air, and talking a deal of nonsense concerning matters of which I do not pretend to know either much or little—not that I mean to speak disparagingly of any one who is a student of natural philosophy. I should be very sorry if Meletus could bring so grave a charge against me. But the simple truth is, O Athenians, that I have nothing to do with physical speculations. Very many of those here present are witnesses to the truth of this, and to them I appeal. Speak then, you who have heard me, and tell your neighbours whether any of you have ever known me hold forth in few words or in many upon such matters. . . . You hear their answer. And from what they say of this part of the charge you will be able to judge of the truth of the rest.

As little foundation is there for the report that I am a teacher, and take money; this accusation has no more truth in it than the other. Although, if a man were really able to instruct mankind, to receive money for giving instruc-tion would, in my opinion, be an honour to him. There is Gorgias of Leontium, and Prodicus of Ceos, and Hippias of Elis, who go the round of the cities, and are able to persuade the young men to leave their own citizens by whom [20] they might be taught for nothing, and come to them whom they not only pay, but are thankful if they may be allowed to pay them. There is at this time a Par-ian philosopher residing in Athens, of whom I have heard; and I came to hear of him in this way:—I came across a man who has spent a world of money on the Sophists, Callias, the son of Hipponicus, and knowing that he had sons, I asked him: 'Callias,' I said, 'if your two sons were foals or calves, there would be no difficulty in finding some one to put over them; we should hire a trainer of horses, or a farmer probably, who would improve and perfect them in their own proper virtue and excellence; but as they are human beings, whom are you thinking of placing over them? Is there any one who understands human and political virtue? You must have thought about the matter, for you have sons; is there any one?' 'There is,' he said. 'Who is he?' said I; 'and of what country? and what does he charge?' 'Evenus the Parian,' he replied; 'he is the man, and his charge is five minae.' Happy is Evenus, I said to myself, if he really has this wisdom, and teaches at such a moderate charge. Had I the same, I should have been very proud and conceited; but the truth is that I have no knowledge of the kind.

I dare say, Athenians, that some one among you will reply, 'Yes, Socrates, but what is the origin of these accusations which are brought against you; there must have been something strange which you have been doing? All these rumours and this talk about you would never have arisen if you had been like other men: tell us, then, what is the cause of them, for we should be sorry to judge hastily of you.' Now I regard this as a fair challenge, and I will endeavour to explain to you the reason why I am called wise and have such an evil fame. Please to attend then. And although some of you may think that I am joking, I declare that I will tell you the entire truth. Men of Athens, this reputation of mine has come of a certain sort of wisdom which I possess. If you ask me what kind of wisdom, I reply, wisdom such as may perhaps be attained by man, for to that extent I am inclined to believe that I am wise; whereas the persons of whom I was speaking have a superhuman wisdom, which I may fail to describe, because I have it not myself; and he who says that I have, speaks falsely, and is taking away my character. And here, O men of Athens, I must beg you not to interrupt me, even if I seem to say something extravagant. For the word which I will speak is not mine. I will refer you to a witness who is worthy of credit; that witness shall be the God of Delphi—he will tell you about my wisdom, if I have any, and of what sort it is. You must have known Chaerephon; he was early [21] a friend of mine, and also a friend of yours, for he shared in the recent exile of the people, and returned with you. Well, Chaerephon, as you know, was very impetuous in all his doings, and he went to Delphi and boldly asked the oracle to tell him whether—as I was saying, I must beg you not to interrupt—he asked the oracle to tell him whether any one was wiser than I was, and the Pythian prophetess answered, that there was no man wiser. Chaerephon is dead himself; but his brother, who is in court, will confirm the truth of what I am saying.

Why do I mention this? Because I am going to explain to you why I have such an evil name. When I heard the answer, I said to myself, What can the god mean? and what is the interpretation of his riddle? for I know that I have no wisdom, small or great. What then can he mean when he says that I am the wisest of men? And yet he is a god, and cannot lie; that would be against his nature. After long consideration, I thought of a method of trying the question. I reflected that if I could only find a man wiser than myself, then I might go to the god with a refutation in my hand. I should say to him, 'Here is a man who is wiser than I am; but you said that I was the wisest.' Accordingly I went to one who had the reputation of wisdom, and observed him—his name I need not mention; he was a politician whom I selected for examination—and the result was as follows: When I began to talk with him, I could not help thinking that he was not really wise, although he was thought wise by many, and still wiser by himself; and thereupon I tried to explain to him that he thought himself wise, but was not really wise; and the consequence was that he hated me, and his enmity was shared by several who were present and heard me. So I left him, saying to myself, as I went away: Well, although I do not suppose that either of us knows anything really beautiful and good. I am better off than he is,—for he knows nothing, and thinks that he knows; I neither know nor think that I know. In this latter particular, then, I seem to have slightly the advantage of him. Then I went to another who had still higher pretensions to wisdom, and my conclusion was exactly the same. Whereupon I made another enemy of him, and of many others besides him.

Then I went to one man after another, being not unconscious of the enmity which I provoked, and I lamented and feared this: but necessity was laid upon me,—the word of God, I thought, ought to be considered first. And I said to myself, Go I must to all who appear to know, and find out the meaning of the oracle. And I swear to you, Athenians, [22] by the dog I swear!—for I must tell you the truth—the result of my mission was just this: I found that the men most in repute were all but the most foolish; and that others less esteemed were really wiser and better. I will tell you the tale of my wanderings and of the 'Herculean' labours, as I may call them, which I endured only to find at last the oracle irrefutable. After the politicians, I went to the poets; tragic, dithyrambic, and all sorts. And there, I said to myself, you will be instantly detected; now you will find out that you are more ignorant than they are. Accordingly, I took them some of the most elaborate passages in their own writings, and asked what was the meaning of them—thinking that they would teach me something. Will you believe me? I am almost ashamed to confess the truth, but I must say that there is hardly a person present who would not have talked better about their poetry than they did themselves. Then I knew that not by wisdom do poets write poetry, but by a sort of genius and inspiration; they are like diviners or soothsayers who also say many fine things, but do not understand the meaning of them. The poets appeared to me to be much in the same case; and I further observed that upon the strength of their poetry they believed themselves to be the wisest of men in other things in which they were not wise. So I departed, conceiving myself to be superior to them for the same reason that I was superior to the politicians.

At last I went to the artisans, for I was conscious that I knew nothing at all, as I may say, and I was sure that they knew many fine things; and here I was not mistaken, for they did know many things of which I was ignorant, and in this they certainly were wiser than I was. But I observed that even the good artisans fell into the same error as the poets;—because they were good workmen they thought that they also knew all sorts of high matters, and this defect in them overshadowed their wisdom; and therefore I asked myself on behalf of the oracle, whether I would like to be as I was, neither having their knowledge nor their ignorance, or like them in both; and I made answer to myself and to the oracle that I was better off as I was.

This inquisition has led to my having many enemies of [23] the worst and most dangerous kind, and has given occasion also to many calumnies. And I am called wise, for my hearers always imagine that I myself possess the wisdom which I find wanting in others: but the truth is, O men of Athens, that God only is wise; and by his answer he intends to show that the wisdom of men is worth little or nothing; he is not speaking of Socrates, he is only using my name by way of illustration, as if he said, He, O men, is the wisest, who, like Socrates, knows that his wisdom is in truth worth nothing. And so I go about the world, obedient to the god, and search and make enquiry into the wisdom of any one, whether citizen or stranger, who appears to be wise; and if he is not wise, then in vindication of the oracle I show him that he is not wise; and my occupation quite absorbs me, and I have no time to give either to any public matter of interest or to any concern of my own, but I am in utter poverty by reason of my devotion to the god.

There is another thing:—young men of the richer classes, who have not much to do, come about me of their own accord; they like to hear the pretenders examined, and they often imitate me, and proceed to examine others; there are plenty of persons, as they quickly discover, who think that they know something, but really know little or nothing; and then those who are examined by them instead of being angry with themselves are angry with me: This confounded Socrates, they say; this villainous misleader of youth!—and then if somebody asks them, Why, what evil does he practise or teach? they do not know, and cannot tell; but in order that they may not appear to be at a loss, they repeat the ready-made charges which are used against all philosophers about teaching things up in the clouds and under the earth, and having no gods, and making the worse appear the better cause; for they do not like to confess that their pretence of knowledge has been detected—which is the truth; and as they are numerous and ambitious and energetic, and are drawn up in battle array and have persuasive tongues, they have filled your ears with their loud and inveterate calumnies. And this is the reason why my three accusers, Meletus and Anytus and Lycon, have set upon me; Meletus, who has a quarrel with me on behalf of the poets; Anytus, on behalf of the craftsmen and politicians; Lycon, on behalf of the rhetoricians: and as I said [24] at the beginning, I cannot expect to get rid of such a mass of calumny all in a moment. And this, O men of Athens, is the truth and the whole truth; I have concealed nothing, I have dissembled nothing. And yet, I know that my plainness of speech makes them hate me, and what is their hatred but a proof that I am speaking the truth? Hence has arisen the prejudice against me; and this is the reason of it, as you will find out either in this or in any future enquiry.

I have said enough in my defence against the first class of my accusers; I turn to the second class. They are headed by Meletus, that good man and true lover of his country, as he calls himself. Against these, too, I must try to make a defence:—Let their affidavit be read: it contains something of this kind: It says that Socrates is a doer of evil, who corrupts the youth; and who does not believe in the gods of the state, but has other new divinities of his own. Such is the charge; and now let us examine the particular counts. He says that I am a doer of evil, and corrupt the youth; but I say, O men of Athens, that Meletus is a doer of evil, in that he pretends to be in earnest when he is only in jest, and is so eager to bring men to trial from a pretended zeal and interest about matters in which he really never had the smallest interest. And the truth of this I will endeavour to prove to you.

Come hither, Meletus, and let me ask a question of you. You think a great deal about the improvement of youth?

Yes, I do.

Tell the judges, then, who is their improver; for you must know, as you have taken the pains to discover their corrupter, and are citing and accusing me before them. Speak, then, and tell the judges who their improver is.—Observe, Meletus, that you are silent, and have nothing to say. But is not this rather disgraceful, and a very considerable proof of what I was saying, that you have no interest in the matter? Speak up, friend, and tell us who their improver is.

The laws.

But that, my good sir, is not my meaning. I want to know who the person is, who, in the first place, knows the laws.

The judges, Socrates, who are present in court.

What, do you mean to say, Meletus, that they are able to instruct and improve youth?

Certainly they are.

What, all of them, or some only and not others?

All of them.

By the goddess Herè, that is good news! There are plenty of improvers, then. And what do you say of the [25] audience,—do they improve them?

Yes, they do.

And the senators?

Yes, the senators improve them.

But perhaps the members of the assembly corrupt them?—or do they too improve them?

They improve them.

Then every Athenian improves and elevates them; all with the exception of myself; and I alone am their corrupter? Is that what you affirm?

That is what I stoutly affirm.

I am very unfortunate if you are right. But suppose I ask you a question: How about horses? Does one man do them harm and all the world good? Is not the exact opposite the truth? One man is able to do them good, or at least not many;—the trainer of horses, that is to say, does them good, and others who have to do with them rather injure them? Is not that true, Meletus, of horses, or of any other animals? Most assuredly it is; whether you and Anytus say yes or no. Happy indeed would be the condition of youth if they had one corrupter only, and all the rest of the world were their improvers. But you, Meletus, have sufficiently shown that you never had a thought about the young: your carelessness is seen in your not caring about the very things which you bring against me.

And now, Meletus, I will ask you another question—by Zeus I will: Which is better, to live among bad citizens, or among good ones? Answer, friend, I say; the question is one which may be easily answered. Do not the good do their neighbours good, and the bad do them evil?

Certainly.

And is there any one who would rather be injured than benefited by those who live with him? Answer, my good friend, the law requires you to answer—does any one like to be injured?

Certainly not.

And when you accuse me of corrupting and deteriorating the youth, do you allege that I corrupt them intentionally or unintentionally?

Intentionally, I say.

But you have just admitted that the good do their neighbours good, and the evil do them evil. Now, is that a truth which your superior wisdom has recognized thus early in life, and am I, at my age, in such darkness and ignorance as not to know that if a man with whom I have to live is corrupted by me, I am very likely to be harmed by him; and yet I corrupt him, and intentionally, too—so you say, although neither I nor any other human being is ever likely to be convinced by you. But either I do not corrupt them, or [26] I corrupt them unintentionally; and on either view of the case you lie. If my offence is unintentional, the law has no cognizance of unintentional offences: you ought to have taken me privately, and warned and admonished me; for if I had been better advised, I should have left off doing what I only did unintentionally—no doubt I should; but you would have nothing to say to me and refused to teach me. And now you bring me up in this court, which is a place not of instruction, but of punishment.

It will be very clear to you, Athenians, as I was saying, that Meletus has no care at all, great or small, about the matter. But still I should like to know, Meletus, in what I am affirmed to corrupt the young. I suppose you mean, as I infer from your indictment, that I teach them not to acknowledge the gods which the state acknowledges, but some other new divinities or spiritual agencies in their stead. These are the lessons by which I corrupt the youth, as you say.

Yes, that I say emphatically.

Then, by the gods, Meletus, of whom we are speaking, tell me and the court, in somewhat plainer terms, what you mean! for I do not as yet understand whether you affirm that I teach other men to acknowledge some gods, and therefore that I do believe in gods, and am not an entire atheist—this you do not lay to my charge,—but only you say that they are not the same gods which the city recognizes—the charge is that they are different gods. Or, do you mean that I am an atheist simply, and a teacher of atheism?

I mean the latter—that you are a complete atheist.

What an extraordinary statement! Why do you think so, Meletus? Do you mean that I do not believe in the godhead of the sun or moon, like other men?

I assure you, judges, that he does not: for he says that the sun is stone, and the moon earth.

Friend Meletus, you think that you are accusing Anaxagoras: and you have but a bad opinion of the judges, if you fancy them illiterate to such a degree as not to know that these doctrines are found in the books of Anax-agoras the Clazomenian, which are full of them. And so, forsooth, the youth are said to be taught them by Socrates, when there are not unfrequently exhi-bitions of them at the theatre (price of admission one drachma at the most); and they might pay their money, and laugh at Socrates if he pretends to father these extraordinary views. And so, Meletus, you really think that I do not believe in any god?

I swear by Zeus that you believe absolutely in none at all.

Nobody will believe you, Meletus, and I am pretty sure that you do not believe yourself. I cannot help thinking, men of Athens, that Meletus is reck-less and impudent, and that he has written this indictment in a spirit of mere wantonness and youthful bravado. Has he not compounded a [27] riddle, think-ing to try me? He said to himself:—I shall see whether the wise Socrates will discover my facetious contradiction, or whether I shall be able to deceive him and the rest of them. For he certainly does appear to me to contradict himself in the indictment as much as if he said that Socrates is guilty of not believing in the gods, and yet of believing in them—but this is not like a person who is in earnest.

I should like you, O men of Athens, to join me in examining what I con-ceive to be his inconsistency; and do you, Meletus, answer. And I must remind the audience of my request that they would not make a disturbance if I speak in my accustomed manner:

Did ever man, Meletus, believe in the existence of human things, and not of human beings? . . . I wish, men of Athens, that he would answer, and not be always trying to get up an interruption. Did ever any man believe in horse-manship, and not in horses? or in flute-playing, and not in flute-players? No, my friend; I will answer to you and to the court, as you refuse to answer for yourself. There is no man who ever did. But now please to answer the next question: Can a man believe in spiritual and divine agencies, and not in spirits or demigods?

He cannot.

How lucky I am to have extracted that answer, by the assistance of the court! But then you swear in the indictment that I teach and believe in divine or spiritual agencies (new or old, no matter for that); at any rate, I believe in spiritual agencies,—so you say and swear in the affidavit; and yet if I believe in divine beings, how can I help believing in spirits or demigods;—must I not? To be sure I must; and therefore I may assume that your silence gives consent. Now what are spirits or demigods? are they not either gods or the sons of gods?

Certainly they are.

But this is what I call the facetious riddle invented by you: the demigods or spirits are gods, and you say first that I do not believe in gods, and then again that I do believe in gods; that is, if I believe in demigods. For if the demigods are the illegitimate sons of gods, whether by the nymphs or by any other moth-ers, of whom they are said to be the sons—what human being will ever believe that there are no gods if they are the sons of gods? You might as well affirm the existence of mules, and deny that of horses and asses. Such nonsense, Meletus, could only have been intended by you to make trial of me. You have put this into the indictment because you had nothing real of which to accuse me. But no one who has a particle of understanding will ever be convinced by you that the same men can believe in divine and superhuman things, and yet not believe that [28] there are gods and demigods and heroes.

I have said enough in answer to the charge of Meletus: any elaborate defence is unnecessary; but I know only too well how many are the enmities which I have incurred, and this is what will be my destruction if I am destroyed;—not Meletus, nor yet Anytus, but the envy and detraction of the world, which has been the death of many good men, and will probably be the death of many more; there is no danger of my being the last of them.

Some one will say: And are you not ashamed, Socrates, of a course of life which is likely to bring you to an untimely end? To him I may fairly answer: There you are mistaken: a man who is good for anything ought not to calculate the chance of living or dying; he ought only to consider whether in doing anything he is doing right or wrong—acting the part of a good man or of a bad. Whereas, upon your view, the heroes who fell at Troy were not good for much, and the son of Thetis above all, who altogether despised danger in comparison with disgrace; and when he was so eager to slay Hector, his goddess mother said to him, that if he avenged his companion Patroclus, and slew Hector, he would die himself—'Fate,' she said, in these or the like words, 'waits for you next after Hector;' he, receiving this warning, utterly despised danger and death, and instead of fearing them, feared rather to live in dishonour, and not to avenge his friend. 'Let me die forthwith,' he replies, 'and be avenged of my enemy, rather than abide here by the beaked ships, a laughing-stock and a burden of the earth.' Had Achilles any thought of death and danger? For wherever a man's place is, whether the place which he has chosen or that in which he has been placed by a commander, there he ought to remain in the hour of danger; he should not think of death or of anything but of disgrace. And this, O men of Athens, is a true saying.

Strange, indeed, would be my conduct, O men of Athens, if I who, when I was ordered by the generals whom you chose to command me at Potidaea and Amphipolis and Delium, remained where they placed me, like any other man, facing death—if now, when, as I conceive and imagine, God orders me to fulfil the philosopher's mission of searching into myself and other men, I were to desert my post through fear [29] of death, or any other fear; that would indeed be strange, and I might justly be arraigned in court for denying the existence of the gods, if I disobeyed the oracle because I was afraid of death, fancying that I was wise when I was not wise. For the fear of death is indeed the pretence of wisdom, and not real wisdom, being a pretence of knowing the unknown; and no one knows whether death, which men in their fear apprehend to be the

greatest evil, may not be the greatest good. Is not this ignorance of a disgraceful sort, the ignorance which is the conceit that a man knows what he does not
know? And in this respect only I believe myself to differ from men in general,
and may perhaps claim to be wiser than they are:—that whereas I know but
little of the world below, I do not suppose that I know: but I do know that injustice and disobedience to a better, whether God or man, is evil and dishonourable, and I will never fear or avoid a possible good rather than a certain evil.
And therefore if you let me go now, and are not convinced by Anytus, who said
that since I had been prosecuted I must be put to death; (or if not that I ought
never to have been prosecuted at all); and that if I escape now, your sons will
all be utterly ruined by listening to my words—if you say to me, Socrates, this
time we will not mind Anytus, and you shall be let off, but upon one condition,
that you are not to enquire and speculate in this way any more, and that if you
are caught doing so again you shall die;—if this was the condition on which
you let me go, I should reply: Men of Athens, I honour and love you; but I
shall obey God rather than you, and while I have life and strength I shall never
cease from the practice and teaching of philosophy, exhorting any one whom
I meet and saying to him after my manner: You, my friend,—a citizen of the
great and mighty and wise city of Athens,—are you not ashamed of heaping up
the greatest amount of money and honour and reputation, and caring so little
about wisdom and truth and the greatest improvement of the soul, which you
never regard or heed at all? And if the person with whom I am arguing, says:
Yes, but I do care; then I do not leave him or let him go at once; but I proceed
to interrogate and examine and cross-examine him, and if I think that he has
no virtue in him, but only says that he has, I reproach him with undervaluing
the [30] greater, and overvaluing the less. And I shall repeat the same words to
every one whom I meet, young and old, citizen and alien, but especially to the
citizens, inasmuch as they are my brethren. For know that this is the command
of God; and I believe that no greater good has ever happened in the state than
my service to the God. For I do nothing but go about persuading you all, old
and young alike, not to take thought for your persons or your properties, but
first and chiefly to care about the greatest improvement of the soul. I tell you
that virtue is not given by money, but that from virtue comes money and every
other good of man, public as well as private. This is my teaching, and if this is
the doctrine which corrupts the youth, I am a mischievous person. But if any
one says that this is not my teaching, he is speaking an untruth. Wherefore, O
men of Athens, I say to you, do as Anytus bids or not as Anytus bids, and either
acquit me or not; but whichever you do, understand that I shall never alter my
ways, not even if I have to die many times.

Men of Athens, do not interrupt, but hear me; there was an understanding
between us that you should hear me to the end: I have something more to say,
at which you may be inclined to cry out; but I believe that to hear me will be
good for you, and therefore I beg that you will not cry out. I would have you

know, that if you kill such an one as I am, you will injure yourselves more than you will injure me. Nothing will injure me, not Meletus nor yet Anytus—they cannot, for a bad man is not permitted to injure a better than himself. I do not deny that Anytus may, perhaps, kill him, or drive him into exile, or deprive him of civil rights; and he may imagine, and others may imagine, that he is inflicting a great injury upon him: but there I do not agree. For the evil of doing as he is doing—the evil of unjustly taking away the life of another—is greater far.

And now, Athenians, I am not going to argue for my own sake, as you may think, but for yours, that you may not sin against the God by condemning me, who am his gift to you. For if you kill me you will not easily find a successor to me, who, if I may use such a ludicrous figure of speech, am a sort of gadfly, given to the state by God; and the state is a great and noble steed who is tardy in his motions owing to his very size, and requires to be stirred into life. I am that gadfly which God has attached to the state, and all day long [31] and in all places am always fastening upon you, arousing and persuading and reproaching you. You will not easily find another like me, and therefore I would advise you to spare me. I dare say that you may feel out of temper (like a person who is suddenly awakened from sleep), and you think that you might easily strike me dead as Anytus advises, and then you would sleep on for the remainder of your lives, unless God in his care of you sent you another gadfly. When I say that I am given to you by God, the proof of my mission is this:—if I had been like other men, I should not have neglected all my own concerns or patiently seen the neglect of them during all these years, and have been doing yours, coming to you individually like a father or elder brother, exhorting you to regard virtue; such conduct, I say, would be unlike human nature. If I had gained anything, or if my exhortations had been paid, there would have been some sense in my doing so; but now, as you will perceive, not even the impudence of my accusers dares to say that I have ever exacted or sought pay of any one; of that they have no witness. And I have a sufficient witness to the truth of what I say—my poverty.

Some one may wonder why I go about in private giving advice and busying myself with the concerns of others, but do not venture to come forward in public and advise the state. I will tell you why. You have heard me speak at sundry times and in divers places of an oracle or sign which comes to me, and is the divinity which Meletus ridicules in the indictment. This sign, which is a kind of voice, first began to come to me when I was a child; it always forbids but never commands me to do anything which I am going to do. This is what deters me from being a politician. And rightly, as I think. For I am certain, O men of Athens, that if I had engaged in politics, I should have perished long ago, and done no good either to you or to myself. And do not be offended at my telling you the truth: for the truth is, that no man who goes to war with you or any other multitude, honestly striving against the many lawless and unrighteous [32] deeds which are done in a state, will save his life; he who will fight for the right, if he would live even for a brief space, must have a private station and not a public one.

I can give you convincing evidence of what I say, not words only, but what you value far more—actions. Let me relate to you a passage of my own life which will prove to you that I should never have yielded to injustice from any fear of death, and that 'as I should have refused to yield' I must have died at once. I will tell you a tale of the courts, not very interesting perhaps, but nevertheless true. The only office of state which I ever held, O men of Athens, was that of senator: the tribe Antiochis, which is my tribe, had the presidency at the trial of the generals who had not taken up the bodies of the slain after the battle of Arginusae; and you proposed to try them in a body, contrary to law, as you all thought afterwards; but at the time I was the only one of the Prytanes who was opposed to the illegality, and I gave my vote against you; and when the orators threatened to impeach and arrest me, and you called and shouted, I made up my mind that I would run the risk, having law and justice with me, rather than take part in your injustice because I feared imprisonment and death. This happened in the days of the democracy. But when the oligarchy of the Thirty was in power, they sent for me and four others into the rotunda, and bade us bring Leon the Salaminian from Salamis, as they wanted to put him to death. This was a specimen of the sort of commands which they were always giving with the view of implicating as many as possible in their crimes; and then I showed, not in word only but in deed, that, if I may be allowed to use such an expression, I cared not a straw for death, and that my great and only care was lest I should do an unrighteous or unholy thing. For the strong arm of that oppressive power did not frighten me into doing wrong; and when we came out of the rotunda the other four went to Salamis and fetched Leon, but I went quietly home. For which I might have lost my life, had not the power of the Thirty shortly afterwards come to an end. And many will witness to my words.

Now do you really imagine that I could have survived all these years, if I had led a public life, supposing that like a good man I had always maintained the right and had made justice, as I ought, the first thing? No indeed, men of Athens, neither I nor any other man. But I have been [33] always the same in all my actions, public as well as private, and never have I yielded any base compliance to those who are slanderously termed my disciples, or to any other. Not that I have any regular disciples. But if any one likes to come and hear me while I am pursuing my mission, whether he be young or old, he is not excluded. Nor do I converse only with those who pay; but any one, whether he be rich or poor, may ask and answer me and listen to my words; and whether he turns out to be a bad man or a good one, neither result can be justly imputed to me; for I never taught or professed to teach him anything. And if any one says that he has ever learned or heard anything from me in private which all the world has not heard, let me tell you that he is lying.

But I shall be asked, Why do people delight in continually conversing with you? I have told you already, Athenians, the whole truth about this matter: they like to hear the cross-examination of the pretenders to wisdom; there is amusement in it. Now this duty of cross-examining other men has been imposed upon me by God; and has been signified to me by oracles, visions, and in every way in which the will of divine power was ever intimated to any one. This is true, O Athenians; or, if not true, would be soon refuted. If I am or have been corrupting the youth, those of them who are now grown up and have become sensible that I gave them bad advice in the days of their youth should come forward as accusers, and take their revenge; or if they do not like to come themselves, some of their relatives, fathers, brothers, or other kinsmen, should say what evil their families have suffered at my hands. Now is their time. Many of them I see in the court. There is Crito, who is of the same age and of the same deme with myself, and there is Critobulus his son, whom I also see. Then again there is Lysanias of Sphettus, who is the father of Aeschines—he is present; and also there is Antiphon of Cephisus, who is the father of Epigenes; and there are the brothers of several who have associated with me. There is Nicostratus the son of Theosdotides, and the brother of Theodotus (now Theodotus himself is dead, and therefore he, at any rate, will not seek to stop him); and there is Paralus the son of Demodocus, who had a brother Theages; [34] and Adeimantus the son of Ariston, whose brother Plato is present; and Aeantodorus, who is the brother of Apollodorus, whom I also see. I might mention a great many others, some of whom Meletus should have produced as witnesses in the course of his speech; and let him still produce them, if he has forgotten—I will make way for him. And let him say, if he has any testimony of the sort which he can produce. Nay, Athenians, the very opposite is the truth. For all these are ready to witness on behalf of the corrupter, of the injurer of their kindred, as Meletus and Anytus call me; not the corrupted youth only—there might have been a motive for that—but their uncorrupted elder relatives. Why should they too support me with their testimony? Why, indeed, except for the sake of truth and justice, and because they know that I am speaking the truth, and that Meletus is a liar.

Well, Athenians, this and the like of this is all the defence which I have to offer. Yet a word more. Perhaps there may be some one who is offended at me, when he calls to mind how he himself on a similar, or even a less serious occasion, prayed and entreated the judges with many tears, and how he produced his children in court, which was a moving spectacle, together with a host of relations and friends; whereas I, who am probably in danger of my life, will do none of these things. The contrast may occur to his mind, and he may be set against me, and vote in anger because he is displeased at me on this account. Now if there be such a person among you,—mind, I do not say that there is,—to him I may fairly reply: My friend, I am a man, and like other men, a creature of flesh and blood, and not 'of wood or stone,' as Homer says;

and I have a family, yes, and sons, O Athenians, three in number, one almost a man, and two others who are still young; and yet I will not bring any of them hither in order to petition you for an acquittal. And why not? Not from any self-assertion or want of respect for you. Whether I am or am not afraid of death is another question, of which I will not now speak. But, having regard to public opinion, I feel that such conduct would be discreditable to myself, and to you, and to the whole state. One who has reached my years, and who has a name for wisdom, ought not to demean himself. Whether this opinion of me be deserved or not, at any rate the world has decided that Socrates is in some way superior to other men. And if those [35] among you who are said to be superior in wisdom and courage, and any other virtue, demean themselves in this way, how shameful is their conduct! I have seen men of reputation, when they have been condemned, behaving in the strangest manner: they seemed to fancy that they were going to suffer something dreadful if they died, and that they could be immortal if you only allowed them to live; and I think that such are a dishonour to the state, and that any stranger coming in would have said of them that the most eminent men of Athens, to whom the Athenians themselves give honour and command, are no better than women. And I say that these things ought not to be done by those of us who have a reputation; and if they are done, you ought not to permit them; you ought rather to show that you are far more disposed to condemn the man who gets up a doleful scene and makes the city ridiculous, than him who holds his peace.

But, setting aside the question of public opinion, there seems to be something wrong in asking a favour of a judge, and thus procuring an acquittal, instead of informing and convincing him. For his duty is, not to make a present of justice, but to give judgment; and he has sworn that he will judge according to the laws, and not according to his own good pleasure; and we ought not to encourage you, nor should you allow yourselves to be encouraged, in this habit of perjury—there can be no piety in that. Do not then require me to do what I consider dishonourable and impious and wrong, especially now, when I am being tried for impiety on the indictment of Meletus. For if, O men of Athens, by force of persuasion and entreaty I could overpower your oaths, then I should be teaching you to believe that there are no gods, and in defending should simply convict myself of the charge of not believing in them. But that is not so—far otherwise. For I do believe that there are gods, and in a sense higher than that in which any of my accusers believe in them. And to you and to God I commit my cause, to be determined by you as is best for you and me.

What to look for now: What is the jury's vote? As the trial moves to the penalty phase, Socrates suggests an alternative to the accusers' proposed death penalty. What is that alternative? On what grounds does Socrates defend that alternative? Why would exile or silence not be acceptable to him?

There are many reasons why I am not grieved, O men of [36] Athens, at the vote of condemnation. I expected it, and am only surprised that the votes are so nearly equal; for I had thought that the majority against me would have been far larger; but now, had thirty votes gone over to the other side, I should have been acquitted. And I may say, I think, that I have escaped Meletus. I may say more; for without the assistance of Anytus and Lycon, any one may see that he would not have had a fifth part of the votes, as the law requires, in which case he would have incurred a fine of a thousand drachmae.

And so he proposes death as the penalty. And what shall I propose on my part, O men of Athens? Clearly that which is my due. And what is my due? What return shall be made to the man who has never had the wit to be idle during his whole life; but has been careless of what the many care for—wealth, and family interests, and military offices, and speaking in the assembly, and magistracies, and plots, and parties. Reflecting that I was really too honest a man to be a politician and live, I did not go where I could do no good to you or to myself; but where I could do the greatest good privately to every one of you, thither I went, and sought to persuade every man among you that he must look to himself, and seek virtue and wisdom before he looks to his private interests, and look to the state before he looks to the interests of the state; and that this should be the order which he observes in all his actions. What shall be done to such an one? Doubtless some good thing, O men of Athens, if he has his reward; and the good should be of a kind suitable to him. What would be a reward suitable to a poor man who is your benefactor, and who desires leisure that he may instruct you? There can be no reward so fitting as maintenance in the Prytaneum, O men of Athens, a reward which he deserves far more than the citizen who has won the prize at Olympia in the horse or chariot race, whether the chariots were drawn by two horses or by many. For I am in want, and he has enough; and he only gives you the appearance of happiness, and I give you the reality. And if I am to estimate the penalty fairly, I should say that maintenance in the [37] Prytaneum is the just return.

Perhaps you think that I am braving you in what I am saying now, as in what I said before about the tears and prayers. But this is not so. I speak rather because I am convinced that I never intentionally wronged any one, although I cannot convince you—the time has been too short; if there were a law at Athens, as there is in other cities, that a capital cause should not be decided in one day, then I believe that I should have convinced you. But I cannot in a moment refute great slanders; and, as I am convinced that I never wronged another, I will assuredly not wrong myself. I will not say of myself that I deserve any evil, or propose any penalty. Why should I? Because I am afraid of the penalty of death which Meletus proposes? When I do not know whether death is a good or an evil, why should I propose a penalty which would certainly be an evil? Shall I say imprisonment? And why should I live in prison, and be the slave of the magistrates of the year—of the Eleven? Or shall the penalty be a fine, and imprisonment until the fine is paid? There is the same objection. I should have to lie in prison, for money I have none, and cannot pay. And if I say exile (and this may possibly be the penalty which you will affix), I must indeed be blinded by the love of life, if I am so irrational as to expect that when you, who are my own citizens, cannot endure my discourses and words, and have found them so grievous and odious that you will have no more of them, others are likely to endure me. No indeed, men of Athens, that is not very likely. And what a life should I lead, at my age, wandering from city to city, ever changing my place of exile, and always being driven out! For I am quite sure that wherever I go, there, as here, the young men will flock to me; and if I drive them away, their elders will drive me out at their request; and if I let them come, their fathers and friends will drive me out for their sakes.

Some one will say: Yes, Socrates, but cannot you hold your tongue, and then you may go into a foreign city, and no one will interfere with you? Now I have great difficulty in making you understand my answer to this. For if I tell you that to do as you say would be a disobedience to the God, and therefore that I cannot hold my tongue, you will not [38] believe that I am serious; and if I say again that daily to discourse about virtue, and of those other things about which you hear me examining myself and others, is the greatest good of man, and that the unexamined life is not worth living, you are still less likely to believe me. Yet I say what is true, although a thing of which it is hard for me to persuade you. Also, I have never been accustomed to think that I deserve to suffer any harm. Had I money I might have estimated the offence at what I was able to pay, and not have been much the worse. But I have none, and therefore I must ask you to proportion the fine to my means. Well, perhaps I could afford a mina, and therefore I propose that penalty: Plato, Crito, Critobulus, and Apollodorus, my friends here, bid me say thirty minae, and they will be the sureties. Let thirty minae be the penalty; for which sum they will be ample security to you.

What to look for now: *The jury chooses the death penalty and Socrates responds. What does he say to those who condemned him? To those who would have acquitted him, what argument does Socrates present that death is not to be feared? What are his final words to the assembly about death?*

Not much time will be gained, O Athenians, in return for the evil name which you will get from the detractors of the city, who will say that you killed Socrates, a wise man; for they will call me wise, even although I am not wise, when they want to reproach you. If you had waited a little while, your desire would have been fulfilled in the course of nature. For I am far advanced in years, as you may perceive, and not far from death. I am speaking now not to all of you, but only to those who have condemned me to death. And I have another thing to say to them: You think that I was convicted because I had no words of the sort which would have procured my acquittal—I mean, if I had thought fit to leave nothing undone or unsaid. Not so; the deficiency which led to my conviction was not of words—certainly not. But I had not the boldness or impudence or inclination to address you as you would have liked me to do, weeping and wailing and lamenting, and saying and doing many things which you have been accustomed to hear from others, and which, as I maintain, are unworthy of me. I thought at the time that I ought not to do anything common or mean when in danger: nor do I now repent of the style of my defence; I would rather die having spoken after my manner, than speak in your manner and live. For neither in war nor yet at law ought I or any man to use every way of escaping death. [39] Often in battle there can be no doubt that if a man will throw away his arms, and fall on his knees before his pursuers, he may escape death; and in other dangers there are other ways of escaping death, if a man is willing to say and do anything. The difficulty, my friends, is not to avoid death, but to avoid unrighteousness; for that runs faster than death. I am old and move slowly, and the slower runner has overtaken me, and my accusers are keen and quick, and the faster runner, who is unrighteousness, has overtaken them. And now I depart hence condemned by you to suffer the penalty of death,—they too go their ways condemned by the truth to suffer the penalty of villainy and wrong; and I must abide by my award—let them abide by theirs. I suppose that these things may be regarded as fated,—and I think that they are well.

And now, O men who have condemned me, I would fain prophesy to you; for I am about to die, and in the hour of death men are gifted with prophetic power. And I prophesy to you who are my murderers, that immediately after my departure punishment far heavier than you have inflicted on me will surely await you. Me you have killed because you wanted to escape the accuser, and not to give an account of your lives. But that will not be as you suppose: far otherwise. For I say that there will be more accusers of you than there are now; accusers whom hitherto I have restrained: and as they are younger they will be more inconsiderate with you, and you will be more offended at them. If you think that by killing men you can prevent some one from censuring your evil lives, you are mistaken; that is not a way of escape which is either possible or honourable; the easiest and the noblest way is not to be disabling others, but to be improving yourselves. This is the prophecy which I utter before my departure to the judges who have condemned me.

Friends, who would have acquitted me, I would like also to talk with you about the thing which has come to pass, while the magistrates are busy, and before I go to the place at which I must die. Stay then a little, for we may as well talk [40] with one another while there is time. You are my friends, and I should like to show you the meaning of this event which has happened to me. O my judges—for you I may truly call judges—I should like to tell you of a wonderful circumstance. Hitherto the divine faculty of which the internal oracle is the source has constantly been in the habit of opposing me even about trifles, if I was going to make a slip or error in any matter; and now as you see there has come upon me that which may be thought, and is generally believed to be, the last and worst evil. But the oracle made no sign of opposition, either when I was leaving my house in the morning, or when I was on my way to the court, or while I was speaking, at anything which I was going to say; and yet I have often been stopped in the middle of a speech, but now in nothing I either said or did touching the matter in hand has the oracle opposed me. What do I take to be the explanation of this silence? I will tell you. It is an intimation that what has happened to me is a good, and that those of us who think that death is an evil are in error. For the customary sign would surely have opposed me had I been going to evil and not to good.

Let us reflect in another way, and we shall see that there is great reason to hope that death is a good; for one of two things—either death is a state of nothingness and utter unconsciousness, or, as men say, there is a change and migration of the soul from this world to another. Now if you suppose that there is no consciousness, but a sleep like the sleep of him who is undisturbed even by dreams, death will be an unspeakable gain. For if a person were to select the night in which his sleep was undisturbed even by dreams, and were to compare with this the other days and nights of his life, and then were to tell us how many days and nights he had passed in the course of his life better and more pleasantly than this one, I think that any man, I will not say a private man, but even the great king will not find many such days or nights, when compared with the others. Now if death be of such a nature, I say that to die is gain; for eternity is then only a single night. But if death is the journey to another place, and there, as men say, all the dead abide, what good, O my friends and judges, can be greater than this? If indeed when the pilgrim arrives in the world below, he is delivered from the [41] professors of justice in this world, and finds the true judges who are said to give judgment there, Minos and Rhadamanthus and Aeacus and Triptolemus, and other sons of God who were righteous in their own life, that pilgrimage will be worth making. What would not a man give if he might converse with Orpheus and Musaeus and Hesiod and Homer? Nay, if this be true, let me die again and again. I myself, too, shall have a wonderful interest in there meeting and conversing with Palamedes, and Ajax the son of Telamon, and any other ancient hero who has suffered death through an unjust judgment; and there will be no small pleasure, as I think, in comparing my own sufferings with theirs. Above all, I shall then be able to continue my search into true and false knowledge; as in this world, so also in the next; and I shall find out who is wise, and who pretends to be wise, and is not. What would not a man give, O judges, to be able to examine the leader of the great Trojan expedition; or Odysseus or Sisyphus, or numberless others, men and women too! What infinite delight would there be in conversing with them and asking them questions! In another world they do not put a man to death for asking questions: assuredly not. For besides being happier than we are, they will be immortal, if what is said is true.

Wherefore, O judges, be of good cheer about death, and know of a certainty, that no evil can happen to a good man, either in life or after death. He and his are not neglected by the gods; nor has my own approaching end happened by mere chance. But I see clearly that the time had arrived when it was better for me to die and be released from trouble; wherefore the oracle gave no sign. For which reason, also, I am not angry with my condemners, or with my accusers; they have done me no harm, although they did not mean to do me any good; and for this I may gently blame them.

Still I have a favour to ask of them. When my sons are grown up, I would ask you, O my friends, to punish them; and I would have you trouble them, as I have troubled you, if they seem to care about riches, or anything, more than about virtue; or if they pretend to be something when they are really nothing,—then reprove them, as I have reproved you, for not caring about that for which they ought to care, and thinking that they are something when they are really [42] nothing. And if you do this, both I and my sons will have received justice at your hands.

The hour of departure has arrived, and we go our ways—I to die, and you to live. Which is better God only knows.

SOCIETY AND
POLITICS

CRITO (399–380? BC)

Plato

Plato—*see p. 24.*

What to look for: *Crito hopes to convince Socrates to escape. What is the urgency? What reasons does Crito offer? How are we to regard the opinion of the many? Why? Upon what two premises (regarding the value of opinion and the value of life) does Socrates base his reasoning? Is it ever right to injure? Would Socrates' escape injure the state? What is the relationship between Socrates and the state? Have his actions created an implied contract that he must obey the laws? If he is found to have broken the laws, is he obligated to accept the punishment? If he were to escape, would he then be guilty of corrupting the youth? If he is a victim, is he a victim of the laws? If not, of whom?*

PERSONS OF THE DIALOGUE: Socrates, Crito.
SCENE: Socrates' prison cell

Socrates: [Stephanus 43] Why have you come at this hour, Crito? it must be quite early?

Crito: Yes, certainly.

S: What is the exact time?

C: The dawn is breaking.

S: I wonder that the keeper of the prison would let you in.

C: He knows me, because I often come, Socrates; moreover, I have done him a kindness.

S: And are you only just arrived?

C: No, I came some time ago.

S: Then why did you sit and say nothing, instead of at once awakening me?

"Crito," by Plato, from *The Dialogues of Plato: Translated into English with Analyses and Introductions.* Trans. B. Jowett. 3rd ed. Vol. 2. (Oxford: Oxford University Press, 1892).

C: I should not have liked myself, Socrates, to be in such great trouble and unrest as you are—indeed I should not: I have been watching with amazement your peaceful slumbers; and for that reason I did not awake you, because I wished to minimize the pain. I have always thought you to be of a happy disposition; but never did I see anything like the easy, tranquil manner in which you bear this calamity.

S: Why, Crito, when a man has reached my age he ought not to be repining at the approach of death.

C: And yet other old men find themselves in similar misfortunes, and age does not prevent them from repining.

S: That is true. But you have not told me why you come at this early hour.

C: I come to bring you a message which is sad and painful; not, as I believe, to yourself, but to all of us who are your friends, and saddest of all to me.

S: What? Has the ship come from Delos, on the arrival of which I am to die?

C: No, the ship has not actually arrived, but she will probably be here today, as persons who have come from Sunium tell me that they left her there; and therefore tomorrow, Socrates, will be the last day of your life.

S: Very well, Crito; if such is the will of God, I am willing; but my belief is that there will be a delay of a day.

C: Why do you think so? [44]

S: I will tell you. I am to die on the day after the arrival of the ship.

C: Yes; that is what the authorities say.

S: But I do not think that the ship will be here until tomorrow; this I infer from a vision which I had last night, or rather only just now, when you fortunately allowed me to sleep.

C: And what was the nature of the vision?

S: There appeared to me the likeness of a woman, fair and comely, clothed in bright raiment, who called to me and said: O Socrates,
'The third day hence to fertile Phthia shalt thou go.' [Homer]

C: What a singular dream, Socrates!

S: There can be no doubt about the meaning, Crito, I think.

C: Yes; the meaning is only too clear. But, oh! my beloved Socrates, let me entreat you once more to take my advice and escape. For if you die I shall not only lose a friend who can never be replaced, but there is another evil: people who do not know you and me will believe that I might have saved you if I had been willing to give money, but that I did not care. Now, can there be a worse disgrace than this—that I should be thought to value money more than the life of a friend? For the many will not be persuaded that I wanted you to escape, and that you refused.

S: But why, my dear Crito, should we care about the opinion of the many? Good men, and they are the only persons who are worth considering, will think of these things truly as they occurred.

C: But you see, Socrates, that the opinion of the many must be regarded, for what is now happening shows that they can do the greatest evil to any one who has lost their good opinion.

S: I only wish it were so, Crito; and that the many could do the greatest evil; for then they would also be able to do the greatest good—and what a fine thing this would be! But in reality they can do neither; for they cannot make a man either wise or foolish; and whatever they do is the result of chance.

C: Well, I will not dispute with you; but please to tell me, Socrates, whether you are not acting out of regard to me and your other friends: are you not afraid that if you escape from prison we may get into trouble with the informers for having stolen you away, and lose either the whole or a great part of [45] our property; or that even a worse evil may happen to us? Now, if you fear on our account, be at ease; for in order to save you, we ought surely to run this, or even a greater risk; be persuaded, then, and do as I say.

S: Yes, Crito, that is one fear which you mention, but by no means the only one.

C: Fear not—there are persons who are willing to get you out of prison at no great cost; and as for the informers, they are far from being exorbitant in their demands—a little money will satisfy them. My means, which are certainly ample, are at your service, and if you have a scruple about spending all mine, here are strangers who will give you the use of theirs; and one of them, Simmias the Theban, has brought a large sum of money for this very purpose; and Cebes and many others are prepared to spend their money in helping you to escape. I say, therefore, do not hesitate on our account, and do not say, as you did in the court, that you will have a difficulty in knowing what to do with yourself anywhere else. For men will love you in other places to which you may go, and not in Athens only; there are friends of mine in Thessaly, if you like to go to them, who will value and protect you, and no Thessalian will give you any trouble. Nor can I think that you are at all justified, Socrates, in betraying your own life when you might be saved; in acting thus you are playing into the hands of your enemies, who are hurrying on your destruction. And further I should say that you are deserting your own children; for you might bring them up and educate them; instead of which you go away and leave them, and they will have to take their chance; and if they do not meet with the usual fate of orphans, there will be small thanks to you. No man should bring children into the world who is unwilling to persevere to the end in their nurture and education. But you appear to be choosing the easier part, not the better and manlier, which would have been more becoming in one who professes to care for virtue in all his actions, like yourself. And indeed, I am ashamed not only of you, but of us who are your friends, when I reflect that the whole business will be attributed entirely to our want of courage. The trial need never have come on, or might have been managed differently; and this last act, or crowning folly, will seem to have occurred through our negligence and cowardice, who might have saved you, if we had been good for [46] anything; and you might have saved yourself, for there was no difficulty at all. See now, Socrates, how sad and discreditable are the consequences, both to us and you. Make up your mind then, or rather have your mind already made up, for the time of deliberation is over, and there is only one thing to be done, which must be done this very night, and if we delay at all will be no longer practicable or possible; I beseech you therefore, Socrates, be persuaded by me, and do as I say.

S: Dear Crito, your zeal is invaluable, if a right one; but if wrong, the greater the zeal the greater the danger; and therefore we ought to consider whether I shall or shall not do as you say. For I am and always have been one of those natures who must be guided by reason, whatever the reason may be which upon reflection appears to me to be the best; and now that this chance has befallen me, I cannot repudiate my own words: the principles which I have hitherto honoured and revered I still honour, and unless we can at once find other and better principles, I am certain not to agree with you; no, not even if the power of the multitude could inflict many more imprisonments, confiscations, deaths, frightening us like children with hobgoblin terrors. What will be the fairest way of considering the question? Shall I return to your old argument about the opinions of men?—we were saying that some of them are to be regarded, and others not. Now were we right in maintaining this before I was condemned? And has the argument which was once good now proved to be talk for the sake of talking—mere childish nonsense? That is what I want to consider with your help, Crito:—whether, under my present circumstances, the argument appears to be in any way different or not; and is to be allowed by me or disallowed. That argument, which, as I believe, is maintained by many persons of authority, was to the effect, as I was saying, that the opinions of some men are to be regarded, and of other men not to be. Now [47] you, Crito, are not going to die tomorrow—at least, there is no human probability of this—and therefore you are disinterested and not liable to be deceived by the circumstances in which you are placed. Tell me then, whether I am right in saying that some opinions, and the opinions of some men only, are to be valued, and that other opinions, and the opinions of other men, are not to be valued. I ask you whether I was right in maintaining this?

C: Certainly.

S: The good are to be regarded, and not the bad?

C: Yes.

S: And the opinions of the wise are good, and the opinions of the unwise are evil?

C: Certainly.

S: And what was said about another matter? Is the pupil who devotes himself to the practice of gymnastics supposed to attend to the praise and blame and opinion of every man, or of one man only—his physician or trainer, whoever he may be?

C: Of one man only.

S: And he ought to fear the censure and welcome the praise of that one only, and not of the many?

C: Clearly so.

S: And he ought to act and train, and eat and drink in the way which seems good to his single master who has understanding, rather than according to the opinion of all other men put together?

C: True.

S: And if he disobeys and disregards the opinion and approval of the one, and regards the opinion of the many who have no understanding, will he not suffer evil?

C: Certainly he will.

S: And what will the evil be, whither tending and what affecting, in the disobedient person?

C: Clearly, affecting the body; that is what is destroyed by the evil.

S: Very good; and is not this true, Crito, of other things which we need not separately enumerate? In questions of just and unjust, fair and foul, good and evil, which are the subjects of our present consultation, ought we to follow the opinion of the many and to fear them; or the opinion of the one man who has understanding? ought we not to fear and reverence him more than all the rest of the world: and if we desert him shall we not destroy and injure that principle in us which may be assumed to be improved by justice and deteriorated by injustice;—there is such a principle?

C: Certainly there is, Socrates.

S: Take a parallel instance:—if, acting under the advice of those who have no understanding, we destroy that which is improved by health and is deteriorated by disease, would life be worth having? And that which has been destroyed is—the body?

C: Yes.

S: Could we live, having an evil and corrupted body?

C: Certainly not.

S: And will life be worth having, if that higher part of man be destroyed, which is improved by justice and depraved by injustice? Do we suppose that principle, whatever it [48] may be in man, which has to do with justice and injustice, to be inferior to the body?

C: Certainly not.

S: More honourable than the body?

C: Far more.

S: Then, my friend, we must not regard what the many say of us: but what he, the one man who has understanding of just and unjust, will say, and what the truth will say. And therefore you begin in error when you advise that we should regard the opinion of the many about just and unjust, good and evil, honourable and dishonourable. — 'Well,' some one will say, 'but the many can kill us.'

C: Yes, Socrates; that will clearly be the answer.

S: And it is true: but still I find with surprise that the old argument is unshaken as ever. And I should like to know whether I may say the same of another proposition—that not life, but a good life, is to be chiefly valued?

C: Yes, that also remains unshaken.

S: And a good life is equivalent to a just and honourable one—that holds also?

C: Yes, it does.

S: From these premises I proceed to argue the question whether I ought or ought not to try and escape without the consent of the Athenians: and if I am clearly right in escaping, then I will make the attempt; but if not, I will abstain. The other considerations which you mention, of money and loss of character and the duty of educating one's children, are, I fear, only the doctrines of the multitude, who would be as ready to restore people to life, if they were able, as they are to put them to death—and with as little reason. But now, since the argument has thus far prevailed, the only question which remains to be considered is, whether we shall do rightly either in escaping or in suffering others to aid in our escape and paying them in money and thanks, or whether in reality we shall not do rightly; and if the latter, then death or any other calamity which may ensue on my remaining here must not be allowed to enter into the calculation.

C: I think that you are right, Socrates; how then shall we proceed?

S: Let us consider the matter together, and do you either refute me if you can, and I will be convinced; or else cease, my dear friend, from repeating to me that I ought to escape against the wishes of the Athenians: for I highly value your attempts to persuade me to do so, but I may not be persuaded against my own better judgement. And now please to consider my first position, and try how you can [49] best answer me.

C: I will.

S: Are we to say that we are never intentionally to do wrong, or that in one way we ought and in another way we ought not to do wrong, or is doing wrong always evil and dishonourable, as I was just now saying, and as has been already acknowledged by us? Are all our former admissions which were made within a few days to be thrown away? And have we, at our age, been earnestly discoursing with one another all our life long only to discover that we are no better than children? Or, in spite of the opinion of the many, and in spite of consequences whether better or worse, shall we insist on the truth of what was then said, that injustice is always an evil and dishonour to him who acts unjustly? Shall we say so or not?

C: Yes.

S: Then we must do no wrong?

C: Certainly not.

S: Nor when injured injure in return, as the many imagine; for we must injure no one at all?

C: Clearly not.

S: Again, Crito, may we do evil?

C: Surely not, Socrates.

And what of doing evil in return for evil, which is the morality of the many—is that just or not?

C: Not just.

S: For doing evil to another is the same as injuring him?

C: Very true.

S: Then we ought not to retaliate or render evil for evil to any one, whatever evil we may have suffered from him. But I would have you consider, Crito, whether you really mean what you are saying. For this opinion has never been held, and never will be held, by any considerable number of persons; and those who are agreed and those who are not agreed upon this point have no common ground, and can only despise one another when they see how widely they differ. Tell me, then, whether you agree with and assent to my first principle, that neither injury nor retaliation nor warding off evil by evil is ever right. And shall that be the premiss of our argument? Or do you decline and dissent from this? For so I have ever thought, and continue to think; but, if you are of another opinion, let me hear what you have to say. If, however, you remain of the same mind as formerly, I will proceed to the next step.

C: You may proceed, for I have not changed my mind.

S: Then I will go on to the next point, which may be put in the form of a question:—Ought a man to do what he admits to be right, or ought he to betray the right?

C: He ought to do what he thinks right.

S: But if this is true, what is the application? In [50] leaving the prison against the will of the Athenians, do I wrong any? or rather do I not wrong those whom I ought least to wrong? Do I not desert the principles which were acknowledged by us to be just—what do you say?

C: I cannot tell, Socrates; for I do not know.

S: Then consider the matter in this way:—Imagine that I am about to play truant (you may call the proceeding by any name which you like), and the laws and the government come and interrogate me: 'Tell us, Socrates,' they say; 'what are you about? are you not going by an act of yours to overturn us—the laws, and the whole state, as far as in you lies? Do you imagine that a state can subsist and not be overthrown, in which the decisions of law have no power, but are set aside and trampled upon by individuals?' What will be our answer, Crito, to these and the like words? Any one, and especially a rhetorician, will have a good deal to say on behalf of the law which requires a sentence to be carried out. He will argue that this law should not be set aside; and shall we reply, 'Yes; but the state has injured us and given an unjust sentence.' Suppose I say that?

C: Very good, Socrates.

S: 'And was that our agreement with you?' the law would answer; 'or were you to abide by the sentence of the state?' And if I were to express my astonishment at their words, the law would probably add: 'Answer, Socrates, instead of opening your eyes—you are in the habit of asking and answering questions. Tell us,—What complaint have you to make against us which justifies you in attempting to destroy us and the state? In the first place did we not bring you into existence? Your father married your mother by our aid and begat you. Say whether you have any objection to urge against those of us who regulate marriage?' None, I should reply. 'Or against those of us who after birth regulate the nurture and education of children, in which you also were trained? Were not the laws, which have the charge of education, right in commanding your father to train you in music and gymnastic?' Right, I should reply. 'Well then, since you were brought into the world and nurtured and educated by us, can you deny in the first place that you are our child and slave, as your fathers were before you? And if this is true you are not on equal terms with us; nor can you think that you have a right to do to us what we are doing to you. Would you have any right to strike or revile or do any other evil to your father or your master, if you had one, because you have been struck or reviled by him, or received some other evil at his hands?—you would not say this? And because we think right to [51] destroy you, do you think that you have any right to destroy us in return, and your country as far as in you lies? Will you, O professor of true virtue, pretend that you are justified in this? Has a philosopher like you failed to discover that our country is more to be valued and higher and holier far than mother or father or any ancestor, and more to be regarded in the eyes of the gods and of men of understanding? also to be soothed, and gently and reverently entreated when angry, even more than a father, and either to be persuaded, or if not persuaded, to be obeyed? And when we are punished by her, whether with imprisonment or stripes, the punishment is to be endured in silence; and if she lead us to wounds or death in battle, thither we follow as is right; neither may any one yield or retreat or leave his rank, but whether in battle or in a court of law, or in any other place, he must do what his city and his country order him; or he must change their view of what is just: and if he may do no violence to his father or mother, much less may he do violence to his country.' What answer shall we make to this, Crito? Do the laws speak truly, or do they not?

C: I think that they do.

S: Then the laws will say: 'Consider, Socrates, if we are speaking truly that in your present attempt you are going to do us an injury. For, having brought you into the world, and nurtured and educated you, and given you and every other citizen a share in every good which we had to give, we further proclaim to any Athenian by the liberty which we allow him, that if he does not like us when he has become of age and has seen the ways of the city, and made our acquaintance, he may go where he pleases and take his goods with him. None of us laws will forbid him or interfere with him. Any one who does not like us and the city, and who wants to emigrate to a colony or to any other city, may go where he likes, retaining his property. But he who has experience of the manner in which we order justice and administer the state, and still remains, has entered into an implied contract that he will do as we command him. And he who disobeys us is, as we maintain, thrice wrong; first, because in disobeying us he is disobeying his parents; secondly, because we are the authors of his education; thirdly, because he has made an agreement with us that he [52] will duly obey our commands; and he neither obeys them nor convinces us that our commands are unjust; and we do not rudely impose them, but give him the alternative of obeying or convincing us:—that is what we offer, and he does neither.

'These are the sort of accusations to which, as we were saying, you, Socrates, will be exposed if you accomplish your intentions; you, above all other Athenians.' Suppose now I ask, why I rather than anybody else? they will justly retort upon me that I above all other men have acknowledged the agreement. 'There is clear proof,' they will say, 'Socrates, that we and the city were not displeasing to you. Of all Athenians you have been the most constant resident in the city, which, as you never leave, you may be supposed to love. For you never went out of the city either to see the games, except once when you went to the Isthmus, or to any other place unless when you were on military service; nor did you travel as other men do. Nor had you any curiosity to know other states or their laws: your affections did not go beyond us and our state; we were your special favourites, and you acquiesced in our government of you; and here in this city you begat your children, which is a proof of your satisfaction. Moreover, you might in the course of the trial, if you had liked, have fixed the penalty at banishment; the state which refuses to let you go now would have let you go then. But you pretended that you preferred death to exile, and that you were not unwilling to die. And now you have forgotten these fine sentiments, and pay no respect to us the laws, of whom you are the destroyer; and are doing what only a miserable slave would do, running away and turning your back upon the compacts and agreements which you made as a citizen. And first of all answer this very question: Are we right in saying that you agreed to be governed according to us in deed, and not in word only? Is that true or not?' How shall we answer, Crito? Must we not assent?

C: We cannot help it, Socrates.

S: Then will they not say: 'You, Socrates, are breaking the covenants and agreements which you made with us at your leisure, not in any haste or under any compulsion or deception, but after you have had seventy years to think of them, during which time you were at liberty to leave the city, if we were not to your mind, or if our covenants appeared to you to be unfair. You had your choice, and might have gone either to Lacedaemon or Crete, both which states are often praised by you for their good government, or to some other Hellenic or foreign state. Whereas you, [53] above all other Athenians, seemed to be so fond of the state, or, in other words, of us her laws (and who would care about a state which has no laws?), that you never stirred out of her; the halt, the blind, the maimed were not more stationary in her than you were. And now you run away and forsake your agreements. Not so, Socrates, if you will take our advice; do not make yourself ridiculous by escaping out of the city.

'For just consider, if you transgress and err in this sort of way, what good will you do either to yourself or to your friends? That your friends will be driven into exile and deprived of citizenship, or will lose their property, is tolerably certain; and you yourself, if you fly to one of the neighbouring cities, as, for example, Thebes or Megara, both of which are well governed, will come to them as an enemy, Socrates, and their government will be against you, and all patriotic citizens will cast an evil eye upon you as a subverter of the laws, and you will confirm in the minds of the judges the justice of their own condemnation of you. For he who is a corrupter of the laws is more than likely to be a corrupter of the young and foolish portion of mankind. Will you then flee from well-ordered cities and virtuous men? and is existence worth having on these terms? Or will you go to them without shame, and talk to them, Socrates? And what will you say to them? What you say here about virtue and justice and institutions and laws being the best things among men? Would that be decent of you? Surely not. But if you go away from well-governed states to Crito's friends in Thessaly, where there is great disorder and licence, they will be charmed to hear the tale of your escape from prison, set off with ludicrous particulars of the manner in which you were wrapped in a goatskin or some other disguise, and metamorphosed as the manner is of runaways; but will there be no one to remind you that in your old age you were not ashamed to violate the most sacred laws from a miserable desire of a little more life? Perhaps not, if you keep them in a good temper; but if they are out of temper you will hear many degrading things; you will live, but how?—as the flatterer of all men, and the servant of all men; and doing what?—eating and drinking in Thessaly, having gone abroad in order that you may get a dinner. And where will be your fine sentiments [54] about justice and virtue? Say that you wish to live for the sake of your children—you want to bring them up and educate them—will you take them into Thessaly and deprive them of Athenian citizenship? Is this the benefit which you will confer upon them? Or are you under the impression that they will be better cared for and educated here if you are still alive, although absent from them; for your friends will take care of them? Do you fancy that if you are an inhabitant of Thessaly they will take care of them, and if you are an inhabitant of the other world that they will not take care of them? Nay; but if they who call themselves friends are good for anything, they will—to be sure they will.

'Listen, then, Socrates, to us who have brought you up. Think not of life and children first, and of justice afterwards, but of justice first, that you may be justified before the princes of the world below. For neither will you nor any that belong to you be happier or holier or juster in this life, or happier in another, if you do as Crito bids. Now you depart in innocence, a sufferer and not a doer of evil; a victim, not of the laws but of men. But if you go forth, returning evil for evil, and injury for injury, breaking the covenants and agreements which you have made with us, and wronging those whom you ought least of all to wrong, that is to say, yourself, your friends, your country, and us, we shall be angry with you while you live, and our brethren, the laws in the world below, will receive you as an enemy; for they will know that you have done your best to destroy us. Listen, then, to us and not to Crito.'

This, dear Crito, is the voice which I seem to hear murmuring in my ears, like the sound of the flute in the ears of the mystic; that voice, I say, is humming in my ears, and prevents me from hearing any other. And I know that anything more which you may say will be vain. Yet speak, if you have anything to say.

C: I have nothing to say, Socrates.

S: Leave me then, Crito, to fulfil the will of God, and to follow whither he leads.

HUMAN FLOURISHING AND THE IDEAL STATE (350? BC)

Aristotle

Aristotle (384–322 BC) was born in the Greek colony of Stagira in Macedonia. His father, Nicomachus, was court physician to the king, Amyntas II. At 17or 18, Aristotle began twenty years at Plato's Academy. After Plato's death, the Academy changed focus, leading Aristotle to accept the invitation of friends to live first at Assos and then Lesbos. During this time, he focused on zoological research. In his early 40s, Aristotle became tutor to the young man who would become Alexander the Great of Macedonia. In 335, at the age of 49, Aristotle returned to Athens where he founded his own school, the Lyceum. There he conducted research on many subjects and built the first great library of antiquity. Anti-Macedonian feeling, arising at the death of Alexander in 323, caused Aristotle to retire to Chalcis, where he died a year later. Contemporaries described him as thin, bald, sardonic, and speaking with a lisp. Though certainly Plato's most brilliant student, Aristotle could hardly have been more different than his teacher. Whereas Plato loved abstract ideas, Aristotle was meticulous, practical, and down to earth. Their diametrically opposed ideas about reality and the nature of knowledge introduced a division among schools that endured well into the 1800s. Though they disagreed about almost everything, each held the greatest of respect for the other, and each became among the most influential philosophers of all time.

What to look for: In his massive work, Politics, Aristotle analyzes whatever is relevant to government and the state. The state, he finds, "is not a community of living beings only, but a community of equals, aiming at the best life possible" [1328b]. The best government, therefore, is the one that brings about the best life possible. In his Ethics, Aristotle argued that the best life is one that maximizes eudaimonia—a state of general well-being (usually translated as "happiness" or "flourishing") that includes both physical and emotional health. In this selection (from the

*end of Book VII), Aristotle considers what regulations on family life will
best lead to the highest state of well-being. First, one must consider the
health of babies. What is the relationship between healthy marriages and
healthy babies? At what ages should persons marry? Why? What prena-
tal and infant care should be required? What education is appropriate
at what ages of youth? What does Aristotle advocate regarding infant
abandonment, abortion, and adultery? Is Aristotle correct in thinking
that the regulations he proposes would indeed produce the best chance
for the best (family) life possible?*

Since the legislator should begin by considering how the frames [bodies] of
the children whom he is rearing may be as good as possible, his first care will
be about marriage—at what age should his citizens marry, and who are fit to
marry? In legislating on this subject he ought to consider the persons and their
relative ages, that there may be no disproportion in them, and that they may
not differ in their bodily powers, as will be the case if the man is still able to
beget children while the woman is unable to bear them, or the woman able to
bear while the man is unable to beget, for from these causes arise quarrels and
differences between married persons. Secondly, he must consider the time at
which the children will succeed to their parents; there ought not to be too great
an interval of age, for then the parents will be too old to derive any pleasure
from their affection, or to be of any use to them. [Bekker 1335a][1] Nor ought
they to be too nearly of an age; to youthful marriages there are many objections—the children will be wanting in respect to the parents, who will seem
to be their contemporaries, and disputes will arise in the management of the
household. Thirdly, and this is the point from which we digressed, the legislator must mold to his will the frames of newly-born children. Almost all these
objects may be secured by attention to one point. Since the time of generation
is commonly limited within the age of seventy years in the case of a man, and
of fifty in the case of a woman, the commencement of the union should conform to these periods. The union of male and female when too young is bad
for the procreation of children; in all other animals the offspring of the young
are small and ill-developed, and generally of the female sex, and therefore also
in man, as is proved by the fact that in those cities in which men and women

---

[1]Aristotle's works are normally referenced to a two-volume Greek edition published in 1831
by Immanuel Bekker (1785–1871). The volumes had continuous pagination (pp. 1–789 in v.1;
pp 791–1462 in v.2) with Greek text appearing in two columns ("a" and "b") with line numbers (5,
10, 15, etc.) printed between the columns. A full "Bekker number" reference includes the page,
column, and line number(s). Here, bracketed numbers indicate the Bekker page and column.

"Human Flourishing and the Ideal State," by Aristotle, from *The Politics of Aristotle: Translated
into English with Introduction, Marginal Analysis, Essays, Notes and Indices.* Trans. B. Jowett.
Vol. 1. (Oxford: Clarendon Press, 1885).

are accustomed to marry young, the people are small and weak; in childbirth also younger women suffer more, and more of them die; some persons say that this was the meaning of the response once given to the Troezenians—['Shear not the young field,']—the oracle really meant that many died because they married too young; it had nothing to do with the ingathering of the harvest. It also conduces to temperance not to marry too soon; for women who marry early are apt to be wanton; and in men too the bodily frame is stunted if they marry while they are growing (for there is a time when the growth of the body ceases). Women should marry when they are about eighteen years of age, and men at seven and thirty; then they are in the prime of life, and the decline in the powers of both will coincide. Further, the children, if their birth takes place at the time that may reasonably be expected, will succeed in their prime, when the fathers are already in the decline of life, and have nearly reached their term of three-score years and ten.

Thus much of the age proper for marriage: the season of the year should also be considered; according to our present custom, people generally limit marriage to the season of winter, and they are right. The precepts of physicians and natural philosophers about generation should also be studied by the parents themselves; the physicians give good advice about the right age of the body, and [1335b] the natural philosophers about the winds; of which they prefer the north to the south.

What constitution in the parent is most advantageous to the offspring is a subject which we will hereafter consider when we speak of the education of children, and we will only make a few general remarks at present. The temperament of an athlete is not suited to the life of a citizen, or to health, or to the procreation of children, any more than the valetudinarian or exhausted constitution, but one which is in a mean between them. A man's constitution should be inured to labour, but not to labour which is excessive or of one sort only, such as is practised by athletes; he should be capable of all the actions of a freeman. These remarks apply equally to both parents.

Women who are with child should be careful of themselves; they should take exercise and have a nourishing diet. The first of these prescriptions the legislator will easily carry into effect by requiring that they shall take a walk daily to some temple, where they can worship the gods who preside over birth. Their minds, however, unlike their bodies, they ought to keep unexercised, for the offspring derive their natures from their mothers as plants do from the earth.

As to the exposure and rearing of children, let there be a law that no deformed child shall live, but where there are too many (for in our state population has a limit), when couples have children in excess, and the state of feeling is averse to the exposure of offspring, let abortion be procured before sense and life have begun; what may or may not be lawfully done in these cases depends on the question of life and sensation.

And now, having determined at what ages men and women are to begin their union, let us also determine how long they shall continue to beget and bear offspring for the state; men who are too old, like men who are too young, produce children who are defective in body and mind; the children of very old men are weakly. The limit, then, should be the age which is the prime of their intelligence, and this in most persons, according to the notion of some poets who measure life by periods of seven years, is about fifty; at four or five years later, they should cease from having families; and from that time forward only cohabit with one another for the sake of health, or for some similar reason.

As to adultery, let it be held disgraceful for any man or woman to be unfaithful when they are married, and called husband and wife. If during the time of bearing [1336a] children anything of the sort occur, let the guilty person be punished with a loss of privileges in proportion to the offence.

After the children have been born, the manner of rearing them may be supposed to have a great effect on their bodily strength. It would appear from the example of animals, and of those nations who desire to create the military habit, that the food which has most milk in it is best suited to human beings; but the less wine the better, if they would escape diseases. Also all the motions to which children can be subjected at their early age are very useful. But in order to preserve their tender limbs from distortion, some nations have had recourse to mechanical appliances which straighten their bodies. To accustom children to the cold from their earliest years is also an excellent practice, which greatly conduces to health, and hardens them for military service. Hence many barbarians have a custom of plunging their children at birth into a cold stream; others, like the Celts, clothe them in a light wrapper only. For human nature should be early habituated to endure all which by habit it can be made to endure; but the process must be gradual. And children, from their natural warmth, may be easily trained to bear cold. Such care should attend them in the first stage of life.

The next period lasts to the age of five; during this no demand should be made upon the child for study or labour, lest its growth be impeded; and there should be sufficient motion to prevent the limbs from being inactive. This can be secured, among other ways, by amusement, but the amusement should not be vulgar or tiring or riotous. The Directors of Education, as they are termed, should be careful what tales or stories the children hear, for the sports of children are designed to prepare the way for the business of later life, and should be for the most part imitations of the occupations which they will hereafter pursue in earnest. Those are wrong who [like Plato] in the Laws attempt to check the loud crying and screaming of children, for these contribute towards their growth, and, in a manner, exercise their bodies. Straining the voice has an effect similar to that produced by the retention of the breath in violent exertions. Besides other duties, the Directors of Education should have an eye to their bringing up, and should take care that they are left as little as possible with slaves. For until they are seven years old they [1336b] must live at home; and therefore, even at this early age, all that is mean and low should be banished from their sight and hearing. Indeed, there is nothing which the legislator should be more careful to drive away than indecency of speech; for the light utterance of shameful words is akin to shameful actions. The young especially should never be allowed to repeat or hear anything of the sort. A freeman who is found saying or doing what is forbidden, if he be too young as yet to have the privilege of a place at the public tables, should be disgraced and beaten, and an elder person degraded as his slavish conduct deserves. And since we do not allow improper language, clearly we should also banish pictures or tales which are indecent. Let the rulers take care that there be no image or picture representing unseemly actions, except in the temples of those Gods at whose festivals the law permits even ribaldry, and whom the law also permits to be worshipped by persons of mature age on behalf of themselves, their children, and their wives. But the legislator should not allow youth to be hearers of satirical Iambic verses or spectators of comedy until they are of an age to sit at the public tables and to drink strong wine; by that time education will have armed them against the evil influences of such representations.

We have made these remarks in a cursory manner,—they are enough for the present occasion; but hereafter we will return to the subject and after a fuller discussion determine whether such liberty should or should not be granted, and in what way granted, if at all. Theodorus, the tragic actor, was quite right in saying that he would not allow any other actor, not even if he were quite second-rate, to enter before himself, because the spectators grew fond of the voices which they first heard. And the same principle of association applies universally to things as well as persons, for we always like best whatever comes first. And therefore youth should be kept strangers to all that is bad, and especially to things which suggest vice or hate. When the five years have passed away, during the two following years they must look on at the pursuits which they are hereafter to learn. There are two periods of life into which education has to be divided, from seven to the age of puberty, and onwards to the age of one and twenty. [1337a] [The poets] who divide ages by sevens are not always right: we should rather adhere to the divisions actually made by nature; for the deficiencies of nature are what art and education seek to fill up.

Let us then first enquire if any regulations are to be laid down about children, and secondly, whether the care of them should be the concern of the state or of private individuals, which latter is in our own day the common custom, and in the third place, what these regulations should be.

THE STATE OF NATURE AND NATURAL LAW (1651/1839)[1]

Thomas Hobbes

Thomas Hobbes (1588–1679) was born in Wiltshire, England. His father, a poor vicar, fled town after involvement in a fight outside his church, leaving his children to be reared by their uncle. Hobbes received an excellent early education and, at 15, entered Magdalen College, Oxford. There, he excelled in language studies and graduated in 1608. He then became companion and tutor to the son of William Cavendish (3rd Earl of Devonshire). In this role, he traveled over much of Europe where he became exposed to scientific and critical methods quite different from those of his Scholastic education. Upon Cavendish's death, Hobbes spent three years, mainly in Paris (as tutor to the son of Sir Gervase Clifton), where his interest in philosophy blossomed. Hobbes then returned to the Cavendish family to tutor the son of his first charge. During the next seven years, he expanded his knowledge of philosophy, visiting Florence, attending regular philosophical debates in Paris, and corresponding with René Descartes. In 1640, caught up in the turmoil that led to the English Civil War (1642–1651), Hobbes fled to Paris, where the exodus of Royalists increased his political interests. In Paris (where, in 1656, he briefly tutored Prince Charles of Wales), Hobbes wrote his most important works. The last of these, Leviathan (1651), almost immediately put Hobbes among the most praised and reviled thinkers of his day. Accused of atheism, egoism, and heresy, Hobbes was forced to flee Paris for England and appeal to the revolutionary government for protection. With the restoration of the Monarchy in 1660, Hobbes was at serious risk of prosecution; however, his former pupil, now King Charles II, granted him a pension of £100 and provided protection, especially when the Commons introduced a bill against atheism and profaneness, which specifically targeted Leviathan. From about age 60, Hobbes began to suffer from a shaking palsy, which worsened over the years. He continued to publish until a paralytic stroke brought on his death at age 91.

---

[1] First edition:1651; this selection is taken from the edition of 1839.

What to look for: In this selection from <u>Leviathan</u>, Hobbes discusses what life would be like with no government. In such a "state of nature," Hobbes claims, men are equal in both body and mind. How does he defend this claim? What three causes of conflict arise from this equality? What commodities are lacking in the state of nature? What five-word phrase describes the life of man? How does present experience fit with Hobbes analysis? Does a "state of nature" exist even today?

CHAPTER XIII.

Of the Natural Condition of Mankind as Concerning Their Felicity, and Misery.

NATURE hath made men so equal, in the faculties of the body, and mind; as that though there be found one man sometimes manifestly stronger in body, or of quicker mind than another; yet when all is reckoned together, the difference between man, and man, is not so considerable, as that one man can thereupon claim to himself any benefit, to which another may not pretend, as well as he. For as to the strength of body, the weakest has strength enough to kill the strongest, either by secret machination, or by confederacy with others, that are in the same danger with himself.

And as to the faculties of the mind, setting aside the arts grounded upon words, and especially that skill of proceeding upon general, and infallible rules, called science; which very few have, and but in few things; as being not a native faculty, born with us; nor attained, as prudence, while we look after somewhat else, I find yet a greater equality amongst men, than that of strength. For prudence, is but experience; which equal time, equally bestows on all men, in those things they equally apply themselves unto. That which may perhaps make such equality incredible, is but a vain conceit of one's own wisdom, which almost all men think they have in a greater degree, than the vulgar; that is, than all men but themselves, and a few others, whom by fame, or for concurring with themselves, [111]² they approve. For such is the nature of men, that howsoever they may acknowledge many others to be more witty, or more eloquent, or more learned; yet they will hardly believe there be many so wise as themselves; for they see their own wit at hand, and other men's at a distance.

---

²Referencing for Hobbes is not entirely standardized. For *Leviathan*, some scholars use the pagination or Chapter and paragraph number from the original 1651 edition, but Hobbes writings are also commonly referenced to the volume and page number in Molesworth's *English Works of Thomas Hobbes*—the source of this selection. Here, the bracketed numbers indicate the page in volume III; a full citation would read "Molesworth III, 111."

"The State of Nature and Natural Law," by Thomas Hobbes, from *Leviathan: The English Works of Thomas Hobbes of Malmesbury, Now First Collected and Edited*. Ed. Sir William Molesworth. Vol 3. (London: J. Bohn, 1839-45).

But this proveth rather that men are in that point equal, than unequal. For there is not ordinarily a greater sign of the equal distribution of any thing, than that every man is contented with his share.

From this equality of ability, ariseth equality of hope in the attaining of our ends. And therefore if any two men desire the same thing, which nevertheless they cannot both enjoy, they become enemies; and in the way to their end, which is principally their own conservation, and sometimes their delectation only, endeavour to destroy, or subdue one another. And from hence it comes to pass, that where an invader hath no more to fear, than another man's single power; if one plant, sow, build, or possess a convenient seat, others may probably be expected to come prepared with forces united, to dispossess, and deprive him, not only of the fruit of his labour, but also of his life, or liberty. And the invader again is in the like danger of another.

And from this diffidence of one another, there is no way for any man to secure himself, so reasonable, as anticipation; that is, by force, or wiles, to master the persons of all men he can, so long, till he see no other power great enough to endanger him: and this is no more than his own conservation requireth, and is generally allowed. Also because there be some, that taking pleasure in [112] contemplating their own power in the acts of conquest, which they pursue farther than their security requires; if others, that otherwise would be glad to be at ease within modest bounds, should not by invasion increase their power, they would not be able, long time, by standing only on their defence, to subsist. And by consequence, such augmentation of dominion over men being necessary to a man's conservation, it ought to be allowed him.

Again, men have no pleasure, but on the contrary a great deal of grief, in keeping company, where there is no power able to over-awe them all. For every man looketh that his companion should value him, at the same rate he sets upon himself: and upon all signs of contempt, or undervaluing, naturally endeavours, as far as he dares, (which amongst them that have no common power to keep them in quiet, is far enough to make them destroy each other), to extort a greater value from his contemners, by damage; and from others, by the example.

So that in the nature of man, we find three principal causes of quarrel. First, competition; secondly, diffidence; thirdly, glory.

The first, maketh men invade for gain; the second, for safety; and the third, for reputation. The first use violence, to make themselves masters of other men's persons, wives, children, and cattle; the second, to defend them; the third, for trifles, as a word, a smile, a different opinion, and any other sign of undervalue, either direct in their persons, or by reflection in their kindred, their friends, their nation, their profession, or their name.

Hereby it is manifest, that during the time men [113] live without a common power to keep them all in awe, they are in that condition which is called war; and such a war, as is of every man, against every man. For WAR, consisteth not in battle only, or the act of fighting; but in a tract of time, wherein the will to contend by battle is sufficiently known: and therefore the notion of *time*, is to be considered in the nature of war; as it is in the nature of weather. For as the nature of foul weather, lieth not in a shower or two of rain; but in an inclination thereto of many days together: so the nature of war, consisteth not in actual fighting; but in the known disposition thereto, during all the time there is no assurance to the contrary. All other time is PEACE.

Whatsoever therefore is consequent to a time of war, where every man is enemy to every man; the same is consequent to the time, wherein men live without other security, than what their own strength, and their own invention shall furnish them withal. In such condition, there is no place for industry; because the fruit thereof is uncertain: and consequently no culture of the earth; no navigation, nor use of the commodities that may be imported by sea; no commodious building; no instruments of moving, and removing, such things as require much force; no knowledge of the face of the earth; no account of time; no arts; no letters; no society; and which is worst of all, continual fear, and danger of violent death; and the life of man, solitary, poor, nasty, brutish, and short.

It may seem strange to some man, that has not well weighed these things; that nature should thus dissociate, and render men apt to invade, and destroy [114] one another: and he may therefore, not trusting to this inference, made from the passions, desire perhaps to have the same confirmed by experience. Let him therefore consider with himself, when taking a journey, he arms himself, and seeks to go well accompanied; when going to sleep, he locks his doors; when even in his house he locks his chests; and this when he knows there be laws, and public officers, armed, to revenge all injuries shall be done him; what opinion he has of his fellow-subjects, when he rides armed; of his fellow citizens, when he locks his doors; and of his children, and servants, when he locks his chests. Does he not there as much accuse mankind by his actions, as I do by my words? But neither of us accuse man's nature in it. The desires, and other passions of man, are in themselves no sin. No more are the actions, that proceed from those passions, till they know a law that forbids them: which till laws be made they cannot know: nor can any law be made, till they have agreed upon the person that shall make it.

It may peradventure be thought, there was never such a time, nor condition of war as this; and I believe it was never generally so, over all the world: but there are many places, where they live so now. For the savage people in many places of America, except the government of small families, the concord whereof dependeth on natural lust, have no government at all; and live at this day in that brutish manner, as I said before. Howsoever, it may be perceived what manner of life there would be, where there were no common power to fear, by the manner of life, which men that have [115] formerly lived under a peaceful government, use to degenerate into, in a civil war.

But though there had never been any time, wherein particular men were in a condition of war one against another; yet in all times, kings, and persons of sovereign authority, because of their independency, are in continual jealousies, and in the state and posture of gladiators; having their weapons pointing, and their eyes fixed on one another; that is, their forts, garrisons, and guns upon the frontiers of their kingdoms; and continual spies upon their neighbours; which is a posture of war. But because they uphold thereby, the industry of their subjects; there does not follow from it, that misery, which accompanies the liberty of particular men.

To this war of every man, against every man, this also is consequent; that nothing can be unjust. The notions of right and wrong, justice and injustice have there no place. Where there is no common power, there is no law: where no law, no injustice. Force, and fraud, are in war the two cardinal virtues. Justice, and injustice are none of the faculties neither of the body, nor mind. If they were, they might be in a man that were alone in the world, as well as his senses, and passions. They are qualities, that relate to men in society, not in solitude. It is consequent also to the same condition, that there be no propriety, no dominion, no *mine* and *thine* distinct; but only that to be every man's, that he can get; and for so long, as he can keep it. And thus much for the ill condition, which man by mere nature is actually placed in; though with a possibility to come out of it, [116] consisting partly in the passions, partly in his reason.

The passions that incline men to peace, are fear of death; desire of such things as are necessary to commodious living; and a hope by their industry to obtain them. And reason suggesteth convenient articles of peace, upon which men may be drawn to agreement. These articles, are they, which otherwise are called the Laws of Nature: whereof I shall speak more particularly, in the two following chapters.

What to look for now: *What is a right of nature? What is liberty? What is a law of nature? What is the difference between right and law? In the state of nature, to what does every man have a right? What is the first law of nature? What is the second law of nature? What must we give up in order to gain peace? What must we not give up, even in order to gain peace? What are the differences between transferring and renouncing?*

CHAPTER XIV.
Of the First and Second Natural Laws, and of Contracts.

THE RIGHT OF NATURE, which writers commonly call *jus naturale,* is the liberty each man hath, to use his own power, as he will himself, for the preservation of his own nature; that is to say, of his own life; and consequently, of doing any thing, which in his own judgment, and reason, he shall conceive to be the aptest means thereunto.

By LIBERTY, is understood, according to the proper signification of the word, the absence of external impediments: which impediments, may oft take away part of a man's power to do what he would; but cannot hinder him from using the power left him, according as his judgment, and reason shall dictate to him.

A LAW OF NATURE, *lex naturalis,* is a precept or general rule, found out by reason, by which a [117]man is forbidden to do that, which is destructive of his life, or taketh away the means of preserving the same; and to omit that, by which he thinketh it may be best preserved. For though they that speak of this subject, use to confound *jus,* and *lex, right* and *law:* yet they ought to be distinguished; because RIGHT, consisteth in liberty to do, or to forbear; whereas LAW, determineth, and bindeth to one of them: so that law, and right, differ as much, as obligation, and liberty; which in one and the same matter are inconsistent.

And because the condition of man, as hath been declared in the precedent chapter, is a condition of war of every one against every one; in which case every one is governed by his own reason; and there is nothing he can make use of, that may not be a help unto him, in preserving his life against his enemies; it followeth, that in such a condition, every man has a right to every thing; even to one another's body. And therefore, as long as this natural right of every man to every thing endureth, there can be no security to any man, how strong or wise soever he be, of living out the time, which nature ordinarily alloweth men to live. And consequently it is a precept, or general rule of reason, *that every man, ought to endeavour peace, as far as he has hope of obtaining it; and when he cannot obtain it, that he may seek, and use, all helps, and advantages of war.* The first branch of which rule, containeth the first, and fundamental law of nature; which is, *to seek peace, and follow it.* The second, the sum of the right of nature; which is, *by all means we can, to defend ourselves.*

From this fundamental law of nature, by which [118] men are commanded to endeavour peace, is derived this second law; *that a man be willing, when others are so too, as far-forth, as for peace, and defence of himself he shall think it necessary, to lay down this right to all things; and be contented with so much liberty against other men, as he would allow other men against himself.* For as long as every man holdeth this right, of doing any thing he liketh; so long are all men in the condition of war. But if other men will not lay down their right, as well as he; then there is no reason for any one, to divest himself of his: for that were to expose himself to prey, which no man is bound to, rather than to dispose himself to peace. This is that law of the Gospel; *whatsoever you require that others should do to you, that do ye to them.* And that law of all men, *quod tibi fieri non vis, alteri ne feceris.* [Do not do unto others what you do not want done unto you.]

To *lay down* a man's *right* to any thing, is to *divest* himself of the *liberty,* of hindering another of the benefit of his own right to the same. For he that renounceth, or passeth away his right, giveth not to any other man a right which he had not before; because there is nothing to which every man had not right by nature: but only standeth out of his way, that he may enjoy his own original right, without hindrance from him; not without hindrance from another. So that the effect which redoundeth to one man, by another man's defect of right, is but so much diminution of impediments to the use of his own right original.

Right is laid aside, either by simply renouncing it; or by transferring it to another. By *simply* RENOUNCING; when he cares not to whom the [119] benefit thereof redoundeth. By TRANSFERRING; when he intendeth the benefit thereof to some certain person, or persons. And when a man hath in either manner abandoned, or granted away his right; then is he said to be OBLIGED, or BOUND, not to hinder those, to whom such right is granted, or abandoned, from the benefit of it: and that he *ought,* and it is his DUTY, not to make void that voluntary act of his own: and that such hindrance is INJUSTICE, and INJURY, as being *sine jure* [without right]; the right being before renounced, or transferred. So that *injury,* or *injustice,* in the controversies of the world, is somewhat like to that, which in the disputations of scholars is called *absurdity.* For as it is there called an absurdity, to contradict what one maintained in the beginning: so in the world, it is called injustice, and injury, voluntarily to undo that, which from the beginning he had voluntarily done. The way by which a man either simply renounceth, or transferreth his right, is a declaration, or signification, by some voluntary and sufficient sign, or signs, that he doth so renounce, or transfer; or hath so renounced, or transferred the same, to him that accepteth it. And these signs are either words only, or actions only; or, as it happeneth most often, both words, and actions. And the same are the BONDS, by which men are bound, and obliged: bonds, that have their strength, not from their own nature, for nothing is more easily broken than a man's word, but from fear of some evil conseuence upon the rupture.

Whensoever a man transferreth his right, or renounceth it; it is either in consideration of some [120] right reciprocally transferred to himself; or for some other good he hopeth for thereby. For it is a voluntary act: and of the voluntary acts of every man, the object is some *good to himself.* And therefore there be some rights, which no man can be understood by any words, or other signs, to have abandoned, or transferred. As first a man cannot lay down the right of resisting them, that assault him by force, to take away his life; because he cannot be understood to aim thereby, at any good to himself. The same may be said of wounds, and chains, and imprisonment; both because there is no benefit consequent to such patience; as there is to the patience of suffering another to be wounded, or imprisoned: as also because a man cannot tell, when he seeth men proceed against him by violence, whether they intend his death or not. And lastly the motive, and end for which this renouncing, and transferring of right is introduced, is nothing else but the security of a man's person, in his life, and in the means of so preserving life, as not to be weary of it. And therefore if a man by words, or other signs, seem to despoil himself of the end, for which those signs were intended; he is not to be understood as if he meant it, or that it was his will; but that he was ignorant of how such words and actions were to be interpreted.

LIMITS ON GOVERNMENT (1689/1764)[1]

John Locke

John Locke (1632–1704) bore the same name as his father, a county lawyer who had been active in the early part of the English Civil War. His mother came from a family of tanners. Both parents were Puritans. At age 15, Locke was named a King's Scholar at the prestigious Westminster School in London. Upon graduation, he entered Christ Church, Oxford, where the classical curriculum annoyed him. He preferred the modern and experimental philosophies being pursued at other colleges and the newly created Royal Society. At 24, Locke completed the bachelor's program; he received a master's degree two years later. Locke then accepted temporary lectureships in Greek and in Rhetoric at Oxford, but declined any permanent appointment as accepting would require him to join a religious order. During his years in Oxford, Locke worked with Robert Boyle, Robert Hooke, and other important scientists of the day. His medical studies led (in 1867) to a position in London as personal physician to the 1st Earl of Shaftesbury, a controversial political figure. (Locke's treatment of a serious liver infection apparently saved Shaftesbury's life.) Locke continued medical studies under the tutelage of Thomas Sydenham, an individual who much influenced Locke's approach to philosophical thinking. During this time, Locke produced the first draft of his Essay Concerning Human Understanding. *(He received the Bachelor of Medicine qualification in 1674.)*

In the 1670s, Shaftesbury's patronage led to Locke's service as Secretary to both the Board of Trade and Plantations and the Lords and Proprietors of the Carolinas. This, together with the rise of Shaftesbury to the Lord Chancellorship (1672) and subsequent fall from power (1675), nurtured Locke's political interests and influenced his philosophical views on economics on government. Locke traveled in France from 1675 until Shaftesbury's political fortunes improved in 1679. Back in

---

[1]First edition 1689; this selection is taken from the sixth reprinting (1764), the one that was widely read in the American colonies on the eve of the Revolution.

England, Locke began to work on his Two Treatises of Government. In 1683, under suspicion of involvement in the Rye House Plot, Locke fled to Holland, where he remained until the Glorious Revolution of 1688 over-threw James II and replaced him with the Dutchman, William of Orange (William III). Upon returning from exile, Locke quickly published (in 1689/1690) the Essay, the Treatises, and a Letter Concerning Toleration. The Essay, with its revolutionary ideas about the nature of and basis for knowledge, became perhaps the most widely read philosophical book of its generation and brought Locke considerable fame. He occupied much of his remaining life working on revised editions that responded to both admirers and critics. The Treatises, published anonymously with the hope to avoid controversy over its revolutionary ideas about natu-ral rights and government, greatly influenced Voltaire, Rousseau, and Jefferson and provided inspiration for the American and French revo-lutions. (Locke's words are easily found embedded in both the United States' Declaration of Independence and Constitution.)

In 1691, Locke moved to a country house in Essex. There he was something of an intellectual hero to the Whigs and engaged in discussion with the likes of Isaac Newton. Another stint with the Board of Trade (from 1696 to 1700) preceded his final four years during which he suf-fered steadily deteriorating health. Locke never married.

What to look for: *Mirroring Hobbes, Locke considers the state of nature. As you read, think about the similarities and the differences between these two wherever they overlap respecting the following questions: What are the powers that persons possess in the state of nature? Why would someone give up any freedom or power that s/he possesses in the state of nature? What exactly does Locke mean by "property?" What is the chief reason that persons unite into commonwealths? What three important (governmental) functions are missing in the state of nature? What powers does one give up in order to unite in commonwealth? Are these to be given up totally? If not, how much can be properly given up? To whom (or what) does one grant these powers? Why does one do so? What are the three forms of commonwealth? Which of the three basic functions of government is supreme? Why? What are four basic restric-tions on legislative power? What is the origin of these restrictions? Is it wise to have a full-time legislature? Why (not)? What is the federative power of government? Why are federative and executive powers usually placed into one office?*

"Limits on Government," by John Locke, from *Two Treatises of Government*. Ed. Thomas Hollis. 6th ed. (London: A. Millar et al., 1764).

CHAP. IX.

Of the Ends of Political Society and Government.

§. 123. IF man in the state of nature be so free, as has been said; if he be absolute lord of his own person and possessions, equal to the greatest, and subject to no body, why will he part with his freedom? why will he give up this empire, and subject himself to the dominion and controul of any other power? To which it is obvious to answer, that though in the state of nature he hath such a right, yet the enjoyment of it is very uncertain, and constantly exposed to the invasion of others: for all being kings as [306] much as he, every man his equal, and the greater part no strict observers of equity and justice, the enjoyment of the property he has in this state is very unsafe, very unsecure. This makes him willing to quit a condition, which, however free, is full of fears and continual dangers: and it is not without reason, that he seeks out, and is willing to join in society with others, who are already united, or have a mind to unite, for the mutual *preservation* of their lives, liberties and estates, which I call by the general name, *property.*

§. 124. The great and *chief end,* therefore, of men's uniting into common-wealths, and putting themselves under government, *is the preservation of their property.* To which in the state of nature there are many things wanting.

First, There wants an *established,* settled, known *law,* received and allowed by common consent to be the standard of right and wrong, and the common measure to decide all controversies between them: for though the law of nature be plain and intelligible to all rational creatures; yet men being biased by their interest, as well as ignorant for want of study of it, are not apt to allow of it as a law binding to them in the application of it to their particular cases.

§. 125. *Secondly,* In the state of nature there wants *a known and indifferent judge,* with authority to determine all differences according [307] to the established law: for every one in that state being both judge and executioner of the law of nature, men being partial to themselves, passion and revenge is very apt to carry them too far, and with too much heat, in their own cases; as well as negligence, and unconcernedness, to make them too remiss in other men's.

§. 126. *Thirdly,* In the state of nature there often wants *power* to back and support the sentence when right, and to *give* it due *execution.* They who by any injustice offended, will seldom fail, where they are able, by force to make good their injustice; such resistance many times makes the punishment dangerous, and frequently destructive, to those who attempt it.

§. 127. Thus mankind, notwithstanding all the privileges of the state of nature, being but in an ill condition, while they remain in it, are quickly driven into society. Hence it comes to pass, that we seldom find any number of men live any time together in this state. The inconveniencies that they are therein exposed to, by the irregular and uncertain exercise of the power every man has of punishing the transgressions of others, make them take sanctuary under the established laws of government, and therein seek *the preservation of their property.* It is this makes them so willingly give up every one his single power of punishing, to be [308]exercised by such alone, as shall be appointed to it amongst them; and by such rules as the community, or those authorized by them to that purpose, shall agree on. And in this we have the original *right and rise of both the legislative and executive power,* as well as of the governments and societies themselves.

§. 128. For in the state of nature, to omit the liberty he has of innocent delights, a man has two powers.

The first is to do whatsoever he thinks fit for the preservation of himself, and others within the permission of the *law of nature:* by which law, common to them all, he and all the rest of *mankind are one community,* make up one society, distinct from all other creatures. And were it not for the corruption and vitiousness of degenerate men, there would be no need of any other; no necessity that men should separate from this great and natural community, and by positive agreements combine into smaller and divided associations.

The other power a man has in the state of nature, is the *power to punish the crimes* committed against that law. Both these he gives up, when he joins in a private, if I may so call it, or particular politic society, and incorporates into any common-wealth, separate from the rest of mankind. [309]

§. 129. The first *power,* viz. *of doing whatsoever be thought for the preservation of himself,* and the rest of mankind, *he gives up* to be regulated by laws made by the society, so far forth as the preservation of himself, and the rest of that society shall require; which laws of the society in many things confine the liberty he had by the law of nature.

§. 130. *Secondly,* The *power of punishing he wholly gives up,* and engages his natural force, (which he might before employ in the execution of the law of nature, by his own single authority, as he thought fit) to assist the executive power of the society, as the law thereof shall require: for being now in a new state, wherein he is to enjoy many conveniences, from the labour, assistance, and society of others in the same community, as well as protection from its whole strength; he is to part also with as much of his natural liberty, in providing for himself, as the good, prosperity, and safety of the society shall require; which is not only necessary, but just, since the other members of the society do the like.

§. 131. But though men, when they enter into society, give up the equality, liberty, and executive power they had in the state of nature, into the hands of the society, to be so far disposed of by the legislative, as the good of the society shall require; yet it being [310] only with an intention in every one the better to preserve himself, his liberty and property; (for no rational creature can be supposed to change his condition with an intention to be worse) the power of the society, or *legislative* constituted by them, can *never be supposed to extend farther, than the common good;* but is obliged to secure every one's property, by providing against those three defects above mentioned, that made the state of nature so unsafe and uneasy. And so whoever has the legislative or supreme power of any common-wealth, is bound to govern by established *standing laws,* promulgated and known to the people, and not by extemporary decrees; by *indifferent* and upright *judges,* who are to decide controversies by those laws; and to employ the force of the community at home, *only in the execution of such laws,* or abroad to prevent or redress foreign injuries, and secure the community from inroads and invasion. And all this to be directed to no other *end,* but the *peace, safety,* and *public good* of the people.

CHAP. X.

Of the Forms of a Common-wealth.

§. 132. THE majority having, as has been shewed, upon men's first uniting into society, the whole power of the community [311] naturally in them, may employ all that power in making laws for the community from time to time, and executing those laws by officers of their own appointing; and then the *form* of the government is a perfect *democracy:* or else may put the power of making laws into the hands of a few select men, and their heirs or successors; and then it is an *oligarchy:* or else into the hands of one man, and then it is a *monarchy:* if to him and his heirs, it is an *hereditary monarchy:* if to him only for life, but upon his death the power only of nominating a successor to return to them; an *elective monarchy.* And so accordingly of these the community may make compounded and mixed forms of government, as they think good. And if the legislative power be at first given by the majority to one or more persons only for their lives, or any limited time, and then the supreme power to revert to them again; when it is so reverted, the community may dispose of it again anew into what hands they please, and so constitute a new form of government: for the *form of government depending upon the placing the* supreme power, which is *the legislative,* it being impossible to conceive that an inferior power should prescribe to a superior, or any but the supreme make laws, according as the power of making laws is placed, such is the *form of the common-wealth.*[312]

§. 133. By *common-wealth,* I must be understood all along to mean, not a democracy, or any form of government, but *any independent community,* which the *Latines* signified by the word *civitas,* to which the word which best answers in our language, is *common-wealth,* and most properly expresses such a society of men, which community or city in *English* does not; for there may be subordinate communities in a government; and city amongst us has a quite different notion from common-wealth: and therefore, to avoid ambiguity, I crave leave to use the word *common-wealth* in that sense, in which I find it used by king *James the first;* and I take it to be its genuine signification; which if any body dislike, I consent with him to change it for a better.

CHAP. XI.

Of the Extent of the Legislative Power.

§. 134. THE great end of men's entering into society, being the enjoyment of their properties in peace and safety, and the great instrument and means of that being the laws established in that society; the *first and fundamental positive law* of all common-wealths *is the establishing of the legislative* power; as the *first and fundamental natural* [313] *law,* which is to govern even the legislative itself, *is the preservation of the society,* and (as far as will consist with the public good) of every person in it. This *legislative* is not only *the supreme power* of the common-wealth, but sacred and unalterable in the hands where the community have once placed it; nor can any edict of any body else, in what form soever conceived, or by what power soever backed, have the force and obligation of a *law,* which has not its *sanction from* that *legislative* which the public has chosen and appointed: for without this the law could not have that, which is absolutely necessary to its being a *law, the consent of the society,* over whom no body can have a power to make laws, but by their own consent, and by authority received [314] from them; and therefore all the *obedience,* which by the most solemn ties any one can be obliged *to* pay, ultimately terminates in this *supreme power,* and is directed by those laws which it enacts: nor can any oaths to any foreign power whatsoever, or any domestic subordinate power, discharge any member of the society from his *obedience to the legislative,* acting pursuant to their trust; nor oblige him to any obedience contrary to the laws so enacted, or farther than they do allow; it being ridiculous to imagine one can be tied ultimately to *obey* any *power* in the society, which is not the *supreme.*

§. 135. Though the *legislative,* whether placed in one or more, whether it be always in being, or only by intervals, though it be the *supreme* power in every common-wealth; yet,

First, It is *not,* nor can possibly be absolutely *arbitrary* over the lives and fortunes of the people: for it being but the joint power of every member of the society given up to that person, or assembly, which is legislator; it can be no more than those persons had in a state of nature before they entered into society, and gave up to the community: for no body can transfer to another more power than he has in himself; and no body has an absolute arbitrary power over himself, or over any other, to destroy his own life, or take away the life or property of another. A man, [315] as has been proved, cannot subject himself to the arbitrary power of another; and having in the state of nature no arbitrary power over the life, liberty, or possession of another, but only so much as the law of nature gave him for the preservation of himself, and the rest of mankind; this is all he doth, or can give up to the common-wealth, and by it to the *legislative power,* so that the legislative can have no more than this. Their power, in the utmost bounds of it, is *limited to the public good* of the society. It is a power, that hath no other end but preservation, and therefore can never have a right to destroy, enslave, or designedly to impoverish the subjects. The obligations of the law of nature cease not in society, but only in many cases are drawn closer, and have by human laws [316] known penalties annexed to them, to inforce their observation. Thus the law of nature stands as an eternal rule to all men, *legislators* as well as others. The *rules* that they make for other men's actions, must, as well as their own and other men's actions, be conformable to the law of nature, *i.e.* to the will of God, of which that is a declaration, and the *fundamental law of nature being the preservation of mankind,* no human sanction can be good, or valid against it.

§. 136. *Secondly,* The *legislative,* or supreme authority, cannot assume to its self a power to rule by extemporary arbitrary decrees, but *is bound to dispense justice,* and decide the rights of the subject *by promulgated standing laws, and known authorized judges:* for the law of nature being unwritten, and so no where to be found but in the minds of men, they who through passion or interest shall miscite, or misapply it, cannot so easily be convinced of their mistake where there is no established judge: and so it serves not, as it ought, to determine the rights, and fence the [317] properties of those that live under it, especially where every one is judge, interpreter, and executioner of it too, and that in his own case: and he that has right on his side, having ordinarily but his own single strength, hath not force enough to defend himself from injuries, or to punish delinquents. To avoid these inconveniencies, which disorder men's properties in the state of nature, men unite into societies, that they may have the united strength of the whole society to secure and defend their properties, and may have *standing rules* to bound it, by which every one may know what is his. To this end it is that men give up all their natural power to the society which they enter into, and the community put the legislative power into such hands as they think fit, with this trust, that they shall be governed by *declared laws,* or else their peace, quiet, and property will still be at the same uncertainty, as it was in the state of nature.

§. 137. Absolute arbitrary power, or governing without *settled standing laws,* can neither of them consist with the ends of society and government, which men would not quit the freedom of the state of nature for, and tie themselves up under, were it not to preserve their lives, liberties and fortunes, and by *stated rules* of right and property to secure their peace and quiet. It cannot be supposed that they should intend, had they a power [318] so to do, to give to any one, or more, an *absolute arbitrary power* over their persons and estates, and put a force into the magistrate's hand to execute his unlimited will arbitrarily upon them. This were to put themselves into a worse condition than the state of nature, wherein they had a liberty to defend their right against the injuries of others, and were upon equal terms of force to maintain it, whether invaded by a single man, or many in combination. Whereas by supposing they have given up themselves to the *absolute arbitrary power* and will of a legislator, they have disarmed themselves, and armed him, to make a prey of them when he pleases; he being in a much worse condition, who is exposed to the arbitrary power of one man, who has the command of 100,000, than he that is exposed to the arbitrary power of 100,000 single men; no body being secure, that his will, who has such a command, is better than that of other men, though his force be 100,000 times stronger. And therefore, whatever form the commonwealth is under, the ruling power ought to govern by *declared* and *received laws,* and nor by extemporary dictates and undetermined resolutions: for then mankind will be in a far worse condition than in the state of nature, if they shall have armed one, or a few men with the joint power of a multitude, to force them to obey at pleasure the exorbitant [319] and unlimited decrees of their sudden thoughts, or unrestrained, and till that moment unknown wills, without having any measures set down which may guide and justify their actions: for all the power the government has, being only for the good of the society, as it ought not to be *arbitrary* and at pleasure, so it ought to be exercised by *established and promulgated laws;* that both the people may know their duty, and be safe and secure within the limits of the law; and the rulers too kept within their bounds, and not be tempted, by the power they have in their hands, to employ it to such purposes, and by such measures, as they would not have known, and own not willingly.

§. 138. *Thirdly,* The *supreme power cannot take* from any man any part of his *property* without his own consent: for the preservation of property being the end of government, and that for which men enter into society, it necessarily supposes and requires, that the people should *have property,* without which they must be supposed to lose that, by entering into society, which was the end for which they entered into it; too gross an absurdity for any man to own. *Men* therefore *in society having property,* they have such a right to the goods, which by the law of the community are their's, that no body hath a right to take their substance or any part of it from them, without their own consent: without [320] this they have no *property* at all; for I have truly no *property* in that, which another can by right take from me, when he pleases, against my consent. Hence it is a mistake to think, that the *supreme or legislative power* of any common-wealth, can do what it will, and dispose of the estates of the subject *arbitrarily,* or take any part of them at pleasure. This is not much to be feared in governments where the *legislative* consists, wholly or in part, in assemblies which are variable, whose members, upon the dissolution of the assembly, are subjects under the common laws of their country, equally with the rest. But in governments, where the *legislative* is in one lasting assembly always in being, or in one man, as in absolute monarchies, there is danger still, that they will think themselves to have a distinct interest from the rest of the community; and so will be apt to increase their own riches and power, by taking what they think fit from the people: for a man's *property* is not at all secure, tho' there be good and equitable laws to set the bounds of it between him and his fellow subjects, if he who commands those subjects have power to take from any private man, what part he pleases of his *property,* and use and dispose of it as he thinks good.

§. 139. But *government,* into whatsoever hands it is put, being, as I have before shewed, intrusted with this condition, and *for this* [321]*end,* that men might have and secure their *properties;* the prince, or senate, however it may have power to make laws, for the regulating of *property* between the subjects one amongst another, yet can never have a power to take to themselves the whole, or any part of the subjects *property,* without their own consent: for this would be in effect to leave them no *property* at all. And to let us see, that even *absolute power,* where it is necessary, is *not arbitrary* by being absolute, but is still limited by that reason, and confined to those ends, which required it in some cases to be absolute, we need look no farther than the common practice of martial discipline: for the preservation of the army, and in it of the whole common-wealth, requires an *absolute obedience* to the command of every superior officer, and it is justly death to disobey or dispute the most dangerous or unreasonable of them; but yet we see, that neither the serjeant, that could command a soldier to march up to the mouth of a cannon, or stand in a breach, where he is almost sure to perish, can command that soldier to give him one penny of his money; nor the *general,* that can condemn him to death for deserting his post, or for not obeying the most desperate orders, can yet, with all his *absolute power* of life and death, dispose of one farthing of that soldier's estate, or seize one jot of his goods; whom yet he can command any thing, and [322] hang for the least disobedience; because such a blind obedience is necessary to that end, for which the commander has his power, *viz.* the preservation of the rest; but the disposing of his goods has nothing to do with it.

§. 140. It is true, governments cannot be supported without great charge, and it is fit every one who enjoys his share of the protection, should pay out of his estate his proportion for the maintenance of it. But still it must be with his own consent, *i.e.* the consent of the majority, giving it either by themselves, or their representatives chosen by them: for if any one shall claim a *power to lay* and levy *taxes* on the people, by his own authority, and without such consent of the people, he thereby invades the *fundamental law of property,* and subverts the end of government: for what property have I in that, which another may by right take, when he pleases, to himself?

§. 141. *Fourthly,* The *legislative cannot transfer the power of making laws* to any other hands: for it being but a delegated power from the people, they who have it cannot pass it over to others. The people alone can appoint the form of the common-wealth, which is by constituting the legislative, and appointing in whose hands that shall be. And when the people have said, We will submit to rules, and be governed by *laws* made by such men, and in such forms, no body else can [323] say other men shall make *laws* for them; nor can the people be bound by any *laws,* but such as are enacted by those whom they have chosen, and authorized to make *laws* for them. The power of the *legislative,* being derived from the people by a positive voluntary grant and institution, can be no other than what that positive grant conveyed, which being only to make *laws,* and not to make *legislators,* the *legislative* can have no power to transfer their authority of making laws, and place it in other hands.

§. 142. These are the *bounds* which the trust, that is put in them by the society, and the law of God and nature, have *set to the legislative* power of every common-wealth, in all forms of government.

First, They are to govern by *promulgated established laws,* not to be varied in particular cases, but to have one rule for rich and poor, for the favourite at court, and the country man at plough.

Secondly, These *laws* also ought to be designed *for* no other end ultimately, but *the good of the people.*

Thirdly, They must *not raise taxes* on the *property of the people, without the consent of the people,* given by themselves, or their deputies. And this properly concerns only such governments where the *legislative* is always in being, or at least where the people have not reserved any part of the legislative to [324] deputies, to be from time to time chosen by themselves.

Fourthly, The *legislative* neither must *nor can transfer the power of making laws* to any body else, or place it any where, but where the people have.

CHAP. XII.

Of the Legislative, Executive, and Federative Power of the Common-wealth.

§. 143. THE *legislative* power is that, which has a right *to direct how the force of the common-wealth* shall be employed for preserving the community and the members of it. But because those laws which are constantly to be executed, and whose force is always to continue, may be made in a little time; therefore there is no need, that the *legislative* should be always in being, not having always business to do. And because it may be too great a temptation to human frailty, apt to grasp at power, for the same persons, who have the power of making laws, to have also in their hands the power to execute them, whereby they may exempt themselves from obedience to the laws they make, and suit the law, both in its making, and execution, to their own private advantage, and thereby come to have a distinct interest from the rest of the community, [325] contrary to the end of society and government: therefore in well-ordered common-wealths, where the good of the whole is so considered, as it ought, the *legislative* power is put into the hands of divers persons, who duly assembled, have by themselves, or jointly with others, a power to make laws, which when they have done, being separated again, they are themselves subject to the laws they have made; which is a new and near tie upon them, to take care, that they make them for the public good.

§. 144. But because the laws, that are at once, and in a short time made, have a constant and lasting force, and need a *perpetual execution,* or an attendance thereunto; therefore it is necessary there should be a *power always in being,* which should see to the *execution* of the laws that are made, and remain in force. And thus the *legislative* and *executive power* come often to be separated.

§. 145. There is another *power* in every common-wealth, which one may call *natural,* because it is that which answers to the power every man naturally had before he entered into society: for though in a common-wealth the members of it are distinct persons still in reference to one another, and as such are governed by the laws of the society; yet in reference to the rest of mankind, they make one body, which is, as every member of it before was, still in the state of [326] nature with the rest of mankind. Hence it is, that the controversies that happen between any man of the society with those that are out of it, are managed by the public; and an injury done to a member of their body, engages the whole in the reparation of it. So that under this consideration, the whole community is one body in the state of nature, in respect of all other states or persons out of its community.

§. 146. This therefore contains the power of war and peace, leagues and alliances, and all the transactions, with all persons and communities without the common-wealth, and may be called *federative,* if any one pleases. So the thing be understood, I am indifferent as to the name.

§. 147. These two powers, *executive* and *federative,* though they be really distinct in themselves, yet one comprehending the *execution* of the municipal laws of the society *within* its self, upon all that are parts of it; the other the management of the *security and interest of the public without,* with all those that it may receive benefit or damage from, yet they are always almost united. And though this *federative power* in the well or ill management of it be of great moment to the common-wealth, yet it is much less capable to be directed by antecedent, standing, positive laws, than the *executive;* and so must necessarily be left to the prudence and wisdom [327] of those, whose hands it is in, to be managed for the public good: for the *laws* that concern subjects one amongst another, being to direct their actions, may well enough *precede* them. But what is to be done in reference to *foreigners,* depending much upon their actions, and the variation of designs and interests, must be *left* in great part *to* the *prudence* of those, who have this power committed to them, to be managed by the best of their skill, for the advantage of the common-wealth.

§. 148. Though, as I said, the *executive* and *federative power* of every community be really distinct in themselves, yet they are hardly to be separated, and placed at the same time, in the hands of distinct persons: for both of them requiring the force of the society for their exercise, it is almost impracticable to place the force of the common-wealth in distinct, and not subordinate hands; or that the *executive* and *federative power* should be *placed* in persons, that might act separately, whereby the force of the public would be under different commands: which would be apt some time or other to cause disorder and ruin.

LIBERTY (1859)

John Stuart Mill

John Stuart Mill (1806–1873) was born in London, England, the eldest of nine children of Scottish historian/economist/philosopher James Mill (1773–1836). The senior Mill, with advice from utilitarian philosopher and social reformer Jeremy Bentham, gave John Stuart a most extraordinary upbringing—one designed to produce a genius who would be a powerful advocate for utilitarianism. The lad was kept separate from children (other than his siblings). At just 3 years of age, he began learning Greek. By 8, he had read works of Aesop, Xenophon, and Herodotus, had begun learning Latin, algebra, and Euclid, and assumed schoolmaster's duties to his younger siblings. By 10, he was reading Plato and becoming familiar with the classical writings of Horace, Virgil, Ovid, Tacitus, Homer, Dionysus, Sophocles, Euripides, Aristophanes, and Thucydides that were commonly read in the universities of the time. He also studied poetry and was allowed to read novels and natural science. At 12, Mill undertook serious study of scholastic logic, reading Aristotle in Greek. At 13, he became acquainted with the economic work of Adam Smith and David Ricardo, friends of his father who often discussed their work with the teenager. At 14, Mill was sent to stay with Bentham's brother in southern France. There he was tutored in higher mathematics and attended classes in chemistry and zoology at the <u>Faculté des Sciences</u> in Montpellier. Mill also spent time in Paris, where his father's connections brought him into contact with prominent Parisian economists and socialists. At 17, Mill declined to take Anglican orders (a requirement for study at Oxford or Cambridge) and instead began a 35-year career at British East India Company (where he rose through the ranks to become Chief of Office shortly before the British Government takeover). At 18, Mill published his first article. At 20, he began to question his views and suffered a nervous breakdown (which he later attributed to the physical and mental rigor of his upbringing, including suppression of normal childhood feelings). As his depression diminished, he took an interest in romantic poetry and positivism. Mill published extensively in radical journals, including the <u>Westminster Review</u>, which he bought and used to support progressive, reformist politicians. At 45, Mill married Harriet Taylor, his *close friend of twenty years. Taylor herself had a brilliant mind and was a strong influence on Mill's thought. Only seven years into the marriage, Mill lost his wife to illness. To be near her grave, Mill took a house in Avignon, France, and subsequently divided his time between that place and London. At 59, Mill was elected to Parliament, thus beginning a very brief political career. The same year, Mill became Lord Rector at the University of St. Andrews in Scotland. Both positions lasted only two years. In Parliament, Mill was the first member to call for women to be given the right to vote. Throughout his productive life, in both words and action, Mill strongly advocated for progressive policies including abolition of the slave trade, universal suffrage, proportional representation, prison reform, labor unions, and farm cooperatives. A few days before his 67th birth anniversary, an infection took Mill's life. His grave is in Avignon, next to Harriet's.*

What to look for: *This selection comes from* <u>On Liberty</u>, *a work that Mill and his wife, Harriet Taylor, wrote jointly. What are their answers to the following questions: What is the principal question in human affairs? How is this question ordinarily answered? What reasons back up the ordinary answer? What is the true origin of "self-evident" principles? What is the single principle that should govern the dealings of society with the individual as to compulsion and control? Are there limits to this principle? What liberty exists if the principle is violated? What liberties does the principle entail? How is liberty threatened?*

. . . There is a limit to the legitimate interference of collective opinion with individual independence: and to find that limit, and maintain it against encroachment, is as indispensable to a good condition of human affairs, as protection against political despotism.

But though this proposition is not likely to be contested in general terms, the practical question, where to place the limit—how to make the fitting adjustment between individual independence and social control—is a subject on which nearly everything remains to be done. All that makes existence valuable to any one, depends on the enforcement of restraints upon the actions of other people. Some rules of conduct, therefore, must be imposed, by law in the first place, and by opinion on many things which are not fit subjects for the operation of law. What these rules should be, is the principal question in human affairs; but if we except a few of the most obvious cases, it is one of those which least progress has been made in resolving. No two ages, and scarcely

"Liberty," by John Stuart Mill, from *On Liberty*. 2nd ed. (London: John W. Parker and Son, West Strand, 1859).

any two countries, have decided it alike; and the decision of one age or country is a wonder to another. Yet the people of any given age and country no more suspect any difficulty in it, than if it were a subject on which mankind had always been agreed. The rules [15][1] which obtain among themselves appear to them self-evident and self-justifying. This all but universal illusion is one of the examples of the magical influence of custom, which is not only, as the proverb says, a second nature, but is continually mistaken for the first. The effect of custom, in preventing any misgiving respecting the rules of conduct which mankind impose on one another, is all the more complete because the subject is one on which it is not generally considered necessary that reasons should be given, either by one person to others, or by each to himself. People are accustomed to believe, and have been encouraged in the belief by some who aspire to the character of philosophers, that their feelings, on subjects of this nature, are better than reasons, and render reasons unnecessary. The practical principle which guides them to their opinions on the regulation of human conduct, is the feeling in each person's mind that everybody should be required to act as he, and those with whom he sympathizes, would like them to act. No one, indeed, acknowledges to himself that his standard of judgment is his own liking; but an opinion on a point of conduct, not supported by reasons, can only count as one person's preference; and if the reasons, when given, are a mere appeal to a similar preference felt by other people, it is still only many people's liking instead of one. To an ordinary man, however, his own preference, [16] thus supported, is not only a perfectly satisfactory reason, but the only one he generally has for any of his notions of morality, taste, or propriety, which are not expressly written in his religious creed; and his chief guide in the interpretation even of that. Men's opinions, accordingly, on what is laudable or blamable, are affected by all the multifarious causes which influence their wishes in regard to the conduct of others, and which are as numerous as those which determine their wishes on any other subject. Sometimes their reason—at other times their prejudices or superstitions: often their social affections, not seldom their antisocial ones, their envy or jealousy, their arrogance or contemptuousness: but most commonly, their desires or fears for themselves—their legitimate or illegitimate self-interest. Wherever there is an ascendant class, a large portion of the morality of the country emanates from its class interests, and its feelings of class superiority. The morality between Spartans and Helots, between planters and negroes, between princes and subjects, between nobles and roturiers, between men and women, has been for the most part the creation of these class interests and feelings: and the sentiments thus generated, react in turn upon the moral feelings of the members of the ascendant class, in their relations among themselves. Where, on the other hand, a class, formerly ascendant, has lost [17] its ascendancy, or where its ascendancy is unpopular, the prevailing moral

---

[1]Bracketed numbers indicate pages in the 1859 edition from which this selection is taken.

sentiments frequently bear the impress of an impatient dislike of superiority.
Another grand determining principle of the rules of conduct, both in act and for-
bearance, which have been enforced by law or opinion, has been the servility of
mankind towards the supposed preferences or aversions of their temporal masters, or of their gods. This servility, though essentially selfish, is not hypocrisy;
it gives rise to perfectly genuine sentiments of abhorrence; it made men burn
magicians and heretics. Among so many baser influences, the general and obvious interests of society have of course had a share, and a large one, in the direction of the moral sentiments: less, however, as a matter of reason, and on their
own account, than as a consequence of the sympathies and antipathies which
grew out of them: and sympathies and antipathies which had little or nothing to
do with the interests of society, have made themselves felt in the establishment
of moralities with quite as great force.

The likings and dislikings of society, or of some powerful portion of it,
are thus the main thing which has practically determined the rules laid down
for general observance, under the penalties of law or opinion. And in general,
those who have been in advance of society in thought and feeling have left this
condition of things unassailed in [18] principle, however they may have come
into conflict with it in some of its details. They have occupied themselves
rather in inquiring what things society ought to like or dislike, than in questioning whether its likings or dislikings should be a law to individuals. They
preferred endeavouring to alter the feelings of mankind on the particular points
on which they were themselves heretical, rather than make common cause in
defence of freedom, with heretics generally. The only case in which the higher
ground has been taken on principle and maintained with consistency, by any
but an individual here and there, is that of religious belief: a case instructive in
many ways, and not least so as forming a most striking instance of the fallibil-
ity of what is called the moral sense: for the *odium theologicum*, in a sincere
bigot, is one of the most unequivocal cases of moral feeling. Those who first
broke the yoke of what called itself the Universal Church, were in general as
little willing to permit difference of religious opinion as that church itself. But
when the heat of the conflict was over, without giving a complete victory to any
party, and each church or sect was reduced to limit its hopes to retaining possession of the ground it already occupied; minorities, seeing that they had no
chance of becoming majorities, were under the necessity of pleading to those
whom they could not convert, for permission to differ. It is accordingly [19] on
this battle-field, almost solely, that the rights of the individual against society
have been asserted on broad grounds of principle, and the claim of society to
exercise authority over dissentients, openly controverted. The great writers to
whom the world owes what religious liberty it possesses, have mostly asserted
freedom of conscience as an indefeasible right, and denied absolutely that a
human being is accountable to others for his religious belief. Yet so natural
to mankind is intolerance in whatever they really care about, that religious

freedom has hardly anywhere been practically realized, except where religious indifference, which dislikes to have its peace disturbed by theological quarrels, has added its weight to the scale. In the minds of almost all religious persons, even in the most tolerant countries, the duty of toleration is admitted with tacit reserves. One person will bear with dissent in matters of church government, but not of dogma; another can tolerate everybody, short of a Papist or a Unitarian; another, every one who believes in revealed religion; a few extend their charity a little further, but stop at the belief in a God and in a future state. Wherever the sentiment of the majority is still genuine and intense, it is found to have abated little of its claim to be obeyed.

In England, from the peculiar circumstances of our political history, though the yoke of opinion is [20] perhaps heavier, that of law is lighter, than in most other countries of Europe; and there is considerable jealousy of direct interference, by the legislative or the executive power, with private conduct; not so much from any just regard for the independence of the individual, as from the still subsisting habit of looking on the government as representing an opposite interest to the public. The majority have not yet learnt to feel the power of the government their power, or its opinions their opinions. When they do so, individual liberty will probably be as much exposed to invasion from the government, as it already is from public opinion. But, as yet, there is a considerable amount of feeling ready to be called forth against any attempt of the law to control individuals in things in which they have not hitherto been accustomed to be controlled by it; and this with very little discrimination as to whether the matter is, or is not, within the legitimate sphere of legal control; insomuch that the feeling, highly salutary on the whole, is perhaps quite as often misplaced as well grounded in the particular instances of its application. There is, in fact, no recognised principle by which the propriety or impropriety of government interference is customarily tested. People decide according to their personal preferences. Some, whenever they see any good to be done, or evil to be remedied, would willingly instigate the government [21] to undertake the business; while others prefer to bear almost any amount of social evil, rather than add one to the departments of human interests amenable to governmental control. And men range themselves on one or the other side in any particular case, according to this general direction of their sentiments; or according to the degree of interest which they feel in the particular thing which it is proposed that the government should do, or according to the belief they entertain that the government would, or would not, do it in the manner they prefer; but very rarely on account of any opinion to which they consistently adhere, as to what things are fit to be done by a government. And it seems to me that in consequence of this absence of rule or principle, one side is at present as often wrong as the other; the interference of government is, with about equal frequency, improperly invoked and improperly condemned.

The object of this Essay is to assert one very simple principle, as entitled to govern absolutely the dealings of society with the individual in the way of compulsion and control, whether the means used be physical force in the form of legal penalties, or the moral coercion of public opinion. That principle is, that the sole end for which mankind are warranted, individually or collectively, in interfering with the liberty of action [22] of any of their number, is self-protection. That the only purpose for which power can be rightfully exercised over any member of a civilized community, against his will, is to prevent harm to others. His own good, either physical or moral, is not a sufficient warrant. He cannot rightfully be compelled to do or forbear because it will be better for him to do so, because it will make him happier, because, in the opinions of others, to do so would be wise, or even right. These are good reasons for remonstrating with him, or reasoning with him, or persuading him, or entreating him, but not for compelling him, or visiting him with any evil in case he do otherwise. To justify that, the conduct from which it is desired to deter him must be calculated to produce evil to some one else. The only part of the conduct of any one, for which he is amenable to society, is that which concerns others. In the part which merely concerns himself, his independence is, of right, absolute. Over himself, over his own body and mind, the individual is sovereign.

It is, perhaps, hardly necessary to say that this doctrine is meant to apply only to human beings in the maturity of their faculties. We are not speaking of children, or of young persons below the age which the law may fix as that of manhood or womanhood. Those who are still in a state to require being taken care of by others, must be protected [23] against their own actions as well as against external injury. For the same reason, we may leave out of consideration those backward states of society in which the race itself may be considered as in its nonage. The early difficulties in the way of spontaneous progress are so great, that there is seldom any choice of means for overcoming them; and a ruler full of the spirit of improvement is warranted in the use of any expedients that will attain an end, perhaps otherwise unattainable. Despotism is a legitimate mode of government in dealing with barbarians, provided the end be their improvement, and the means justified by actually effecting that end. Liberty, as a principle, has no application to any state of things anterior to the time when mankind have become capable of being improved by free and equal discussion. Until then, there is nothing for them but implicit obedience to an Akbar or a Charlemagne, if they are so fortunate as to find one. But as soon as mankind have attained the capacity of being guided to their own improvement by conviction or persuasion (a period long since reached in all nations with whom we need here concern ourselves), compulsion, either in the direct form or in that of pains and penalties for non-compliance, is no longer admissible as a means to their own good, and justifiable only for the security of others.

It is proper to state that I forego any advantage [24] which could be derived to my argument from the idea of abstract right, as a thing independent of utility.

I regard utility as the ultimate appeal on all ethical questions; but it must be utility in the largest sense, grounded on the permanent interests of man as a progressive being. Those interests, I contend, authorize the subjection of individual spontaneity to external control, only in respect to those actions of each, which concern the interest of other people. If any one does an act hurtful to others, there is a *primâ facie* case for punishing him, by law, or, where legal penalties are not safely applicable, by general disapprobation. There are also many positive acts for the benefit of others, which he may rightfully be compelled to perform; such as, to give evidence in a court of justice; to bear his fair share in the common defence, or in any other joint work necessary to the interest of the society of which he enjoys the protection; and to perform certain acts of individual beneficence, such as saving a fellow-creature's life, or interposing to protect the defenceless against ill-usage, things which whenever it is obviously a man's duty to do, he may rightfully be made responsible to society for not doing. A person may cause evil to others not only by his actions but by his inaction, and in either case he is justly accountable to them for the injury. The latter case, it is true, requires a much more [25] cautious exercise of compulsion than the former. To make any one answerable for doing evil to others, is the rule; to make him answerable for not preventing evil, is, comparatively speaking, the exception. Yet there are many cases clear enough and grave enough to justify that exception. In all things which regard the external relations of the individual, he is *de jure* amenable to those whose interests are concerned, and if need be, to society as their protector. There are often good reasons for not holding him to the responsibility; but these reasons must arise from the special expediencies of the case: either because it is a kind of case in which he is on the whole likely to act better, when left to his own discretion, than when controlled in any way in which society have it in their power to control him; or because the attempt to exercise control would produce other evils, greater than those which it would prevent. When such reasons as these preclude the enforcement of responsibility, the conscience of the agent himself should step into the vacant judgment seat, and protect those interests of others which have no external protection; judging himself all the more rigidly, because the case does not admit of his being made accountable to the judgment of his fellow-creatures.

But there is a sphere of action in which society, as distinguished from the individual, has, if any, [26] only an indirect interest; comprehending all that portion of a person's life and conduct which affects only himself, or if it also affects others, only with their free, voluntary, and undeceived consent and participation. When I say only himself, I mean directly, and in the first instance: for whatever affects himself, may affect others *through* himself; and the objection which may be grounded on this contingency, will receive consideration in the sequel. This, then, is the appropriate region of human liberty. It comprises, first, the inward domain of consciousness; demanding liberty of conscience, in the most comprehensive sense; liberty of thought and feeling; absolute free-dom of opinion and sentiment on all subjects, practical or speculative, scien-tific, moral, or theological. The liberty of expressing and publishing opinions may seem to fall under a different principle, since it belongs to that part of the conduct of an individual which concerns other people; but, being almost of as much importance as the liberty of thought itself, and resting in great part on the same reasons, is practically inseparable from it. Secondly, the principle requires liberty of tastes and pursuits; of framing the plan of our life to suit our own character; of doing as we like, subject to such consequences as may follow: without impediment from our fellow-creatures, so long as what we do does not harm them, even though[27] they should think our conduct foolish, perverse, or wrong. Thirdly, from this liberty of each individual, follows the liberty, within the same limits, of combination among individuals; freedom to unite, for any purpose not involving harm to others: the persons combining being supposed to be of full age, and not forced or deceived.

No society in which these liberties are not, on the whole, respected, is free, whatever may be its form of government; and none is completely free in which they do not exist absolute and unqualified. The only freedom which deserves the name, is that of pursuing our own good in our own way, so long as we do not attempt to deprive others of theirs, or impede their efforts to obtain it. Each is the proper guardian of his own health, whether bodily, or mental and spiritual. Mankind are greater gainers by suffering each other to live as seems good to themselves, than by compelling each to live as seems good to the rest.

Though this doctrine is anything but new, and, to some persons, may have the air of a truism, there is no doctrine which stands more directly opposed to the general tendency of existing opinion and practice. Society has expended fully as much effort in the attempt (according to its lights) to compel peo-ple to conform to its notions of personal, as of social excellence. The ancient commonwealths thought themselves entitled to practise, and the ancient [28] philosophers countenanced, the regulation of every part of private conduct by public authority, on the ground that the State had a deep interest in the whole bodily and mental discipline of every one of its citizens; a mode of thinking which may have been admissible in small republics surrounded by power-ful enemies, in constant peril of being subverted by foreign attack or internal commotion, and to which even a short interval of relaxed energy and self-command might so easily be fatal, that they could not afford to wait for the salutary permanent effects of freedom. In the modern world, the greater size of political communities, and above all, the separation between spiritual and temporal authority (which placed the direction of men's consciences in other hands than those which controlled their worldly affairs), prevented so great an interference by law in the details of private life; but the engines of moral repression have been wielded more strenuously against divergence from the reigning opinion in self-regarding, than even in social matters; religion, the most powerful of the elements which have entered into the formation of moral feeling, having almost always been governed either by the ambition of a hierarchy, seeking control over every department of human conduct, or by the spirit of Puritanism. And some of those modern reformers who have placed themselves [29] in strongest opposition to the religions of the past, have been noway behind either churches or sects in their assertion of the right of spiritual domination: M. Comte, in particular, whose social system, as unfolded in his *Traité de Politique Positive*, aims at establishing (though by moral more than by legal appliances) a despotism of society over the individual, surpassing anything contemplated in the political ideal of the most rigid disciplinarian among the ancient philosophers.

Apart from the peculiar tenets of individual thinkers, there is also in the world at large an increasing inclination to stretch unduly the powers of society over the individual, both by the force of opinion and even by that of legislation: and as the tendency of all the changes taking place in the world is to strengthen society, and diminish the power of the individual, this encroachment is not one of the evils which tend spontaneously to disappear, but, on the contrary, to grow more and more formidable. The disposition of mankind, whether as rulers or as fellow-citizens to impose their own opinions and inclinations as a rule of conduct on others, is so energetically supported by some of the best and by some of the worst feelings incident to human nature, that it is hardly ever kept under restraint by anything but want of power; and as the power is not declining, but growing, unless a strong barrier of moral conviction can be raised against the mischief, we must expect, in the present circumstances of the world, to see it increase.

CLASS STRUGGLE (1848/1888)

Karl Marx

Karl Heinrich Marx (1818–1883) was the third of seven siblings born to a lawyer who, though descended from a long line of Rabbis, had converted to Lutheranism so that he would be allowed to practice his profession. Marx was homeschooled until the age of 13. At 17, he entered the University of Bohn, where he became president of a drinking society but did not excel academically. After a year, he transferred to Humboldt University in Berlin. There, he became associated with the radical leftist "young Hegelians." At 23, warned that his reputation as a young Hegelian would color the reception of his work in Berlin, Marx completed his Doctorate at the University of Jena. At 25, despite objections from both families, he married Jenny von Westphalen, the educated daughter of a Prussian Baron. After brief stint as editor of a liberal newspaper in Cologne, Marx moved to Paris, an enclave of revolutionaries, to write for radical journals. In Paris, Marx met his lifelong collaborator, Friedrich Engels (1820–1895). In 1845, Marx and Engels, forced out of Paris, moved to Brussels, where they coauthored and published the Communist Manifesto (1848), asserting that class struggles explain human history and predicting rule by the proletariat. After being expelled from Belgium, Marx returned to Paris, where he witnessed the June Days Uprising, following which he returned to Cologne to found a newspaper. After two arrests and acquittals in Cologne, Marx returned to Paris, only to be forced out once again. In 1849 (at age 31), he found refuge in London. For nearly two decades, Marx spend his days in the British Museum, writing (among other things) his masterwork on economics, Capital (Volume I, 1867; Volumes II and III, posthumously) Late in this period, he also devoted much time and energy to the International Workingmen's Association (1864–1876), an organization that sought to unite left-wing political groups and trade unions. For much of this time, his family—four children at first, three more to come—lived in poverty and constant fear of creditors. Though he did earn a minimal income over his decade as a correspondent for the New York Tribune, Marx largely depended on the patronage of Engels for support. During his last decade, Marx suffered declining health. Distress at the death of a daughter and *of his wife hastened his demise. He died stateless, buried in London with the words "Workers of all lands unite"—the final line of the <u>Communist Manifesto</u>—carved on his headstone.*

What to look for: *Mill and Marx both talk about social classes. What are the similarities and the differences between their views on this subject? How does political struggle arise? How did the rise of industry change social class? How has industrialization changed work and its relationship to the worker? Is the present social class structure inevitable?*

CHAPTER I. BOURGEOIS AND PROLETARIANS[1]

The history of all hitherto existing society is the history of class struggles.

Freeman and slave, patrician and plebeian, lord and serf, guild-master and journeyman, in a word, oppressor and oppressed, stood in constant opposition to one another, carried on an uninterrupted, now hidden, now open fight, a fight that each time ended, either in a revolutionary reconstitution of society at large, or in the common ruin of the contending classes.

In the earlier epochs of history, we find almost everywhere a complicated arrangement of society into various orders, a manifold gradation of social rank. In ancient Rome we have patricians, knights, plebeians, slaves; in the Middle Ages, feudal lords, vassals, guild-masters, journeymen, apprentices, serfs; in almost all of these classes, again, subordinate gradations.

The modern bourgeois society that has sprouted from the ruins of feudal society has not done away with class antagonisms. It has but established new classes, new conditions of oppression, new forms of struggle in place of the old ones. Our epoch, the epoch of the bourgeoisie, possesses, however, this distinct feature: it has simplified class antagonisms. Society as a whole is more and more splitting up into two great hostile camps, into two great classes directly facing each other—Bourgeoisie and Proletariat . . . .

The feudal system of industry, in which industrial production was monopolized by closed guilds, now no longer sufficed for the growing wants of the new markets. The manufacturing system took its place. The guild-masters were pushed on one side by the manufacturing middle class; division of labour

---

[1] By bourgeoisie is meant the class of modern capitalists, owners of the means of social production and employers of wage labour. By proletariat, the class of modern wage labourers who, having no means of production of their own, are reduced to selling their labour power in order to live. [Engels, 1888 English edition]

"Class Struggle," by Karl Marx and Frederick Engels, from *Manifesto of the Communist Party.* Trans. Samuel Moore with Frederick Engels. (Waiheke Island: Floating Press, 1888).

between the different corporate guilds vanished in the face of division of labour in each single workshop.

Meantime the markets kept ever growing, the demand ever rising. Even manufacturer no longer sufficed. Thereupon, steam and machinery revolutionized industrial production. The place of manufacture was taken by the giant, Modern Industry; the place of the industrial middle class by industrial millionaires, the leaders of the whole industrial armies, the modern bourgeois.

Modern industry has established the world market, for which the discovery of America paved the way. This market has given an immense development to commerce, to navigation, to communication by land. This development has, in its turn, reacted on the extension of industry; and in proportion as industry, commerce, navigation, railways extended, in the same proportion the bourgeoisie developed, increased its capital, and pushed into the background every class handed down from the Middle Ages.

We see, therefore, how the modern bourgeoisie is itself the product of a long course of development, of a series of revolutions in the modes of production and of exchange.

Each step in the development of the bourgeoisie was accompanied by a corresponding political advance of that class . . . .

The bourgeoisie cannot exist without constantly revolutionizing the instruments of production, and thereby the relations of production, and with them the whole relations of society . . . .

The need of a constantly expanding market for its products chases the bourgeoisie over the entire surface of the globe. It must nestle everywhere, settle everywhere, establish connections everywhere. . . .

The bourgeoisie, by the rapid improvement of all instruments of production, by the immensely facilitated means of communication, draws all, even the most barbarian, nations into civilisation. The cheap prices of commodities are the heavy artillery with which it batters down all Chinese walls, with which it forces the barbarians' intensely obstinate hatred of foreigners to capitulate. It compels all nations, on pain of extinction, to adopt the bourgeois mode of production; it compels them to introduce what it calls civilization into their midst, i.e., to become bourgeois themselves. In one word, it creates a world after its own image . . . .

The weapons with which the bourgeoisie felled feudalism to the ground are now turned against the bourgeoisie itself.

But not only has the bourgeoisie forged the weapons that bring death to itself; it has also called into existence the men who are to wield those weapons—the modern working class—the proletarians.

In proportion as the bourgeoisie, i.e., capital, is developed, in the same proportion is the proletariat, the modern working class, developed—a class of labourers, who live only so long as they find work, and who find work only so long as their labour increases capital. These labourers, who must sell themselves piecemeal, are a commodity, like every other article of commerce, and are consequently exposed to all the vicissitudes of competition, to all the fluctuations of the market.

Owing to the extensive use of machinery, and to the division of labour, the work of the proletarians has lost all individual character, and, consequently, all charm for the workman. He becomes an appendage of the machine, and it is only the most simple, most monotonous, and most easily acquired knack, that is required of him. Hence, the cost of production of a workman is restricted, almost entirely, to the means of subsistence that he requires for maintenance, and for the propagation of his race. But the price of a commodity, and therefore also of labour, is equal to its cost of production. In proportion, therefore, as the repulsiveness of the work increases, the wage decreases. Nay more, in proportion as the use of machinery and division of labour increases, in the same proportion the burden of toil also increases, whether by prolongation of the working hours, by the increase of the work exacted in a given time or by increased speed of machinery, etc.

Modern Industry has converted the little workshop of the patriarchal master into the great factory of the industrial capitalist. Masses of labourers, crowded into the factory, are organized like soldiers. As privates of the industrial army they are placed under the command of a perfect hierarchy of officers and sergeants. Not only are they slaves of the bourgeois class, and of the bourgeois State; they are daily and hourly enslaved by the machine, by the overlooker, and, above all, by the individual bourgeois manufacturer himself. The more openly this despotism proclaims gain to be its end and aim, the more petty, the more hateful and the more embittering it is . . . .

But with the development of industry, the proletariat not only increases in number; it becomes concentrated in greater masses, its strength grows, and it feels that strength more. The various interests and conditions of life within the ranks of the proletariat are more and more equalized, in proportion as machinery obliterates all distinctions of labour, and nearly everywhere reduces wages to the same low level. The growing competition among the bourgeois, and the resulting commercial crises, make the wages of the workers ever more fluctuating. The increasing improvement of machinery, ever more rapidly developing, makes their livelihood more and more precarious; the collisions between individual workmen and individual bourgeois take more and more the character of collisions between two classes. Thereupon, the workers begin to form combinations (Trades' Unions) against the bourgeois; they club together in order to keep up the rate of wages; they found permanent associations in order to make provision beforehand for these occasional revolts. Here and there, the contest breaks out into riots . . . .

Though not in substance, yet in form, the struggle of the proletariat with the bourgeoisie is at first a national struggle. The proletariat of each country must, of course, first of all settle matters with its own bourgeoisie.

In depicting the most general phases of the development of the proletariat, we traced the more or less veiled civil war, raging within existing society, up to the point where that war breaks out into open revolution, and where the violent overthrow of the bourgeoisie lays the foundation for the sway of the proletariat . . . .

Hitherto, every form of society has been based, as we have already seen, on the antagonism of oppressing and oppressed classes . . . .

The essential conditions for the existence and for the sway of the bourgeois class is the formation and augmentation of capital; the condition for capital is wage-labour. Wage-labour rests exclusively on competition between the labourers. The advance of industry, whose involuntary promoter is the bourgeoisie, replaces the isolation of the labourers, due to competition, by the revolutionary combination, due to association. The development of Modern Industry, therefore, cuts from under its feet the very foundation on which the bourgeoisie produces and appropriates products. What the bourgeoisie therefore produces, above all, are its own grave-diggers. Its fall and the victory of the proletariat are equally inevitable.

KNOWLEDGE
AND
REALITY

ALLEGORY OF THE CAVE
(390?–370? BC)
Plato

Plato—see p. 23.

What to look for: *This selection comes from book VIII of* The Republic, *a work written by Plato in his 40s or 50s that focuses on psychology, ethics, and political philosophy, but rests upon Plato's underlying theory of appearance, reality, truth, and opinion. The discussion here between Socrates (who narrates) and Glaucon (Plato's brother) presupposes a theory of reality that is given in the pages immediately before this selection by an "Analogy of the Sun" [508b–509c] and a "Divided Line" [509d–513e]:*

Plato on Appearance and Reality*

Visible World (appearance and illusion)		Intelligible World (reality)	
THE SUN The LIGHT and POWER of the SUN The World of Sight and of things seen		**THE GOOD** The ILLUMINATION & INFLUENCE of the GOOD The World of Mind and of things thought	
A B		C D E	
Images such as Shadows and Reflections	Objects such as Animals and everything that grows or is made.	Thought-Images, Ideas such as of Circles, Squares, Cubes, Numbers	Forms, Ideals such as of Truth, Beauty Justice, Goodness
Sensing CONJECTURE	Sensing BELIEF	Mathematical Thinking UNDERSTANDING	Dialectical Thinking REASONING
OPINION		KNOWLEDGE	
CENTRAL FEATURE: **ALWAYS CHANGING** "seen" with the *occulus corpora*		CENTRAL FEATURE: **NEVER CHANGING** "seen" with the *occulus menti*	

Sensing and thinking are ACTIONS; Conjecture, belief, understanding, and reasoning are FACULTIES
Relative lengths represent degree of clarity, not size of class. AC/CE = AB/BC = CD/DE; hence, BC = CD.
*based on the Analogy of the Sun [Stephanus 508b – 509] and the Divided Line [509d – 513e]   c. cardwell

Carefully picture the cave (den) in your mind. Plato says that **we** *are the prisoners. What does he mean by this? To understand the full implications of the allegory, we must go beyond the details in the story. Imagine the experience of the prisoners. Once a prisoner breaks free of the chains, what will s/he observe/conclude about the relative reality of shadows and objects? What will s/he observe/conclude about the relative speed of change in the appearance of shadows and of objects? What follows regarding the relationship between change and reality? How much would* **total reality** *change? Now, push farther. Plato calls things that do not change "Forms." Examples are Truth, Beauty, and Justice. We "see" such things with our mind's eye, but how can Forms be in the mind to be "seen?" (They cannot come in through the senses because senses depend upon change. Indeed, they cannot be put in the mind since putting involves change!) What must we conclude about the mind? And what of teaching? Is teaching even possible?*

[Socrates narrates his discussion with Glaucon:] And now, I said, let me show in a figure how far our nature is enlightened or unenlightened: —behold! human beings living in an underground den, which has a mouth open towards the light and reaching all along the den; here they have been from their childhood, and have their legs and necks chained so that they cannot move, and can only see before them, being prevented by the chains from turning round their heads. Above and behind them a fire is blazing at a distance, and between the fire and the prisoners there is a raised way; and you will see, if you look, a low wall built along the way, like the screen which marionette players have in front of them, over which they show the puppets.

[Glaucon:] I see.

And do you see, I said, men passing along the wall carrying all sorts of vessels, and statues and figures of animals of made of wood and stone and various materials, which appear [Steph. 515] over the wall? Some of them are talking, others silent.

You have shown me a strange image, and they are strange prisoners.

Like ourselves, I replied; and they see only their own shadows, or the shadows of one another, which the fire throws on the opposite wall of the cave?

True, he said; how could, they see anything but the shadows if they were never allowed to move their heads?

And of the objects which are being carried in like manner they would only see the shadows?

"Allegory of the Cave," by Plato, from *The Republic of Plato: Translated into English with Introduction, Analysis, Marginal Analysis, and Index.* Trans. B. Jowett. 3rd ed. (Oxford: Clarendon Press, 1888).

Yes, he said.

And if they were able to converse with one another, would they not suppose that they were naming what was actually before them?

Very true.

And suppose further that the prison had an echo which came from the other side, would they not be sure to fancy when one of the passers-by spoke that the voice which they heard came from the passing shadow?

No question, he replied.

To them, I said, the truth would be literally nothing but the shadows of the images.

That is certain.

And now look again, and see what will naturally follow if the prisoners are released and disabused of their error. At first, when any of them is liberated and compelled suddenly to stand up and turn his neck round and walk and look towards the light, he will suffer sharp pains; the glare will distress him, and he will be unable to see the realities of which in his former state he had seen the shadows; and then conceive some one saying to him, that what he saw before was an illusion, but that now, when he is approaching nearer to being and his eye is turned towards more real existence, he has a clearer vision,—what will be his reply? And you may further imagine that his instructor is pointing to the objects as they pass and requiring him to name them,—will he not be perplexed? Will he not fancy that the shadows which he formerly saw are truer than the objects which are now shown to him?

Far truer.

And if he is compelled to look straight at the light, will he not have a pain in his eyes which will make him turn away to take refuge in the objects of vision which he can see, and which he will conceive to be in reality clearer than the things which are now being shown to him?

True, he said.

And suppose once more, that he is reluctantly dragged up a steep and rugged ascent, and held fast until he is forced into the presence of the sun himself, is he not likely to be [516] pained and irritated? When he approaches the light his eyes will be dazzled, and he will not be able to see anything at all of what are now called realities.

Not all in a moment, he said.

He will require to grow accustomed to the sight of the upper world. And first he will see the shadows best, next the reflections of men and other objects in the water, and then the objects themselves; then he will gaze upon the light of the moon and the stars and the spangled heaven; and he will see the sky and the stars by night better than the sun or the light of the sun by day?

Certainly.

Last of all he will be able to see the sun, and not mere reflections of him in the water, but he will see him in his own proper place, and not in another; and he will contemplate him as he is.

Certainly.

He will then proceed to argue that this is he who gives the season and the years, and is the guardian of all that is in the visible world, and in a certain way the cause of all things which he and his fellows have been accustomed to behold?

Clearly, he said, he would first see the sun and then reason about him.

And when he remembered his old habitation, and the wisdom of the den and his fellow prisoners, do you not suppose that he would felicitate himself on the change, and pity them?

Certainly, he would.

And if they were in the habit of conferring honours among themselves on those who were quickest to observe the passing shadows and to remark which of them went before, and which followed after, and which were together; and who were therefore best able to draw conclusions as to the future, do you think that he would care for such honours and glories, or envy the possessors of them? Would he not say with Homer,

'Better to be the poor servant of a poor master,'

and to endure anything, rather than think as they do and live after their manner?

Yes, he said, I think that he would rather suffer anything than entertain these false notions and live in this miserable manner.

Imagine once more, I said, such a one coming suddenly out of the sun to be replaced in his old situation; would he not be certain to have his eyes full of darkness?

To be sure, he said.

And if there were a contest, and he had to compete in measuring the shadows with the prisoners who had never [517] moved out of the den, while his sight was still weak, and before his eyes had become steady (and the time which would be needed to acquire this new habit of sight might be very considerable), would he not be ridiculous? Men would say of him that up he went and down he came without his eyes; and that it was better not even to think of ascending; and if any one tried to lose another and lead him up to the light, let them only catch the offender, and they would put him to death.

No question, he said.

This entire allegory, I said, you may now append, dear Glaucon, to the previous argument; the prison-house is the world of sight, the light of the fire is the sun, and you will not misapprehend me if you interpret the journey upwards to be the ascent of the soul into the intellectual world according to my poor belief, which, at your desire, I have expressed—whether rightly or wrongly God knows. But, whether true or false, my opinion is that in the world of knowledge the idea of good appears last of all, and is seen only with an effort; and, when seen, is also inferred to be the universal author of all things beautiful and right, parent of light and of the lord of light in this visible world, and the immediate source of reason and truth in the intellectual; and that this is the power upon which he who would act rationally either in public or private life must have his eye fixed.

I agree, he said, as far as I am able to understand you. Moreover, I said, you must not wonder that those who attain to this beatific vision are unwilling to descend to human affairs; for their souls are ever hastening into the upper world where they desire to dwell; which desire of theirs is very natural, if our allegory may be trusted.

Yes, very natural.

And is there anything surprising in one who passes from divine contemplations to the evil state of man, misbehaving himself in a ridiculous manner; if, while his eyes are blinking and before he has become accustomed to the surrounding darkness, he is compelled to fight in courts of law, or in other places, about the images or the shadows of images of justice, and is endeavouring to meet the conceptions of those who have never yet seen absolute justice?

Anything but surprising, he replied.

Anyone who has common sense will remember that the [518] bewilderments of the eyes are of two kinds, and arise from two causes, either from coming out of the light or from going into the light, which is true of the mind's eye, quite as much as of the bodily eye; and he who remembers this when he sees any one whose vision is perplexed and weak, will not be too ready to laugh ; he will first ask whether that soul of man has come out of the brighter life, and is unable to see because unaccustomed to the dark, or having turned from darkness to the day is dazzled by excess of light. And he will count the one happy in his condition and state of being, and he will pity the other; or, if he have a mind to laugh at the soul which comes from below into the light, there will be more reason in this than in the laugh which greets him who returns from above out of the light into the den.

That, he said, is a very just distinction.

But then, if I am right, certain professors of education must be wrong when they say that they can put a knowledge into the soul which was not there before, like sight into blind eyes.

They undoubtedly say this, he replied.

Whereas, our argument shows that the power and capacity of learning exists in the soul already; and that just as the eye was unable to turn from darkness to light without the whole body, so too the instrument of knowledge can only by the movement of the whole soul be turned from the world of becoming into that of being, and learn by degrees to endure the sight of being, and of the brightest and best of being, or in other words, of the good.

KNOWLEDGE IS RECOLLECTION (390?–370? BC)

Plato

Plato—see p. 23.

What to look for: *Plato has argued that knowledge (of Forms) cannot be taught (because it is already known, residing in minds that have neither beginning nor end). In <u>Meno</u>, Socrates seeks to demonstrate the immortality of the mind by showing that knowledge is remembered, not taught. Questions often serve as a crucial aid to help us recall what we have forgotten. Using only questions, Socrates guides a slave boy through several stages, ultimately to demonstrate knowledge of a bit of sophisticated mathematics. What are these stages and what is Socrates' evaluation of each? Socrates insists that he does not teach . . . that he does nothing more than help the boy to remember. It is easiest to work through the dialog if you draw the figures that Socrates describes. There is only one step that is essential to Socrates' success or failure. What is that step? Does Socrates succeed in showing what he wants to show?*

PERSONS OF THE DIALOGUE:

Meno, Socrates, Meno's slave boy.

Meno: CAN you tell me, Socrates, whether virtue is acquired by teaching or by practice; or if neither by teaching nor by practice, then whether it comes to man by nature, or in what other way?

    . . . .

Socrates: I know, Meno, what you mean; but just see what a tiresome dispute you are introducing. You argue that a man cannot enquire either about that which he knows, or about that which he does not know; for if he knows, he has no need to enquire; and if not, he cannot; for he does not know the very subject about which he is to enquire.

"Knowledge is Recollection," by Plato, from *The Dialogues of Plato: Translated into English with Analyses and Introductions.* Trans. B. Jowett. 3rd ed. Vol. 2. (Oxford: Oxford University Press, 1892).

M: Well, Socrates, and is not the argument sound? [Stephanus 81]

S: I think not.

M: Why not?

S: I will tell you why: I have heard from certain wise men and women who spoke of things divine that—

M: What did they say?

S: They spoke of a glorious truth, as I conceive.

M: What was it? and who were they?

S: Some of them were priests and priestesses, who had studied how they might be able to give a reason of their profession: there have been poets also, who spoke of these things by inspiration, like Pindar, and many others who were inspired. And they say—mark, now, and see whether their words are true—they say that the soul of man is immortal, and at one time has an end, which is termed dying, and at another time is born again, but is never destroyed. And the moral is, that a man ought to live always in perfect holiness. *'For in the ninth year Persephone sends the souls of those from whom she has received the penalty of ancient crime back again from beneath into the light of the sun above, and these are they who become noble kings and mighty men and great in wisdom and are called saintly heroes in after ages.'* The soul, then, as being immortal, and having been born again many times, and having seen all things that exist, whether in this world or in the world below, has knowledge of them all; and it is no wonder that she should be able to call to remembrance all that she ever knew about virtue, and about everything; for as all nature is akin, and the soul has learned all things, there is no difficulty in her eliciting or as men say learning, out of a single recollection all the rest, if a man is strenuous and does not faint; for all enquiry and all learning is but recollection. And therefore we ought not to listen to this sophistical argument about the impossibility of enquiry: for it will make us idle, and is sweet only to the sluggard; but the other saying will make us active and inquisitive. In that confiding, I will gladly enquire with you into the nature of virtue.

M: Yes, Socrates; but what do you mean by saying that we do not learn, and that what we call learning is only a process of recollection? Can you teach me how this is?

S: I told you, Meno, just now that you were a rogue, and now you ask whether I can teach you, when I am saying that [82] there is no teaching, but only recollection; and thus you imagine that you will involve me in a contradiction.

M: Indeed, Socrates, I protest that I had no such intention. I only asked the question from habit; but if you can prove to me that what you say is true, I wish that you would.

S: It will be no easy matter, but I will try to please you to the utmost of my power. Suppose that you call one of your numerous attendants, that I may demonstrate on him.

M: Certainly. Come hither, Boy.

S: He is Greek, and speaks Greek, does he not?

M: Yes, indeed; he was born in the house.

S: Attend now to the questions which I ask him, and observe whether he learns of me or only remembers.

M: I will.

S: Tell me, boy, do you know that a figure like this is a square?

Boy: I do.

S: And you know that a square figure has these four lines equal?

B: Certainly.

S: And these lines which I have drawn through the middle of the square are also equal?

B: Yes.

S: A square may be of any size?

B: Certainly.

S: And if one side of the figure be of two feet, and the other side be of two feet, how much will the whole be? Let me explain: if in one direction the space was of two feet, and in the other direction of one foot, the whole would be of two feet taken once?

B: Yes.

S: But since this side is also of two feet, there are twice two feet?

B: There are.

S: Then the square is of twice two feet?

B: Yes.

S: And how many are twice two feet? count and tell me.

B: Four, Socrates.

S: And might there not be another square twice as large as this, and having like this the lines equal?

B: Yes.

S: And of how many feet will that be?

B: Of eight feet.

S: And now try and tell me the length of the line which forms the side of that double square: this is two feet—what will that be?

B: Clearly, Socrates, it will be double.

S: Do you observe, Meno, that I am not teaching the boy anything, but only asking him questions; and now he fancies that he knows how long a line is necessary in order to produce a figure of eight square feet; does he not?

M: Yes.

S: And does he really know?

M: Certainly not.

S: He only guesses that because the square is double, the line is double.

M: True.

S: Observe him while he recalls the steps in regular order. (*To the Boy.*) Tell me, boy, do you assert that a [83] double space comes from a double line? Remember that I am not speaking of an oblong, but of a figure equal every way, and twice the size of this—that is to say of eight feet; and I want to know whether you still say that a double square comes from a double line?

B: Yes.

S: But does not this line become doubled if we add another such line here?

B: Certainly.

S: And four such lines will make a space containing eight feet?

B: Yes.

S: Let us describe such a figure: Would you not say that this is the figure of eight feet?

B: Yes.

S: And are there not these four divisions in the figure, each of which is equal to the figure of four feet?

B: True.

S: And is not that four times four?

B: Certainly.

S: And four times is not double?

B: No, indeed.

S: But how much?

B: Four times as much.

S: Therefore the double line, boy, has given a space, not twice, but four times as much.

B: True.

S: Four times four are sixteen—are they not?

B: Yes.

S: What line would give you a space of eight feet, as this gives one of sixteen feet;—do you see?

B: Yes.

S: And the space of four feet is made from this half line?

B: Yes.

S: Good; and is not a space of eight feet twice the size of this, and half the size of the other?

B: Certainly.

S: Such a space, then, will be made out of a line greater than this one, and less than that one?

B: Yes; I think so.

S: Very good; I like to hear you say what you think. And now tell me, is not this a line of two feet and that of four?

B: Yes.

S: Then the line which forms the side of eight feet ought to be more than this line of two feet, and less than the other of four feet?

B: It ought.

S: Try and see if you can tell me how much it will be.

B: Three feet.

S: Then if we add a half to this line of two, that will be the line of three. Here are two and there is one; and on the other side, here are two also and there is one: and that makes the figure of which you speak?

B: Yes.

S: But if there are three feet this way and three feet that way, the whole space will be three times three feet?

B: That is evident.

S: And how much are three times three feet?

B: Nine.

S: And how much is the double of four?

B: Eight.

S: Then the figure of eight is not made out of a line of three?

B: No.

S: But from what line?—tell me exactly; and if you [84] would rather not reckon, try and show me the line.

B: Indeed, Socrates, I do not know.

S: Do you see, Meno, what advances he has made in his power of recollection? He did not know at first, and he does not know now, what is the side of a figure of eight feet: but then he thought that he knew, and answered confidently as if he knew, and had no difficulty; now he has a difficulty, and neither knows nor fancies that he knows.

M: True.

S: Is he not better off in knowing his ignorance?

M: I think that he is.

S: If we have made him doubt, and given him the 'torpedo's shock,' have we done him any harm?

M: I think not.

S: We have certainly, as would seem, assisted him in some degree to the discovery of the truth; and now he will wish to remedy his ignorance, but then he would have been ready to tell all the world again and again that the double space should have a double side.

M: True.

S: But do you suppose that he would ever have enquired into or learned what he fancied that he knew, though he was really ignorant of it, until he had fallen into perplexity under the idea that he did not know, and had desired to know?

M: I think not, Socrates.

S: Then he was the better for the torpedo's touch?

M: I think so.

S: Mark now the farther development. I shall only ask him, and not teach him, and he shall share the enquiry with me: and do you watch and see if you find me telling or explaining anything to him, instead of eliciting his opinion. Tell me, boy, is not this a square of four feet which I have drawn?

B: Yes.

S: And now I add another square equal to the former one?

B: Yes.

S: And a third, which is equal to either of them?

B: Yes.

S: Suppose that we fill up the vacant corner?

B: Very good.

S: Here, then, there are four equal spaces?

B: Yes.

S: And how many times larger is this space than this other?

B: Four times.

S: But it ought to have been twice only, as you will remember.

B: True.

S: And does not this line, reaching from corner to corner, [85] bisect each of these spaces?

B: Yes.

S: And are there not here four equal lines which contain this space?

B: There are.

S: Look and see how much this space is.

B: I do not understand.

S: Has not each interior line cut off half of the four spaces?

B: Yes.

S: And how many such spaces are there in this section?

B: Four.

S: And how many in this?

B: Two.

S: And four is how many times two?

B: Twice.

S: And this space is of how many feet?

B: Of eight feet.

S: And from what line do you get this figure?

B: From this.

S: That is, from the line which extends from corner to corner of the figure of four feet?

B: Yes.

S: And that is the line which the learned call the diagonal. And if this is the proper name, then you, Meno's slave, are prepared to affirm that the double space is the square of the diagonal?

B: Certainly, Socrates.

S: What do you say of him, Meno? Were not all these answers given out of his own head?

M: Yes, they were all his own.

S: And yet, as we were just now saying, he did not know?

M: True.

S: But still he had in him those notions of his—had he not?

M: Yes.

S: Then he who does not know may still have true notions of that which he does not know?

M: He has.

S: And at present these notions have just been stirred up in him, as in a dream; but if he were frequently asked the same questions, in different forms, he would know as well as any one at last?

M: I dare say.

S: Without any one teaching him he will recover his knowledge for himself, if he is only asked questions?

M: Yes.

S: And this spontaneous recovery of knowledge in him is recollection?

M: True.

S: And this knowledge which he now has must he not either have acquired or always possessed?

M: Yes.

S: But if he always possessed this knowledge he would always have known; or if he has acquired the knowledge he could not have acquired it in this life, unless he has been taught geometry; for he may be made to do the same with all geometry and every other branch of knowledge. Now, has any one ever taught him all this? You must know about him, if, as you say, he was born and bred in your house.

M: And I am certain that no one ever did teach him.

S: And yet he has the knowledge?

M: The fact, Socrates, is undeniable.

S: But if he did not acquire the knowledge in this life, [86] then he must have had and learned it at some other time?

M: Clearly he must.

S: Which must have been the time when he was not a man?

M: Yes.

S: And if there have been always true thoughts in him, both at the time when he was and was not a man, which only need to be awakened into knowledge by putting questions to him, his soul must have always possessed this knowledge, for he always either was or was not a man?

M: Obviously.

S: And if the truth of all things always existed in the soul, then the soul is immortal. Wherefore be of good cheer, and try to recollect what you do not know, or rather what you do not remember.

M: I feel, somehow, that I like what you are saying.

S: And I, Meno, like what I am saying. Some things I have said of which I am not altogether confident. But that we shall be better and braver and less helpless if we think that we ought to enquire, than we should have been if we indulged in the idle fancy that there was no knowing and no use in seeking to know what we do not know;—that is a theme upon which I am ready to fight, in word and deed, to the utmost of my power.

MEDITATIONS I AND II (1641/1647)

René Descartes

René Descartes [day-CART] (1596–1650) was born in the Loire valley in the town of La Haye (now Descartes), France. His father was a lawyer and magistrate. His mother died when he was just a year old, and he was mainly reared by his grandmother. From age 8 through 16, he studied classics, logic, and Aristotelian philosophy at a Jesuit school where, owing to poor health, he was allowed to stay in bed until 11:00 a.m.— a practice he continued throughout his life. After a brief stay in Paris, where he studied mathematics, Descartes moved to Poitier to obtain (at age 20) a law degree. Descartes did not practice law, however. Instead, he spent six years traveling and experiencing the world. As he walked through Breda, Holland, he met Isaac Beeckman (1588–1637), who became important in turning Descartes' interests to mathematics and physics. When he returned to France, Descartes sold all his property and invested in bonds, the income from which provided a comfortable income for life. After three years, Descartes decided that France was too bustling for him to concentrate on his work, so he returned to Holland. There, he moved from university to university, living in ten different cities over a 21-year period. During these years, Descartes wrote his most important works, contributing to mathematics (Cartesian coordinates), physics (in France, Boyle's law is called Descartes' law), and philosophy (Descartes is called the father of modern philosophy). Aware that his contemporary, Galileo Galilei (1564–1642), was forced to recant Copernicanism and placed under house arrest, Descartes (a devoted Catholic) feared persecution or censure enough that he withheld some work from publication until after his death. (In 1663, 13 years after his death, the Pope put Descartes' works on the index of prohibited books. In 1671, Louis XIV prohibited lectures on Cartesianism.)

A relationship with a servant in Amsterdam gave him a daughter (who died at age 5), but Descartes never married. In 1649, he moved to Sweden to tutor Queen Christina in philosophy. She insisted that her studies start at 5 a.m., a time that did not suit Descartes. With the harsh climate and early hours, he contracted pneumonia and died at age 54. As a Catholic in Protestant Sweden, Descartes was buried in a Stockholm graveyard for orphans and the unbaptized. In 1666, his corpse was moved to the church of Sainte-Geneviève-du-Mont in Paris. A plan during the French Revolution to transfer his remains to the Panthéon may or may not have been carried out. In 1819, the body, said to be lacking a finger and the skull, was entombed at the Abbey of Saint-Germain-des-Prés. One of the five skulls attributed to Descartes is at the Musée de l'Homme [Museum of Man] in Paris.

What to look for: *Descartes seeks a solid foundation for science. What is his initial concern regarding such a foundation? What kinds of beliefs does he need to examine? When are our senses reliable and when do they fail us? What problems do dreams introduce? Are general ideas more reliable than particular ones? Why (not)? Can we depend upon God's goodness to solve the problem? What extreme strategy does Descartes adopt as a way of finding indubitable beliefs? How does the possibility of a malignant demon influence how much we can doubt? What is Descartes' mood at the end of his first meditation?*

MEDITATION I
Of The Things On Which We May Doubt.

SEVERAL years have now elapsed since I first became aware that I had accepted, even from my youth, many false opinions for true, and that consequently what I afterward based on such principles was highly doubtful; and from that time I was convinced of the necessity of undertaking once in my life to rid myself of all the opinions I had adopted, and of commencing anew the work of building from the foundation, if I desired to establish a firm and abiding superstructure in the sciences. But as this enterprise appeared to me to be one of great magnitude, I waited until I had attained an age so mature as to leave me no hope that at any stage of life more advanced I should be better able to execute my design. On this account, I have delayed so long that I should henceforth consider I was doing wrong were I still to consume in deliberation any of the time that now remains for action. Today, then, since I have opportunely freed my mind from all cares [and am happily disturbed by no passions][1], and since I am in the secure possession of leisure in a peaceable retirement, I will at length apply myself earnestly and freely to the general [220][2] overthrow of all my former

---

[1]Square brackets mark additions to the original of the revised French translation.
[2]Bracketed numbers indicate the page of the John Veitch translation (1901) from which this selection is taken.

"Mediations I and II," by René Descartes, from *The Method, Meditations and Philosophy of Descartes: From the Original Texts, with a New Introductory Essay, Historical and Critical.* Trans. John Veitch. Frank Sewall, Introduction. (Washington: M. Walter Dunne, 1901).

opinions. But, to this end, it will not be necessary for me to show that the whole of these are false—a point, perhaps, which I shall never reach; but as even now my reason convinces me that I ought not the less carefully to withhold belief from what is not entirely certain and indubitable, than from what is manifestly false, it will be sufficient to justify the rejection of the whole if I shall find in each some ground for doubt. Nor for this purpose will it be necessary even to deal with each belief individually, which would be truly an endless labor; but, as the removal from below of the foundation necessarily involves the downfall of the whole edifice, I will at once approach the criticism of the principles on which all my former beliefs rested.

All that I have, up to this moment, accepted as possessed of the highest truth and certainty, I received either from or through the senses. I observed, however, that these sometimes misled us; and it is the part of prudence not to place absolute confidence in that by which we have even once been deceived.

But it may be said, perhaps, that, although the senses occasionally mislead us respecting minute objects, and such as are so far removed from us as to be beyond the reach of close observation, there are yet many other of their informations (presentations), of the truth of which it is manifestly impossible to doubt; as for example, that I am in this place, seated by the fire, clothed in a winter dressing gown, that I hold in my hands this piece of paper, with other intimations of the same nature. But how could I deny that I possess these hands and this body, and withal escape being classed with persons in a state of insanity, whose brains are so disordered and clouded by dark bilious vapors as to cause them pertinaciously to assert that they are monarchs when they are in the greatest poverty; or clothed [in gold] and purple when destitute of any covering; or that their head is made of clay, their body of glass, or that they are gourds? I should certainly be not less insane than they, were I to regulate my procedure according to examples so extravagant.

Though this be true, I must nevertheless here consider that I am a man, and that, consequently, I am in the habit of sleeping, and representing to myself in dreams [221] those same things, or even sometimes others less probable, which the insane think are presented to them in their waking moments. How often have I dreamt that I was in these familiar circumstances, that I was dressed, and occupied this place by the fire, when I was lying undressed in bed? At the present moment, however, I certainly look upon this paper with eyes wide awake; the head which I now move is not asleep; I extend this hand consciously and with express purpose, and I perceive it; the occurrences in sleep are not so distinct as all this. But I cannot forget that, at other times I have been deceived in sleep by similar illusions; and, attentively considering those cases, I perceive so clearly that there exist no certain marks by which the state of waking can ever be distinguished from sleep, that I feel greatly astonished; and in amazement I almost persuade myself that I am now dreaming.

Let us suppose, then, that we are dreaming, and that all these particulars— namely, the opening of the eyes, the motion of the head, the forth-putting of the hands—are merely illusions; and even that we really possess neither an entire body nor hands such as we see. Nevertheless it must be admitted at least that the objects which appear to us in sleep are, as it were, painted representations which could not have been formed unless in the likeness of realities; and, therefore, that those general objects, at all events, namely, eyes, a head, hands, and an entire body, are not simply imaginary, but really existent. For, in truth, painters themselves, even when they study to represent sirens and satyrs by forms the most fantastic and extraordinary, cannot bestow upon them natures absolutely new, but can only make a certain medley of the members of different animals; or if they chance to imagine something so novel that nothing at all similar has ever been seen before, and such as is, therefore, purely fictitious and absolutely false, it is at least certain that the colors of which this is composed are real.

And on the same principle, although these general objects, viz, [a body], eyes, a head, hands, and the like, be imaginary, we are nevertheless absolutely necessitated to admit the reality at least of some other objects still more simple and universal than these, of which, just as of certain real colors, all those images of things, whether [222] true and real, or false and fantastic, that are found in our consciousness (cogitatio), are formed.

To this class of objects seem to belong corporeal nature in general and its extension; the figure of extended things, their quantity or magnitude, and their number, as also the place in, and the time during, which they exist, and other things of the same sort. We will not, therefore, perhaps reason illegitimately if we conclude from this that Physics, Astronomy, Medicine, and all the other sciences that have for their end the consideration of composite objects, are indeed of a doubtful character; but that Arithmetic, Geometry, and the other sciences of the same class, which regard merely the simplest and most general objects, and scarcely inquire whether or not these are really existent, contain somewhat that is certain and indubitable: for whether I am awake or dreaming, it remains true that two and three make five, and that a square has but four sides; nor does it seem possible that truths so apparent can ever fall under a suspicion of falsity [or incertitude].

Nevertheless, the belief that there is a God who is all powerful, and who created me, such as I am, has, for a long time, obtained steady possession of my mind. How, then, do I know that he has not arranged that there should be neither earth, nor sky, nor any extended thing, nor figure, nor magnitude, nor place, providing at the same time, however, for [the rise in me of the perceptions of all these objects, and] the persuasion that these do not exist otherwise than as I perceive them? And further, as I sometimes think that others are in error respecting matters of which they believe themselves to possess a perfect knowledge, how do I know that I am not also deceived each time I add together two and three, or number the sides of a square, or form some judgment still more simple, if more simple indeed can be imagined? But perhaps Deity has not been willing that I should be thus deceived, for he is said to be supremely good. If, however, it were repugnant to the goodness of Deity to have created me subject to constant deception, it would seem likewise to be contrary to his goodness to allow me to be occasionally deceived; and yet it is clear that this is permitted. Some, indeed, might perhaps [223] be found who would be disposed rather to deny the existence of a Being so powerful than to believe that there is nothing certain. But let us for the present refrain from opposing this opinion, and grant that all which is here said of a Deity is fabulous: nevertheless, in whatever way it be supposed that I reach the state in which I exist, whether by fate, or chance, or by an endless series of antecedents and consequents, or by any other means, it is clear (since to be deceived and to err is a certain defect) that the probability of my being so imperfect as to be the constant victim of deception, will be increased exactly in proportion as the power possessed by the cause, to which they assign my origin, is lessened. To these reasonings I have assuredly nothing to reply, but am constrained at last to avow that there is nothing of all that I formerly believed to be true of which it is impossible to doubt, and that not through thoughtlessness or levity, but from cogent and maturely considered reasons; so that henceforward, if I desire to discover anything certain, I ought not the less carefully to refrain from assenting to those same opinions than to what might be shown to be manifestly false.

But it is not sufficient to have made these observations; care must be taken likewise to keep them in remembrance. For those old and customary opinions perpetually recur—long and familiar usage giving them the right of occupying my mind, even almost against my will, and subduing my belief; nor will I lose the habit of deferring to them and confiding in them so long as I shall consider them to be what in truth they are, viz, opinions to some extent doubtful, as I have already shown, but still highly probable, and such as it is much more reasonable to believe than deny. It is for this reason I am persuaded that I shall not be doing wrong, if, taking an opposite judgment of deliberate design, I become my own deceiver, by supposing, for a time, that all those opinions are entirely false and imaginary, until at length, having thus balanced my old by my new prejudices, my judgment shall no longer be turned aside by perverted usage from the path that may conduct to the perception of truth. For I am assured that, meanwhile, there will arise neither peril nor error from this course, and that I [224] cannot for the present yield too much to distrust, since the end I now seek is not action but knowledge.

I will suppose, then, not that Deity, who is sovereignly good and the fountain of truth, but that some malignant demon, who is at once exceedingly potent and deceitful, has employed all his artifice to deceive me; I will suppose that the sky, the air, the earth, colors, figures, sounds, and all external things, are nothing better than the illusions of dreams, by means of which this being has laid snares for my credulity; I will consider myself as without hands, eyes, flesh, blood, or any of the senses, and as falsely believing that I am possessed of these; I will continue resolutely fixed in this belief, and if indeed by this means it be not in my power to arrive at the knowledge of truth, I shall at least do what is in my power, viz [suspend my judgment], and guard with settled

purpose against giving my assent to what is false, and being imposed upon by
this deceiver, whatever be his power and artifice.

But this undertaking is arduous, and a certain indolence insensibly leads
me back to my ordinary course of life; and just as the captive, who, perchance,
was enjoying in his dreams an imaginary liberty, when he begins to suspect
that it is but a vision, dreads awakening, and conspires with the agreeable illusions that the deception may be prolonged; so I, of my own accord, fall back
into the train of my former beliefs, and fear to arouse myself from my slumber,
lest the time of laborious wakefulness that would succeed this quiet rest, in
place of bringing any light of day, should prove inadequate to dispel the darkness that will arise from the difficulties that have now been raised.

---

*What to look for now: Descartes begins his second meditation by recon-
sidering all the things he can doubt. Is there anything about which even
the malignant demon could not deceive us? What are the characteristics of extended things? ...of thinking things? What (which of these) is
Descartes? Are there other beliefs about which one could not be mistaken? Are such beliefs about the "outside" world? Why does Descartes
think it important to examine the "piece of wax"? (What exactly is the
"piece of wax"?) What faculty enables Descartes to "see" that the wax
is the <u>same</u> wax both before and after it melts? What is <u>imagination</u>?
What is the difference between <u>seeing</u> and <u>judging</u>? How can/does our
language mislead us? How/why are clarity and distinctness especially
important for Descartes? Has Descartes now found an anchor point from
which to build a foundation for science?*

MEDITATION II.

*Of the Nature of the Human Mind; and that
It is More Easily Known than the Body.*

THE Meditation of yesterday has filled my mind with so many doubts, that it is
no longer in my power to forget them. Nor do I see, meanwhile, any principle
on which they can be resolved; and, just as if I had fallen all of a [225] sudden
into very deep water, I am so greatly disconcerted as to be unable either to
plant my feet firmly on the bottom or sustain myself by swimming on the surface. I will, nevertheless, make an effort, and try anew the same path on which
I had entered yesterday, that is, proceed by casting aside all that admits of the
slightest doubt, not less than if I had discovered it to be absolutely false; and I
will continue always in this track until I shall find something that is certain, or
at least, if I can do nothing more, until I shall know with certainty that there is

nothing certain. Archimedes, that he might transport the entire globe from the place it occupied to another, demanded only a point that was firm and immovable; so, also, I shall be entitled to entertain the highest expectations, if I am fortunate enough to discover only one thing that is certain and indubitable.

I suppose, accordingly, that all the things which I see are false (fictitious); I believe that none of those objects which my fallacious memory represents ever existed; I suppose that I possess no senses; I believe that body, figure, extension, motion, and place are merely fictions of my mind. What is there, then, that can be esteemed true? Perhaps this only, that there is absolutely nothing certain.

But how do I know that there is not something different altogether from the objects I have now enumerated, of which it is impossible to entertain the slightest doubt? Is there not a God, or some being, by whatever name I may designate him, who causes these thoughts, to arise in my mind? But why suppose such a being, for it may be I myself am capable of producing them? Am I, then, at least not something? But I before denied that I possessed senses or a body; I hesitate, however, for what follows from that? Am I so dependent on the body and the senses that without these I cannot exist? But I had the persuasion that there was absolutely nothing in the world, that there was no sky and no earth, neither minds nor bodies; was I not, therefore, at the same time, persuaded that I did not exist? Far from it; I assuredly existed, since I was persuaded. But there is I know not what being, who is possessed at once of the highest power and the deepest cunning, who is constantly employing all his ingenuity in deceiving me. [226] Doubtless, then, I exist, since I am deceived; and, let him deceive me as he may, he can never bring it about that I am nothing, so long as I shall be conscious that I am something. So that it must, in fine, be maintained, all things being maturely and carefully considered, that this proposition *(pronunciatum)* I am, I exist, is necessarily true each time it is expressed by me, or conceived in my mind.

But I do not yet know with sufficient clearness what I am, though assured that I am; and hence, in the next place, I must take care, lest perchance I inconsiderately substitute some other object in room of what is properly myself, and thus wander from truth, even in that knowledge (cognition) which I hold to be of all others the most certain and evident. For this reason, I will now consider anew what I formerly believed myself to be, before I entered on the present train of thought; and of my previous opinion I will retrench all that can in the least be invalidated by the grounds of doubt I have adduced, in order that there may at length remain nothing but what is certain and indubitable. What then did I formerly think I was? Undoubtedly I judged that I was a man. But what is a man? Shall I say a rational animal? Assuredly not; for it would be necessary forthwith to inquire into what is meant by animal, and what by rational, and thus, from a single question, I should insensibly glide into others, and these more difficult than the first; nor do I now possess enough of leisure to warrant me in wasting my time amid subtleties of this sort. I prefer here to attend to the thoughts that sprung up of themselves in my mind, and were inspired by my own nature alone, when I applied myself to the consideration of what I was. In the first place, then, I thought that I possessed a countenance, hands, arms, and all the fabric of members that appears in a corpse, and which I called by the name of body. It further occurred to me that I was nourished, that I walked, perceived, and thought, and all those actions I referred to the soul; but what the soul itself was I either did not stay to consider, or, if I did, I imagined that it was something extremely rare and subtle, like wind, or flame, or ether, spread through my grosser parts. As regarded the body, I did not even doubt of its nature, but thought I distinctly knew it, and if I had wished to describe it according to the notions I then [227] entertained, I should have explained myself in this manner : By body I understand all that can be terminated by a certain figure; that can be comprised in a certain place, and so fill a certain space as therefrom to exclude every other body; that can be perceived either by touch, sight, hearing, taste, or smell; that can be moved in different ways, not indeed of itself, but by something foreign to it by which it is touched [and from which it receives the impression]; for the power of self-motion, as likewise that of perceiving and thinking, I held as by no means pertaining to the nature of body; on the contrary, I was somewhat astonished to find such faculties existing in some bodies.

But [as to myself, what can I now say that I am], since I suppose there exists an extremely powerful, and, if I may so speak, malignant being, whose whole endeavors are directed toward deceiving me? Can I affirm that I possess any one of all those attributes of which I have lately spoken as belonging to the nature of body? After attentively considering them in my own mind, I find none of them that can properly be said to belong to myself. To recount them were idle and tedious. Let us pass, then, to the attributes of the soul. The first mentioned were the powers of nutrition and walking; but, if it be true that I have no body, it is true likewise that I am capable neither of walking nor of being nourished. Perception is another attribute of the soul; but perception too is impossible without the body; besides, I have frequently, during sleep, believed that I perceived objects which I afterward observed I did not in reality perceive. Thinking is another attribute of the soul; and here I discover what properly belongs to myself. This alone is inseparable from me. I am—I exist: this is certain; but how often? As often as I think; for perhaps it would even happen, if I should wholly cease to think, that I should at the same time altogether cease to be. I now admit nothing that is not necessarily true. I am therefore, precisely speaking, only a thinking thing, that is, a mind *(mens sive animus)*, understanding, or reason, terms whose signification was before unknown to me. I am, however, a real thing, and really existent; but what thing? The answer was, a thinking thing. The question now arises, am I aught besides? I will stimulate my imagination with [228] a view to discover whether I am not still something more than a thinking being. Now it in plain I am not the assemblage of members called the human body; I am not a thin and penetrating air diffused through all these members, or wind, or flame, or vapor, or breath, or any of all the things I can imagine; for I supposed that all these were not, and, without changing the supposition, I find that I still feel assured of my existence.

But it is true, perhaps, that those very things which I suppose to be non-existent, because they are unknown to me, are not in truth different from myself whom I know. This is a point I cannot determine, and do not now enter into any dispute regarding it. I can only judge of things that are known to me: I am conscious that I exist, and I who know that I exist inquire into what I am. It is, however, perfectly certain that the knowledge of my existence, thus precisely taken, is not dependent on things, the existence of which is as yet unknown to me: and consequently it is not dependent on any of the things I can feign in imagination. Moreover, the phrase itself, I frame an image (*effingo*), reminds me of my error; for I should in truth frame one if I were to imagine myself to be anything, since to imagine is nothing more than to contemplate the figure or image of a corporeal thing; but I already know that I exist, and that it is possible at the same time that all those images, and in general all that relates to the nature of body, are merely dreams [or chimeras]. From this I discover that it is not more reasonable to say, I will excite my imagination that I may know more distinctly what I am, than to express myself as follows: I am now awake, and perceive something real; but because my perception is not sufficiently clear, I will of express purpose go to sleep that my dreams may represent to me the object of my perception with more truth and clearness. And, therefore, I know that nothing of all that I can embrace in imagination belongs to the knowledge which I have of myself, and that there is need to recall with the utmost care the mind from this mode of thinking, that it may be able to know its own nature with perfect distinctness.

But what, then, am I? A thinking thing, it has been said. But what is a thinking thing? It is a thing that [229] doubts, understands, [conceives], affirms, denies, wills, refuses; that imagines also, and perceives. Assuredly it is not little, if all these properties belong to my nature. But why should they not belong to it? Am I not that very being who now doubts of almost everything; who, for all that, understands and conceives certain things; who affirms one alone as true, and denies the others; who desires to know more of them, and does not wish to be deceived; who imagines many things, sometimes even despite his will; and is likewise percipient of many, as if through the medium of the senses. Is there nothing of all this as true as that I am, even although I should be always dreaming, and although he who gave me being employed all his ingenuity to deceive me? Is there also any one of these attributes that can be properly distinguished from my thought, or that can be said to be separate from myself? For it is of itself so evident that it is I who doubt, I who understand, and I who desire, that it is here unnecessary to add anything by way of rendering it more clear. And I am as certainly the same being who imagines; for although it maybe (as I before supposed) that nothing I imagine is true, still the power of imagination does not cease really to exist in me and to form part of my thought. In fine, I am the same being who perceives, that is, who apprehends certain objects as by the organs of sense, since, in truth, I see light, hear a noise, and feel heat. But it will be said that these presentations are false, and that I am dreaming. Let it be so. At all events it is certain that I seem to see light, hear a noise, and feel heat; this cannot be false, and this is what in me is properly called perceiving *(sentire)*, which is nothing else than thinking. From this I begin to know what I am with somewhat greater clearness and distinctness than heretofore.

But, nevertheless, it still seems to me, and I cannot help believing, that corporeal things, whose images are formed by thought [which fall under the senses], and are examined by the same, are known with much greater distinctness than that I know not what part of myself which is not imaginable; although, in truth, it may seem strange to say that I know and comprehend with greater distinctness things whose existence appears to me doubtful, that are unknown, and do not belong to me, than [230] others of whose reality I am persuaded, that are known to me, and appertain to my proper nature; in a word, than myself. But I see clearly what is the state of the case. My mind is apt to wander, and will not yet submit to be restrained within the limits of truth. Let us therefore leave the mind to itself once more, and, according to it every kind of liberty [permit it to consider the objects that appear to it from without], in order that, having afterward withdrawn it from these gently and opportunely [and fixed it on the consideration of its being and the properties it finds in itself], it may then be the more easily controlled.

Let us now accordingly consider the objects that are commonly thought to be [the most easily, and likewise] the most distinctly known, viz, the bodies we touch and see; not, indeed, bodies in general, for these general notions are usually somewhat more confused, but one body in particular. Take, for example, this piece of wax; it is quite fresh, having been but recently taken from the beehive; it has not yet lost the sweetness of the honey it contained; it still retains somewhat of the odor of the flowers from which it was gathered; its color, figure, size, are apparent (to the sight); it is hard, cold, easily handled; and sounds when struck upon with the finger. In fine, all that contributes to make a body as distinctly known as possible, is found in the one before us. But, while I am speaking, let it be placed near the fire—what remained of the taste exhales, the smell evaporates, the color changes, its figure is destroyed, its size increases, it becomes liquid, it grows hot, it can hardly be handled, and, although struck upon, it emits no sound. Does the same wax still remain after this change? It must be admitted that it does remain; no one doubts it, or judges otherwise. What, then, was it I knew with so much distinctness in the piece of wax? Assuredly, it could be nothing of all that I observed by means of the senses, since all the things that fell under taste, smell, sight, touch, and hearing are changed, and yet the same wax remains. It was perhaps what I now think, viz, that this wax was neither the sweetness of honey, the pleasant odor of flowers, the whiteness, the figure, nor the sound, but only a body that a little before appeared to me conspicuous under these forms, and which is now [231] perceived under others. But, to speak precisely, what is it that I imagine when I think of it in this way? Let it be attentively considered, and, retrenching all that does not belong to the wax, let us see what remains. There certainly remains nothing, except something extended, flexible, and movable. But what is meant by flexible and movable? Is it not that I imagine that the piece of wax, being round, is capable of becoming square, or of passing from a square into a triangular figure? Assuredly such is not the case, because I conceive that it admits of an infinity of similar changes; and I am, moreover, unable to compass this infinity by imagination, and consequently this conception which I have of the wax is not the product of the faculty of imagination. But what now is this extension? Is it not also unknown? for it becomes greater when the wax is melted, greater when it is boiled, and greater still when the heat increases; and I should not conceive [clearly and] according to truth, the wax as it is, if I did not suppose that the piece we are considering admitted even of a wider variety of extension than I ever imagined. I must, therefore, admit that I cannot even comprehend by imagination what the piece of wax is, and that it is the mind alone (*mens*, Lat., *entendement*, F.) which perceives it. I speak of one piece in particular; for as to wax in general, this is still more evident. But what is the piece of wax that can be perceived only by the [understanding or] mind? It is certainly the same which I see, touch, imagine; and, in fine, it is the same which, from the beginning, I believed it to be. But (and this it is of moment to observe) the perception of it is neither an act of sight, of touch, nor of imagination, and never was either of these, though it might formerly seem so, but is simply an intuition (*inspectio*) of the mind, which may be imperfect and confused, as it formerly was, or very clear and distinct, as it is at present, according as the attention is more or less directed to the elements which it contains, and of which it is composed.

But, meanwhile, I feel greatly astonished when I observe [the weakness of my mind, and] its proneness to error. For although, without at all giving expression to what I think, I consider all this in my own mind, words yet occasionally impede my progress, and I am almost [232] led into error by the terms of ordinary language. We say, for example, that we see the same wax when it is before us, and not that we judge it to be the same from its retaining the same color and figure: whence I should forthwith be disposed to conclude that the wax is known by the act of sight, and not by the intuition of the mind alone, were it not for the analogous instance of human beings passing on in the street below, as observed from a window. In this case I do not fail to say that I see the men themselves, just as I say that I see the wax; and yet what do I see from the window beyond hats and cloaks that might cover artificial machines, whose motions might be determined by springs? But I judge that there are human beings from these appearances, and thus I comprehend, by the faculty of judgment alone which is in the mind, what I believed I saw with my eyes.

The man who makes it his aim to rise to knowledge superior to the common, ought to be ashamed to seek occasions of doubting from the vulgar forms of speech: instead, therefore, of doing this, I shall proceed with the matter in hand, and inquire whether I had a clearer and more perfect perception of the piece of wax when I first saw it, and when I thought I knew it by means of the external sense itself, or, at all events, by the common sense *(sensus communis)*, as it is called, that is, by the imaginative faculty; or whether I rather apprehend it more clearly at present, after having examined with greater care, both what it is, and in what way it can be known. It would certainly be ridiculous to entertain any doubt on this point. For what, in that first perception, was there distinct? What did I perceive which any animal might not have perceived? But when I distinguish the wax from its exterior forms, and when, as if I had stripped it of its vestments, I consider it quite naked, it is certain, although some error may still be found in my judgment, that I cannot, nevertheless, thus apprehend it without possessing a human mind.

But, finally, what shall I say of the mind itself, that is, of myself? for as yet I do not admit that I am anything but mind. What, then! I who seem to possess so distinct an apprehension of the piece of wax, do I not know [233] myself, both with greater truth and certitude, and also much more distinctly and clearly? For if I judge that the wax exists because I see it, it assuredly follows, much more evidently, that I myself am or exist, for the same reason: for it is possible that what I see may not in truth be wax, and that I do not even possess eyes with which to see anything; but it cannot be that when I see, or, which comes to the same thing, when I think I see, I myself who think am nothing. So likewise, if I judge that the wax exists because I touch it, it will still also follow that I am; and if I determine that my imagination, or any other cause, whatever it be, persuades me of the existence of the wax, I will still draw the same conclusion. And what is here remarked of the piece of wax, is applicable to all the other things that are external to me. And further, if the [notion or] perception of wax appeared to me more precise and distinct, after that not only sight and touch, but many other causes besides, rendered it manifest to my apprehension, with how much greater distinctness must I now know myself, since all the reasons that contribute to the knowledge of the nature of wax, or of any body whatever, manifest still better the nature of my mind? And there are besides so many other things in the mind itself that contribute to the illustration of its nature, that those dependent on the body, to which I have here referred, scarcely merit to be taken into account.

But, in conclusion, I find I have insensibly reverted to the point I desired; for, since it is now manifest to me that bodies themselves are not properly perceived by the senses nor by the faculty of imagination, but by the intellect alone; and since they are not perceived because they are seen and touched, but only because they are understood [or rightly comprehended by thought], I readily discover that there is nothing more easily or clearly apprehended than my own mind. But because it is difficult to rid one's self so promptly of an opinion to which one has been long accustomed, it will be desirable to tarry for some time at this stage, that, by long continued meditation, I may more deeply impress upon my memory this new knowledge.

IDEAS IN THE UNDERSTANDING (1689)

John Locke

John Locke: see p. 87.

What to look for: What is Locke's purpose in this essay? What is an advantage of knowing the scope and limits to knowledge? Should we reject the doctrine of innate ideas if we can discover how all knowledge may be attained through experience? Why (not)? What counterexamples does Locke offer to challenge the notion that there is universal assent to supposedly innate ideas? If there are no innate ideas, what can we say of the mind at birth? How is the mind "furnished?" How do "universal" ideas form? What are primary qualities? What are secondary qualities? How are they related? What test can be used to distinguish whether a particular quality is primary or secondary?

BOOK I—CHAP. I
Introduction

§ 1. Since it is the understanding, that sets man above the rest of sensible beings, and gives him all the advantage and dominion, which he has over them; it is certainly a subject, even for its nobleness, worth our labour to inquire into. The understanding, like the eye, whilst it makes us see and perceive all other things, takes no notice of itself; and it requires art and pains to set it at a distance, and make it its own object. But, whatever be the difficulties that lie in the way of this inquiry; whatever it be, that keeps us so much in the dark to ourselves; sure I am, that all the light we can let in upon our own minds, all the acquaintance we can make with our own understandings, will not only be very pleasant, but bring us great advantage, in directing our thoughts in the search of other things.

"Ideas in the Understanding," by John Locke, from *The Works of John Locke in Nine Volumes.* Vol. 1, *An Essay concerning Human Understanding, Part 1.* (Edinburgh: C. and J. Rivington et al, 1824).

§ 2. This, therefore, being my purpose, to inquire into the original, certainty, and extent of human knowledge; together with the grounds and degrees of belief, opinion, and assent . . .

§ 3. It is, therefore, worth while to search out the bounds between opinion and knowledge; and examine by what measures, in things, whereof we have no certain knowledge, we ought to regulate our assent, and moderate our persuasions . . .

§ 4. If, by this enquiry into the nature of the understanding, I can discover the powers thereof; how far they reach; to what things they are in any degree proportionate; and where they fail us: I suppose it may be of use to prevail with the busy mind of man, to be more cautious in meddling with things exceeding its comprehension; to stop when it is at the utmost extent of its tether; and to sit down in a quiet ignorance of those things, which, upon examination, are found to be beyond the reach of our capacities. We should not then perhaps be so forward, out of an affectation of an universal knowledge, to raise questions, and perplex ourselves and others with disputes about things, to which our understandings are not suited; and of which we cannot frame in our minds any clear or distinct perceptions, or whereof (as it has perhaps too often happened) we have not any notions at all. If we can find out how far the understanding can extend its view, how far it has faculties to attain certainty, and in what cases it can only judge and guess; we may learn to content ourselves with what is attainable by us in this state . . .

§ 7. This was that which gave the first rise to this essay concerning the understanding. For I thought that the first step towards satisfying several enquiries, the mind of man was very apt to run into, was to take a survey of our own understandings, examine our own powers, and see to what things they were adapted. Till that was done, I suspected we began at the wrong end, and in vain sought for satisfaction in a quiet and sure possession of truths that most concerned us, whilst we let loose our thoughts into the vast ocean of being; as if all that boundless extent were the natural and undoubted possession of our understandings, wherein there was nothing exempt from its decisions, or that escaped its comprehension. Thus men extending their enquiries beyond their capacities, and letting their thoughts wander into those depths, where they can find no sure footing; it is no wonder, that they raise questions, and multiply disputes, which, never coming to any clear resolution, are proper only to continue and increase their doubts, and to confirm them at last in perfect scepticism. Whereas, were the capacities of our understandings well considered, the extent of our knowledge once discovered, and the horizon found, which sets the bounds between the enlightened and dark parts of things, between what is, and what is not comprehensible by us; men would perhaps with less scruple acquiesce in the avowed ignorance of the one, and employ their thoughts and discourse with more advantage and satisfaction in the other . . .

§ 8. Thus much I thought necessary to say concerning the occasion of this enquiry into human understanding. But, before I proceed on to what I have thought on this subject, I must here in the entrance beg pardon of my reader for the frequent use of the word "idea," which he will find in the following treatise. It being that term, which, I think, serves best to stand for whatsoever is the object of the understanding when a man thinks; I have used it to express whatever is meant by phantasm, notion, species, or whatever it is which the mind can be employed about in thinking; and I could not avoid frequently using it. . .

CHAP. II
No Innate Principles in the Mind

§ 1. It is an established opinion amongst some men, that there are in the understanding certain innate principles; some primary notions, κοιναί ἔννοιαι, characters, as it were, stamped upon the mind of man, which the soul receives in its very first being; and brings into the world with it. It would be sufficient to convince unprejudiced readers of the falseness of this supposition, if I should only shew (as I hope I shall in the following parts of this discourse) how men, barely by the use of their natural faculties, may attain to all the knowledge they have, without the help of any innate impressions; and may arrive at certainty, without any such original notions or principles. For I imagine any one will easily grant, that it would be impertinent to suppose, the ideas of colours innate in a creature, to whom God hath given sight, and a power to receive them by the eyes, from external objects: and no less unreasonable would it be to attribute several truths to the impressions of nature, and innate characters, when we may observe in ourselves faculties, fit to attain as easy and certain knowledge of them, as if they were originally imprinted on the mind.

But because a man is not permitted without censure to follow his own thoughts in the search of truth, when they lead him ever so little out of the common road; I shall set down the reasons that made me doubt of the truth of that opinion, as an excuse for my mistake, if I be in one; which I leave to be considered by those, who, with me, dispose themselves to embrace truth, wherever they find it.

§ 2. There is nothing more commonly taken for granted, than that there are certain principles, both speculative and practical (for they speak of both) universally agreed upon by all mankind: which therefore, they argue, must needs be constant impressions, which the souls of men receive in their first beings, and which they bring into the world with them, as necessarily and really as they do any of their inherent faculties.

§ 3. This argument, drawn from universal consent, has this misfortune in it, that if it were true in matter of fact, that there were certain truths, wherein all mankind agreed, it would not prove them innate, if there can be any other way shewn, how men may come to that universal agreement, in the things they do consent in; which I presume may be done.

§ 4. But, which is worse, this argument of universal consent, which is made use of to prove innate principles, seems to me a demonstration that there are none such; because there are none to which all mankind give an universal assent. I shall begin with the speculative, and instance in those magnified principles of demonstration; "whatsoever is, is;" and, "it is impossible for the same thing to be, and not to be;" which, of all others, I think have the most allowed title to innate. These have so settled a reputation of maxims universally received, that it will, no doubt, be thought strange, if any one should seem to question it. But yet I take liberty to say, that these propositions are so far from having an universal assent, that there are a great part of mankind to whom they are not so much as known.

§ 5. For, first, it is evident, that all children and idiots have not the least apprehension or thought of them; and the want of that is enough to destroy that universal assent, which must needs be the necessary concomitant of all innate truths: it seeming to me near a contradiction, to say, that there are truths imprinted on the soul, which it perceives or understands not; imprinting, if it signify any thing, being nothing else, but the making certain truths to be perceived. For to imprint any thing on the mind, without the mind's perceiving it, seems to me hardly intelligible. If therefore children and idiots have souls, have minds, with those impressions upon them, they must unavoidably perceive them, and necessarily know and assent to these truths: which since they do not, it is evident that there are no such impressions. For if they are not notions naturally imprinted, how can they be innate? and if they are notions imprinted, how can they be unknown? To say a notion is imprinted on the mind, and yet at the same time to say, that the mind is ignorant of it, and never yet took notice of it, is to make this impression nothing. No proposition can be said to be in the mind, which it never yet knew, which it was never yet conscious of. For if any one may, then, by the same reason, all propositions that are true, and the mind is capable of ever assenting to, may be said to be in the mind, and to be imprinted: since, if any one can be said to be in the mind, which it never yet knew, it must be only, because it is capable of knowing it, and so the mind is of all truths it ever shall know. Nay, thus truths may be imprinted on the mind, which it never did, nor ever shall know: for a man may live long, and die at last in ignorance of many truths, which his mind was capable of knowing, and that with certainty. So that if the capacity of knowing, be the natural impression contended for, all the truths a man ever comes to know, will, by this account, be every one of them innate; and this great point will amount to no more, but only to a very improper way of speaking; which, whilst it pretends to assert the contrary, says nothing different from those, who deny innate principles. For nobody, I think, ever denied that the mind was capable of knowing several truths. The capacity, they say, is innate, the knowledge acquired. But then to what end such contest for certain innate maxims? If truths can be imprinted on the understanding without being perceived, I can see no difference there can be, between any truths the mind is capable of knowing, in respect of their original: they must all be innate, or all adventitious: in vain shall a man go about to distinguish them. He [16] therefore, that talks of innate notions in the understanding, cannot (if he intend thereby any distinct sort of truths) mean such truths to be in the understanding, as it never perceived, and is yet wholly ignorant of. For if these words (to be in the understanding) have any propriety, they signify to be understood: so that, to be in the understanding, and not to be understood; to be in the mind, and never to be perceived; is all one, as to say, any thing is, and is not, in the mind or understanding. If therefore these two propositions, "whatsoever is, is;" and "it is impossible for the same thing to be, and not to be," are by nature imprinted, children cannot be ignorant of them; infants, and all that have souls, must necessarily have them in their understandings, know the truth of them, and assent to it. . . .

§ 15. The senses at first let in particular ideas, and furnish the yet empty cabinet; and the mind by degrees growing familiar with some of them, they are lodged in the memory, and names got to them. Afterwards the mind, proceeding farther, abstracts them, and by degrees learns the use of general names. In this manner the mind comes to be furnished with ideas and language, the materials about which to exercise its discursive faculty: and the use of reason becomes daily more visible, as these materials, that give it employment, increase. But though the having of general ideas, and the use of general words and reason, usually grow together; yet, I see not, how this any way proves them innate. The knowledge of some truths, I confess, is very early in the mind; but in a way that shows them not to be innate. For, if we will observe, we shall find it still to be about ideas, not innate, but acquired: It being about those first which are imprinted by external things, with which infants have earliest to do, which make the most frequent impressions on their senses. In ideas thus got, the mind discovers that some agree, and others differ, probably as soon as it has any use of memory; as soon as it is able to retain and perceive distinct ideas. But whether it be then, or no, this is certain, it does so, long before it has the use of words, or comes to that, which we commonly call "the use of reason." For a child knows as certainly, before it can speak, the difference between the ideas of sweet and bitter (i. e. that sweet is not bitter) as it knows afterwards (when it comes to speak) that wormwood and sugar-plums are not the same thing.

§ 16. A child knows not that three and four are equal to seven, till he comes to be able to count seven, and has got the name and idea of equality: and then, upon explaining those words, he presently assents to, or rather perceives the truth of that proposition. But neither does he then readily assent, because it is an innate truth, nor was his assent wanting till then, because he wanted the use of reason; but the truth of it appears to him, as soon as he has settled in his mind the clear and distinct ideas, that these names stand for: and then he knows the truth of that proposition, upon the same grounds, and by the same means, that he knew before, that a rod and a cherry are not the same thing; and upon the same grounds also, that he may come to know afterwards, "that it is impossible for the same thing to be, and not to be," as shall be more fully shown hereafter. So that the later it is before any one comes to have those general ideas, about which those maxims are; or to know the signification of those general terms that stand for them; or to put together in his mind the ideas they stand for; the later also will it be before he comes to assent to those maxims, whose terms, with the ideas they stand for, being no more innate than those of a cat or a weasel, he must stay till time and observation have acquainted him with them; and then he will be in a capacity to know the truth of these maxims, upon the first occasion that shall make him put together those ideas in his mind, and observe whether they agree or disagree, according as is expressed in those propositions. And therefore it is, that a man knows that eighteen and nineteen are equal to thirty-seven, by the same self-evidence, that he knows one and two to be equal to three: yet a child knows this not so soon as the other; not for want of the use of reason, but because the ideas the words eighteen, nineteen, and thirty-seven stand for, are not so soon got, as those which are signified by one, two, and three . . .

BOOK II—CHAP. VIII
Some farther Considerations concerning our Simple Ideas

§ 8. Whatsoever the mind perceives in itself, or is the immediate object of perception, thought, or understanding, that I call idea; and the power to produce any idea in our mind I call quality of the subject wherein that power is. Thus a snow-ball having the power to produce in us the ideas of white, cold, and round, the powers to produce those ideas in us, as they are in the snow-ball, I call qualities; and as they are sensations or perceptions in our understandings, I call them ideas: which ideas, if I speak of sometimes, as in the things themselves, I would be understood to mean those qualities in the objects which produce them in us.

§ 9. Qualities thus considered in bodies are, first, such as are utterly inseparable from the body, in what estate soever it be; such as in all the alterations and changes it suffers, all the force can be used upon it, it constantly keeps; and such as sense constantly finds in every particle of matter which has bulk enough to be perceived, and the mind finds inseparable from every particle of matter, though less than to make itself singly be perceived by our senses, v. g. Take a grain of wheat, divide it into two parts, each part has still solidity, extension, figure, and mobility; divide it again, and it retains still the same qualities; and so divide it on till the parts become insensible, they must retain still each of them all those qualities. For division (which is all that a mill, or pestle, or any other body does upon another, in reducing it to insensible parts) can never take away either solidity, extension, figure, or mobility from any body, but only makes two or more distinct separate masses of matter, of that which was but one before: all which distinct masses, reckoned as so many distinct bodies, after division make a certain number. These I call original or primary qualities of body, which I think we may observe to produce simple ideas in us, viz. solidity, extension, figure, motion or rest, and number.

§ 10. Secondly, such qualities which in truth are nothing in the objects themselves, but powers to produce various sensations in us by their primary qualities, i. e. by the bulk, figure, texture, and motion of their insensible parts, as colours, sounds, tastes, &c. these I call secondary qualities. To these might be added a third sort, which are allowed to be barely powers, though they are as much real qualities in the subject, as those which I, to comply with the common way of speaking, call qualities, but for distinction, secondary qualities. For the power in fire to produce a new colour, or consistency, in wax or clay, by its primary qualities, is as much a quality in fire, as the power it has to produce in me a new idea or sensation of warmth or burning, which I felt not before by the same primary qualities, viz. the bulk, texture, and motion of its insensible parts.

TO BE IS TO BE PERCEIVED (1713)[1]

George Berkeley

George Berkeley ["BARK-lee"] (1685–1753) was born at the family home, Dysart Castle, in County Kilkenny, Ireland. (His family was of minor English Nobility, but Berkeley always considered himself to be Irish.) In 1700 (at age 15), he entered Trinity College, Dublin, where he earned a bachelor degree in 1704 and a masters in 1707 (becoming a Junior Fellow). In 1709, he published <u>An Essay towards a New Theory of Vision</u>, *a significant contribution to the psychology of vision. He was ordained an Anglican priest in 1710, the same year he published* <u>A Treatise Concerning the Principles of Human Knowledge</u>. *This was a counterintuitive work, masterfully written, dense with cogent argument defending a view that Berkeley came to call* <u>immaterialism</u>. *Three years later, Berkeley published* <u>Three Dialogues between Hylas and Philonous</u>, *an effort to make the ideas in the* <u>Principles</u> *more accessible. Between 1710 and 1714, Berkeley interrupted his time at Trinity with trips to the continent and to London, where he associated with literary figures such as Jonathan Swift (1667–1745), Joseph Addison (1672–1719), Sir Richard Steele (1709–1729), and Alexander Pope (1688–1744). Upon completing his doctorate in 1717, Berkley rose to Senior Fellow at Trinity. In 1721, he earned a second doctorate (in Divinity) and took holy orders in the Church of Ireland. In 1724, he left Trinity to become Anglican Dean of the city of Derry, but was so involved in work to establish a seminary in Bermuda that he was never in residence. In 1728, he married the daughter of the Lord Chief Justice of Ireland. The couple purchased Whitehall Plantation in Newport, Rhode Island (USA), expecting to establish a seminary. In America, Berkeley met a number of prominent intellectuals, served as acting cleric, and wrote a work defending Christianity against the challenges of materialism. When funding that had been promised for the seminary failed to come, the Berkeleys returned (in 1731) to London. There he helped establish a home for abandoned children, wrote an influential, cutting critique of the foundations of Newton's differential*

---

[1] Spelling has been changed to conform more closely with modern American usage. The eighteenth-century custom of capitalizing nouns has been retained.

calculus, produced brilliant analyses of Descartes, Malebranche, Locke, and Hobbes, and published a raft of revisions and defenses of his own work. In 1734, Berkeley was appointed Bishop of Clone, an economically poor Anglican diocese in predominantly Catholic Ireland. During his 18 years there, he was generally perceived as a good bishop, concerned with the well-being of both Protestants and Catholics. At Clone, he wrote a very popular book concerning the medicinal virtues of pine-tar-water and of contemplating God. In 1752, Berkeley retired to Oxford. He planned to oversee the education of his son George—one of three surviving children—but died suddenly (at age 67) shortly after the move. He is buried in Oxford in Christ Church Cathedral. The city of Berkeley, California—current pronunciation has evolved to suit American English—and a residential college at Yale University are named in his honor.

What to look for: *Descartes saw the world as made up of both* <u>res cogitans</u> *(minds and the ideas in them) and* <u>res extensa</u> *(material stuff/matter). Locke held that the external world comprised material substance accurately characterized by primary qualities. Berkeley sets out to show that contradiction and skepticism arise from these beliefs. He defends the theses that "to be is to be perceived" (esse est percipi) and that "there is no such thing as material substance." As you read the dialogue, notice how Berkeley develops these interlaced points. Be sure you are clear on exactly what* <u>sensible things</u> *are. What is left if you remove all sensible qualities? Does Berkeley indeed show that material stuff is not sensible? Does Berkeley show that Locke's primary qualities are in fact secondary qualities? What is the real world made up of if Berkeley is correct? ("Hylas" comes from the Greek for "matter" and "Philonous" comes from the Greek for "lover of mind.")*

THE FIRST DIALOGUE.

Hylas: [2]² . . . I was considering the odd Fate of those Men who . . . , pretended either to believe nothing at all, or to believe the most extravagant Things in the World. This however might be born, if their Paradoxes and Skepticism did not draw after them some Consequences of general Disadvantage to Mankind . . . [3]

Philonous: I entirely agree with you, as to the ill Tendency of the affected Doubts of some Philosophers, and fantastical Conceits of others . . .

---

² Bracketed numbers indicate pages in the 1713 edition.

"To Be is To Be Perceived," by George Berkeley, from *Three Dialogues Between Hylas and Philonous*. (London: G. James, for Henry Clements, at the Half-Moon, in St. Paul's Churchyard, 1713).

H: I am glad to find there was nothing in the Accounts I heard of you.

P: Pray, what were those?

H: You were represented in last Night's Conversation, as one who maintained the most extravagant Opinion that ever entered into the Mind of Man, *viz.* That there is no such Thing as *material Substance* in the World. [4]

P: That there is no such Thing as what Philosophers call *Material Substance,* I am seriously persuaded: But if I were made to see any thing Absurd or Skeptical in this, I should then have the same Reason to renounce this, that I imagine I have now to reject the contrary Opinion.

H: What! can any Thing be more fantastical, more repugnant to common Sense, or a more manifest Piece of Skepticism, than to believe there is no such Thing as *Matter?*

P: Softly, good *Hylas.* What if it should prove, that you, who hold there is, are by Virtue of that Opinion a greater *Skeptic,* and maintain more Paradoxes and Repugnancies to common Sense, than I who believe no such Thing?

H: You may as soon persuade me, The Part is greater than the Whole, as that, in order to avoid Absurdity and Skepticism, I should ever be obliged to give up my Opinion in this Point.

P: Well then, are you content to admit that Opinion for true, which upon Examination shall appear most agreeable to common Sense, and remote from Skepticism?

H: With all my Heart . . . [5]

P: Pray, *Hylas,* what do you mean by a *Skeptic?*

H: I mean what all Men mean, one that doubts of every Thing.

P: He then who entertains no Doubt concerning some particular Point, with regard to that Point, cannot be thought a *Skeptic.*

H: I agree with you . . .

P: How comes it then, *Hylas,* that you pronounce me a *Skeptic,* because I deny what you affirm, *viz.* the Existence of Matter? Since, for ought you can tell, I am as peremptory in my Denial, as you in your Affirmation. [6]

H: Hold, *Philonous* . . . I said, indeed, that a *Skeptic* was one who doubted of every Thing; but I should have added, or who denies the Reality and Truth of Things.

P: What Things? . . .

H: What think you of distrusting the Senses, of denying the real Existence of sensible Things, or pretending to know nothing of them. Is not this sufficient to denominate a Man a *Skeptic?*

P: Shall we therefore examine which of us it is that denies the Reality of Sensible Things, or professes the greatest Ignorance of them; since, if I take you rightly, he is to be esteemed the greatest *Skeptic?*

H: That is what I desire.

P: What mean you by Sensible Things?

H: Those Things which are perceived by the Senses. Can you imagine that I mean any thing else?

P: Pardon me, *Hylas,* if I am desirous clearly to apprehend your Notions, since this [7] may much shorten our Inquiry . . . Are those Things only perceived by the Senses which are perceived immediately? Or may those Things properly be said to be *Sensible,* which are perceived mediately, or not without the Intervention of others?

H: I do not sufficiently understand you.

P: In reading a Book, what I immediately perceive are the Letters, but mediately, or by means of these, are suggested to my Thoughts the Notions of God, Virtue, Truth, &c. Now, that the Letters are truly Sensible Things, or perceived by Sense, there is no doubt: But I would know whether you take the Things suggested by them to be so too.

H: No certainly, it were absurd to think *God* or *Virtue* Sensible Things, tho' they may be signified and suggested to the Mind by Sensible Marks, with which they have an arbitrary Connection.

P: It seems then, that by *Sensible Things* you mean those only which can be perceived immediately by Sense.

H: Right.

P: Does it not follow from this, that tho' I see one part of the Sky Red, and another Blue, and that my Reason doth thence evidently conclude there must be some Cause of that Diversity of Colors, yet that Cause [8] cannot be said to be a Sensible Thing, or perceived by the Sense of Seeing?

H: It does.

P: In like manner, tho' I hear Variety of Sounds, yet I cannot be said to hear the Causes of those Sounds.

H: You cannot.

P: And when by my Touch I perceive a thing to be hot and heavy, I cannot say with any Truth or Propriety, that I feel the Cause of its Heat or Weight.

H: To prevent any more Questions of this kind, I tell you once for all, that by *Sensible Things* I mean those only which are perceived by Sense, and that in truth the Senses perceive nothing which they do not perceive immediately: for they make no Inferences. The Deducing therefore of Causes or Occasions from Effects and Appearances, which alone are perceived by Sense, entirely relates to Reason.

P: This Point then is agreed between us, That *sensible things are those only which are immediately perceived by Sense.* You will farther inform me, whether we immediately perceive by Sight, any thing beside Light, and Colors, and Figures: or by Hearing, any thing but Sounds: by the Palate, any thing beside Tastes: by the Smell, beside Odors: or by the Touch, more than tangible Qualities. [9]

H: We do not.

P: It seems, therefore, that if you take away all sensible Qualities, there remains nothing sensible.

H: I grant it.

P: Sensible things, therefore, are nothing else but so many sensible Qualities, or Combinations of sensible Qualities.

H: Nothing else . . .

P: Does the Reality of sensible things consist in being perceived? or, is it something distinct from their being perceived, and that bears no relation to the Mind?

H: To *exist* is one thing, and to be *perceived* is another.

P: I speak with regard to sensible things only: And of these I ask, Whether by their real Existence you mean a Subsistence exterior to the Mind, and distinct from their being perceived?

H: I mean a real, absolute Being, distinct from, and without any relation to, their being perceived. . . . . [15]

P: Can any Doctrine be true that necessarily leads a Man into an Absurdity?

H: Without doubt, it cannot.

P: Is it not an Absurdity to think, that the same thing should be at the same time both cold and warm?

H: It is.

P: Suppose now, one of your Hands hot, and the other cold, and that they are both at once put into the same Vessel of Water, in an intermediate State; will not the Water seem cold to one Hand, and warm to the other?

H: It will.

P: Ought we not, therefore, by your Principles to conclude, it is really both cold and warm at the same time, that is, according to your own Concession, to believe an Absurdity.

H: I confess, it seems so. [16]

P: Consequently, the Principles themselves are false, since you have granted, that no true Principle leads to an Absurdity.

H: But after all, can any thing be more absurd than to say, *there is no Heat in the Fire?*

P: To make the Point still clearer; tell me, whether in two Cases exactly alike, we ought not to make the same Judgment?

H: We ought.

P: When a Pin pricks your Finger, does it not rend and divide the Fibers of your Flesh?

H: It does.

P: And when a Coal burns your Finger, does it any more?

H: It does not.

P: Since, therefore, you neither judge the Sensation itself occasioned by the Pin, nor any thing like it to be in the Pin; you should not, conformably to what you have now granted, judge the Sensation, occasioned by the Fire, or any thing like it, to be in the Fire.

H: Well, since it must be so, I . . . acknowlege, that Heat and Cold are only Sensations existing in our Minds: But there still remain Qualities enough to secure the Reality of external Things. [17]

P: But, what will you say, *Hylas,* if it shall appear that the Case is the same
    with regard to all other sensible Qualities, and that they can no more be
    supposed to exist without the Mind, than Heat and Cold?

H: Then, indeed, you will have done something to the purpose; but that is
    what I despair of seeing proved.

P: Let us examine them in Order. What think you of Tastes, do they exist
    without the Mind, or no?

H: Can any Man in his Senses doubt whether Sugar is sweet, or Wormwood
    bitter?

P: Inform me, *Hylas.* Is a sweet Taste a particular kind of Pleasure or pleasant
    Sensation, or is it not?

H: It is.

P: And is not Bitterness some kind of Uneasiness or Pain?

H: I grant it.

P: If, therefore, Sugar and Wormwood are unthinking corporeal Substances
    existing without the Mind, how can Sweetness and Bitterness, that is,
    Pleasure and Pain, agree to them?

H: Hold, *Philonous,* I now see what it was deluded me all this time. You
    asked whether Heat and Cold, Sweetness and Bitterness, were not par-
    ticular Sorts of Pleasure and Pain; to which I answered simply, [18] that
    they were. Whereas I should have thus distinguished: Those Qualities, as
    perceived by us, are Pleasures or Pains, but not as existing in the external
    Objects. We must not therefore conclude absolutely, that there is no Heat
    in the Fire, or Sweetness in the Sugar, but only that Heat or Sweetness, as
    perceived by us, are not in the Fire or Sugar. What say you to this?

P: I say it is nothing to the Purpose. Our Discourse proceeded altogether
    concerning Sensible Things, which you defined to be the Things we *imme-
    diately perceive by our Senses.* Whatever other Qualities, therefore, you
    speak of, as distinct from these, I know nothing of them, neither do they
    at all belong to the Point in Dispute. You may, indeed, pretend to have
    discovered certain Qualities which you do not perceive, and assert those
    insensible Qualities exist in Fire and Sugar. But . . . do you acknowledge
    that Heat and Cold, Sweetness and Bitterness, (meaning those Qualities
    which are perceived by the Senses) do not exist without the Mind.

H: I see it is to no purpose to hold out, so I give up the Cause as to those men-
    tioned Qualities: Though I profess it sounds oddly, to say that Sugar is not
    sweet. [19]

P: But for your farther Satisfaction, take this along with you: That which at
    other times seems sweet, shall, to a distempered Palate, appear bitter. And
    nothing can be plainer, than that divers Persons perceive different Tastes in
    the same Food, since that which one Man delights in, another abhors. And
    how could this be, if the Taste was something really inherent in the Food?

H: I acknowledge I know not how.

P: In the next place, Odors are to be considered. And with regard to these, I would fain know, whether what has been said of Tastes does not exactly agree to them? Are they not so many pleasing or displeasing Sensations?

H: They are.

P: Can you then conceive it possible that they should exist in an unperceiving Thing?

H: I cannot . . .

P: May we not, therefore, conclude of Smells, as of the other forementioned Qualities, that they cannot exist in any but a perceiving Substance or Mind?

H: I think so. [20]

P: Then as to Sounds, what must we think of them: Are they Accidents really inherent in external Bodies, or not?

H: That they inhere not in the sonorous Bodies, is plain from hence; because a Bell struck in the exhausted Receiver of an Air-Pump, sends forth no Sound. The Air, therefore, must be thought the Subject of Sound.

P: What Reason is there for that, *Hylas?*

H: Because when any Motion is raised in the Air, we perceive a Sound greater or lesser, in Proportion to the Air's Motion; but without some Motion in the Air, we never hear any Sound at all.

P: And, granting that we never hear a Sound but when some Motion is produced in the Air, yet I do not see how you can infer from thence, that the Sound itself is in the Air.

H: It is this very Motion in the external Air, that produces in the Mind the Sensation of *Sound.* For, striking on the Drum of the Air, it causes a Vibration, which by the Auditory Nerves being communicated to the Brain, the Soul is thereupon affected with the Sensation called *Sound.*

P: What! is Sound then a Sensation?

H: I tell you, as perceived by us, it is a particular Sensation in the Mind. [21]

P: And can any Sensation exist without the Mind?

H: No certainly.

P: How then can Sound, being a Sensation, exist in the Air, if by the *Air* you mean a senseless Substance existing without the Mind?

H: You must distinguish, *Philonous,* between Sound as it is perceived by us, and as it is in itself; or (which is the same thing) between the Sound we immediately perceive, and that which exists without us. The former, indeed, is a particular kind of Sensation, but the latter is merely a Vibrative or Undulatory Motion in the Air.

P: I thought I had already obviated that Distinction, by the Answer I gave when you were applying it in a like Case before. But to say no more of that; Are you sure then that Sound is really nothing but Motion?

H: I am.

P: Whatever therefore agrees to real Sound, may with Truth be attributed to Motion.

H: It may.

P: It is then good Sense to speak of *Motion,* as of a thing that is *loud, sweet, acute, grave,* &c.

H: I see you are resolved not to understand me. Is it not evident, those Accidents or Modes belong only to sensible Sound, or [22] *Sound* in the Common Acceptation of the Word, but not to *Sound* in the Real and Philosophic Sense, which, as I just now told you, is nothing but a certain Motion of the Air?

P: It seems then there are two Sorts of Sound, the one Vulgar, or that which is heard, the other Philosophical and Real.

H: Even so.

P: And the latter consists in Motion.

H: I told you so before.

P: Tell me, *Hylas,* to which of the Senses, think you, the Idea of Motion belong: To the Hearing?

H: No certainly, but to the Sight and Touch.

P: It should follow then, that according to you, real Sounds may possibly be *seen* or *felt,* but never *heard.*

H: Look you, *Philonous,* you may if you please make a Jest of my Opinion, but that will not alter the Truth of Things. I own, indeed, the Inferences you draw me into, sound something oddly; but common Language, you know, is framed by, and for the Use of, the Vulgar: we must not therefore wonder, if Expressions, adapted to exact Philosophic Notions, seem uncouth and out of the way.

P: Is it come to that? I assure you I imagine myself to have gained no small [23] Point, since you make so light of departing from common Phrases and Opinions; it being a main Part of our Inquiry, to examine whose Notions are widest of the common Road, and most repugnant to the general Sense of the World. But, can you think it no more than a Philosophical Paradox, to say that *real Sounds are never heard,* and that the Idea of them is obtained by some other Sense. And is there nothing in this contrary to Nature, and the Truth of Things?

H: To deal ingenuously, I do not like it. And after the Concessions already made, I had as good grant that Sounds too have no real Being without the Mind.

P: And, I hope, you will make no Difficulty to acknowledge the same of Colors.

H: Pardon me: the Case of Colors is very different. Can any thing be plainer, than that we see them on the Objects?

P: The Objects you speak of are, I suppose, corporeal Substances existing without the Mind.

H: They are.

P: And, have true and real Colors inhering in them?

H: Each visible Object has that Color which we see in it.

P: How! Is there any thing visible but what we perceive by Sight?

P: There is not. [24]

H: And, do we perceive any thing by Sense, which we do not perceive immediately?

H: How often must I be obliged to repeat the same thing? I tell you, we do not.

P: Have Patience, good *Hylas;* and tell me once more, whether there is any thing immediately perceived by the Senses, except sensible Qualities. I know, you asserted there was not: But I would now be informed, whether you still persist in the same Opinion.

H: I do.

P: Pray, is your corporeal Substance either a sensible Quality, or made up of sensible Qualities?

H: What a Question that is! who ever thought it was?

P: My Reason for asking was, because in saying, *each visible Object has that Color which we see in it,* you make visible Objects to be corporeal Substances; which implies either that corporeal Substances are sensible Qualities, or else, that there is something beside sensible Qualities perceived by Sight: But, as this Point was formerly agreed between us, and is still maintained by you, it is a clear Consequence, that your corporeal Substance is nothing distinct from sensible Qualities. [25]

H: You may draw as many absurd Consequences as you please, and endeavor to perplex the plainest things; but you shall never persuade me out of my Senses. I clearly understand my own Meaning.

P: I wish you would make me understand it too. But, since you are unwilling to have your Notion of corporeal Substance examined, I shall urge that Point no farther. Only be pleased to let me know, whether the same Colors which we see, exist in external Bodies, or some other.

H: The very same.

P: What! are then the beautiful Red and Purple we see on yonder Clouds, really in them? Or, do you imagine, they have in themselves any other Form, than that of a dark Mist, or Vapor?

H: I must own, *Philonous,* those Colors are not really in the Clouds, as they seem to be at this Distance. They are only apparent Colors.

P: *Apparent* call you them; how shall we distinguish these apparent Colors from real?

H: Very easily. Those are to be thought apparent, which, appearing only at a distance, vanish upon a nearer Approach.

P: And those, I suppose, are to be thought real, which are discovered by the most near and exact Survey.

H: Right. [26]

P: Is the nearest and exactest Survey, made by help of a Microscope, or by the naked Eye?

H: By a Microscope, doubtless.

P: But a Microscope often discovers Colors in an Object different from those
     perceived by the unassisted Sight. And in case we had Microscopes, mag-
     nifying to any assigned Degree; it is certain, that no Object whatsoever,
     viewed thro' them, would appear in the same Color which it exhibits to the
     naked Eye.

H: And, what will you conclude from all this? You cannot argue, that there are
     really and naturally no Colors on Objects: because, by artificial Manage-
     ments they may be altered, or made to vanish.

P: I think it may evidently be concluded from your own Concessions, that
     all the Colors we see with our naked Eyes, are only apparent as those on
     the Clouds, since they vanish upon a more close and accurate Inspection,
     which is afforded us by a Microscope. . . . [28]

P: The Point will be past all doubt, if you consider, that in case Colors were
     real Properties or Affections inherent in external Bodies, they could admit
     of no Alteration, without some Change wrought in the very Bodies them-
     selves: But, is it not evident from what has been said, that, upon the Use
     of Microscopes, upon a Change happening in the Humors of the Eye, or a
     Variation of Distance, without any manner of real Alteration in the Thing
     itself, the Colors of any Object are either changed, or totally disappear?
     Nay, all other Circumstances remaining the same, change but the Situation
     of some Objects, and they shall present different Colors to the Eye. The
     same thing happens upon viewing an Object in various Degrees of Light.
     And what is more known, than that the same Bodies appear differently
     colored by Candle-light, from what they do in the open Day? . . . [29] And
     now tell me, whether you are still of Opinion, that every Body has its true
     real Color inhering in it[?] . . .

H: I own myself entirely satisfied, that they are all equally apparent; and that
     there is no such thing as Color really inhering in external Bodies, but that it
     is altogether in the Light. And what confirms me in this Opinion is, that in
     proportion to the Light, Colors are still more or less vivid; and if there be
     no Light, then are there no Colors perceived. Besides, allowing there are
     Colors on external Objects, yet, how is it possible for us to perceive them?
     For no external Body affects the Mind, unless it act first on our Organs
     of Sense. But the only Action of Bodies is Motion; and Motion cannot
     be communicated otherwise than by Impulse. A distant Object, therefore,
     cannot act on the Eye, nor, consequently, make [30] itself, or its Proper-
     ties perceivable to the Soul. Whence it plainly follows, that it is immedi-
     ately some contiguous Substance, which operating on the Eye, occasions
     a Perception of Colors: And such is Light.

P: How! is Light then a Substance?

H: I tell you, *Philonous,* external Light is nothing but a thin, fluid Substance,
     whose minute Particles being agitated with a brisk Motion, and in various

Manners reflected from the different Surfaces of outward Objects to the Eyes, communicate different Motions to the Optic Nerves; which being propagated to the Brain, cause therein various Impressions: And these are attended with the Sensations of Red, Blue, Yellow, &c.

P: It seems then, the Light does no more than shake the Optic Nerves.

H: Nothing else.

P: And consequent to each particular Motion of the Nerves, the Mind is affected with a Sensation, which is some particular Color.

H: Right.

P: And these Sensations have no Existence without the Mind.

H: They have not.

P: How then do you affirm, that Colors are in the Light, since by *Light* you understand a corporeal Substance external to the Mind? [31]

H: Light and Colors, as immediately perceived by us, I grant cannot exist without the Mind. But in themselves, they consist entirely in the Motions and Configurations of certain insensible Particles of Matter.

P: Colors then, in the vulgar Sense, or taken for the immediate Objects of Sight, cannot agree to any but a perceiving Substance.

H: That is what I say.

P: Well then, since you give up the Point as to those sensible Qualities, which are alone thought Colors by all Mankind beside, you may hold what you please with regard to those invisible ones of the Philosophers. It is not my Business to dispute about them; only I would advise you to think, whether, considering the Inquiry we are upon, it be prudent for you to affirm, *the Red and Blue which we see are not real Colors, but certain unknown Motions and Figures which no Man ever did or can see are truly so.* Are not these shocking Notions, and are not they subject to as many ridiculous Inferences, as those you before renounced in the Case of Sounds?

H: I frankly own, *Philonous,* that it is in vain to stand out any longer. Colors, Sounds, Tastes, in a word, all those termed *Secondary Qualities,* have certainly no Existence without the Mind. But by this [32] Acknowlegement, I must not be supposed to derogate any thing from the Reality of Matter, or external Objects, seeing it is no more than several Philosophers maintain, who nevertheless are the farthest imaginable from denying Matter. For the clearer Understanding of this, you must know, sensible Qualities are by Philosophers divided into *Primary* and *Secondary.* The former are Extension, Figure, Solidity, Gravity, Motion, and Rest; and these they hold exist really in Bodies. The latter are those above enumerated; or, briefly, all sensible Qualities beside, the Primary, which they assert are only so many Sensations or Ideas existing no where but in the Mind. But all this, I doubt not, you are already apprised of. For my part, I have been a long time sensible there was such an Opinion current among Philosophers, but was never thoroughly convinced of its Truth till now.

P: You are still then of Opinion, that Extension and Figures are inherent in external unthinking Substances.

H: I am.

P: But, what if the same Arguments which are brought against Secondary Qualities, will hold good against these also?

H: Why, then I shall be obliged to think, they too exist only in the Mind. [33]

P: Is it your Opinion, the very Figure and Extension which you perceive by Sense, exist in the outward Object or material Substance?

H: It is . . . [34]

P: Again, have you not acknowledged that no real inherent Property of any Object can be changed, without some Change in the thing itself?

H: I have.

P: But as we approach to or recede from an Object, the visible Extension varies, being at one Distance ten or a hundred times greater than at another. Does it not therefore follow from hence likewise, that it is not really inherent in the Object?

H: I own I am at a Loss what to think. [35]

P: Your Judgment will soon be determined, if you will venture to think as freely with relation to this Quality, as you have done in respect of the rest. Was it not admitted as a good Argument, that neither Heat nor Cold was in the Water, because it seemed warm to one Hand, and cold to the other?

H: It was.

P: Is it not the very same Reasoning to conclude, there is no Extension or Figure in an Object, because to one Eye it shall seem little, smooth, and round, when at the same time it appears to the other, great, uneven, and angular?

H: The very same. But does this latter Fact ever happen?

P: You may at any time make the Experiment, by looking with one Eye bare, and with the other thro a Microscope.

H: I know not how to maintain it, and yet I am loath to give up *Extension,* I see so many odd Consequences following upon such a Concession.

P: *Odd,* say you? After the Concessions already made, I hope you will stick at nothing for its Oddness.

H: I give up the Point for the present, reserving still a Right to retract my Opinion, in case I shall hereafter discover any false Step in my Progress to it. [36]

P: That is a Right you cannot be denied. Figures and Extension being dispatched, we proceed next to *Motion.* Can a real Motion in any external Body be, at the same time, both very swift and very slow?

H: It cannot.

P: Is not the Motion of a Body swift in a reciprocal Proportion to the time it takes up in describing any given Space? Thus a Body that describes a Mile in an Hour, moves three times faster than it would in case it described only a Mile in three Hours.

H: I agree with you.

P: And is not Time measured by the Succession of Ideas in our Minds?

H: It is.

P: And is it not possible Ideas should succeed one another twice as fast in your Mind, as they do in mine, or in that of some Spirit of another Kind.

H: I own it.

P: Consequently the same Body may to another seem to perform its Motion over any Space, in half the time that it does to you. And the same Reasoning will hold as to any other Proportion: That is to say, according to your Principles (since the Motions perceived are both really in the Object) it is possible one and the same Body shall be really moved, the same way, at once, both very swift, and very slow. How is this consistent [37] either with common Sense, or what you just now granted?

H: I have nothing to say to it.

P: Then as for *Solidity;* either you do not mean any sensible Quality by that Word, and so it is beside our Inquiry: Or if you do, it must be either Hardness or Resistance. But both the one and the other are plainly relative to our Senses: It being evident, that what seems hard to one Animal, may appear soft to another, who hath greater Force and Firmness of Limbs. Nor is it less plain, that the Resistance I feel is not in the Body.

H: I own, the very Sensation of Resistance, which is all you immediately perceive, is not in the Body, but the Cause of that Sensation is.

P: But, the Causes of our Sensations are not Things immediately perceived, and therefore not sensible. This Point I thought had been already determined.

H: I own it was; but you will pardon me if I seem a little embarrassed: I know not how to quit my old Notions.

P: To help you out, do but consider, that if Extension be once acknowledged to have no Existence without the Mind, the same must necessarily be granted of Motion, Solidity, and Gravity, since they all evidently suppose Extension. It is therefore superfluous to inquire particularly concerning each of [38] them. In denying Extension, you have denied them all to have any real Existence. . . . [39]

H: It is just come into my Head, *Philonous,* that I have somewhere heard of a Distinction between absolute and sensible Extension. Now, though it be acknowledged that *great* and *small,* consisting merely in the Relation which other extended Beings have to the Parts of our own Bodies, do not really inhere in the Substances themselves, yet nothing obliges us to hold the same with regard to *absolute Extension,* which is something abstracted from *great* and *small,* from this or that particular Magnitude or

Figure. So likewise as to Motion, *swift* and *slow* are altogether relative to the Succession of Ideas in our own Minds. But it does not follow, because those Modifications of Motion exist not without the Mind, that therefore absolute Motion abstracted from them does not. . . .

P: These Qualities, therefore, stripped of all sensible Properties, are without all specific and numerical Differences, as the Schools call them.

H: They are. [40]

P: That is to say, they are Extension in general, and Motion in general.

H: Let it be so.

P: But it is a universally received Maxim, that, *Every thing which exists, is particular.* How then can Motion in general, or Extension in general, exist in any corporeal Substance?

H: I will take time to solve your Difficulty.

P: But I think the Point may be speedily decided . . . If you can frame in your Thoughts a distinct abstract Idea of Motion or Extension, divested of all those sensible Modes, as swift and slow, great and small, round and square, and the like, which are acknowledged to exist only in the Mind, I will then yield the Point you contend for. But if you cannot, it will be unreasonable on your Side, to insist any longer upon what you have no Notion of.

H: To confess ingenuously, I cannot.

P: Can you even separate the Ideas of Extension and Motion, from the Ideas of Light and Colors, hard and soft, hot and cold, with the rest of those Qualities which they who make the Distinction, term *Secondary. [41]*

H: What! Is it not an easy Matter, to consider Extension and Motion by themselves, abstracted from all other sensible Qualities? Pray, how do the Mathematicians treat of them?

P: I acknowledge, *Hylas,* it is not difficult to form general Propositions and Reasonings about those Qualities, without mentioning any other; and in this Sense, to consider or treat of them abstractedly. But, how does it follow, that because I can pronounce the Word *Motion,* by itself, I can form the Idea of it in my Mind exclusive of Body? or, because Theorems may be made of Extension and Figures, without any mention of *Great,* or *Small,* or any other sensible Mode or Quality? That, therefore, it is possible such an abstract Idea of Extension, without any particular Size, Color, *&c.* should be distinctly formed, and apprehended by the Mind? Mathematicians treat of Quantity, without regarding what other sensible Qualities it is attended with, as being altogether indifferent to their Demonstrations. But, when laying aside the Words, they contemplate the bare Ideas, I believe you will find, they are not the pure abstracted Ideas of Extension.

H: But, what say you to *pure Intellect?* may not abstracted Ideas be framed by that Faculty? [42]

P: Since I cannot frame abstract Ideas at all, it is plain, I cannot frame them by the Help of *pure Intellect,* whatsoever Faculty you understand by those

Words. Besides, not to inquire into the Nature of pure Intellect, and its spiritual Objects, as *Virtue, Reason, God,* or the like; thus much seems manifest, that sensible Things are only to be perceived by Sense, or represented by the Imagination. Figures, therefore, and Extension, being originally perceived by Sense, do not belong to pure Intellect. But, for your farther Satisfaction, try if you can frame the Idea of any Figure, abstracted from all Particularities of Size, or even from other sensible Qualities.

H: Let me think a little—I do not find that I can.

P: And can you think it possible, that should really exist in Nature, which implies a Repugnancy in its Conception?

H: By no means.

P: Since, therefore, it is impossible, even for the Mind, to disunite the Ideas of Extension and Motion from all other sensible Qualities, does it not follow, that where the one exist, there, necessarily, the other exist likewise?

H: It should seem so.

P: Consequently, the very same Arguments which you admitted, as conclusive against the Secondary Qualities, are, without [43] any farther Application of Force, against the Primary too. Besides, if you will trust your Senses; is it not plain, all sensible Qualities coexist, or, to them, appear as being in the same Place? Do they ever represent a Motion, or Figure, as being divested of all other visible and tangible Qualities?

H: You need say no more on this Head. I am free to own, if there be no secret Error, or Oversight, in our Proceedings hitherto, that all sensible Qualities are alike to be denied Existence without the Mind. But my Fear is, that I have been too liberal in my former Concessions, or overlooked some Fallacy or other. In short, I did not take time to think.

P: For that matter, *Hylas,* you may take what time you please, in reviewing the Progress of our Inquiry. You are at liberty to recover any Slips you might have made, or offer whatever you have omitted, which makes for your first Opinion.

H: One great Oversight I take to be this: That I did not sufficiently distinguish the *Object* from the *Sensation.* Now, tho this latter may not exist without the Mind, yet it will not thence follow, that the former cannot . . . [44] The Sensation I take to be an Act of the Mind perceiving; beside which, there is something perceived; and this I call the *Object.* For Example, there is Red and Yellow on that Tulip. But then, the Act of perceiving those Colors is in me only, and not in the Tulip . . .

P: And, what do you see, beside Color, Figure, and Extension?

H: Nothing.

P: What you would say then is, that the Red and Yellow are coexistent with the Extension; is it not?

H: That is not all; I would say, They have a real Existence without the Mind, in some unthinking Substance.

P: That the Colors are really in the Tulip which I see, is manifest. Neither can it be denied, that this Tulip may exist independent of your Mind, or mine; but that any immediate Object of the Senses, *i. e.* any Idea, or Combination of Ideas, should exist in an unthinking Substance, or exterior to all [45] Minds, is in itself an evident Contradiction. Nor can I imagine how this follows, from what you said just now, *viz.* that the Red and Yellow were on the Tulip *you saw,* since you do not pretend to *see* that unthinking Substance.

H: You have an artful way, *Philonous,* of diverting our Inquiry from the Subject.

P: I see you have no mind to be pressed that way. To return then to your Distinction between *Sensation* and *Object;* if I take you right, you distinguish in every Perception two things, the one an Action of the Mind, the other not.

H: True.

P: And this Action cannot exist in, or belong to any unthinking thing; but, whatever beside is implied in a Perception, may.

H: That is my Meaning.

P: So that if there was a Perception without any Act of the Mind, it were possible such a Perception should exist in an unthinking Substance.

H: I grant it. But it is impossible there should be such a Perception.

P: When is the Mind said to be active?

H: When it produces, puts an end to, or changes any thing.

P: Can the Mind produce, discontinue, or change any thing but by an Act of the Will? [46]

H: It cannot.

P: The Mind, therefore, is to be accounted active in its Perceptions, so far forth as Volition is included in them . . . . Then, as to Seeing, is it not in your Power to open your Eyes, or keep them shut; to turn them this, or that way? [47]

H: Without doubt.

P: But does it, in like manner, depend on your Will, that in looking on this Flower, you perceive *White* rather than any other Color? or, directing your open Eyes toward yonder Part of the Heaven, can you avoid seeing the Sun? or, is Light or Darkness the Effect of your Volition?

H: No, certainly.

P: You are then, in these Respects, altogether Passive.

H: I am.

P: Tell me now, whether *Seeing* consists in perceiving Light and Colors, or in opening and turning the Eyes?

H: Without doubt, in the former.

P: Since, therefore, you are in the very Perception of Light and Colors altogether passive, what is become of that Action you were speaking of, as an Ingredient in every Sensation? And, does it not follow from your own Concessions, that the Perception of Light and Colors, including no Action in it, may exist in an unperceiving Substance? And, is not this a plain Contradiction? . . . .

H: I acknowledge, *Philonous,* that upon a fair Observation of what passes in my Mind, I can discover nothing else, but that I am a thinking Being, affected with Variety of Sensations; neither is it possible to conceive, how a Sensation should exist in an unperceiving Substance. But then, on the other hand, when I look on sensible Things in a different View, considering them as so many Modes and Qualities, I find it necessary to suppose a material *Substratum,* without which they cannot be conceived to exist.

P: *Material Substratum* call you it? Pray, by which of your Senses came you acquainted with that Being?

H: It is not itself sensible; its Modes and Qualities only being perceived by the Senses.

P: I presume then, it was by Reflection and Reason you obtained the Idea of it.

H: I do not pretend to any proper, positive Idea of it. However, I conclude it exists, because Qualities cannot be conceived to exist without a Support. [49]

P: It seems then you have only a relative Notion of it, or that you conceive it not otherwise than by conceiving the Relation it bears to sensible Qualities.

H: Right.

P: Be pleased therefore to let me know wherein that Relation consists.

H: Is it not sufficiently expressed in the Term *Substratum,* or *Substance?*

P: If so, the Word *Substratum* should import, that it is spread under the sensible Qualities or Accidents.

H: True.

P: And consequently under Extension.

H: I own it.

P: It is, therefore, somewhat in its own Nature entirely distinct from Extension.

H: I tell you, Extension is only a Mode, and Matter is something that supports Modes. And is it not evident the Thing supported is different from the thing supporting?

P: So that something distinct from, and exclusive of, Extension, is supposed to be the *Substratum* of Extension.

H: Just so.

P: Answer me, *Hylas.* Can a thing be spread without Extension: or is not the Idea of Extension necessarily included in *Spreading?*

H: It is. [50]

P: Whatsoever, therefore, you suppose spread under any thing, must have in itself an Extension distinct from the Extension of that Thing under which it is spread.

H: It must.

P: Consequently every corporeal Substance, being the *Substratum* of Extension, must have in itself another Extension by which it is qualified to be a

Substratum: And so on to Infinity. And I ask whether this be not absurd in itself, and repugnant to what you granted just now, *viz.* that the *Substratum* was something distinct from, and exclusive of, Extension.

H: Ay, but, *Philonous,* you take me wrong. I do not mean that Matter is *spread* in a gross literal Sense under Extension. The Word *Substratum* is used only to express, in general, the same thing with *Substance.*

P: Well then, let us examine the Relation implied in the Term *Substance.* Is it not that it stands under Accidents?

H: The very same . . . . [51]

P: You tell me, Matter supports or stands under Accidents. How! is it as your Legs support your Body?

H: No; that is the literal Sense.

P: Pray let me know any Sense, literal or not literal, that you understand it in.—How long must I wait for an Answer, *Hylas?*

H: I declare I know not what to say. I once thought I understood well enough what was meant by Matter's supporting Accidents. But now the more I think on it, the less can I comprehend it; in short, I find that I know nothing of it.

P: It seems then you have no Idea at all, neither relative nor positive of Matter; you know neither what it is in itself, nor what Relation it bears to Accidents.

H: I acknowledge it.

P: And yet you asserted, that you could not conceive, how Qualities or Accidents should really exist, without conceiving at the same time a material Support of them.

H: I did.

P: That is to say, when you conceive the real Existence of Qualities, you do withal [52] conceive something which you cannot conceive.

H: It was wrong I own . . .

P: But (to pass by all that hath been [53] hitherto said, and reckon it for nothing, if you will have it so) I am content to put the whole upon this Issue. If you can conceive it possible for any Mixture or Combination of Qualities, or any sensible Object whatever, to exist without the Mind, then I will grant it actually to be so.

H: If it comes to that, the Point will soon be decided. What more easy than to conceive a Tree or House existing by itself, independent of, and unperceived by, any Mind whatsoever? I do, at this present time, conceive them existing after that Manner.

P: How say you, *Hylas,* can you see a thing which is at the same time unseen?

H: No, that were a Contradiction.

P: Is it not as great a Contradiction to talk of *conceiving* a thing which is *unconceived?*

H: It is.

P: The Tree or House, therefore, which you think of, is conceived by you.

H: How should it be otherwise?

P: And what is conceived, is surely in the Mind.

H: Without Question, that which is conceived is in the Mind.

P: How then came you to say, you conceived a House or Tree existing independent and out of all Minds whatsoever? [54]

H: That was, I own, an Oversight; but stay, let me consider what led me into it.—It is a pleasant Mistake enough. As I was thinking of a Tree in a solitary Place, where no one was present to see it, methought that was to conceive a Tree as existing unperceived or unthought of, not considering that I myself conceived it all the while. But now I plainly see, that all I can do is to frame Ideas in my own Mind. I may, indeed, conceive in my own Thoughts the Idea of a Tree, or a House, or a Mountain, but that is all. And this is far from proving, that I can conceive them *existing out of the Minds of all Spirits.*

P: You acknowledge then that you cannot possibly conceive, how any one corporeal sensible Thing should exist otherwise than in a Mind.

H: I do . . .

What to look for now: *Even if we have no direct acquaintance with matter, it may be necessary to assume its existence in order to explain the stability of appearance. After all, ideas are flitting things. In this section, Berkeley argues that stability can be accounted for using only minds and the ideas in them. What is the core argument?*

THE SECOND DIALOGUE . . .

P: To me it is evident, for the Reasons you allow of, that sensible Things cannot exist otherwise than in a Mind or Spirit. Whence I conclude, not that they have no real Existence, but that seeing they depend not on my Thought, and have an Existence distinct from being perceived by me, *there must be some other Mind wherein they exist.* As sure, therefore, as the sensible World really exists, so sure is there an infinite omnipresent Spirit who contains and supports it.

H: What! This is no more than I and all Christians hold; nay, and all others too [75] who believe there is a God, and that he knows and comprehends all Things.

P: Ay, but here lies the Difference. Men commonly believe that all Things are known or perceived by God, because they believed the Being of a God, whereas I, on the other side, immediately and necessarily conclude the Being of a God, because all sensible Things must be perceived by Him.

H: But so long as we all believe the same thing, what matter is it how we come by that Belief?

P: But neither do we agree in the same Opinion. For Philosophers, tho they acknowledge all corporeal Beings to be perceived by God, yet they attribute to them an absolute Subsistence distinct from their being perceived by any Mind whatever, which I do not. Besides, is there no Difference between saying, *There is a God, therefore he perceives all Things:* and saying, *Sensible Things do really exist: and if they really exist, they are necessarily perceived by an infinite Mind: therefore there is an infinite Mind, or God.* This furnishes you with a direct and immediate Demonstration, from a most evident Principle, of the *Being of a God.* Divines and Philosophers had proved, beyond all Controversy, from the Beauty and Usefulness of the several Parts of the Creation, that it was the Workmanship of God. But that, setting aside all [76] Help of Astronomy and natural Philosophy, all Contemplation of the Contrivance, Order, and Adjustment of Things, an infinite Mind should be necessarily inferred from the bare Existence of the sensible World, is an Advantage peculiar to them only who have made this easy Reflection: That the sensible World is that which we perceive by our several Senses; and that nothing is perceived by the Senses beside Ideas; and that no Idea, or Archetype of an Idea, can exist otherwise than in a Mind. You may now, without any laborious Search into the Sciences, without any Subtlety of Reason, or tedious Length of Discourse, oppose and baffle the most strenuous Advocate for Atheism . . . [78] It is evident that the Things I perceive are my own Ideas, and that no Idea can exist, unless it be in a Mind. Nor is it less plain that these Ideas or Things by me perceived, either themselves or their Archetypes exist independently of my Mind, [79] since I know myself not to be their Author, it being out of my Power to determine at Pleasure, what particular Ideas I shall be affected with upon opening my Eyes or Ears. They must therefore exist in some other Mind, whose Will it is they should be exhibited to me. The Things, I say, immediately perceived, are Ideas or Sensations, call them which you will. But how can any Idea or Sensation exist in, or be produced by, any thing but a Mind or Spirit? This, indeed, is inconceivable: and to assert that which is inconceivable, is to talk Nonsense: Is it not?

H: Without doubt.

P: But on the other hand, it is very conceivable that they should exist in, and be produced by, a Spirit; since this is no more than I daily experience in myself, inasmuch as I perceive numberless Ideas; and by an Act of my Will can form a great Variety of them, and raise them up in my Imagination: Tho' it must be confessed, these Creatures of the Fancy are not altogether so distinct, so strong, vivid, and permanent, as those perceived by my Senses, which latter are called *Real Things*. From all which I conclude, *there is a Mind which affects me every Moment with all the sensible Impressions I perceive*. And from the Variety, Order, and Manner of these, I conclude the Author of them to be *wise, powerful, and good, beyond Comprehension. [80]*

CAUSATION (1740)

David Hume

David Hume (1711–1776) was born David Home in Edinburgh, Scotland. (To help the English pronounce his name in the Scottish manner, he adopted the more phonetic "Hume" in 1734.) His barrister father died in 1713, leaving an estate that provided enough income for a comfortable life. Reared by his mother, Hume received a good grounding in Latin and Greek. The Calvinist family regularly attended Church of Scotland, where his uncle was pastor. Hume left home at the unusually early age of 12—some sources say 10—to study law at the University of Edinburgh, a center for studies of Berkeley and Newtonian natural philosophy. At University, Hume came to dislike everything but philosophy and general learning. After three years, believing that the professors gave him nothing that he could not get from books, Hume undertook a self-directed education. At 18, he became convinced that he had made a great discovery and, with some hindrances owing to depression, devoted the next decade to concentrated reading and writing. At 23, after a brief stint working for a sugar merchant in Bristol (England), Hume took residence in Anjou, France, frequenting the library at La Flèche (where Descartes had been educated) and becoming intimately acquainted with French philosophy. There he wrote A Treatise of Human Nature, his most important philosophical work, completed when he was only 26 and published (anonymously) two years later. Hume attributed poor reception of the Treatise—he wrote that it came "dead-born from the Press"—to its length and complexity. He immediately produced a brief abstract as an advertising tool (unsuccessful) and began to write essays and dialogues, forms more suitable to the tastes of his age. In 1741 and 1742, he published (also anonymously) the two-volume Essays, Moral and Political. This work emphasized the role of sentiment in morality, established him as an inspiration for the utilitarian movement, and, in 1746, brought him to candidacy for the Professorship of Ethics and Pneumatical Philosophy at the University of Edinburgh, a position for which he was rejected after local ministers raised accusations of heresy and atheism. (Hume encountered such charges throughout his remaining life, and it again

*cost him an academic position when, some years later, he was point-
edly not considered the Chair of Philosophy at Glasgow.) Hume next
found work as a tutor, then as secretary to General St. Clair (a distant
relative), and then as Aides-de-camp in the Embassy to the Court of
Vienna and Turin. During this time, Hume began a correspondence with
Montesquieu, recast the ideas in the Treatise into Philosophical Essays
Concerning Human Understanding (published anonymously in 1748,
renamed An Enquiry Concerning Human Understanding in 1758), and
wrote Three Essays: Moral, Political, and Literary, the first work that
he published under his own name (1748). The Enquiry was hardly more
successful than the Treatise, but the iconoclastic Three Essays earned
him considerable fame. In 1751, he wrote an Enquiry Concerning the
Principles of Morals as a replacement for the third book of the Treatise.
In 1752, he took employment as librarian for the Faculty of Advocates,
a job that paid little but gave him access to an excellent library. That
year, he published Political Discourses, began work on the Dialogues
Concerning Natural Religion—a work deemed so dangerous that there
was resistance even to its posthumous publication in 1779—and continued historical research (begun in 1745) that would result in publication (in the late 1750s and early '60s) of his History of Great Britain—a
best-selling six-volume work of over one million words that earned him
literary fame and served as the standard history for many years. In 1757,
he published Four Dissertations of which one, "The Natural History of
Religion," argued that classical mythologies are more reasonable and
enlightening than systematic Christian theology. Hume lived in Paris
from 1763 to 1765, where he served as secretary to Lord Hertford and
came to know Voltaire, Diderot, and d'Alembert. Hume also befriended
Jean-Jacques Rousseau, who was living in Switzerland after making
himself quite unwelcome in Paris. Rousseau accepted Hume's invitation
to come to England, but the Frenchman's paranoia made it as impossible
to live in England as in France. In 1767, Hume accepted an appointment in London as Under Secretary of State for the Northern Department, retiring back to Edinburgh the next year. His essays "Of Suicide"
and "Of the Immortality of the Soul" appeared in unauthorized French
translations in 1770. During his last years, Hume mentored Adam Smith.
(He read early drafts of The Wealth of Nations.) In 1776, well into a long
illness and knowing that he was near death, Hume wrote My Own Life, a
brief autobiography and apologia that was published by Smith, his literary executor. Hume died at age 65. His grave on Calton Hill overlooks
New Town, Edinburgh.*

What to look for: *What relation underlies all reasoning involving matters
of fact (scientific reasoning)? What do we actually see when we observe*

a cause-effect event? What do we not see? Is it possible to demonstrate (by reason) that an effect must follow from a cause? Why (not)? Does the "necessity" inherent in our idea of cause and effect come through sensory experience? What actually gives rise to the notion of cause and effect?

[A 8][1] 'Tis evident, that all reasonings concerning *matter of fact* are founded on the relation of cause and effect, and that we can never infer the existence of one object from another, unless they be connected together, either mediately or immediately. In order therefore to understand these reasonings, we must be perfectly acquainted with the idea of a cause; and in order to that, must look about us to find something that is the cause of another.

[A 9] Here is a billiard-ball lying on the table, and another ball moving towards it with rapidity. They strike; and the ball, which was formerly at rest, now acquires a motion. This is as perfect an instance of the relation of cause and effect as any which we know, either by sensation or reflection. Let us therefore examine it. 'Tis evident, that the two balls touched one another before the motion was communicated, and that there was no interval betwixt the shock and the motion. *Contiguity* in time and place is therefore a requisite circumstance to the operation of all causes. 'Tis evident likewise, that the motion, which was the cause, is prior to the motion, which was the effect. *Priority* in time is therefore another requisite circumstance in every cause. But this is not all. Let us try any other balls of the same kind in a like situation, and we shall always find, that the impulse of the one produces motion in the other. Here therefore is a *third* circumstance, *viz.* that of a *constant conjunction* betwixt the cause and effect. Every object like the cause, produces always some object like the effect. Beyond these three circumstances of contiguity, priority, and constant conjunction, I can discover nothing in this cause. The first ball is in motion; touches the second; immediately the second is in motion: and when I try the experiment with the same or like balls, in the same or like circumstances, I find, that upon the motion and touch of the one ball, motion always follows in the other. In whatever shape I turn this matter, and however I examine it, I can find nothing farther.

[A 10] This is the case when both the cause and effect are present to the senses. Let us now see upon what our inference is founded, when we conclude from the one that the other has existed or will exist. Suppose I see a ball moving in a straight line towards another, I immediately conclude, that they will shock, and that the second will be in motion. This is the inference from cause

---

[1] Scholars commonly reference this work with an "A" [for *Abstract*] followed by the paragraph number. Paragraph numbers were not in the original.

"Causation," by David Hume, from *An Abstract Of A Book Lately Published; Entituled, A Treatise Of Human Nature, &c.* (London: C. Borbet, at Addison's Head, over-against St. Dunstan's Church, in Fleet-street, 1740).

to effect; and of this nature are all our reasonings in the conduct of life: on this is founded all our belief in history: and from hence is derived all philosophy, excepting only geometry and arithmetic. If we can explain the inference from the shock of two balls, we shall be able to account for this operation of the mind in all instances.

[A 11] Were a man, such as *Adam*, created in the full vigor of understanding, without experience, he would never be able to infer motion in the second ball from the motion and impulse of the first. It is not any thing that reason sees in the cause, which makes us *infer* the effect. Such an inference, were it possible, would amount to a demonstration, as being founded merely on the comparison of ideas. But no inference from cause to effect amounts to a demonstration. Of which there is this evident proof. The mind can always *conceive* any effect to follow from any cause, and indeed any event to follow upon another: whatever we *conceive* is possible, at least in a metaphysical sense: but wherever a demonstration takes place, the contrary is impossible, and implies a contradiction. There is no demonstration, therefore, for any conjunction of cause and effect. And this is a principle, which is generally allowed by philosophers.

[A 12] It would have been necessary, therefore, for *Adam* (if he was not inspired) to have had *experience* of the effect, which followed upon the impulse of these two balls. He must have seen, in several instances, that when the one ball struck upon the other, the second always acquired motion. If he had seen a sufficient number of instances of this kind, whenever he saw the one ball moving towards the other, he would always conclude without hesitation, that the second would acquire motion. His understanding would anticipate his sight, and form a conclusion suitable to his past experience.

[A 13] It follows, then, that all reasonings concerning cause and effect, are founded on experience, and that all reasonings from experience are founded on the supposition, that the course of nature will continue uniformly the same. We conclude, that like causes, in like circumstances, will always produce like effects. It may now be worth while to consider, what determines us to form a conclusion of such infinite consequence.

[A 14]'Tis evident, that *Adam* with all his science, would never have been able to *demonstrate*, that the course of nature must continue uniformly the same, and that the future must be conformable to the past. What is possible can never be demonstrated to be false; and 'tis possible the course of nature may change, since we can conceive such a change. Nay, I will go farther, and assert, that he could not so much as prove by any *probable* arguments, that the future must be conformable to the past. All probable arguments are built on the supposition, that there is this conformity betwixt the future and the past, and therefore can never prove it. This conformity is a *matter of fact*, and if it must be proved, will admit of no proof but from experience. But our experience in the past can be a proof of nothing for the future, but upon a supposition, that there is a resemblance betwixt them. This therefore is a point, which can admit of no proof at all, and which we take for granted without any proof.

[A 15] We are determined by custom alone to suppose the future conformable to the past. When I see a billiard-ball moving towards another, my mind is immediately carry'd by habit to the usual effect, and anticipates my sight by conceiving the second ball in motion. There is nothing in these objects, abstractly considered, and independent of experience, which leads me to form any such conclusion: and even after I have had experience of many repeated effects of this kind, there is no argument, which determines me to suppose, that the effect will be conformable to past experience. The powers, by which bodies operate, are entirely unknown. We perceive only their sensible qualities: and what *reason* have we to think, that the same powers will always be conjoined with the same sensible qualities?

[A 16] 'Tis not, therefore, reason, which is the guide of life, but custom. That alone determines the mind, in all instances, to suppose the future conformable to the past. However easy this step may seem, reason would never, to all eternity, be able to make it.

[A 17] This is a very curious discovery, but leads us to others, that are still more curious. *When I see a billiard ball moving towards another, my mind is immediately carry'd by habit to the usual effect, and anticipates my sight by conceiving the second ball in motion.* But is this all? Do I nothing but conceive the motion of the second ball? No surely. I also believe that it will move. What then is this *belief*? And how does it differ from the simple conception of any thing? Here is a new question unthought of by philosophers.

[A 18] When a demonstration convinces me of any proposition, it not only makes me conceive the proposition, but also makes me sensible, that 'tis impossible to conceive any thing contrary. What is demonstratively false implies a contradiction; and what implies a contradiction cannot be conceived. But with regard to any matter of fact, however strong the proof may be from experience, I can always conceive the contrary, tho' I cannot always believe it. The belief, therefore, makes some difference betwixt the conception to which we assent, and that to which we do not assent.

[A 19] To account for this, there are only two hypotheses. It may be said, that belief joins some new idea to those which we may conceive without assenting to them. But this hypothesis is false. For *first*, no such idea can be produced. When we simply conceive an object, we conceive it in all its parts. We conceive it as it might exist, tho' we do not believe it to exist. Our belief of it would discover no new qualities. We may paint out the entire object in imagination without believing it. We may set it, in a manner, before our eyes, with every circumstance of time and place. 'Tis the very object conceived as it might exist; and when we believe it, we can do no more.

[A 20] *Secondly,* The mind has a faculty of joining all ideas together, which involve not a contradiction; and therefore if belief consisted in some idea, which we add to the simple conception, it would be in a man's power, by adding this idea to it, to believe any thing, which he can conceive.

[A 21] Since therefore belief implies a conception, and yet is something more; and since it adds no new idea to the conception; it follows, that it is a different manner of conceiving an object; *something* that is distinguishable to the feeling, and depends not upon our will, as all our ideas do. My mind runs by habit from the visible object of one ball moving towards another, to the usual effect of motion in the second ball. It not only conceives that motion, but *feels* something different in the conception of it from a mere reverie of the imagination. The presence of this visible object, and the constant conjunction of that particular effect, render the idea different to the *feeling* from those loose ideas, which come into the mind without any introduction. This conclusion seems a little surprising; but we are led into it by a chain of propositions, which admit of no doubt. To ease the reader's memory I shall briefly resume them. No matter of fact can be proved but from its cause or its effect. Nothing can be known to be the cause of another but by experience. We can give no reason for extending to the future our experience in the past; but are entirely determined by custom, when we conceive an effect to follow from its usual cause. But we also believe an effect to follow, as well as conceive it. This belief joins no new idea to the conception. It only varies the manner of conceiving, and makes a difference to the feeling or sentiment. Belief, therefore, in all matters of fact arises only from custom, and is an idea conceived in a peculiar *manner*.

A COPERNICAN REVOLUTION FOR KNOWLEDGE (1781/1787)

Immanuel Kant

Immanuel Kant—see p. 3.

What to look for: Kant wrote that reading Hume on causality "shook me from my dogmatic slumbers." Kant's solution to Hume's problem appears in the "Preface" (just below), but it won't make much sense until you have digested the rest of the selection. Does all knowledge arise from *experience? What is* a priori *knowledge and what is the difference between the pure and impure examples? What must one examine to determine whether a claim is* analytic *or* synthetic*? What must one examine to determine whether a claim is* a priori *or* a posteriori*? These distinctions generate four possible categories for a claim:*

Type of claim	A priori	A posteriori
Analytic		
Synthetic		

What are examples of each type of claim (if examples exist)? In which category do claims regarding relations of ideas fall? In which category do claims regarding matters of fact fall? And finally—the question addressed in the "Preface"—how are synthetic a priori claims possible? If Kant is correct, is the principle of causation (and science) justified?

PREFACE

. . . It has hitherto been assumed that our cognition must conform to the objects; but all attempts to ascertain anything about these objects *a priori*, by means of conceptions, and thus to extend the range of our knowledge, have

"A Copernican Revolution for Knowledge," by Immanuel Kant, from *The Critique Of Pure Reason*. Trans. J. M. D. Meiklejohn (London: Henry G. Bohn, York Street, Covent Garden. 1855).

been rendered abortive by this assumption. Let us then make the experiment whether we may not be more successful in metaphysics, if we assume that the objects must conform to our cognition. This appears, at all events, to accord better with the *possibility* of our gaining the end we have in view, that is to say, of arriving at the cognition of [xxiv] objects *a priori*, of determining something with respect to these objects, before they are given to us. We here propose to do just what Copernicus did in attempting to explain the celestial movements. When he found that he could make no progress by assuming that all the heavenly bodies revolved round the spectator, he reversed the process, and tried the experiment of assuming that the spectator revolved, while the stars remained at rest. We may make the same experiment with regard to the intuition of objects. If the intuition must conform to the nature of the objects, I do not see how we can know anything of them *a priori*. If, on the other hand, the object conforms to the nature of our faculty of intuition, I can then easily conceive the possibility of such an *a priori* knowledge. . . .

Konigsberg, April 1787.

INTRODUCTION
I.—Of the difference between pure and empirical knowledge

That all our knowledge begins with experience there can be no doubt. For how is it possible that the faculty of cognition should be awakened into exercise otherwise than by means of objects which affect our senses, and partly of themselves produce representations, partly rouse our powers of understanding into activity, to compare to connect, or to separate these, and so to convert the raw material of our sensuous impressions into a knowledge of objects, which is called experience? In respect of time, therefore, no knowledge of ours is antecedent to experience, but begins with it.

But, though all our knowledge begins with experience, it by no means follows that all arises out of experience. For, on the contrary, it is quite possible that our empirical knowledge is a compound of that which we receive through impressions, and that which the faculty of cognition supplies from itself (sensuous impressions giving merely the *occasion*), an addition which we cannot distinguish from the original element given by sense, till long practice has made us attentive to, and skilful in separating it. It is, therefore, a question which requires close investigation, and not to be answered at first sight, whether there exists a knowledge altogether independent of experience, and even of all sensuous impressions? Knowledge of this kind is called *a priori*, in contradistinction to empirical knowledge, which has its sources *a posteriori*, that is, in experience.

But the expression, "*a priori*," is not as yet definite enough adequately to indicate the whole meaning of the question above started. For, in speaking of knowledge which [2] has its sources in experience, we are wont to say, that this or that may be known *a priori*, because we do not derive this knowledge imme- diately from experience, but from a general rule, which, however, we have itself borrowed from experience. Thus, if a man undermined his house, we say, "he might know *a priori* that it would have fallen;" that is, he needed not to have waited for the experience that it did actually fall. But still, *a priori*, he could not know even this much. For, that bodies are heavy, and, consequently, that they fall when their supports are taken away, must have been known to him previously, by means of experience.

By the term "knowledge *a priori*," therefore, we shall in the sequel under- stand, not such as is independent of this or that kind of experience, but such as is absolutely so of all experience. Opposed to this is empirical knowledge, or that which is possible only *a posteriori*, that is, through experience. Knowl- edge *a priori* is either pure or impure. Pure knowledge *a priori* is that with which no empirical element is mixed up. For example, the proposition, "Every change has a cause," is a proposition *a priori*, but impure, because change is a conception which can only be derived from experience.

II.—The Human Intellect, even in an Unphilosophical State, is in Possession of Certain Cognitions "a priori".

The question now is as to a criterion, by which we may securely distinguish a pure from an empirical cognition. Experience no doubt teaches us that this or that object is constituted in such and such a manner, but not that it could not possibly exist otherwise. Now, in the first place, if we have a proposition which contains the idea of necessity in its very conception, it is a if, moreover, it is not derived from any other proposition, unless from one equally involving the idea of necessity, it is absolutely priori. Secondly, an empirical judgement never exhibits strict and absolute, but only assumed and comparative universality (by induction); therefore, the most we can say is—so far as we have hitherto observed, there is no exception to this or that rule. If, on the other hand, a judgement carries with it strict and absolute universality, that is, admits of no possible exception, [3] it is not derived from experience, but is valid absolutely *a priori*.

Empirical universality is, therefore, only an arbitrary extension of validity, from that which may be predicated of a proposition valid in most cases, to that which is asserted of a proposition which holds good in all; as, for example, in the affirmation, "All bodies are heavy." When, on the contrary, strict universal- ity characterizes a judgement, it necessarily indicates another peculiar source of knowledge, namely, a faculty of cognition *a priori*. Necessity and strict universality, therefore, are infallible tests for distinguishing pure from empiri- cal knowledge, and are inseparably connected with each other. But as in the use of these criteria the empirical limitation is sometimes more easily detected than the contingency of the judgement, or the unlimited universality which we attach to a judgement is often a more convincing proof than its necessity, it may be advisable to use the criteria separately, each being by itself infallible.

Now, that in the sphere of human cognition we have judgements which are necessary, and in the strictest sense universal, consequently pure *a priori*, it will be an easy matter to show. If we desire an example from the sciences, we need only take any proposition in mathematics. If we cast our eyes upon the commonest operations of the understanding, the proposition, "Every change must have a cause," will amply serve our purpose. In the latter case, indeed, the conception of a cause so plainly involves the conception of a necessity of connection with an effect, and of a strict universality of the law, that the very notion of a cause would entirely disappear, were we to derive it, like Hume, from a frequent association of what happens with that which precedes; and the habit thence originating of connecting representations—the necessity inherent in the judgement being therefore merely subjective. Besides, without seeking for such examples of principles existing *a priori* in cognition, we might easily show that such principles are the indispensable basis of the possibility of experience itself, and consequently prove their existence *a priori*. For whence could our experience itself acquire certainty, if all the rules on which it depends were themselves empirical, and consequently fortuitous? No one, therefore, can admit the validity of the use [4] of such rules as first principles. But, for the present, we may content ourselves with having established the fact, that we do possess and exercise a faculty of pure *a priori* cognition; and, secondly, with having pointed out the proper tests of such cognition, namely, universality and necessity.

Not only in judgements, however, but even in conceptions, is an *a priori* origin manifest. For example, if we take away by degrees from our conceptions of a body all that can be referred to mere sensuous experience—colour, hardness or softness, weight, even impenetrability—the body will then vanish; but the space which it occupied still remains, and this it is utterly impossible to annihilate in thought. Again, if we take away, in like manner, from our empirical conception of any object, corporeal or incorporeal, all properties which mere experience has taught us to connect with it, still we cannot think away those through which we cogitate it as substance, or adhering to substance, although our conception of substance is more determined than that of an object. Compelled, therefore, by that necessity with which the conception of substance forces itself upon us, we must confess that it has its seat in our faculty of cognition *a priori* . . .

IV.—Of the Difference Between Analytical and Synthetical Judgements.

In all judgements wherein the relation of a subject to the predicate is cogitated (I mention affirmative judgements only here; the application to negative will be very easy), this relation is possible in two different ways. Either the predicate B belongs to the subject A, as somewhat which is contained (though covertly) in the conception A; or the predicate B lies completely out of the conception A, although it stands in connection with it. In the first instance, I term the judgement analytical, in the second, synthetical. Analytical judgements (affirmative) are therefore those in which the connection of the predicate with the subject is cogitated through identity; those in which this connection is cogitated without identity, are called synthetical judgements. The former may be called *explicative*, the latter *augmentative* judgements; because the former add in the predicate nothing to the conception of the subject, but only analyse it into its constituent conceptions, which were thought already in the subject, although in a confused manner; the latter add to our conceptions of the subject a predicate which was not contained in it, and which no analysis could ever have discovered therein. For example, when I say, "All bodies are extended," this is an analytical judgement. For I need not go beyond the conception of *body* in order to find extension connected with it, but merely analyse the conception, that is, become conscious of the manifold properties which I think in that conception, in order to discover this predicate in it: it is therefore an analytical judgement. On the other hand, when I say, "All bodies are heavy," the predicate is something totally different from that which I think in the mere conception of a body. By the addition of such a predicate, therefore, it becomes a synthetical judgement.

Judgements of experience, as such, are always synthetical. For it would be absurd to think of grounding an analytical judgement on experience, because in forming such a judgement I need not go out of the sphere of my conceptions, [8] and therefore recourse to the testimony of experience is quite unnecessary. That "bodies are extended" is not an empirical judgement, but a proposition which stands firm *a priori*. For before addressing myself to experience, I already have in my conception all the requisite conditions for the judgement, and I have only to extract the predicate from the conception, according to the principle of contradiction, and thereby at the same time become conscious of the necessity of the judgement, a necessity which I could never learn from experience. On the other hand, though at first I do not at all include the predicate of weight in my conception of body in general, that conception still indicates an object of experience, a part of the totality of experience, to which I can still add other parts; and this I do when I recognize by observation that bodies are heavy. I can cognize beforehand by analysis the conception of body through the characteristics of extension, impenetrability, shape, etc., all which are cogitated in this conception. But now I extend my knowledge, and looking back on experience from which I had derived this conception of body, I find weight at all times connected with the above characteristics, and therefore I synthetically add to my conceptions this as a predicate, and say, "All bodies are heavy." Thus it is experience upon which rests the possibility of the synthesis of the predicate of weight with the conception of body, because both conceptions, although the one is not contained in the other, still belong to one another (only contingently, however), as parts of a whole, namely, of experience, which is itself a synthesis of intuitions.

But to synthetical judgements *a priori*, such aid is entirely wanting. If I go out of and beyond the conception A, in order to recognize another B as connected with it, what foundation have I to rest on, whereby to render the synthesis possible? I have here no longer the advantage of looking out in the sphere of experience for what I want. Let us take, for example, the proposition, "Everything that happens has a cause." In the conception of *something that happens*, I indeed think an existence which a certain time antecedes, and from this I can derive analytical judgements. But the conception of a cause lies quite out of the above conception, and indicates something entirely different from "that which [9] happens," and is consequently not contained in that conception. How then am I able to assert concerning the general conception—"that which happens"—something entirely different from that conception, and to recognize the conception of cause although not contained in it, yet as belonging to it, and even necessarily? what is here the unknown = X, upon which the understanding rests when it believes it has found, out of the conception A a foreign predicate B, which it nevertheless considers to be connected with it? It cannot be experience, because the principle adduced annexes the two representations, cause and effect, to the representation existence, not only with universality, which experience cannot give, but also with the expression of necessity, therefore completely *a priori* and from pure conceptions. Upon such synthetical, that is augmentative propositions, depends the whole aim of our speculative knowledge *a priori*; for although analytical judgements are indeed highly important and necessary, they are so, only to arrive at that clearness of conceptions which is requisite for a sure and extended synthesis, and this alone is a real acquisition.

V.—In all Theoretical Sciences of Reason, Synthetical Judgements "a priori" are contained as Principles.

1. Mathematical judgements are always synthetical. Hitherto this fact, though incontestably true and very important in its consequences, seems to have escaped the analysts of the human mind, nay, to be in complete opposition to all their conjectures. For as it was found that mathematical conclusions all proceed according to the principle of contradiction (which the nature of every apodeictic certainty requires), people became persuaded that the fundamental principles of the science also were recognized and admitted in the same way. But the notion is fallacious; for although a synthetical proposition can certainly be discerned by means of the principle of contradiction, this is possible only when another synthetical proposition precedes, from which the latter is deduced, but never of itself.

Before all, be it observed, that proper mathematical propositions are always judgements *a priori*, and not empirical, because they carry along with them the conception of necessity, [10] which cannot be given by experience. If this be demurred to, it matters not; I will then limit my assertion to pure mathematics, the very conception of which implies that it consists of knowledge altogether non-empirical and *a priori*.

We might, indeed at first suppose that the proposition $7 + 5 = 12$ is a merely analytical proposition, following (according to the principle of contradiction) from the conception of a sum of seven and five. But if we regard it more narrowly, we find that our conception of the sum of seven and five contains nothing more than the uniting of both sums into one, whereby it cannot at all be cogitated what this single number is which embraces both. The conception of twelve is by no means obtained by merely cogitating the union of seven and five; and we may analyse our conception of such a possible sum as long as we will, still we shall never discover in it the notion of twelve. We must go beyond these conceptions, and have recourse to an intuition which corresponds to one of the two – our five fingers, for example, or like Segner in his Arithmetic five points, and so by degrees, add the units contained in the five given in the intuition, to the conception of seven. For I first take the number 7, and, for the conception of 5 calling in the aid of the fingers of my hand as objects of intuition, I add the units, which I before took together to make up the number 5, gradually now by means of the material image my hand, to the number 7, and by this process, I at length see the number 12 arise. That 7 should be added to 5, I have certainly cogitated in my conception of a sum $= 7 + 5$, but not that this sum was equal to 12. Arithmetical propositions are therefore always synthetical, of which we may become more clearly convinced by trying large numbers. For it will thus become quite evident that, turn and twist our conceptions as we may, it is impossible, without having recourse to intuition, to arrive at the sum total or product by means of the mere analysis of our conceptions. Just as little is any principle of pure geometry analytical. "A straight line between two points is the shortest," is a synthetical proposition. For my conception of *straight* contains no notion of *quantity*, but is merely *qualitative*. The conception of the shortest is therefore fore wholly an addition, and by no analysis can it be extracted from our conception of a straight line. Intuition [11] must therefore here lend its aid, by means of which, and thus only, our synthesis is possible.

Some few principles preposited by geometricians are, indeed, really analytical, and depend on the principle of contradiction. They serve, however, like identical propositions, as links in the chain of method, not as principles— for example, $a = a$, the whole is equal to itself, or $(a+b) > a$, the whole is greater than its part. And yet even these principles themselves, though they derive their validity from pure conceptions, are only admitted in mathematics because they can be presented in intuition. What causes us here commonly to believe that the predicate of such apodeictic judgements is already contained in our conception, and that the judgement is therefore analytical, is merely the equivocal nature of the expression. We must join in thought a certain predicate to a given conception, and this necessity cleaves already to the conception.

But the question is, not what we must join in thought to the given conception, but what we really think therein, though only obscurely, and then it becomes manifest that the predicate pertains to these conceptions, necessarily indeed, yet not as thought in the conception itself, but by virtue of an intuition, which must be added to the conception.

2. The science of natural philosophy (physics) contains in itself synthetical judgements *a priori*, as principles. I shall adduce two propositions. For instance, the proposition, "In all changes of the material world, the quantity of matter remains unchanged"; or, that, "In all communication of motion, action and reaction must always be equal." In both of these, not only is the necessity, and therefore their origin *a priori* clear, but also that they are synthetical propositions. For in the conception of matter, I do not cogitate its permanency, but merely its presence in space, which it fills. I therefore really go out of and beyond the conception of matter, in order to think on to it something *a priori*, which I did not think in it. The proposition is therefore not analytical, but synthetical, and nevertheless conceived *a priori*; and so it is with regard to the other propositions of the pure part of natural philosophy.

3. As to metaphysics, even if we look upon it merely as an attempted science, yet, from the nature of human reason, an [12] indispensable one, we find that it must contain synthetical propositions *a priori*. It is not merely the duty of metaphysics to dissect, and thereby analytically to illustrate the conceptions which we form *a priori* of things; but we seek to widen the range of our *a priori* knowledge. For this purpose, we must avail ourselves of such principles as add something to the original conception—something not identical with, nor contained in it, and by means of synthetical judgements *a priori*, leave far behind us the limits of experience; for example, in the proposition, "the world must have a beginning," and such like. Thus metaphysics, according to the proper aim of the science, consists merely of synthetical propositions *a priori*.

GOD

AN ONTOLOGICAL PROOF OF GOD'S EXISTENCE (1077–1078)

St. Anselm

St. Anselm of Canterbury (1033–1109) was born Anselmus Candiae Genavae in Aosta, Kingdom of Burgundy [now northern Italy], into an aristocratic, propertied family. His father was of a notably harsh nature. His prudent mother saw to Anselm's religious instruction. At 15, the lad desired to become a monk, but his father prevented him from doing so. At 23, after the death of his mother, unable to further endure his father's harshness, Anselm set off across the Alps to wander through Burgundy, and France . In Normandy, he met Lanfranc (1005?–1089), a prominent theologian and dialectician at the Benedictine Abbey of Bec. The following year (1060), with Lanfranc's encouragement, Anselm entered the Abbey as a Novice. Three years after that, Lanfranc relocated to Caen and Anselm was elected Prior. At Bec, Anselm devoted himself to scholarship (the works of Augustine and Boethius particularly influenced him), to writing philosophical dialogues—De grammatico [The Grammarian] (1059-1060), De veritate [On Truth], De libertate arbitrii [On Freedom of Choice], and De casu diaboli [On the Fall of the Devil], (1080–1086)—and to setting out his important theistic proofs—the Monologion (1075–1076) and the Proslogion (1077–1078). When the Abbot of Bec died in 1078, Anselm succeeded to the office. Under his leadership, Bec became one of Europe's most important seats of learning. In 1093, Anselm's reputation as counselor to the nobility brought him an invitation to visit England. There, contrary to his wishes, King William II of England appointed him to the highly prestigious position of Archbishop of Canterbury. Anselm's concerns proved real: the King constantly sought to appropriate church lands and income. In 1097, while in Rome, in an effort to settle some of the King's ecclesiastical problems, Anselm was exiled from England. Henry I (who became King at the death of William in 1100) recalled Anselm, but proved as adamant about control of the church as William had been. In 1103, Anselm again set out for Rome to resolve conflicts between Church and King and was again exiled. His return to Canterbury in 1107 came only after the Pope threatened the King with excommunication. Throughout the tumult at Canterbury, Anselm continued to write theology intimately intertwined with philosophy. His work, which sought to find a rational foundation for faith, has greatly influenced Church doctrine. He was canonized by the Roman Catholic Church in 1494 and declared a Doctor of the Church in 1720. Anselm is generally recognized as the founder of Scholasticism. And even today, his ontological argument for the existence of God engenders hot debate among scholars.

What to look for: *Anselm wastes no words; especially at the outset, readers need to ponder nearly every sentence to soak in the meaning and/or understand the argument. What are Anselm's two objectives? What is the definition of "God?" To deny that God exists, what must the fool understand? What does he not understand? Which is greater, to exist in reality or to exist only in thought? Is it self-contradictory to deny God's existence? Which is greater, to exist contingently or to exist necessarily? Is it possible to think of God as not existing? Why (not)? How is it possible for the fool to deny that God exists? What recurring strategy serves Anselm in discovering God's qualities? What are the clearest of these qualities? How does Anselm explain that God can perceive even though He has no body? How can God be both omnipotent and yet unable to do many things? How can God lack passion and yet be compassionate? How can God be both righteous and compassionate? Where and how does Anselm reach his limit of understanding? How and why does he revise the definition of "God?"*

CHAPTER II.
Truly there is a God, although the fool hath said in his heart,
There is no God.

And so, Lord, do thou, who dost give understanding to faith, give me, so far as thou knowest it to be profitable, to understand that thou art as we believe; and that thou art that which we believe. And, indeed, we believe that thou art a being than which nothing greater can be conceived. Or is there no such nature, since the fool hath said in his heart, there is no God? (Psalms xiv. 1). But, at any rate, this very fool, when he hears of this being of which I speak—a being than which nothing greater can be conceived—understands what he hears, and what he understands is in his understanding; although he does not understand it to exist.

"An Ontological Proof of God's Existence," by Saint Anselm, from *Proslogium; Monologium; An Appendix in Behalf of the Fool by Gaunilon; and Cur Deus Homo.* Trans. Sidney Norton Deane (Chicago: Open Court, 1903).

For, it is one thing for an object to be in the understanding, and another to understand that the object exists. When a painter first conceives of what he will afterwards perform, he has it in his understanding, but he does not yet understand it to be, because he has not yet performed it. But after he has made the painting, he both has it in his understanding, and he understands that it exists, because he has made it. [8]

Hence, even the fool is convinced that something exists in the understanding, at least, than which nothing greater can be conceived. For, when he hears of this, he understands it. And whatever is understood, exists in the understanding. And assuredly that, than which nothing greater can be conceived, cannot exist in the understanding alone. For, suppose it exists in the understanding alone: then it can be conceived to exist in reality; which is greater.

Therefore, if that, than which nothing greater can be conceived, exists in the understanding alone, the very being, than which nothing greater can be conceived, is one, than which a greater can be conceived. But obviously this is impossible. Hence, there is no doubt that there exists a being, than which nothing greater can be conceived, and it exists both in the understanding and in reality.

CHAPTER III.

God cannot be conceived not to exist.—God is that, than which nothing greater can be conceived.—That which can be conceived not to exist is not God.

And it assuredly exists so truly, that it cannot be conceived not to exist. For, it is possible to conceive of a being which cannot be conceived not to exist; and this is greater than one which can be conceived not to exist. Hence, if that, than which nothing greater can be conceived, can be conceived not to exist, it is not that, than which nothing greater can be conceived. But this is an irreconcilable contradiction. There is, then, so truly a being than which nothing greater can be conceived to exist, that it cannot even [9] be conceived not to exist; and this being thou art, O Lord, our God.

So truly, therefore, dost thou exist, O Lord, my God, that thou canst not be conceived not to exist; and rightly. For, if a mind could conceive of a being better than thee, the creature would rise above the Creator; and this is most absurd. And, indeed, whatever else there is, except thee alone, can be conceived not to exist. To thee alone, therefore, it belongs to exist more truly than all other beings, and hence in a higher degree than all others. For, whatever else exists does not exist so truly, and hence in a less degree it belongs to it to exist. Why, then, has the fool said in his heart, there is no God (Psalms xiv. 1), since it is so evident, to a rational mind, that thou dost exist in the highest degree of all? Why, except that he is dull and a fool?

CHAPTER IV.

*How the fool has said in his heart what cannot be conceived.—A thing may
be conceived in two ways: (1) when the word signifying it is conceived;
(2) when the thing itself is understood As far as the word goes,
God can be conceived not to exist; in reality he cannot.*

But how has the fool said in his heart what he could not conceive; or how is it
that he could not conceive what he said in his heart? since it is the same to say
in the heart, and to conceive.

But, if really, nay, since really, he both conceived, because he said in his
heart; and did not say in his heart, because he could not conceive; there is more
than one way in which a thing is said in the heart or conceived. For, in one
sense, an object is conceived, [10] when the word signifying it is conceived;
and in another, when the very entity, which the object is, is understood.

In the former sense, then, God can be conceived not to exist; but in the latter, not at all. For no one who understands what fire and water are can conceive
fire to be water, in accordance with the nature of the facts themselves, although
this is possible according to the words. So, then, no one who understands what
God is can conceive that God does not exist; although he says these words in
his heart, either without any or with some foreign, signification. For, God is
that than which a greater cannot be conceived. And he who thoroughly understands this, assuredly understands that this being so truly exists, that not even
in concept can it be non-existent. Therefore, he who understands that God so
exists, cannot conceive that he does not exist.

I thank thee, gracious Lord, I thank thee; because what I formerly believed
by thy bounty, I now so understand by thine illumination, that if I were unwilling to believe that thou dost exist, I should not be able not to understand this
to be true.

CHAPTER V.

*God is whatever it is better to be than not to be; and he, as the only
self-existent being, creates all things from nothing.*

What art thou, then, Lord God, than whom nothing greater can be conceived?
But what art thou, except that which, as the highest of all beings, alone exists
through itself, and creates all other things from nothing? For, whatever is
not this is less than a thing which can be conceived of. But this cannot be
conceived [11] of thee. What good, therefore, does the supreme Good lack,
through which every good is? Therefore, thou art just, truthful, blessed, and
whatever it is better to be than not to be. For it is better to be just than not just;
better to be blessed than not blessed.

CHAPTER VI.

How God is sensible (sensibilis) although he is not a body—God is
sensible, omnipotent, compassionate, passionless; for it is better to be
these than not be He who in any way knows, is not improperly
said in some sort to feel

But, although it is better for thee to be sensible, omnipotent, compassionate, passionless, than not to be these things; how art thou sensible, if thou art not a body; or omnipotent, if thou hast not all powers; or at once compassionate and passionless? For, if only corporeal things are sensible, since the senses encompass a body and are in a body, how art thou sensible, although thou art not a body, but a supreme Spirit, who is superior to body? But, if feeling is only cognition, or for the sake of cognition,—for he who feels obtains knowledge in accordance with the proper functions of his senses; as through sight, of colors; through taste, of flavors,—whatever in any way cognises is not inappropriately said, in some sort, to feel.

Therefore, O Lord, although thou art not a body, yet thou art truly sensible in the highest degree in respect of this, that thou dost cognise all things in the highest degree; and not as an animal cognises, through a corporeal sense. [12]

CHAPTER VII.

How he is omnipotent, although there are many things of which he is
not capable.—To be capable of being corrupted, or of lying, is not power,
but impotence. God can do nothing by virtue of impotence, and nothing
has power against him.

But how art thou omnipotent, if thou art not capable of all things? Or, if thou canst not be corrupted, and canst not lie, nor make what is true, false—as, for example, if thou shouldst make what has been done not to have been done, and the like—how art thou capable of all things? Or else to be capable of these things is not power, but impotence. For, he who is capable of these things is capable of what is not for his good, and of what he ought not to do; and the more capable of them he is, the more power have adversity and perversity against him; and the less has he himself against these.

He, then, who is thus capable is so not by power, but by impotence. For, he is not said to be able because he is able of himself, but because his impotence gives something else power over him. Or, by a figure of speech, just as many words are improperly applied, as when we use "to be" for "not to be," and "to do" for what is really "not to do," or "to do nothing." For, often we say to a man who denies the existence of something: "It is as you say it to be," though it might seem more proper to say, "It is not, as you say it is not." In the same way, we say: "This man sits just as that man does," or, "This man rests just as that man does"; although to sit is not to do anything, and to rest is to do nothing.

So, then, when one is said to have the power of [13] doing or experiencing what is not for his good, or what he ought not to do, impotence is understood in the word power. For, the more he possesses this power, the more powerful are adversity and perversity against him, and the more powerless is he against them.

Therefore, O Lord, our God, the more truly art thou omnipotent, since thou art capable of nothing through impotence, and nothing has power against thee.

CHAPTER VIII.

How he is compassionate and passionless God is compassionate, in terms of our experience, because we experience the effect of compassion. God is not compassionate, in terms of his own being, because he does not experience the feeling (affectus) of compassion.

But how art thou compassionate, and, at the same time, passionless? For, if thou art passionless, thou dost not feel sympathy; and if thou dost not feel sympathy, thy heart is not wretched from sympathy for the wretched; but this it is to be compassionate. But if thou art not compassionate, whence cometh so great consolation to the wretched? How, then, art thou compassionate and not compassionate, O Lord, unless because thou art compassionate in terms of our experience, and not compassionate in terms of thy being.

Truly, thou art so in terms of our experience, but thou art not so in terms of thine own. For, when thou beholdest us in our wretchedness, we experience the effect of compassion, but thou dost not experience the feeling. Therefore, thou art both compassionate, because thou dost save the wretched, and spare those [14] who sin against thee; and not compassionate, because thou art affected by no sympathy for wretchedness.

CHAPTER IX.

How the all-just and supremely just God spares the wicked, and justly pities the wicked He is better who is good to the righteous and the wicked than he who is good to the righteous alone. Although God is supremely just, the source of his compassion is hidden. God is supremely compassionate, because he is supremely just He saveth the just, because justice goes with them, he frees sinners by the authority of justice. God spares the wicked out of justice; for it is just that God, than whom none is better or more powerful, should be good even to the wicked, and should make the wicked good If God ought not to pity, he pities unjustly. But this it is impious to suppose. Therefore, God justly pities.

But how dost thou spare the wicked, if thou art all just and supremely just? For how, being all just and supremely just, dost thou aught that is not just? Or, what justice is that to give him who merits eternal death everlasting life? How, then, gracious Lord, good to the righteous and the wicked, canst thou save the wicked, if this is not just, and thou dost not aught that is not just? Or, since thy goodness is incomprehensible, is this hidden in the unapproachable light wherein thou dwellest? Truly, in the deepest and most secret parts of thy goodness is hidden the fountain whence the stream of thy compassion flows.

For thou art all just and supremely just, yet thou art kind even to the wicked, even because thou art all supremely good. For thou wouldst be less good if thou wert not kind to any wicked being. For, he who is good, both to the righteous and the wicked, is better than he who is good to the wicked alone; [15] and he who is good to the wicked, both by punishing and sparing them, is better than he who is good by punishing them alone. Therefore, thou art compassionate, because thou art all supremely good. And, although it appears why thou dost reward the good with goods and the evil with evils; yet this, at least, is most wonderful, why thou, the all and supremely just, who lackest nothing, bestowest goods on the wicked and on those who are guilty toward thee.

The depth of thy goodness, O God! The source of thy compassion appears, and yet is not clearly seen! We see whence the river flows, but the spring whence it arises is not seen. For, it is from the abundance of thy goodness that thou art good to those who sin against thee; and in the depth of thy goodness is hidden the reason for this kindness.

For, although thou dost reward the good with goods and the evil with evils, out of goodness, yet this the concept of justice seems to demand. But, when thou dost bestow goods on the evil, and it is known that the supremely Good hath willed to do this, we wonder why the supremely Just has been able to will this.

O compassion, from what abundant sweetness and what sweet abundance dost thou well forth to us! O boundless goodness of God, how passionately should sinners love thee! For thou savest the just, because justice goeth with them; but sinners thou dost free by the authority of justice. Those by the help of their deserts; these, although their deserts oppose. Those by acknowledging the goods thou hast granted; these by pardoning the evils thou hatest. O boundless goodness, which dost so exceed all understanding, let that compassion come upon me, which proceeds [16] from thy so great abundance! Let it flow upon me, for it wells forth from thee. Spare, in mercy; avenge not, in justice.

For, though it is hard to understand how thy compassion is not inconsistent with thy justice; yet we must believe that it does not oppose justice at all, because it flows from goodness, which is no goodness without justice; nay, that it is in true harmony with justice. For, if thou art compassionate only because thou art supremely good, and supremely good only because thou art supremely just, truly thou art compassionate even because thou art supremely just. Help me, just and compassionate God, whose light I seek; help me to understand what I say.

Truly, then, thou art compassionate even because thou art just. Is, then, thy compassion born of thy justice? And dost thou spare the wicked, therefore, out of justice? If this is true, my Lord, if this is true, teach me how it is. Is it because it is just, that thou shouldst be so good that thou canst not be conceived better; and that thou shouldst work so powerfully that thou canst not be conceived more powerful? For what can be more just than this? Assuredly it could not be that thou shouldst be good only by requiting (*retribuendo*) and not by sparing, and that thou shouldst make good only those who are not good, and not the wicked also. In this way, therefore, it is just that thou shouldst spare the wicked, and make good souls of evil.

Finally, what is not done justly ought not to be done; and what ought not to be done is done unjustly. If, then, thou dost not justly pity the wicked, thou oughtest not to pity them. And, if thou oughtest not to pity them, thou pityest them unjustly. And if [17] it is impious to suppose this, it is right to believe that thou justly pityest the wicked.

CHAPTER X.

How he justly punishes and justly spares the wicked.—God, in sparing the wicked, is just, according to his own nature, because he does what is consistent with his goodness; but he is not just, according to our nature, because he does not inflict the punishment deserved.

But it is also just that thou shouldst punish the wicked. For what is more just than that the good should receive goods, and the evil, evils? How, then, is it just that thou shouldst punish the wicked, and, at the same time, spare the wicked? Or, in one way, dost thou justly punish, and, in another, justly spare them? For, when thou punishest the wicked, it is just, because it is consistent with their deserts; and when, on the other hand, thou sparest the wicked, it is just, not because it is compatible with their deserts, but because it is compatible with thy goodness.

For, in sparing the wicked, thou art as just, according to thy nature, but not according to ours, as thou art compassionate, according to our nature, and not according to thine; seeing that, as in saving us, whom it would be just for thee to destroy, thou art compassionate, not because thou feelest an affection (*affectum*), but because we feel the effect (*effectum*); so thou art just, not because thou requitest us as we deserve, but because thou dost that which becomes thee as the supremely good Being. In this way, therefore, without contradiction thou dost justly punish and justly spare. [18]

CHAPTER XI.

How all the ways of God are compassion and truth; and yet God is just in all his ways—We cannot comprehend why, of the wicked, he saves these rather than those, through his supreme goodness; and condemns those rather than these, through his supreme justice.

But, is there any reason why it is not also just, according to thy nature, O Lord, that thou shouldst punish the wicked? Surely it is just that thou shouldst be so just that thou canst not be conceived more just; and this thou wouldst in no wise be if thou didst only render goods to the good, and not evils to the evil For, he who requiteth both good and evil according to their deserts is more just than he who so requites the good alone. It is, therefore, just, according to thy nature, O just and gracious God, both when thou dost punish and when thou sparest.

Truly, then, all the paths of the Lord are mercy and truth (Psalms xxv. 10); and yet the Lord is righteous in all his ways (Psalms cxlv. 17). And assuredly without inconsistency: For, it is not just that those whom thou dost will to punish should be saved, and that those whom thou dost will to spare should be condemned. For that alone is just which thou dost will; and that alone unjust which thou dost not will. So, then, thy compassion is born of thy justice.

For it is just that thou shouldst be so good that thou art good in sparing also; and this may be the reason why the supremely Just can will goods for the veil. But if it can be comprehended in any way why thou canst will to save the wicked, yet by no consideration can we comprehend why, of those who are [19] alike wicked, thou savest some rather than others, through supreme goodness; and why thou dost condemn the latter rather than the former, through supreme justice.

So, then, thou art truly sensible (*sensibilis*), omnipotent, compassionate, and passionless, as thou art living, wise, good, blessed, eternal: and whatever it is better to be than not to be.

. . . .

CHAPTER XV.

He is greater than can be conceived.

Therefore, O Lord, thou art not only that than which a greater cannot be conceived, but thou art a being greater than can be conceived. For, since it can be conceived that there is such a being, if thou art not this very being, a greater than thou can be conceived. But this is impossible.

DEMONSTRATIONS THAT GOD EXISTS (1265–1274)[1]

St. Thomas Aquinas

St. Thomas Aquinas (1225?–1274) was born in Roccasecca, Italy, in the castle of his parents, the Count and Countess of Aquino. At age 5, Thomas was sent to be educated at the Benedictine monastery at Monte Cassino (where his Uncle was Abbott). At 13, because of changes in the political climate, he moved to a Benedictine monastery in Naples and, at 16, began studies at the University of Naples. At Naples, he secretly joined a Dominican Order, which so upset his family that they took him captive for a year while they tried to rid him of his new beliefs. At age 20, Aquinas began studies in Cologne, where he earned the bachelor of theology degree in 1248 and was ordained in 1250. He then went to study under Albertus Magnus in Paris, where he earned his doctorate. In 1256, Aquinas began his career of writing, teaching, lecturing on theology, and preaching throughout France and Italy, often with his friend St. Bonaventure of Bagnoregio (1221–1274). He was advisor to the pontiff and to King Louis VIII (of France) on affairs of state. In addition to preaching every day, Aquinas wrote homilies, disputations, and lectures and worked on his <u>Summa Theologica</u>, a masterpiece that merged the recently rediscovered work of Aristotle with Christian theology. Though offered important posts such as Archbishop of Naples and Abbot of Monte Cassino, Aquinas declined. In 1270, the Bishop of Paris issued an edict that condemned theology derived from Aristotle or Arabic commentators such as Averroës, specifically targeting Aquinas. While investigations proceeded in Paris, the Dominicans moved Aquinas to Italy. In 1274, while traveling to attend the Second Council of Lyons (which hoped to resolve differences between the Greek and Latin churches), Aquinas became ill. He died at the Cistercian monastery of Fossa Nuova. Three years later (1277), the Bishops of Paris and of Oxford issued a detailed edict condemning a series of Thomas's theses as heretical.

---

[1] Traditional dating puts *Summa Contra Gentiles* at around 1260–1264; recent scholarship puts it around 1270–1273. *Summa Theologica* seems to have been written around 1265–1274. This reading is drawn from both works.

Consequently, Aquinas was posthumously excommunicated. Forty-seven years later, however, Aquinas was declared (by Pope John XXII in Avignon) to be a saint of the Catholic Church. Aquinas' theology grew in importance. In 1568, he was named a Doctor of the Church. In 1879, Pope Leo XIII declared Aquinas' theology to be a definitive exposition of Catholic doctrine and directed clergy to base their theological positions on the teachings of Aquinas. He is now widely thought to be the Roman Catholic Church's greatest philosopher-theologian.

What to look for: *What are the two sources of knowledge about divine things? How must the apologist direct his responses to different sorts of "questioners?" Can genuine revelation ever conflict with reason? Why is it necessary to demonstrate (by reason) that God exists? What problems does Aquinas have with ontological arguments? Can you find a lineage for the other arguments? How would Anselm likely respond to Aquinas' responses to the ontological argument? What is the significance for the ontological argument that things be "posited in the same way?" What is the reasoning in each of the five proofs that Aquinas offers? Do the premises that Aquinas gives in some of his arguments contradict each other? What properties of God do Aquinas' arguments support?*

CHAPTER IX

The order and manner of procedure in the present work

[1][2] It is clearly apparent . . . that the intention of the wise man ought to be directed toward the twofold truth of divine things, and toward the destruction of the errors that are contrary to this truth. One kind of divine truth the investigation of the reason is competent to reach, whereas the other surpasses every effort of the reason . . .

[2] Now, to make the first kind of divine truth known, we must proceed through demonstrative arguments, by which our adversary may become convinced. However, since such arguments are not available for the second

---

[2] Paragraph numbers were not in original.

This selection is a compilation from two sources:

"Demonstrations that God Exists," by St. Thomas Aquinas, compiled from: *Summa Contra Gentiles, Book One: God,* by Thomas Acquinas. Trans. Anton C. Pegis. (New York: Hanover House, 1955).

and,

The "Summa Theologica" of St. Thomas Aquinas, Part I QQ I.-XXVI. Trans. Fathers of the English Dominican Province. 2nd ed. Vol. 1. (London: Burns Oates and Washbourne, 1920) kind of divine truth, our intention should not be to convince our adversary by arguments: it should be to answer his arguments against the truth; for, as we have shown, the natural reason cannot be contrary to the truth of faith.

The sole way to overcome an adversary of divine truth is from the authority of Scripture—an authority divinely confirmed by miracles. For that which is above the human reason we believe only because God has revealed it . . . .

[4] We are aiming, then, to set out following the way of the reason and to inquire into what the human reason can investigate about God . . .

[5] Now, among the inquiries that we must undertake concerning God in Himself, we must set down in the beginning that whereby His Existence is demonstrated, as the necessary foundation of the whole work. For, if we do not demonstrate that God exists, all consideration of divine things is necessarily suppressed.

CHAPTER X
The opinion of those who say that the existence of God,
being self-evident, cannot be demonstrated

[1] There are some persons to whom the inquiry seeking to demonstrate that God exists may perhaps appear superfluous. These are the persons who assert that the existence of God is self-evident, in such wise that its contrary cannot be entertained in the mind. It thus appears that the existence of God cannot be demonstrated, as may be seen from the following arguments.

[2] Those propositions are said to be self-evident that are known immediately upon the knowledge of their terms. Thus, as soon as you know the nature of a whole and the nature of a part, you know immediately that every whole is greater than its part. The proposition God exists is of this sort. For by the name God we understand something than which a greater cannot be thought. This notion is formed in the intellect by one who hears and understands the name God. As a result, God must exist already at least in the intellect. But He cannot exist solely in the intellect, since that which exists both in the intellect and in reality is greater than that which exists in the intellect alone. Now, as the very definition of the name points out, nothing can be greater than God. Consequently, the proposition that God exists is self-evident, as being evident from the very meaning of the name God.

[3] Again, it is Possible to think that something exists whose non-existence cannot be thought. Clearly, such a being is greater than the being whose non-existence can be thought. Consequently, if God Himself could be thought not to be, then something greater than God could be thought. This, however, is contrary to the definition of the name God. Hence, the proposition that God exists is self-evident.

[4] Furthermore, those propositions ought to be the most evident in which the same thing is predicated of itself, for example, man is man, or whose predicates are included in the definition of their subjects, for example, Man is

an animal. Now, in God, as will be shown in a later chapter, it is pre-eminently the case that His being is His essence, so that to the question what is He? and to the question is He? the answer is one and the same. Thus, in the proposition God exists, the predicate is consequently either identical with the subject or at least included in the definition of the subject. Hence, that God exists is self-evident.

[5] What is naturally known is known through itself, for we do not come to such propositions through an effort of inquiry. But the proposition that God exists is naturally known since, as will be shown later on, the desire of man naturally tends towards God as towards the ultimate end. The proposition that God exists is, therefore, self-evident.

[6] There is also the consideration that that through which all the rest are known ought itself to be self-evident. Now, God is of this sort. For just as the light of the sun is the principle of all visible perception, so the divine light is the principle of all intelligible knowledge; since the divine light is that in which intelligible illumination is found first and in its highest degree. That God exists, therefore, must be self-evident.

[7] These, then, and others like them are the arguments by which some think that the proposition God exists is so self-evident that its contrary cannot be entertained by the mind.

CHAPTER XI
A refutation of the above mentioned opinion and a solution
of the arguments

[1] In part, the above opinion arises from the custom by which from their earliest days people are brought up to hear and to call upon the name of God. Custom, and especially custom in a child comes to have the force of nature. As a result, what the mind is steeped in from childhood it clings to very firmly, as something known naturally and self-evidently.

[2] In part, however, the above opinion comes about because of a failure to distinguish between that which is self-evident in an absolute sense and that which is self-evident in relation to us. For assuredly that God exists is, absolutely speaking, self-evident, since what God is is His own being. Yet, because we are not able to conceive in our minds that which God is, that God exists remains unknown in relation to us. So, too, that every whole is greater than its part is, absolutely speaking, self-evident; but it would perforce be unknown to one who could not conceive the nature of a whole. Hence it comes about, as it is said in *Metaphysics* II [Ia, 1], that "our intellect is related to the most knowable things in reality as the eye of an owl is related to the sun."

[3] And, contrary to the Point made by the first argument, it does not follow immediately that, as soon as we know the meaning of the name God,

the existence of God is known. It does not follow first because it is not known to all, even including those who admit that God exists, that God is that than which a greater cannot be thought. After all, many ancients said that this world itself was God. Furthermore, no such inference can be drawn from the interpretations of the name God to be found in Damascene [*De fide orthodoxa* I, 9]. What is more, granted that everyone should understand by the name God something than which a greater cannot be thought, it will still not be necessary that there exist in reality something than which a greater cannot be thought. For a thing and the definition of a name are posited in the same way. Now, from the fact that that which is indicated by the name God is conceived by the mind, it does not follow that God exists save only in the intellect. Hence, that than which a greater cannot be thought will likewise not have to exist save only in the intellect. From this it does not follow that there exists in reality something than which a greater cannot be thought. No difficulty, consequently, befalls anyone who posits that God does not exist. For that something greater can be thought than anything given in reality or in the intellect is a difficulty only to him who admits that there is something than which a greater cannot be thought in reality.

[4] Nor, again, is it necessary, as the second argument advanced, that something greater than God can be thought if God can be thought not to be. For that He can be thought not to be does not arise either from the imperfection or the uncertainty of His own being, since this is in itself most manifest. It arises, rather, from the weakness of our intellect, which cannot behold God Himself except through His effects and which is thus led to know His existence through reasoning.

[5] This enables us to solve the third argument as well. For just as it is evident to us that a whole is greater than a part of itself, so to those seeing the divine essence in itself it is supremely self-evident that God exists because His essence is His being. But, because we are not able to see His essence, we arrive at the knowledge of His being, not through God Himself, but through His effects.

[6] The answer to the fourth argument is likewise clear. For man naturally knows God in the same way as he naturally desires God. Now, man naturally desires God in so far as he naturally desires beatitude, which is a certain likeness of the divine goodness. On this basis, it is not necessary that God considered in Himself be naturally known to man, but only a likeness of God. It remains, therefore, that man is to reach the knowledge of God through reasoning by way of the likenesses of God found in His effects.

[7] So, too, with the fifth argument, an easy solution is available. For God is indeed that by which all things are known, not in the sense that they are not known unless He is known (as obtains among self-evident principles), but because all our knowledge is caused in us through His influence.

CHAPTER XII
The opinion of those who say that the existence of God cannot be
demonstrated but is held by faith alone

[1] There are others who hold a certain opinion, contrary to the position mentioned above, through which the efforts of those seeking to prove the existence of God would likewise be rendered futile. For they say that we cannot arrive at the existence of God through the reason; it is received by way of faith and revelation alone.

[2] What led some persons to hold this view was the weakness of the arguments which had been brought forth by others to prove that God exists.

[3] Nevertheless, the present error might erroneously find support in its behalf in the words of some philosophers who show that in God essence and being are identical, that is, that that which answers to the question what is it? is identical with that which answers to the question is it? Now, following the way of the reason we cannot arrive at a knowledge of what God is. Hence, it seems likewise impossible to demonstrate by the reason that God exists . . . .

[5] Again, if, as is shown in the *Posterior Analytics* [I, 18], the knowledge of the principles of demonstration takes its origin from sense, whatever transcends all sense and sensibles seems to be indemonstrable. That God exists appears to be a proposition of this sort and is therefore indemonstrable.

[6] The falsity of this opinion is shown to us, first, from the art of demonstration which teaches us to arrive at causes from their effects. Then, it is shown to us from the order of the sciences. For, as it is said in the *Metaphysics* [IV, 3], if there is no knowable substance higher than sensible substance, there will be no science higher than physics. It is shown, thirdly, from the pursuit of the philosophers, who have striven to demonstrate that God exists. Finally, it is shown to us by the truth in the words of the Apostle Paul: "For the invisible things of God... are clearly seen, being understood by the things that are made" (Rom. 1:20).

[7] Nor, contrary to the first argument, is there any problem in the fact that in God essence and being are identical. For this is understood of the being by which God subsists in Himself. But we do not know of what sort this being is, just as we do not know the divine essence. The reference is not to the being that signifies the composition of intellect. For thus the existence of God does fall under demonstration; this happens when our mind is led from demonstrative arguments to form such a proposition of God whereby it expresses that He exists . . . .

[9] It is thereby likewise evident that, although God transcends all sensible things and the sense itself, His effects, on which the demonstration proving His existence is based, are nevertheless sensible things. And thus, the origin of our knowledge in the sense applies also to those things that transcend the sense.

CHAPTER XIII
Arguments in proof of the existence of God

[1] We have now shown that the effort to demonstrate the existence of God is not a vain one. We shall therefore proceed to set forth the arguments by which both philosophers and Catholic teachers have proved that God exists.[3]

· · · ·

The existence of God can be proved in five ways.

The first and more manifest way is the argument from motion. It is certain, and evident to our senses, that in the world some things are in motion. Now whatever is in motion is put in motion by another, for nothing can be in motion except it is in potentiality to that towards which it is in motion; whereas a thing moves inasmuch as it is in act. For motion is nothing else than the reduction of something from potentiality to actuality. But nothing can be reduced from potentiality to actuality, except by something in a state of actuality. Thus that which is actually hot, as fire, makes wood, which is potentially hot, to be actually hot, and thereby moves and changes it. Now it is not possible that the same thing should be at once in actuality and potentiality in the same [25] respect, but only in different respects. For what is actually hot cannot simultaneously be potentially hot; but it is simultaneously potentially cold. It is therefore impossible that in the same respect and in the same way a thing should be both mover and moved, *i.e.*, that it should move itself. Therefore, whatever is in motion must be put in motion by another. If that by which it is put in motion be itself put in motion, then this also must needs be put in motion by another, and that by another again. But this cannot go on to infinity, because then there would be no first mover, and, consequently, no other mover; seeing that subsequent movers move only inasmuch as they are put in motion by the first mover; as the staff moves only because it is put in motion by the hand. Therefore it is necessary to arrive at a first mover, put in motion by no other; and this everyone understands to be God.

The second way is from the nature of the efficient cause. In the world of sense we find there is an order of efficient causes. There is no case known (neither is it, indeed, possible) in which a thing is found to be the efficient cause of itself; for so it would be prior to itself, which is impossible. Now in efficient causes it is not possible to go on to infinity, because in all efficient causes following in order, the first is the cause of the intermediate cause, and

---

[3] *Summa Contra Gentiles* continues with an extensive discussion of proofs for the existence of God. Here, however, we switch to Aquinas' much more compact discussion of the same subject given in Book I, Question 2, Article 3 of his *Summa Theologica*.

the intermediate is the cause of the ultimate cause, whether the intermediate cause be several, or one only. Now to take away the cause is to take away the effect. Therefore, if there be no first cause among efficient causes, there will be no ultimate, nor any intermediate cause. But if in efficient causes it is possible to go on to infinity, there will be no first efficient cause, neither will there be an ultimate effect, nor any intermediate efficient causes; all of which is plainly false. Therefore it is necessary to admit a first efficient cause, to which everyone gives the name of God.

The third way is taken from possibility and necessity, and runs thus. We find in nature things that are possible to be and not to be, since they are found to be generated, and [26] to corrupt, and consequently, they are possible to be and not to be. But it is impossible for these always to exist, for that which is possible not to be at some time is not. Therefore, if everything is possible not to be, then at one time there could have been nothing in existence. Now if this were true, even now there would be nothing in existence, because that which does not exist only begins to exist by something already existing. Therefore, if at one time nothing was in existence, it would have been impossible for anything to have begun to exist; and thus even now nothing would be in existence—which is absurd. Therefore, not all beings are merely possible, but there must exist something the existence of which is necessary. But every necessary thing either has its necessity caused by another, or not. Now it is impossible to go on to infinity in necessary things which have their necessity caused by another, as has been already proved in regard to efficient causes. Therefore we cannot but postulate the existence of some being having of itself its own necessity, and not receiving it from another, but rather causing in others their necessity. This all men speak of as God.

The fourth way is taken from the gradation to be found in things. Among beings there are some more and some less good, true, noble, and the like. But 'more' and 'less' are predicated of different things, according as they resemble in their different ways something which is the maximum, as a thing is said to be hotter according as it more nearly resembles that which is hottest; so that there is something which is truest, something best, something noblest, and, consequently, something which is uttermost being; for those things that are greatest in truth are greatest in being, as it is written in *Metaph.* ii. Now the maximum in any genus is the cause of all in that genus; as fire, which is the maximum of heat, is the cause of all hot things. Therefore there must also be something which is to all beings the cause of their being, goodness, and every other perfection; and this we call God.

The fifth way is taken from the governance of the world. [27] We see that things which lack intelligence, such as natural bodies, act for an end, and this is evident from their acting always, or nearly always, in the same way, so as to obtain the best result. Hence it is plain that not fortuitously, but designedly, do they achieve their end. Now whatever lacks intelligence cannot move towards an end, unless it be directed by some being endowed with knowledge and intelligence; as the arrow is shot to its mark by the archer. Therefore some intelligent being exists by whom all natural things are directed to their end; and this being we call God.

ANALOGY AND THE ARGUMENT FROM DESIGN (1779)

David Hume

David Hume—see p. 175.

What to look for: Cleanthes, the first speaker in this dialogue, defends the view that God's nature and existence can be known through nature and that the design of the universe is sufficient evidence for both. The second speaker, Demea, seems to accept a first-cause argument for existence (as in Aquinas), but contends that we simply cannot know God's nature. He cites scripture to support this view. Like Cleanthes, Philo insists that claims about God be backed up by evidence, but he argues that the evidence is insufficient to show either God's existence or His nature. Try to follow the arguments that each presents. What are Cleanthes' views on skepticism? How does Cleanthes' "design argument" go? What general issues arise with argument by analogy? What additional problems arise when one analogue is a part of the other? What is Cleanthes' contention about analogies used in science? What is Philo's response?

D 1.9[1]—[Cleanthes:] To whatever length any one may push his speculative principles of skepticism, he must act, I own, and live, and converse like other men; and for this conduct he is not obliged to give any other reason, than the absolute necessity he lies under of so doing. If he ever carries his speculations farther than this necessity constrains him, and philosophises, either on natural or moral subjects, he is allured by a certain pleasure and satisfaction, which he finds in employing himself after that manner. He considers besides, that every one, even in common life, is constrained to have more or less of this philosophy; that from our earliest infancy we make continual advances in forming more general principles of conduct and reasoning; that the larger

---

[1] Scholars commonly reference this work with a "D" [for *Dialogues*] followed by the part and paragraph number. Paragraph numbers were not in the original.

"Analogy and the Argument from Design," by David Hume, from *Dialogues concerning Natural Religion*. (London and Edinburgh: published on the authority of Hume's nephew, David Hume the younger, in accordance with Hume's instructions, 1779).

experience we acquire, and the stronger reason we are endued with, we always render our principles the more general and comprehensive; and that what we call *philosophy* is nothing but a more regular and methodical operation of the same kind. To philosophize on such subjects is nothing essentially different from reasoning on common life; and we may only expect greater stability, if not greater truth, from our philosophy, on account of its exacter and more scrupulous method of proceeding.

D 1.10—But when we look beyond human affairs and the properties of the surrounding bodies: When we carry our speculations into the two eternities, before and after the present state of things; into the creation and formation of the universe; the existence and properties of spirits; the powers and operations of one universal spirit, existing without beginning and without end; omnipotent, omniscient, immutable, infinite, and incomprehensible: We must be far removed from the smallest tendency to skepticism not to be apprehensive, that we have here got quite beyond the reach of our faculties. So long as we confine our speculations to trade, or morals, or politics, or criticism, we make appeals, every moment, to common sense and experience, which strengthen our philosophical conclusions, and remove (at least, in part) the suspicion, which we so justly entertain with regard to every reasoning, that is very subtle and refined. But in theological reasonings, we have not this advantage; while at the same time we are employed upon objects, which, we must be sensible, are too large for our grasp, and of all others, require most to be familiarized to our apprehension. We are like foreigners in a strange country, to whom every thing must seem suspicious, and who are in danger every moment of transgressing against the laws and customs of the people, with whom they live and converse. We know not how far we ought to trust our vulgar methods of reasoning in such a subject; since, even in common life and in that province, which is peculiarly appropriated to them, we cannot account for them, and are entirely guided by a kind of instinct or necessity in employing them. . . .

D 1.13—There is indeed a kind of brutish and ignorant skepticism, as you well observed, which gives the vulgar a general prejudice against what they do not easily understand, and makes them reject every principle, which requires elaborate reasoning to prove and establish it. This species of skepticism is fatal to knowledge, not to religion; since we find, that those who make greatest profession of it, give often their assent, not only to the great truths of Theism, and natural theology, but even to the most absurd tenets, which a traditional superstition has recommended to them. They firmly believe in witches; though they will not believe nor attend to the most simple proposition of Euclid. But the refined and philosophical sceptics fall into an inconsistence of an opposite nature. They push their researches into the most abstruse corners of science; and their assent attends them in every step, proportioned to the evidence, which they meet with. They are even obliged to acknowledge, that the most abstruse and remote objects are those, which are best explained by philosophy.

Light is in reality anatomized: The true system of the heavenly bodies is discovered and ascertained. But the nourishment of bodies by food is still an inexplicable mystery: The cohesion of the parts of matter is still incomprehensible. These sceptics, therefore, are obliged, in every question, to consider each particular evidence apart, and proportion their assent to the precise degree of evidence, which occurs. This is their practice in all natural, mathematical, moral, and political science. And why not the same, I ask, in the theological and religious? Why must conclusions of this nature be alone rejected on the general presumption of the insufficiency of human reason, without any particular discussion of the evidence? Is not such an unequal conduct a plain proof of prejudice and passion?. . . .

D 1.17—And here we may observe, continued he, turning himself towards Demea, a pretty curious circumstance in the history of the sciences. After the union of philosophy with the popular religion, upon the first establishment of Christianity, nothing was more usual, among all religious teachers, than declamations against reason, against the senses, against every principle, derived merely from human research and enquiry. All the topics of the ancient Academics were adopted by the Fathers; and thence propagated for several ages in every school and pulpit throughout Christendom. The Reformers embraced the same principles of reasoning, or rather declamation; and all panegyrics on the excellency of faith were sure to be interlarded with some severe strokes of satire against natural reason. A celebrated prelate too, of the Romish communion, a man of the most extensive learning, who wrote a demonstration of Christianity, has also composed a treatise, which contains all the cavils of the boldest and most determined Pyrrhonism. Locke seems to have been the first Christian, who ventured openly to assert, that *faith* was nothing but a species of *reason*, that religion was only a branch of philosophy, and that a chain of arguments, similar to that which established any truth in morals, politics, or physics, was always employed in discovering all the principles of theology, natural and revealed. . . .

D 2.1—I must own, Cleanthes, said Demea, that nothing can more surprise me, than the light, in which you have, all along, put this argument. By the whole tenor of your discourse, one would imagine that you were maintaining the Being of a God, against the cavils of Atheists and Infidels; and were necessitated to become a champion for that fundamental principle of all religion. But this, I hope, is not, by any means, a question among us. No man; no man, at least, of common sense, I am persuaded, ever entertained a serious doubt with regard to a truth, so certain and self-evident. The question is not concerning the BEING, but the NATURE of GOD. This I affirm, from the infirmities of human understanding, to be altogether incomprehensible and unknown to us. The essence of that supreme mind, his attributes, the manner of his existence, the very nature of his duration; these and every particular, which regards so divine a Being, are mysterious to men. Finite, weak, and blind creatures, we ought to humble ourselves in his august presence, and, conscious of our frailties, adore in silence his infinite perfections, which eye hath not seen, ear hath not heard, neither hath it entered into the heart of man to conceive. They are covered in a deep cloud from human curiosity: It is profaneness to attempt penetrating through these sacred obscurities: And next to the impiety of denying his existence, is the temerity of prying into his nature and essence, decrees and attributes.

D 2.2—But lest you should think, that my *piety* has here got the better of my *philosophy*, I shall support my opinion, if it needs any support, by a very great authority. I might cite all the divines almost, from the foundation of Christianity, who have ever treated of this or any other theological subject: But I shall confine myself, at present, to one equally celebrated for piety and philosophy. It is Father Malebranche, who, I remember, thus expresses himself. "One ought not so much (says he) to call God a spirit, in order to express positively what he is, as in order to signify that he is not matter. He is a Being infinitely perfect: Of this we cannot doubt. But in the same manner as we ought not to imagine, even supposing him corporeal, that he is clothed with a human body, as the Anthropomorphites asserted, under colour that that figure was the most perfect of any; so neither ought we to imagine, that the Spirit of God has human ideas, or bears any resemblance to our spirit; under colour that we know nothing more perfect than a human mind. We ought rather to believe, that as he comprehends the perfections of matter without being material. . . . . he comprehends also the perfections of created spirits, without being spirit, in the manner we conceive spirit: That his true name is, *He that is*, or in other words, Being without restriction, All Being, the Being infinite and universal."

D 2.3—After so great an authority, Demea, replied Philo, as that which you have produced, and a thousand more, which you might produce, it would appear ridiculous in me to add my sentiment, or express my approbation of your doctrine. But surely, where reasonable men treat these subjects, the question can never be concerning the *Being*, but only the *Nature* of the Deity. The former truth, as you well observe, is unquestionable and self-evident. Nothing exists without a cause; and the original cause of this universe (whatever it be) we call GOD; and piously ascribe to him every species of perfection. Whoever scruples this fundamental truth, deserves every punishment, which can be inflicted among philosophers, to wit, the greatest ridicule, contempt and disapprobation. But as all perfection is entirely relative, we ought never to imagine, that we comprehend the attributes of this divine Being, or to suppose, that his perfections have any analogy or likeness to the perfections of a human creature. Wisdom, Thought, Design, Knowledge; these we justly ascribe to him; because these words are honourable among men, and we have no other language or other conceptions, by which we can express our adoration of him. But let us beware, lest we think, that our ideas any wise correspond to his perfections, or that his attributes have any resemblance to these qualities among men. He is infinitely superior to our limited view and comprehension; and is more the object of worship in the temple than of disputation in the schools.

D 2.4—In reality, Cleanthes, continued he, there is no need of having recourse to that affected skepticism, so displeasing to you, in order to come at this determination. Our ideas reach no farther than our experience: We have no experience of divine attributes and operations: I need not conclude my syllogism: You can draw the inference yourself. And it is a pleasure to me (and I hope to you too) that just reasoning and sound piety here concur in the same conclusion, and both of them establish the adorably mysterious and incomprehensible nature of the Supreme Being.

D 2.5—Not to lose any time in circumlocutions, said Cleanthes, addressing himself to Demea, much less in replying to the pious declamations of Philo; I shall briefly explain how I conceive this matter. Look round the world: contemplate the whole and every part of it: You will find it to be nothing but one great machine, subdivided into an infinite number of lesser machines, which again admit of subdivisions, to a degree beyond what human senses and faculties can trace and explain. All these various machines, and even their most minute parts, are adjusted to each other with an accuracy, which ravishes into admiration all men, who have ever contemplated them. The curious adapting of means to ends, throughout all nature, resembles exactly, though it much exceeds, the productions of human contrivance; of human design, thought, wisdom, and intelligence. Since therefore the effects resemble each other, we are led to infer, by all the rules of analogy, that the causes also resemble; and that the Author of Nature is somewhat similar to the mind of man; though possessed of much larger faculties, proportioned to the grandeur of the work, which he has executed. By this argument a posteriori, and by this argument alone, do we prove at once the existence of a Deity, and his similarity to human mind and intelligence.

D 2.6—I shall be so free, Cleanthes, said Demea, as to tell you, that from the beginning I could not approve of your conclusion concerning the similarity of the Deity to men; still less can I approve of the mediums, by which you endeavour to establish it. What! No demonstration of the Being of a God! No abstract arguments! No proofs a priori! Are these, which have hitherto been so much insisted on by philosophers, all fallacy, all sophism? Can we reach no farther in this subject than experience and probability? I will not say, that this is betraying the cause of a Deity: But surely, by this affected candor, you give advantages to Atheists, which they never could obtain, by the mere dint of argument and reasoning.

D 2.7—What I chiefly scruple in this subject, said Philo, is not so much, that all religious arguments are by Cleanthes reduced to experience, as that they appear not to be even the most certain and irrefragable of that inferior kind. That a stone will fall, that fire will burn, that the earth has solidity, we have observed a thousand and a thousand times; and when any new instance of this nature is presented, we draw without hesitation the accustomed inference.

The exact similarity of the cases gives us a perfect assurance of a similar event; and a stronger evidence is never desired nor sought after. But where-ever you depart, in the least, from the similarity of the cases, you diminish proportionably the evidence; and may at last bring it to a very weak *analogy*, which is confessedly liable to error and uncertainty. After having experienced the circulation of the blood in human creatures, we make no doubt, that it takes place in Titius and Maevius: But from its circulation in frogs and fishes, it is only a presumption, though a strong one, from analogy, that it takes place in men and other animals. The analogical reasoning is much weaker, when we infer the circulation of the sap in vegetables from our experience, that the blood circulates in animals; and those, who hastily followed that imperfect analogy, are found, by more accurate experiments, to have been mistaken.

D 2.8—If we see a house, Cleanthes, we conclude, with the greatest certainty, that it had an architect or builder; because this is precisely that species of effect, which we have experienced to proceed from that species of cause. But surely you will not affirm, that the universe bears such a resemblance to a house, that we can with the same certainty infer a similar cause, or that the analogy is here entire and perfect. The dissimilitude is so striking, that the utmost you can here pretend to is a guess, a conjecture, a presumption concerning a similar cause; and how that pretension will be received in the world, I leave you to consider.

D 2.9—It would surely be very ill received, replied Cleanthes; and I should be deservedly blamed and detested, did I allow, that the proofs of a Deity amounted to no more than a guess or conjecture. But is the whole adjustment of means to ends in a house and in the universe so slight a resemblance? The economy of final causes? The order, proportion, and arrangement of every part? Steps of a stair are plainly contrived, that human legs may use them in mounting; and this inference is certain and infallible. Human legs are also contrived for walking and mounting; and this inference, I allow, is not altogether so certain, because of the dissimilarity which you remark; but does it, therefore, deserve the name only of presumption or conjecture?

D 2.10—Good God! cried Demea, interrupting him, where are we? Zealous defenders of religion allow, that the proofs of a Deity fall short of perfect evidence! And you, Philo, on whose assistance I depended, in proving the adorable mysteriousness of the Divine Nature, do you assent to all these extravagant opinions of Cleanthes? For what other name can I give them? Or why spare my censure, when such principles are advanced, supported by such an authority, before so young a man as Pamphilus?

D 2.11—You seem not to apprehend, replied Philo, that I argue with Cleanthes in his own way; and by showing him the dangerous consequences of his tenets, hope at last to reduce him to our opinion. But what sticks most with you, I observe, is the representation which Cleanthes has made of the argument *a posteriori*; and finding, that that argument is likely to escape your hold and vanish into air, you think it so disguised, that you can scarcely believe it to be set in its true light. Now, however much I may dissent, in other respects, from the dangerous principles of Cleanthes, I must allow, that he has fairly represented that argument; and I shall endeavour so to state the matter to you, that you will entertain no farther scruples with regard to it.

D 2.12—Were a man to abstract from every thing which he knows or has seen, he would be altogether incapable, merely from his own ideas, to determine what kind of scene the universe must be, or to give the preference to one state or situation of things above another. For as nothing which he clearly conceives, could be esteemed impossible or implying a contradiction, every chimera of his fancy would be upon an equal footing; nor could he assign any just reason, why he adheres to one idea or system, and rejects the others, which are equally possible.

D 2.13—Again; after he opens his eyes, and contemplates the world, as it really is, it would be impossible for him, at first, to assign the cause of any one event; much less, of the whole of things or of the universe. He might set his Fancy a rambling; and she might bring him in an infinite variety of reports and representations. These would all be possible; but being all equally possible, he would never, of himself, give a satisfactory account for his preferring one of them to the rest. Experience alone can point out to him the true cause of any phenomenon.

D 2.14—Now according to this method of reasoning, Demea, it follows (and is, indeed, tacitly allowed by Cleanthes himself) that order, arrangement, or the adjustment of final causes is not, of itself, any proof of design; but only so far as it has been experienced to proceed from that principle. For aught we can know *a priori*, matter may contain the source or spring of order originally, within itself, as well as mind does; and there is no more difficulty in conceiving, that the several elements, from an internal unknown cause, may fall into the most exquisite arrangement, than to conceive that their ideas, in the great, universal mind, from a like internal, unknown cause, fall into that arrangement. The equal possibility of both these suppositions is allowed. But by experience we find, (according to Cleanthes) that there is a difference between them. Throw several pieces of steel together, without shape or form; they will never arrange themselves so as to compose a watch: Stone, and mortar, and wood, without an architect, never erect a house. But the ideas in a human mind, we see, by an unknown, inexplicable oeconomy, arrange themselves so as to form the plan of a watch or house. Experience, therefore, proves, that there is an original principle of order in mind, not in matter. From similar effects we infer similar causes. The adjustment of means to ends is alike in the universe, as in a machine of human contrivance. The causes, therefore, must be resembling.

D 2.15—I was from the beginning scandalized, I must own, with this resemblance, which is asserted, between the Deity and human creatures; and must conceive it to imply such a degradation of the Supreme Being as no sound

Theist could endure. With your assistance, therefore, Demea, I shall endeavour to defend what you justly call the adorable mysteriousness of the Divine Nature, and shall refute this reasoning of Cleanthes; provided he allows, that I have made a fair representation of it.

D 2.16—When Cleanthes had assented, Philo, after a short pause, proceeded in the following manner.

D 2.17—That all inferences, Cleanthes, concerning fact, are founded on experience, and that all experimental reasonings are founded on the supposition, that similar causes prove similar effects, and similar effects similar causes; I shall not, at present, much dispute with you. But observe, I entreat you, with what extreme caution all just reasoners proceed in the transferring of experiments to similar cases. Unless the cases be exactly similar, they repose no perfect confidence in applying their past observation to any particular phenomenon. Every alteration of circumstances occasions a doubt concerning the event; and it requires new experiments to prove certainly, that the new circumstances are of no moment or importance. A change in bulk, situation, arrangement, age, disposition of the air, or surrounding bodies; any of these particulars may be attended with the most unexpected consequences: And unless the objects be quite familiar to us, it is the highest temerity to expect with assurance, after any of these changes, an event similar to that which before fell under our observation. The slow and deliberate steps of philosophers, here, if any where, are distinguished from the precipitate march of the vulgar, who, hurried on by the smallest similitude, are incapable of all discernment or consideration.

D 2.18—But can you think, Cleanthes, that your usual phlegm and philosophy have been preserved in so wide a step as you have taken, when you compared to the universe houses, ships, furniture, machines; and from their similarity in some circumstances inferred a similarity in their causes? Thought, design, intelligence, such as we discover in men and other animals, is no more than one of the springs and principles of the universe, as well as heat or cold, attraction or repulsion, and a hundred others, which fall under daily observation. It is an active cause, by which some particular parts of nature, we find, produce alterations on other parts. But can a conclusion, with any propriety, be transferred from parts to the whole? Does not the great disproportion bar all comparison and inference? From observing the growth of a hair, can we learn any thing concerning the generation of a man? Would the manner of a leaf's blowing, even though perfectly known, afford us any instruction concerning the vegetation of a tree?

D 2.19—But allowing that we were to take the *operations* of one part of nature upon another for the foundation of our judgement concerning the *origin* of the whole (which never can be admitted) yet why select so minute, so weak, so bounded a principle as the reason and design of animals is found to be upon this planet? What peculiar privilege has this little agitation of the brain which we call *thought*, that we must thus make it the model of the whole universe? Our partiality in our own favour does indeed present it on all occasions; but sound philosophy ought carefully to guard against so natural an illusion.

D 2.20—So far from admitting, continued Philo, that the operations of a part can afford us any just conclusion concerning the origin of the whole, I will not allow any one part to form a rule for another part, if the latter be very remote from the former. Is there any reasonable ground to conclude, that the inhabitants of other planets possess thought, intelligence, reason, or any thing similar to these faculties in men? When Nature has so extremely diversified her manner of operation in this small globe; can we imagine, that she incessantly copies herself throughout so immense a universe? And if thought, as we may well suppose, be confined merely to this narrow corner, and has even there so limited a sphere of action; with what propriety can we assign it for the original cause of all things? The narrow views of a peasant, who makes his domestic oeconomy the rule for the government of kingdoms, is in comparison a pardonable sophism.

D 2.21—But were we ever so much assured, that a thought and reason, resembling the human, were to be found throughout the whole universe, and were its activity elsewhere vastly greater and more commanding than it appears in this globe: yet I cannot see, why the operations of a world, constituted, arranged, adjusted, can with any propriety be extended to a world, which is in its embryo-state, and is advancing towards that constitution and arrangement. By observation, we know somewhat of the economy, action, and nourishment of a finished animal; but we must transfer with great caution that observation to the growth of a fetus in the womb, and still more, to the formation of an animalcule in the loins of its male parent. Nature, we find, even from our limited experience, possesses an infinite number of springs and principles, which incessantly discover themselves on every change of her position and situation. And what new and unknown principles would actuate her in so new and unknown a situation, as that of the formation of a universe, we cannot, without the utmost temerity, pretend to determine.

D 2.22—A very small part of this great system, during a very short time, is very imperfectly discovered to us: and do we thence pronounce decisively concerning the origin of the whole?

D 2.23—Admirable conclusion! Stone, wood, brick, iron, brass, have not, at this time, in this minute globe of earth, an order or arrangement without human art and contrivance: therefore the universe could not originally attain its order and arrangement, without something similar to human art. But is a part of nature a rule for another part very wide of the former? Is it a rule for the whole? Is a very small part a rule for the universe? Is nature in one situation, a certain rule for nature in another situation, vastly different from the former?

D 2.24—And can you blame me, Cleanthes, if I here imitate the prudent reserve of Simonides, who, according to the noted story, being asked by Hiero,

What God was? desired a day to think of it, and then two days more; and after that manner continually prolonged the term, without ever bringing in his definition or description? Could you even blame me, if I had answered at first, *that I did not know*, and was sensible that this subject lay vastly beyond the reach of my faculties? You might cry out sceptic and rallier as much as you pleased: but having found, in so many other subjects, much more familiar, the imperfections and even contradictions of human reason, I never should expect any success from its feeble conjectures, in a subject, so sublime, and so remote from the sphere of our observation. When two *species* of objects have always been observed to be conjoined together, I can *infer*, by custom, the existence of one, where-ever I *see* the existence of the other: and this I call an argument from experience. But how this argument can have place, where the objects, as in the present case, are single, individual, without parallel, or specific resemblance, may be difficult to explain. And will any man tell me with a serious countenance, that an orderly universe must arise from some thought and art, like the human; because we have experience of it? To ascertain this reasoning, it were requisite, that we had experience of the origin of worlds; and it is not sufficient surely, that we have seen ships and cities arise from human art and contrivance. . . . .

D 2.25—Philo was proceeding in this vehement manner, somewhat between jest and earnest, as it appeared to me; when he observed some signs of impatience in Cleanthes, and then immediately stopped short. What I had to suggest, said Cleanthes, is only that you would not abuse terms, or make use of popular expressions to subvert philosophical reasonings. You know, that the vulgar often distinguish reason from experience, even where the question relates only to matter of fact and existence; though it is found, where that *reason* is properly analyzed, that it is nothing but a species of experience. To prove by experience the origin of the universe from mind is not more contrary to common speech than to prove the motion of the earth from the same principle. And a caviller might raise all the same objections to the Copernican system, which you have urged against my reasonings. Have you other earths, might he say, which you have seen to move? Have . . . .

D 2.26—Yes! cried Philo, interrupting him, we have other earths. Is not the moon another earth, which we see to turn round its centre? Is not Venus another earth, where we observe the same phenomenon? Are not the revolutions of the sun also a confirmation, from analogy, of the same theory? All the planets, are they not earths, which revolve about the sun? Are not the satellites moons, which move round Jupiter and Saturn, and along with these primary planets, round the sun? These analogies and resemblances, with others, which I have not mentioned, are the sole proofs of the Copernican system: and to you it belongs to consider, whether you have any analogies of the same kind to support your theory.

D 2.27—In reality, Cleanthes, continued he, the modern system of astronomy is now so much received by all enquirers, and has become so essential a part even of our earliest education, that we are not commonly very scrupulous in examining the reasons, upon which it is founded. It is now become a matter of mere curiosity to study the first writers on that subject, who had the full force of prejudice to encounter, and were obliged to turn their arguments on every side, in order to render them popular and convincing. But if we peruse Galilaeo's famous Dialogues concerning the system of the world, we shall find, that that great genius, one of the sublimest that ever existed, first bent all his endeavours to prove, that there was no foundation for the distinction commonly made between elementary and celestial substances. The schools, proceeding from the illusions of sense, had carried this distinction very far; and had established the latter substances to be ingenerable, incorruptible, unalterable, impassable; and had assigned all the opposite qualities to the former. But Galilaeo, beginning with the moon, proved its similarity in every particular to the earth; its convex figure, its natural darkness when not illuminated, its density, its distinction into solid and liquid, the variations of its phases, the mutual illuminations of the earth and moon, their mutual eclipses, the inequalities of the lunar surface, &c. After many instances of this kind, with regard to all the planets, men plainly saw, that these bodies became proper objects of experience; and that the similarity of their nature enabled us to extend the same arguments and phenomena from one to the other.

D 2.28—In this cautious proceeding of the astronomers, you may read your own condemnation, Cleanthes; or rather may see, that the subject in which you are engaged exceeds all human reason and enquiry. Can you pretend to show any such similarity between the fabric of a house, and the generation of a universe? Have you ever seen Nature in any such situation as resembles the first arrangement of the elements? Have worlds ever been formed under your eye? and have you had leisure to observe the whole progress of the phenomenon, from the first appearance of order to its final consummation? If you have, then cite your experience, and deliver your theory.

THE WAGER (1657–1662)

Blaise Pascal

Blaise Pascal (1623–1662) was born in Clermont-Ferrand, in central France. His aristocrat father was a local judge who was much interested in science and mathematics. His mother died when he was 3. In 1631, his father sold his legal position—a common practice—and invested the proceeds in a government bond that promised a comfortable income and enabled the family to move to Paris. Pascal's father, using his own original methods, educated his three children in grammar, Latin, Spanish, and mathematics, at which Blaise proved to be a prodigy. At 11 or 12, he was allowed to attend (as a silent onlooker) gatherings of the greatest mathematicians and scientists (including Roberval, Gassendi, Fermat, and Descartes), hosted by Père Marin Mersenne (1588–1648) at the <u>Académie Parisienne</u>. At 16, Pascal submitted a now-famous essay on conic sections that, based on Pascal's age, Descartes simply discarded.

About this time, the costs of war led Cardinal Richelieu to default on the government's bonds, sharply reducing the family's income. Owing to his opposition to Richelieu's fiscal policies, Pascal's father was forced to flee Paris and leave his children to be cared for by Madame Sainctot, a neighbor who hosted one of the most glittering intellectual salons in France. Fortunately, after about a year, Pascal's father was restored to Richelieu's good graces and was appointed commissioner of taxes in Rouen. In Rouen, at 18, Pascal invented a machine that could add and subtract numbers. (He built more than 50 of them.) Around this time, Pascal came to suffer from a nerve disease that kept him in nearly constant pain. Nevertheless, throughout the 1640s and early '50s, he produced his most famous work on probabilities, hydrodynamics (inventing the syringe and hydraulic press), and hydrostatics. At 24 (in 1647), Pascal suffered a disabling paralytic attack and (with his sister) moved to Paris in search of medical treatment. In Paris, his condition improved a bit, and though he fell victim to bouts of hypochondria, anger, and depression, he continued to work. An initially short-lived interest in Jansenism (a splinter of Catholicism that emphasized original sin, predestination, and divine grace) led to his first theological writings. In science, working with Descartes, Pascal extended Torricelli's experiments with barometers and wrote "Expériences nouvelles touchant la vide" [New Experiments with the Vacuum], a paper that challenged the then predominant notion that vacuums do not exist in nature. Over the years, Pascal corresponded with Fermat about division of stakes in gambling. They developed a calculus of probabilities that Pascal partially laid out in his "Traité du triangle arithmétique" [Treatise on the Arithmetical Triangle]. Unpublished during his lifetime, it laid the foundations of modern probability theory and is today generally regarded as his most important mathematical work. He completed it in 1654 when he was just 31. That same year, his father passed away, his sister joined a Jansenist convent at Port Royal, and he had a mystical experience that revitalized his religious commitment. In 1655, he followed his sister to Port Royal, where he lived in a monastery for four years, devoting his time to religion rather than science. There, he wrote "Lettres provincials" [Provincial Letters] (1656–1657). Published under a pseudonym, it critiqued the Catholic Church's casuistry and moral double standards and was instantly successful. (The book was burned in 1660; today, it is widely accepted as having set a new literary standard for French prose and as having a big impact on Voltaire and Rousseau.) After his return to Paris, Pascal maintained an ascetic lifestyle and continued to work on both science and religion. In 1659 (at age 36), he became seriously ill but rejected the help of physicians on the grounds that illness is "the natural state of Christians." His condition steadily worsened; he died in his 39th year. Shortly before his death, Pascal designed the public transit system for Paris that was put in operation in 1662. Over his short and pain-filled life, Pascal produced an amazing body of important work in both mathematics and religion, much of it published posthumously. Among the posthumous publications is his most important philosophical/religious work, "Pensées" ["Thoughts"] (1670), a fragmentary work that he had begun at Port Royal in 1657 (as "Apologie de la religion Chrétienne" [Christian apology]) and had worked on to the end.

What to look for: How does custom limit our understanding? How is it possible for God to be both infinite and without parts? What is required to know a thing's existence? Its nature? Can we know either God's existence or His nature by use of reason? Why (not)? Should we condemn those who fail to prove God's existence? Should we condemn those who believe on insufficient evidence (remember Clifford!)? Why (not)? Why do we have no choice but to wager on God's existence? What are the expected payoffs if you bet on God by believing versus those if you bet against God by not believing?

	God Exists	God does not exist
Believe		
Do not believe		

Which is the better bet? Few (if any) nonbelievers can simply decide to believe; how can they come to place the better bet? If God cannot be experienced through reason, how is God experienced?

89.[1] Custom is our nature. He who is accustomed to the faith believes in it, can no longer fear hell, and believes in nothing else. He who is accustomed to believe that the king is terrible . . . etc. Who doubts, then, that our soul, being accustomed to see number, space, motion, believes that and nothing else?

231. Do you believe it to be impossible that God is infinite, without parts? Yes. I wish therefore to show you an infinite and indivisible thing. It is a point moving everywhere with an infinite velocity; for it is one in all places and is all totality in every place. Let this effect of nature, which previously seemed to you impossible, make you know that there may be others of which you are still ignorant. Do not draw this conclusion from your experiment, that there remains nothing for you to know; but rather that there remains an infinity for you to know.

233. Infinite—nothing.—Our soul is cast into a body, where it finds number, dimension. Thereupon it reasons, and calls this nature necessity, and can believe nothing else.

Unity joined to infinity adds nothing to it, no more than one foot to an infinite measure. The finite is annihilated in the presence of the infinite, and becomes a pure nothing. So our spirit before God, so our justice before divine justice . . .

We know that there is an infinite, and are ignorant of its nature. As we know it to be false that numbers are finite, it is therefore true that there is an infinity in number. But we do not know what it is. It is false that it is even, it is false that it is odd; for the addition of a unit can make no change in its nature. Yet it is a number, and every number is odd or even (this is certainly true of every finite number). So we may well know that there is a God without knowing what He is. Is there not one substantial truth, seeing there are so many things which are not the truth itself?

---

[1] Numbers are those given by Léon Brunschvicg.

"The Wager," by Blaise Pascal, from *The Thoughts of Blaise Pascal*. Trans. W.F. Trotter, from the edition prepared by Léon Brunschvicg. (London: Gollanez, 1904).

We know then the existence and nature of the finite, because we also are finite and have extension. We know the existence of the infinite and are ignorant of its nature, because it has extension like us, but not limits like us. But we know neither the existence nor the nature of God, because He has neither extension nor limits.

But by faith we know His existence; in glory we shall know His nature. Now, I have already shown that we may well know the existence of a thing, without knowing its nature.

Let us now speak according to natural lights.

If there is a God, He is infinitely incomprehensible, since, having neither parts nor limits, He has no affinity to us. We are then incapable of knowing either what He is or if He is. This being so, who will dare to undertake the decision of the question? Not we, who have no affinity to Him.

Who then will blame Christians for not being able to give a reason for their belief, since they profess a religion for which they cannot give a reason? They declare, in expounding it to the world, that it is a foolishness, *stultitiam*; [1 Cor. 1:21] and then you complain that they do not prove it! If they proved it, they would not keep their word; it is in lacking proofs that they are not lacking in sense. "Yes, but although this excuses those who offer it as such and takes away from them the blame of putting it forward without reason, it does not excuse those who receive it." Let us then examine this point, and say, "God is, or He is not." But to which side shall we incline? Reason can decide nothing here. There is an infinite chaos which separated us. A game is being played at the extremity of this infinite distance where heads or tails will turn up. What will you wager? According to reason, you can do neither the one thing nor the other; according to reason, you can defend neither of the propositions.

Do not, then, reprove for error those who have made a choice; for you know nothing about it. "No, but I blame them for having made, not this choice, but a choice; for again both he who chooses heads and he who chooses tails are equally at fault, they are both in the wrong. The true course is not to wager at all."

Yes; but you must wager. It is not optional. You are embarked. Which will you choose then? Let us see. Since you must choose, let us see which interests you least. You have two things to lose, the true and the good; and two things to stake, your reason and your will, your knowledge and your happiness; and your nature has two things to shun, error and misery. Your reason is no more shocked in choosing one rather than the other, since you must of necessity choose. This is one point settled. But your happiness? Let us weigh the gain and the loss in wagering that God is. Let us estimate these two chances. If you gain, you gain all; if you lose, you lose nothing. Wager, then, without hesitation that He is. "That is very fine. Yes, I must wager; but I may perhaps wager too much." Let us see. Since there is an equal risk of gain and of loss, if you had only to gain two lives, instead of one, you might still wager. But if there were three lives to gain, you would have to play (since you are under the necessity of playing), and you would be imprudent, when you are forced to play, not to chance your life to gain three at a game where there is an equal risk of loss and gain. But there is an eternity of life and happiness. And this being so, if there were an infinity of chances, of which one only would be for you, you would still be right in wagering one to win two, and you would act stupidly, being obliged to play, by refusing to stake one life against three at a game in which out of an infinity of chances there is one for you, if there were an infinity of an infinitely happy life to gain. But there is here an infinity of an infinitely happy life to gain, a chance of gain against a finite number of chances of loss, and what you stake is finite. It is all divided; where-ever the infinite is and there is not an infinity of chances of loss against that of gain, there is no time to hesitate, you must give all. And thus, when one is forced to play, he must renounce reason to preserve his life, rather than risk it for infinite gain, as likely to happen as the loss of nothingness.

For it is no use to say it is uncertain if we will gain, and it is certain that we risk, and that the infinite distance between the certainly of what is staked and the uncertainty of what will be gained, equals the finite good which is certainly staked against the uncertain infinite. It is not so, as every player stakes a certainty to gain an uncertainty, and yet he stakes a finite certainty to gain a finite uncertainty, without transgressing against reason. There is not an infinite distance between the certainty staked and the uncertainty of the gain; that is untrue. In truth, there is an infinity between the certainty of gain and the certainty of loss. But the uncertainty of the gain is proportioned to the certainty of the stake according to the proportion of the chances of gain and loss. Hence it comes that, if there are as many risks on one side as on the other, the course is to play even; and then the certainty of the stake is equal to the uncertainty of the gain, so far is it from fact that there is an infinite distance between them. And so our proposition is of infinite force, when there is the finite to stake in a game where there are equal risks of gain and of loss, and the infinite to gain. This is demonstrable; and if men are capable of any truths, this is one.

"I confess it, I admit it. But, still, is there no means of seeing the faces of the cards?" Yes, Scripture and the rest, etc. "Yes, but I have my hands tied and my mouth closed; I am forced to wager, and am not free. I am not released, and am so made that I cannot believe. What, then, would you have me do?"

True. But at least learn your inability to believe, since reason brings you to this, and yet you cannot believe. Endeavour, then, to convince yourself, not by increase of proofs of God, but by the abatement of your passions. You would like to attain faith and do not know the way; you would like to cure yourself of unbelief and ask the remedy for it. Learn of those who have been bound like you, and who now stake all their possessions. These are people who know the way which you would follow, and who are cured of an ill of which you would be cured. Follow the way by which they began; by acting as if they believed, taking the holy water, having masses said, etc. Even this will naturally make you believe, and deaden your acuteness. "But this is what I am afraid of." And why? What have you to lose?

But to show you that this leads you there, it is this which will lessen the passions, which are your stumbling-blocks.

The end of this discourse.—Now, what harm will befall you in taking this side? You will be faithful, humble, grateful, generous, a sincere friend, truthful. Certainly you will not have those poisonous pleasures, glory and luxury; but will you not have others? I will tell you that you will thereby gain in this life, and that, at each step you take on this road, you will see so great certainty of gain, so much nothingness in what you risk, that you will at last recognize that you have wagered for something certain and infinite, for which you have given nothing.

"Ah! This discourse transports me, charms me," etc.

If this discourse pleases you and seems impressive, know that it is made by a man who has knelt, both before and after it, in prayer to that Being, infinite and without parts, before whom he lays all he has, for you also to lay before Him all you have for your own good and for His glory, that so strength may be given to lowliness.

277. The heart has its reasons, which reason does not know. We feel it in a thousand things. I say that the heart naturally loves the Universal Being, and also itself naturally, according as it gives itself to them; and it hardens itself against one or the other at its will. You have rejected the one and kept the other. Is it by reason that you love yourself?

278. It is the heart which experiences God, and not the reason.

279. Faith is a gift of God; do not believe that we said it was a gift of reasoning. Other religions do not say this of their faith. They only gave reasoning in order to arrive at it, and yet it does not bring them to it.

535. We owe a great debt to those who point out faults. For they mortify us. They teach us that we have been despised. They do not prevent our being so in the future; for we have many other faults for which we may be despised. They prepare for us the exercise of correction and freedom from fault.

THE WILL TO BELIEVE (1896)

William James

William James (1842–1910) was born at Astor House in New York City, the son of Henry James Sr., an independently wealthy, eccentric theologian and friend to the intellectual elites of his day. (The novelist Henry James was William's younger brother.) The James children were educated by tutors in New York and in Europe. William's early interests were split between art and science. At 16, he studied painting with William Morris Hunt while the family was living in Newport, RI. At 19, he entered Harvard University's Lawrence Scientific School; three years later, he transferred to the medical school. James interrupted his medical education to join an expedition to the Amazon and again to seek a cure in Germany for some health issues. (He and his siblings suffered aliments of the eyes, back, stomach, and skin as well as bouts of suicidal depression.) While in Germany, he realized that his real interests were in philosophy and the budding field of psychology. Thus, after completing his medical degree, he chose not to practice medicine. Instead, he built an academic career at Harvard, first as instructor in physiology and anatomy (1873), then as assistant professor of psychology (1876), assistant professor of philosophy (1881), and full professor (1885). He held an endowed chair in psychology from 1889 until 1897, at which time he returned to philosophy, taking emeritus status in 1907. Remarkably, James never had formal training in philosophy. In the early 1870s, he engaged in philosophical discussions as part of a group at Harvard known as the Metaphysical Club. He and fellow members Charles Sanders Peirce (1839–1914), Oliver Wendell Holmes (1841–1935), and Chauncey Wright (1830–1875) all became important in the American Pragmatism movement. James also became acquainted with the seminal work in psychology of Hermann Helmholtz (1821–1894) in Germany and Pierre Janet (1859–1947) in France. In 1878, James started on a 12-year project writing <u>Principles of Psychology</u> (1890), a tour de force that helped define the discipline and became for many years its standard textbook. He also wrote influential books on educational psychology, religious experience, and mysticism and is often credited (instead of Freud) with the discovery of the subconscious. He was a founder of the American Society for Psychical Research *and an advocate of alternative healing. Seeds of his philosophy appear in many of his psychological works. Following his retirement, James continued to lecture and published his most important philosophical works: <u>Pragmatism: a New Name for Some Old Ways of Thinking</u> (1907), <u>A Pluralistic Universe</u> (1909), <u>The Meaning of Truth</u> (1909), and <u>Essays in Radical Empiricism</u> (published posthumously in 1912). James' students included Theodore Roosevelt (26th President of the USA), George Santayana (philosopher and novelist), W. E. B. Du Bois (civil rights campaigner), G. Stanley Hall (psychologist and educator), Gertrude Stein (writer and feminist), and C. I. Lewis (philosopher). His work influenced a number of both contemporary and later-generation philosophers, including John Dewey (1859–1952), Edmund Husserl (1859–1938), Bertrand Russell (1872–1970), and Ludwig Wittgenstein (1889–1951). James suffered severe cardiac pain during his last years. Experimental treatments in Europe did not help. He died at his home in Chocorua, New Hampshire, world famous both as psychologist and as philosopher.*

What to look for: *James is very careful to define all his terms, including " hypothesis" and "option" and explain their varieties. Be sure you understand all the distinctions. What does James say about the (psychological) origin of and justification for humans' beliefs? What does he mean by our "passional" nature? What is his analysis and evaluation of Pascal and Clifford? Exactly what thesis does James defend? How do "empiricists" and "absolutists" see belief differently? What two competing goals do we all have in believing? How does this competition help us understand the differences between Pascal and Clifford? How does it give James a justification for his thesis? In what sort of cases might prior belief be necessary to bring about a truth? In what three areas do <u>genuine</u> options, undecidable on intellectual grounds, arise? If we allow belief on insufficient evidence for ourselves, how must we each treat others who disagree with us regarding that belief?*

THE WILL TO BELIEVE.[1]

In the recently published Life by Leslie Stephen of his brother, Fitz-James, there is an account of a school to which the latter went when he was a boy. The

---

[1]An Address to the Philosophical Clubs of Yale and Brown Universities, delivered in April and May of this year, the Yale introduction being the one preserved. I ought perhaps to say, at the outset, that I owe my confidence in my position to the writings of Charles Renouvier.

"The Will to Believe," by William James, from *The New World – A Quarterly Review of Ethics and Theology*, Vol. V (1896).

teacher, a certain Mr. Guest, used to converse with his pupils in this wise: "Gurney, what is the difference between justification and sanctification?—Stephen, prove the omnipotence of God!" etc., etc. In the midst of our Harvard Unitarianism and indifference we are prone to imagine that here at good old orthodox Yale your conversation continues to be somewhat of this order . . . [328] And to show you that we at Harvard have not lost all interest in these vital subjects, I have brought with me tonight something like a sermon on justification by faith to read to you—I mean an essay in justification *of* faith, a defense of our right to adopt a believing attitude in religious matters, in spite of the fact that our merely logical intellect may not have been coerced. "The Will to Believe" shall accordingly be the title of my paper.

I have long defended the lawfulness of voluntary faith to my own students; but as soon as they have got well imbued with the logical spirit, they have as a rule refused to admit my contention to be lawful philosophically, even though in point of fact they were personally all the time chock-full of some faith or other themselves. I am all the while, however, so profoundly convinced that my own position is correct, that your invitation has seemed to me a good occasion to make my own statement more clear. Perhaps the Yale mind will be more open than those with which I have hitherto had to deal. I am afraid I must talk for a good hour or more, but I will try to be as little technical as I can, though I must begin by straightway setting up some technical distinctions that will help us in the end.

I.

Let us give the name of *hypothesis* to anything that may be proposed to our belief; and just as the electricians speak of live and dead wires, let us speak of any hypothesis as either *live* or *dead*. A live hypothesis is one which appeals as a real possibility to him to whom it is proposed. If I ask you to believe in the Mahdi, the notion makes no electric connection with your nature, it refuses to scintillate with any credibility at all. As an hypothesis it is completely dead. To an Arab, however (even if he be not one of the Mahdi's followers), the hypothesis is among the mind's possibilities; it is alive. This shows that deadness and liveness in an hypothesis are not intrinsic properties, but relations to the individual thinker. They are measured by his [329] willingness to act. The maximum of liveness in an hypothesis means willingness to act irrevocably. Practically, that means belief; but there is some believing tendency wherever there is willingness to act at all.

Next, let us call the decision between two hypotheses an *option*. Options may be of several kinds. They may be (*a*) *living* or *dead*; (*b*) *forced* or *avoidable*; (*c*) *momentous* or *trivial*; and for our purposes we may call an option a *genuine* option when it is of the forced, living, and momentous kind.

(*a*) A living option is one in which both hypotheses are live ones. If I say to you: "Be a theosophist or be a Mohammedan," it is probably a dead option, because for you neither hypothesis is likely to be alive. But if I say: "Be an agnostic or be a Christian," it is otherwise: trained as you are, each hypothesis makes some appeal, however small, to your belief.

(b) Next, if I say to you: "Choose between going out with your umbrella or without it," I do not offer you a genuine option, for it is not forced. You can easily avoid it by not going out at all. Similarly, if I say, "Either love me or hate me," "Either call my theory true or call it false," your option is avoidable. You may remain indifferent to me, neither loving nor hating, and you may decline to offer any judgment as to my theory. But if I say, "Either accept this truth or go without it," I put on you a forced option, for there is no standing place outside of the alternative. Every dilemma based on a complete logical disjunction, with no possibility of not choosing, is an option of this forced kind.

(c) Finally, if I were Dr. Nansen and proposed to you to join my North Pole expedition, your option would be momentous; for this would probably be your only similar opportunity, and your choice now would either exclude you from the North Pole sort of immortality altogether or put at least the chance of it into your hands. He who refuses to embrace a unique opportunity loses the prize as surely as if he tried and failed. *Per contra*, the option is trivial when the opportunity is not unique, when the stake is insignificant, or when the decision is reversible if it later prove unwise. Such trivial options abound in the scientific life. A chemist finds an hypothesis live enough to spend a year in its verification: he believes in it to that extent. But if his experiments prove inconclusive either way, he is quit for his loss of time, no vital harm being done. It will facilitate our discussion if we keep all these distinctions well in mind. [330]

II.

The next matter to consider is the actual psychology of human opinion. When we look at certain facts, it seems as if our passional and volitional nature lay at the root of all our convictions. When we look at others, it seems as if they could do nothing when the intellect had once said its say. Let us take the latter facts up first.

Does it not seem preposterous on the very face of it to talk of our opinions being modifiable at will? Can our will either help or hinder our intellect in its perceptions of truth? Can we, by just willing it, believe that Abraham Lincoln's existence is a myth, and that the portraits of him in "McClure's Magazine" are all of some one else? Can we, by any effort of our will, or by any strength of wish that it were true, believe ourselves well and about when we are roaring with rheumatism in bed, or feel certain that the sum of the two one-dollar bills in our pocket must be a hundred dollars? We can *say* any of these things, but we are absolutely impotent to believe them; and of just such things is the whole fabric of the truths that we do believe in made up—matters of fact, immediate or remote, as Hume said, and relations between ideas, which are either there or not there for us if we see them so, and which if not there cannot be put there by any action of our own.

In Pascal's Thoughts there is a celebrated passage known in literature as Pascal's wager. In it he tries to force us into Christianity by reasoning as if our concern with truth resembled our concern with the stakes in a game of chance. Translated freely his words are these: You must either believe or not believe that God is —which will you do? Your human reason cannot say. A game is going on between you and the nature of things which, at the day of judgment, will bring out either heads or tails. Weigh what your gains and your losses would be if you should stake all you have on heads, or God's existence: if you win in such case, you gain eternal beatitude; if you lose, you lose nothing at all. If there were an infinity of chances, and only one for God in this wager, still you ought to stake your all on God; for though you surely risk a finite loss by this procedure, any finite loss is reasonable, even a certain one is reasonable, if there is but the possibility of infinite gain. Go, then, and take holy water, and have masses said; belief will come and stupefy your scruples,—*Cela vous fera croire et vous abêtira.* Why should you not? At bottom, what have you to lose? [331]

You probably feel that when religious faith expresses itself thus, in the language of the gaming-table, it is put to its last trumps. Surely Pascal's own personal belief in masses and holy water had far other springs; and this celebrated page of his is but an argument for others, a last desperate snatch at a weapon against the hardness of the unbelieving heart. We feel that a faith in masses and holy water adopted wilfully after such a mechanical calculation would lack the inner soul of faith's reality; and if we were ourselves in the place of the Deity, we should probably take particular pleasure in cutting off believers of this pattern from their infinite reward. It is evident that unless there be some *preëxisting tendency* to believe in masses and holy water, the option offered to the will by Pascal is not a living option. Certainly no Turk ever took to masses and holy water on its account; and even to us here these means of salvation seem such foregone impossibilities that Pascal's logic, invoked for Protestants specifically, leaves us unmoved. As well might the Mahdi write to us, saying, "I am the Expected One whom God has created in his effulgence. You shall be infinitely happy if you confess me; otherwise you shall be cut off from the light of the sun. Weigh, then, your infinite gain if I am genuine against your finite sacrifice if I am not!" His logic would be that of Pascal; but he would vainly use it on us, for the hypothesis he offers us is dead. No tendency to act on it exists in us to any degree.

The talk of believing by our volition seems, then, from one point of view, simply silly. From another point of view it is worse than silly, it is vile. When one turns to the magnificent edifice of the physical sciences, and sees how it was reared; what thousands of disinterested moral lives of men lie buried in its mere foundations; what patience and postponement, what choking down of preference, what submission to the icy laws of outer fact are wrought into its very stones and mortar; how absolutely impersonal it stands in its vast augustness, then how besotted and contemptible seems every little sentimentalist who comes blowing his voluntary smoke-wreaths, and pretending to decide things from out of his private dream! It is to be wondered at that those bred in the rugged and manly school of science should feel like spewing such subjectivism out of their mouths? The whole system of loyalties which grow up in the schools of science go dead against its toleration; so that it is only natural that those who have caught the scientific fever should pass over to the opposite extreme, [332] and write sometimes as if the incorruptibly truthful intellect ought positively to prefer bitterness and unacceptableness to the heart in its cup.

> It fortifies my soul to know
> That, though I perish, Truth is so —

sings Clough, while Huxley exclaims: "My only consolation lies in the reflection that, however bad our posterity may become, so far as they hold by the plain rule of not pretending to believe what they have no reason to believe, because it may be to their advantage so to pretend [the word "pretend" is surely here redundant], they will not have reached the lowest depth of immorality." And that delicious *enfant terrible* Clifford writes; "Belief is desecrated when given to unproved and unquestioned statements for the solace and private pleasure of the believer. . . . Whoso would deserve well of his fellows in this matter will guard the purity of his belief with a very fanaticism of jealous care, lest at any time it should rest on an unworthy object, and catch a stain which can never be wiped away. . . . If [a] belief has been accepted on insufficient evidence [even though the belief be true, as Clifford on the same page explains], the pleasure is a stolen one. . . . It is sinful because it is stolen in defiance of our duty to mankind. That duty is to guard ourselves from such beliefs as from a pestilence which may shortly master our own body and then spread to the rest of the town. . . . It is wrong always, everywhere, and for every one, to believe anything upon insufficient evidence."

III.

All this strikes one as healthy, even when expressed, as by Clifford, with somewhat too much of robustious pathos in the voice. Free-will and simple wishing do seem, in the matter of our credences, to be only fifth wheels to the coach. Yet if any one should thereupon assume that intellectual insight is what remains after wish and will and sentimental preference have taken wing, or that pure reason is what then settles our opinions, he would fly quite as directly in the teeth of the facts.

It is only our already dead hypotheses that our willing nature is unable to bring to life again. But what has made them dead for us is for the most part a previous action of our willing nature of an antagonistic kind. When I say "willing nature," I do not mean only such deliberate volitions as may have set up habits of belief that we cannot now escape from, I mean all such factors [333] of belief as fear and hope, prejudice and passion, imitation and partisanship, the circumpressure of our caste and set. As a matter of fact we find ourselves believing, we hardly know how or why. Mr. Balfour gives the name of "authority" to all those influences, born of the intellectual climate, that make hypotheses possible or impossible for us, alive or dead. In this room, we all believe in molecules and the conservation of energy, in democracy and necessary progress, in Protestant Christianity and the duty of fighting for "the doctrine of the immortal Monroe," all for no reasons worthy of the name. We see into these matters with no more inner clearness, and probably with much less, than any disbeliever in them might possess. His unconventionality would probably have some grounds to show for its conclusions; but for us, not insight, but the *prestige* of the opinions, is what makes the spark shoot from them and light up our sleeping magazines of faith. Our reason is quite satisfied, in 999 cases out of every thousand of us, if it can find a few arguments that will do to recite in case our credulity is criticised by some one else. Our faith is faith in some one else's faith, and in the greatest matters this is most the case. Our belief in truth itself, for instance, that there is a Truth, and that our minds and it are made for each other, what is it but a passionate affirmation of desire, in which our social system backs us up? We want to have a Truth; we want to believe that our experiments and studies and discussions must put us in a continually better and better position towards it; and on this line we agree to fight out our thinking lives. But if a pyrrhonistic skeptic asks us *how we know* all this, can our logic find a reply? No! Certainly it cannot. It is just one volition against another, —we willing to go in for life upon a trust or assumption which he, for his part, does not care to make.[2]

As a rule we disbelieve all facts and theories for which we have no *use*. Clifford's cosmic emotions find no use for Christian feelings. Huxley belabors the bishops because there is no use for sacerdotalism in his scheme of life. Newman, on the contrary, goes over to Romanism, and finds all sorts of reasons good for staying there, because a priestly system is for him an organic appetite and need. Why do so few "scientists" even look at the evidence for telepathy, so called? Because they think, as a leading biologist, now dead, once said to me, that even if such a thing were true, "scientists" ought to band together to keep it suppressed and concealed. It would undo the uniformity of Nature and all [334] sorts of other things without which scientists cannot carry on their pursuits. But if this very man had been shown something which as a

---

[2] Compare the admirable page 310 in S. H. Hodgson's *Time and Space*, London, 1865.

scientist he might *do* with telepathy, he might not only have examined the evidence, but he might even have found it good enough. This very law which the logicians would impose upon us—if I may give the name of logicians to those who would rule out our willing nature here—is based on nothing but their own natural wish to exclude all elements for which they, in their professional quality of logicians, can find no use.

Evidently, then, our non-intellectual nature does influence our convictions. There are passional tendencies and volitions that run before, and others that come after belief, and it is only the latter that are too late for the fair. And they are not too late when the previous passional work has been already in their own direction. Pascal's argument, instead of being powerless, then seems a regular clincher, and is the last stroke needed to make our faith in masses and holy water complete. The state of things is evidently far from simple; and pure insight and logic, whatever they might do ideally, are not the only things that really do produce our creeds.

IV.

Our next duty, having recognized this mixed-up state of affairs, is to ask whether it be simply reprehensible and pathological, or whether, on the contrary, we must treat it as a normal element in making up our minds. The thesis I defend is, briefly stated, this: *Our passional nature must, and lawfully may, decide an option between propositions, whenever it is a genuine option that cannot by its nature be decided on intellectual grounds; for to say, under such circumstances, "Do not decide, but leave the question open," is itself a passional decision, just like deciding "yes" or "no," and is attended with the same risk of losing the truth.* The thesis thus abstractly expressed will, I trust, soon become quite clear. But I must first indulge in a bit more of preliminary work.

V.

It will be observed that for the purposes of this discussion we are on "dogmatic" ground—ground, I mean, which leaves systematic philosophical skepticism altogether out of account. The postulate that there is truth and that it is the destiny of our minds to attain it, we are deliberately resolving to make, though [335] the skeptic will not make it. We part company with him, therefore, absolutely, at this point. But the faith that truth exists and that our minds can find it, may be held in two ways. We may talk of the *empiricist* way and of the *absolutist* way of believing in truth. The absolutists in this matter say that we not only can attain to knowing truth, but we can *know when* we have attained to knowing it; while the empiricists think that although we may attain it, we cannot infallibly know when. To know is one thing, and to know for certain *that* we know is another. One may hold to the first being possible without the second; hence the empiricists and the absolutists, although neither of them is a skeptic in the usual philosophic sense of the term, show very different degrees of dogmatism in their lives.

If we look at the history of opinions, we see that the empiricist tendency has largely prevailed in science, while in philosophy the absolutist tendency has had everything its own way. The characteristic sort of happiness, indeed, which philosophies yield has mainly consisted in the conviction felt by each successive school or system that by it bottom-certitude had been attained. "Other philosophies are collections of opinions, mostly false; *my* philosophy gives standing-ground forever,"—who does not recognize in this the key-note of every system worthy of the name? A system, to be a system at all, must come as a *closed* system, reversible in this or that detail, perchance, but in its essential features never!

Scholastic orthodoxy, to which one must always go when one wishes to find perfectly clear statement, has beautifully elaborated this absolutist conviction in a doctrine which it calls that of "objective evidence." If, for example, I am unable to doubt that I now exist before you, that two is less than three, or that if all men are mortal then I am mortal too, it is because these things illumine my intellect irresistibly. The final ground of this objective evidence possessed by certain propositions is the *adaequatio intellectûs nostri cum rê*. The certitude it brings involves an *aptitudinem ad extorquendum certum assensum* on the part of the truth envisaged, and on the side of the subject a *quietem in cognitione*, when once the object is mentally received, that leaves no possibility of doubt behind; and in the whole transaction nothing operates but the *entitas ipsa* of the object and the *entitas ipsa* of the mind. We slouchy modern thinkers dislike to talk in Latin, indeed, we dislike to talk in set terms at all; but at bottom our own state of mind is very much like this whenever [336] we uncritically abandon ourselves: You believe in objective evidence and I do. Of some things we feel that we are certain: we know, and we know that we do know. There is something that gives a click inside of us, a bell that strikes twelve, when the hands of our mental clock have swept the dial and meet over the meridian hour. The greatest empiricists among us are only empiricists on reflection—when left to their instincts, they dogmatize like infallible popes. When the Cliffords tell us how sinful it is to be Christians on such "insufficient evidence," insufficiency is really the last thing they have in mind. For them the evidence is absolutely sufficient, only it makes the other way. They believe so completely in an anti-Christian order of the universe that there is no living option,—Christianity is a dead hypothesis from the very start.

VI.

But now, since we are all such absolutists by instinct, what in our quality of students of philosophy ought we to do about the fact? Shall we espouse and indorse it? Or shall we treat it as a weakness of our nature from which we must free ourselves, if we can?

I sincerely believe that the latter course is the only one we can follow as reflective men. Objective evidence and certitude are doubtless very fine ideals to play with, but where on this moonlit and dream-visited planet are they found? I am, therefore, myself a complete empiricist so far as my theory of human knowledge goes. I live, to be sure, by the practical faith that we must go on experiencing and thinking over our experience, for only thus can our opinions grow more true. But to hold any one of them, I absolutely don't care which, as if it never could be reinterpretable or corrigible, I believe to be a tremendously mistaken attitude, and I think that the whole history of philosophy will bear me out. There is but one indefectibly certain truth, and that is the truth that pyrrhonistic skepticism itself leaves standing upright, the truth that the present phenomenon of consciousness or datum of experience exists. That, however, is the bare starting-point of knowledge, the mere admission of a stuff to be philosophized about. The various philosophies are but so many attempts at expressing what this stuff really is. And if we repair to our libraries what disagreement do we discover! Where is a certainly true answer found? Apart from abstract propositions of comparison (such as two and two [337] are the same as four), propositions which tell us nothing by themselves about concrete reality, we find no proposition ever regarded by any one as evidently certain that has not either been called a falsehood, or at least had its truth sincerely questioned by some one else. The transcending of the axioms of geometry, not in play but in earnest, by certain of our contemporaries (as Zöllner and Charles H. Hinton), and the rejection of the whole Aristotelian logic by the Hegelians, are striking instances in point.

No concrete test of what is really true has ever been agreed upon. Some make the criterion external to the moment of perception, putting it either in revelation, the *consensus gentium*, the instincts of the heart, or the systematized experience of the race. Others make the perceptive moment its own test—Descartes, for instance, with his clear and distinct ideas guaranteed by the veracity of God; Reid with his "common-sense;" and Kant with his forms of synthetic judgment *a priori*. The inconceivability of the opposite; the capacity to be verified by sense; the possession of complete organic unity or self-relation, realized when a thing is its own other; are standards which, in turn, have been used. The much lauded objective evidence is never triumphantly there, it is a mere aspiration or *Grenzbegriff*, marking the infinitely remote ideal of our thinking life. To claim that certain truths now possess it is simply to say that when you think them true and they *are* true, then their evidence is objective, otherwise it is not. But practically one's conviction that the evidence one goes by is of the real objective brand, is only one more subjective opinion added to the lot. For what a contradictory array of opinions have objective evidence and absolute certitude been claimed! The world is rational through and through—its existence is an ultimate brute fact; there is a personal God—a personal God is inconceivable; there is an extra-mental physical world immediately known—the mind can only know its own ideas; a moral imperative exists—obligation is only the resultant of desires; a permanent spiritual principle is in every one—there are only shifting states of mind; there is an endless chain of causes—there is an absolute first cause; an eternal necessity—a freedom; a purpose—no purpose; a primal One—a primal Many; a universal continuity—an essential discontinuity in things; an infinity—no infinity. There is this—there is that; there is indeed nothing which some one has not thought absolutely true, while his neighbor deemed it absolutely false; and not an absolutist among them seems ever to have considered [338] that the trouble may all the time be essential, and that the intellect, even with truth directly in its grasp, may have no infallible signal for knowing whether it be truth or no. When, indeed, one remembers that the most striking practical application to life of the doctrine of objective certitude has been the conscientious labors of the Holy Office of the Inquisition, one feels less tempted than ever to lend the doctrine a respectful ear.

But please observe, now, that when as empiricists we give up the doctrine of objective certitude, we do not thereby give up the quest or hope of truth itself. We still pin our faith on its existence, and still believe that we gain an ever better position towards it by systematically continuing to roll up experiences and think. Our great difference from the scholastic lies in the way we face. The strength of his system lies in the principles, the origin, the *terminus a quo* of his thought; for us the strength is in the outcome, the upshot, the *terminus ad quem*. Not where it comes from but what it leads to is to decide. It matters not to an empiricist from what quarter an hypothesis may come to him; he may have acquired it by fair means or by foul; passion may have whispered or accident suggested it; but if the total drift of thinking continues to confirm it, that is what he means by its being true.

VII.

One more point, small but important, and our preliminaries are done. There are two ways of looking at our duty in the matter of opinion, ways entirely different, and yet ways about whose difference the theory of knowledge seems hitherto to have shown very little concern. *We must know the truth*; and *we must avoid error*—these are our first and great commandments as would-be knowers; but they are not two ways of stating an identical commandment, they are two separable laws. Although it may indeed happen that, when we believe the truth A, we escape as an incidental consequence from believing the falsehood B, it hardly ever happens that by merely disbelieving the falsehood B, we incidentally must needs believe the truth A. We may, in escaping B, fall into believing other falsehoods, C or D, just as bad as B; or we may escape B by not believing anything at all, not even A. "Believe truth!" "Shun error!"—these, we see, are two materially different laws; and by choosing between them we may color differently our whole intellectual life. We may regard the chase for truth as paramount, and the avoidance of error as secondary; or we may, on the other hand, treat the [339] avoidance of error as more imperative, and let truth take its chance. Clifford, in the instructive passage which I have quoted, exhorts us to the latter course. Believe nothing, he tells us, keep your mind in suspense forever, rather than by closing it on insufficient evidence incur the awful risk of believing lies. You, on the other hand, may think that the risk of being in error is a very small matter when compared with the blessings of real knowledge, and be ready to be duped many times in your investigation rather than postpone indefinitely the chance of guessing true. I myself find it impossible to go with Clifford. We must remember that these feelings of our duty about either truth or error are in any case only expressions of our passional life. Biologically considered, our minds are as ready to grind out falsehood as veracity, and he who says, "Better go without belief forever than believe a lie!" merely shows his own preponderant private horror of becoming a dupe. He may be critical of many of his desires and fears, but this fear he slavishly obeys. He cannot imagine any one questioning its binding force. For my own part, I have also a horror of being duped. But I can believe that worse things than being duped may happen to a man in this world: so Clifford's exhortation has to my ears a thoroughly fantastic sound. It is like a general informing his soldiers that it is better to keep out of battle forever than to risk a single wound. Not so are victories either over enemies or over nature gained. Our errors are surely not such awfully solemn things. In a world where we are so certain to incur them in spite of all our caution, a certain lightness of heart seems healthier than this excessive nervousness on their behalf. At any rate, it seems the fittest thing for the empiricist philosopher.

VIII.

And now, after all this introduction, let us go straight at our question. I have said, and now repeat it, that not only as a matter of fact do we find our passional nature influencing us in our opinions, but that there are some options between opinions in which this influence must be regarded both as an inevitable and as a lawful determinant of our choice.

I fear here that some of you my hearers will begin to scent danger, and lend an inhospitable ear. Two first steps of passion you have indeed had to admit as necessary—we must think so as to avoid dupery, and we must think so as to gain truth—but the surest path to those ideal consummations, you will probably [340] consider, is from now onwards to take no further passional step. Well, of course, I agree as far as the facts will allow. Wherever the option between losing truth and gaining it is not momentous, we can throw the chance of *gaining truth* away, and at any rate save ourselves from any chance of *believing falsehood*, by not making up our minds at all till objective evidence has come. In scientific questions, this is almost always the case. And even in human affairs in general, the need of acting is seldom so urgent that a false belief to act on is better than no belief at all. Law courts, indeed, have to decide on the best evidence attainable for the moment, because a judge's duty is to make law as well as to ascertain it, and (as a learned judge once said to me) few cases are worth spending much time over—the great thing is to have them decided on *any* acceptable principle, and got out of the way. But in our dealings with objective nature we obviously are recorders, not makers, of the truth; and decisions for the mere sake of deciding promptly and getting on to the next business would be wholly out of place. Throughout the breadth of physical nature facts are what they are quite independently of us, and seldom is there any such hurry about them that the risks of being duped by believing a premature theory need be faced. The questions here are always trivial options, the hypotheses are hardly living (at any rate not living for us spectators), the choice between believing truth or falsehood is seldom forced. The attitude of skeptical balance is therefore the absolutely wise one if we wish to escape mistakes. What difference, indeed, does it make to most of us whether we have or have not a theory of the Röntgen rays, whether we believe or not in mind-stuff, or have a conviction about the causality of conscious states? It makes no difference. Such options are not forced on us. On every account it is better not to make them, but still keep weighing reasons *pro et contra* with an indifferent hand. I speak, of course, here of the purely judging mind. For purposes of discovery such indifference is to be less highly recommended, and science would be far less advanced than she is if the passionate desires of individuals to get their own faiths confirmed had been kept out of the game. In fact, if you want an absolute duffer in an investigation, you must, after all, take the man who has no interest whatever in its results. He is the warranted incapable, the positive fool. The most useful investigator, because the most sensitive observer, is always he whose eager interest in one side of the question is balanced by an equally keen nervousness lest [341] he become deceived.[3] Science has organized this nervousness into a regular *technique*, her so-called method of verification; and she has fallen so deeply in love with the method that one may even say she has ceased to care for truth by itself at all. It is only truth as technically verified that interests her. The truth of truths might come in merely affirmative form, and she would decline to touch it. Such truth as that, she might repeat with Clifford, would be stolen in defiance of her duty to mankind. Human passions, however, are stronger than technical rules. "*Le coeur a ses raisons,*" as Pascal says, "*que la raison ne connaît pas;*" and however indifferent to all but the bare rules of the game the umpire, the abstract intellect, may be, the concrete players who furnish him the materials to judge of are usually, each one of them, in love with some pet "live hypothesis" of his own.

---

[3] Compare Wilfrid Ward's Essay, "The Wish to Believe," in his *Witnesses to the Unseen*, Macmillan & Co., 1893.

Let us agree, however, that wherever there is no forced option, the dispassionately judicial intellect, with no pet hypothesis, saving us at any rate from dupery, ought to be our ideal. The question next arises: Are there not *somewhere* forced options in our speculative questions, and can we (as men who may be interested at least as much in positively gaining truth as in merely escaping dupery) always wait with impunity till the coercive evidence shall have arrived? It seems *a priori* improbable that the truth should be so nicely adjusted to our needs and powers as that. In the great boarding-house of nature, the cakes and the butter and the syrup seldom come out so even and leave the plates so clean. Indeed, we should view them with scientific suspicion if they did.

IX.

Moral questions immediately present themselves as questions whose solution cannot wait for sensible proof. A moral question is a question not of what sensibly exists, but of what is good, or would be good if it did exist. Science can tell us what exists; but to compare the *worths*, both of what exists and of what does not exist, we must consult not science, but what Pascal calls our heart. Science herself consults her heart when she lays it down that the infinite ascertainment of fact and correction of false belief are the supreme goods for man. Challenge the statement, and science can only repeat it oracularly, or else prove it by showing that such ascertainment and correction bring man all sorts of other goods [342] which man's heart in turn declares. It is outworn scholasticism to say that "good" is a category that the intellect must first perceive before the heart can follow with its desires; and there is no middle course between letting our passional nature cooperate in our moral beliefs at all.

The question of having moral beliefs at all or not having them is decided by our will. Are our moral preferences true or false, or are they only odd biological phenomena, making things good or bad for *us*, but in themselves indifferent? How can your pure intellect decide? If your heart does not *want* a world of moral reality, your head will assuredly never make you believe in one. Mephistophelian skepticism, indeed, will satisfy the head's play-instincts much better than any rigorous idealism can. Some men (even at the student age) are so naturally cool-hearted that the moralistic hypothesis never has for them any pungent life, and in their supercilious presence the hot young moralist always feels strangely ill at ease. The appearance of knowingness is on their side, of *naïveté* and gullibility on his. Yet, in the inarticulate heart of him, he clings to it that he is not a dupe, and that there is a realm in which (as Emerson says) all their wit and intellectual superiority is no better than the cunning of a fox. Moral skepticism can no more be refuted or proved by logic than intellectual skepticism can. When we stick to it that there is truth (be it of either kind), we do so with our whole nature, and resolve to stand or fall by the results. The skeptic with his whole nature adopts the doubting attitude; but which of us is the wiser, Omniscience only knows.

Turn now from these wide questions of good to a certain class of questions of fact, questions concerning personal relations, states of mind between one man and another. *Do you like me or not?*—for example. Whether you do or not depends, in countless instances, on whether I meet you half-way, am willing to assume that you must like me, and show you trust and expectation. The previous faith on my part in your liking's existence is in such cases what makes your liking come. If I stand aloof, and refuse to budge an inch until I have objective evidence, until you shall have done something apt, as the absolutists say, *ad extorquendum assensum meum*, ten to one your liking never comes. How many women's hearts are vanquished by the mere sanguine insistence of some man that they *must* love him, he will not consent to the hypothesis that they [343] cannot! The desire for a certain kind of truth here brings about that special truth's existence; and so it is in innumerable cases of other sorts. Who gains promotions, boons, appointments, but the man in whose life they are seen to play the part of live hypotheses, who discounts them, sacrifices other things for their sake before they have come, and takes risks for them in advance? His faith acts on the powers above him as a claim, and creates its own verification.

Where faith in a fact, based on need of the fact, can create the fact, that would be an insane logic which should say that faith running ahead of scientific evidence is the "lowest kind of immorality" into which a thinking being can fall. Yet such is the logic by which our scientific absolutists pretend to regulate our lives![4]

X.

In truths dependent on our personal action, then, faith based on desire is certainly a lawful, and possibly an indispensable thing. But now, it will be said, these are all childish human cases, and have nothing to do with great cosmical matters, like the question of religious faith. Let us then pass on to that. Religions differ so much in their accidents that in discussing the religious question

---

[4] Editor: In later versions of this paper, James inserted the following elaboration at the beginning of this paragraph: "A social organism of any sort whatever, large or small, is what it is because each member proceeds to his own duty with a trust that the other members will simultaneously do theirs. Wherever a desired result is achieved by the co-operation of many independent persons, its existence as a fact is a pure consequence of the precursive faith in one another of those immediately concerned. A government, an army, a commercial system, a ship, a college, an athletic team, all exist on this condition, without which not only is nothing achieved, but nothing is even attempted. A whole train of passengers (individually brave enough) will be looted by a few highwaymen, simply because the latter can count on one another, while each passenger fears that if he makes a movement of resistance, he will be shot before any one else backs him up. If we believed that the whole car-full would rise at once with us, we should each severally rise, and train-robbing would never even be attempted. There are, then, cases where a fact cannot come at all unless a preliminary faith exists in its coming."

we must make it very generic and broad. What then do we now mean by the religious hypothesis? Science says things are; morality says some things are better than other things; and religion says essentially two things: –

First, she says that the best things are the more eternal things, the overlapping things, the things in the universe that throw the last stone, so to speak, and say the final word. "Perfection is eternal,"—this phrase of Charles Secrétan seems a good way of putting this first affirmation of religion, an affirmation which obviously cannot yet be verified scientifically at all.

The second affirmation of religion is that we are better off even now *if we believe* that first religious truth.

Now, let us consider what the logical elements of this situation are *in case the religious hypothesis in both its branches be really true*. (Of course, we must admit that possibility at the outset. If we are to discuss the question at all, it must involve a living option. If for any of you religion be a hypothesis that cannot, by any living possibility be true, then you need go no farther. I speak to the "saving remnant" alone.) So proceeding, we see, first, that religion offers itself as a *momentous* option. We are [344] supposed to gain, even now, by our belief, and to lose by our non-belief, a certain vital good. Secondly, religion is a *forced* option, so far as that good goes. We cannot escape the issue by remaining skeptical and waiting for more light, because, although we do avoid error in that way *if religion be untrue*, we lose the good, *if it be true*, just as certainly as if we positively chose to disbelieve. It is as if a man should hesitate indefinitely to ask a certain woman to marry him because he was not perfectly sure that she would prove an angel or a devil after he brought her home. Would he not cut himself off from that particular angel-possibility as decisively as if he went and married some one else? Skepticism, then, is not avoidance of option; it is option of a certain particular kind of risk. *Better risk loss of truth than chance of error*—that is your faith-vetoer's exact position. He is actively playing his stake as much as the believer is; he is backing the field against the religious hypothesis, just as the believer is backing the religious hypothesis against the field. To preach skepticism to us as a duty until "sufficient evidence" for religion be found, is tantamount therefore to telling us, when in presence of the religious hypothesis, that to yield to our fear of its being error is wiser and better than to yield to our hope that it may be true. It is not intellect against all passions, then; it is only intellect with one passion laying down its law. And by what, forsooth, is the supreme wisdom of this passion warranted? And dupery for dupery, what proof is there that dupery through hope is so much worse than dupery through fear? I, for one, can see no proof. And I simply refuse obedience to the scientist's command to imitate his kind of option, in a case where my own stake is important enough to give me the right to choose my own form of risk. If religion be true and the evidence for it be still insufficient, I do not wish, by putting your extinguisher upon my nature (which feels to me as if it had after all some business in this matter), to forfeit my sole chance in life of getting upon the winning side—that chance depending, of course, on my willingness to run the risk of acting as if my passional need of taking the world religiously might be prophetic and right.

All this is on the supposition that it really *may* be prophetic and right, and that, even to us who are discussing the matter, religion is a live hypothesis which may be true. Now, to most of us religion comes in a still further way that makes a veto on our active faith even more illogical. The more perfect and more eternal aspect of the universe is represented in our religions as having personal form. The universe [345] is no longer a mere *It* to us, but a *Thou*, if we are religious; and any relation that may be possible from person to person might be possible here. For instance, although in one sense we are passive portions of the universe, in another we show a curious autonomy, as if we were small active centres on our own account.[5] We feel, too, as if the appeal of religion to us were made to our own active good-will, as if evidence might be forever withheld from us unless we met the hypothesis half-way. To take a trivial illustration: just as a man who in a company of gentlemen made no advances, asked a warrant for every concession, and believed no one's word without proof, would cut himself off by such churlishness from all the social rewards that a more trusting spirit would earn; so here, one who should shut himself up in snarling logicality and try to make the gods extort his recognition willy-nilly, or not get it at all, might cut himself off forever from his only opportunity of making the gods' acquaintance. This feeling, forced on us we know not whence, that by obstinately believing that there *are* gods (although not to do so would be so easy both for our logic and our life) we are doing the universe the deepest service we can, seems part of the living essence of the religious hypothesis. If the hypothesis *were* true in all its parts, including this one, then pure intellectualism, with its veto on our making willing advances, would be an absurdity; and some participation of our sympathetic nature would be logically required. I, therefore, for one cannot see my way to accepting the agnostic rules for truth-seeking, or willfully agree to keep my willing nature out of the game. I cannot do so for this plain reason, that *a code that would absolutely prevent me from acknowledging certain kinds of truth if those kinds of truth were really there, would be an irrational rule.* That for me is the long and short of the formal logic of the situation, no matter what the kinds of truth might materially be.

I confess I do not see how this logic can be escaped. But sad experience makes me fear that some of you may still shrink from radically saying with me, *in abstracto*, that we have the right to believe at our own risk any hypothesis that is live enough to tempt our will. I suspect, however, that if this is so, it is because you have got away from the abstract logical point of view altogether, and are thinking (perhaps without realizing it) of [346] some particular

---

[5] Cf. H. Siebeck, *Lehrbuch der Religionsphilosophie*. Freiburg, 1893 pp. 170 ff.

religious hypothesis which for you is dead. The freedom to "believe what we will" you apply to the case of some patent superstition; and the faith you think of is the faith defined by the schoolboy when he said, "Faith is when you believe something that you know ain't true." I can only repeat that this is misapprehension. *In concreto*, the freedom to believe can only cover living options which the intellect cannot by itself resolve; and living options never seem absurdities to him who has them to consider. When I look at the religious question as it really puts itself to concrete men, when I think of all the possibilities which both practically and theoretically it involves, then this command that we shall put a stopper on our heart, instincts, and courage, and wait—*acting* of course meanwhile more or less as if religion were *not* true[6]—till doomsday, or till such time as our intellect and senses working together may have raked in evidence enough—this command, I say, seems to me the queerest idol ever manufactured in the philosophic cave. Were we scholastic absolutists, there might be more excuse. If we had an infallible intellect with its objective certitudes, we might feel ourselves disloyal to such a perfect organ of knowledge in not trusting to it exclusively, in not waiting for its releasing word. But if we are empiricists, if we believe that no bell in us tolls to let us know for certain when truth is in our grasp, then it seems a piece of idle fantasticality to preach so solemnly our duty of waiting for the bell. Indeed we may wait if we will; but we do so at our peril, as much as if we believed. In *either* case we *act*, taking our life in our hands. No one of us ought to issue vetoes to the other, nor should we bandy words of abuse. We ought, on the contrary, delicately and profoundly to respect one another's mental freedom—then only shall we bring about the intellectual republic; then only shall we have that spirit of inner tolerance without which all our outer tolerance is soulless, and which is empiricism's glory; then only shall we live and let live, in speculative as well as in practical things.

I began by a reference to Sir James Fitz-James Stephen; let me end by a quotation from him. "What do you think of yourself? What do you think of the world?... These are questions with which all must deal as it seems good to them. They are riddles of the Sphinx, and in some way or other we must deal with them. . . . In all important transactions of life we have to take a leap in the dark . . . If we decide to leave the riddles unanswered, that is a choice; if we waver in our answer, that, too, is a choice: but whatever choice we make, we

---

[6] Since belief is measured by action, he who forbids us to believe religion to be true, necessarily also forbids us to act as we should if we did believe it to be true. [Editor: In later versions, James added the following "The whole defense of religious faith hinges upon action. If the action required or inspired by the religious hypothesis is in no way different from that dictated by the naturalistic hypothesis, then religious faith is a pure superfluity, better pruned away, and controversy about its legitimacy is a piece of idle trifling, unworthy of serious minds. I myself believe, of course, that the religious hypothesis gives to the world an expression which specifically determines our reactions, and makes them in a large part unlike what they might be on a purely naturalistic scheme of belief."]

make it at our peril. If a man chooses to turn his back altogether on God and the future, no one can prevent him; no one can show beyond reasonable doubt that he is mistaken. If a man thinks otherwise and acts as he thinks, I do not see that any one can prove that *he* is mistaken. Each must act as he thinks best; and if he is wrong, so much the worse for him. We stand on a mountain pass in the midst of whirling snow and blinding mist, through which we get glimpses now and then of paths which may be deceptive. If we stand still we shall be frozen to death. If we take the wrong road we shall be dashed to pieces. We do not certainly know whether there is any right one. What must we do? 'Be strong and of a good courage.' Act for the best, hope for the best, and take what comes. . . . If death ends all, we cannot meet death better."[7]

William James
Harvard University

---

[7] *Liberty, Equality, Fraternity*, p. 353, 2d edition. London, 1874.

WHY *GOD* ALLOWS EVIL (1996/2010)

Richard Swinburne

Richard Granville Swinburne (1934–) was born in Staffordshire, England. After schooling at Charterhouse, he fulfilled his compulsory national service in the Royal Navy as a Russian translator. At age 20, he received a scholarship to study at Exeter College, Oxford. There, he studied philosophy, politics, and economics, earning the BA degree at age 25. The clarity and rigor of the ordinary-language philosophy taught at Oxford gave him a desire to clarify and justify the claims of Christianity. Intending to become ordained, he took a diploma in theology at St. Steven's House (an Anglican theological college in Oxford) and then devoted his full attention to philosophy. Research fellowships at St John's College, Oxford, and at the University of Leeds enabled Swinburne to study the history and philosophy of the physical and biological sciences. At age 29, he accepted a lectureship at the University of Hull. At Hull, he wrote <u>Space and Time</u> (1968), a book that tied relativity and cosmology into metaphysics; then <u>The Concept of Miracle</u> (1971), his first book on religion; and then <u>An Introduction to Confirmation Theory</u> (1973), an important book on the foundations of probability theory that examined what gives evidence for what. At age 38 (1972), Swinburne accepted appointment as Professor of Philosophy at the University of Keele, where he focused on religion, writing <u>The Coherence of Theism</u> (1977), <u>The Existence of God</u> (1979), and <u>Faith and Reason</u> (1981). His Gifford Lectures (1982–1984) treated the relation of mind and body and led to the publication (with Sidney Shoemaker) of <u>Personal Identity</u> (1984) and <u>The Evolution of the Soul</u> (1986). Following his appointment as Nolloth Professor of the Philosophy of Christian Religion, he undertook to justify the claims of Christian doctrine in <u>Miracles</u> (1989), <u>Responsibility and Atonement</u> (1989), <u>Revelation</u> (1991), <u>The Christian God</u> (1994), <u>Is There a God?</u> (1996), <u>Simplicity as Evidence of Truth</u> (1997), <u>Providence and the Problem of Evil</u> (1998), <u>Epistemic Justification</u> (2001), and <u>The Resurrection of God Incarnate</u> (2003). These are mostly technical works of academic philosophy. A notable exception is

Is There a God?, *a popularized summary of his arguments for the exist-ence of God and the plausibility of belief, now available in 22 languages. Swinburne was elected fellow of the British Academy in 1992. In 1995, he joined the Orthodox Church. He has lectured throughout the world and has accepted several visiting professorships (some in America). He retired in 2002 to emeritus status, but continues to work on updates and revisions of his many works.*

What to look for: *It seems clear to many persons that if an all knowing, all loving, and perfectly good God were to exist, there would not be so much evil in the world. They conclude that such a god does not exist. Swinburne challenges this argument by attempting to show how evil is necessary—perhaps even desirable—in the most desirable world possi-ble. How do moral and natural evil differ? What choices must a god make in designing a universe? Why is it better to let inhabitants be cocreators rather than mere residents? What are the necessary conditions if inhabit-ants are to be cocreators? What are the necessary conditions of signifi-cant free will and what "side effects" necessarily follow? Why must man be depraved? What is the "point" of suffering? Why is it sometimes a privilege to suffer? Is there a limit to suffering? Why does God "hide" from us? How does the free-will defense relate to natural evil? How does Swinburne justify the suffering of animals? Does it make any difference to Swinburne's defense if heaven, as traditionally conceived, actually exists?*

This world . . . contains much evil. An omnipotent God could have prevented this evil, and surely a perfectly good and omnipotent God would have done so. So why is there this evil? Is not its existence strong evidence against the exist-ence of God? It would be unless we can construct what is known as a theodicy, an explanation of why God would allow such evil to occur. I believe that that can be done . . . I emphasize that . . . in writing that God would do this or that, I am not taking for granted the existence of God, but merely claiming that, if there is a God, it is to be expected that he would do certain things, including allowing the occurrence of certain evils; and so, I am claiming, their occur-rence is not evidence against his existence.

It is inevitable that any attempt . . . to construct a theodicy will sound callous, indeed totally insensitive to human suffering . . . I can only ask the reader to believe that I am not totally insensitive to human suffering, and that I do mind about the agony of poisoning, [85] child abuse, bereavement, solitary imprisonment, and marital infidelity as much as anyone else . . . .Yet there is a problem about why God allows evil, and, if the theist does not have (in a cool moment) a satisfactory answer to it, then his belief in God is less than rational, and there is no reason why the atheist should share it. To appreciate the argument of this chapter, each of us needs to stand back a bit from the particular situation of his or her own life and that of close relatives and friends (which can so easily seem the only important thing in the world), and ask very generally what good things would a generous and everlasting God give to human beings in the course of a short earthly life. Of course thrills of pleasure and periods of contentment are good things, and—other things being equal—God would certainly seek to provide plenty of those. But a generous God will seek to give deeper good things than these. He will seek to give us great responsibility for ourselves, each other, and the world, and thus a share in his own creative activity of determining what sort of world it is to be. And he will seek to make our lives valuable, of great use to ourselves and each other. The problem is that **God cannot give us these goods in full measure without allowing much evil on the way** . . .

[T]here are plenty of evils, positive bad states, which God could if he chose remove. I divide these into moral evils and natural evils. I understand by **'natural evil'** all evil which is not deliberately produced by human beings and which is not allowed by human beings to occur as [86] a result of their negligence. Natural evil includes both physical suffering and mental suffering, of animals as well as humans; all the trail of suffering which disease, natural disasters, and accidents unpredictable by humans bring in their train. **'Moral evil'** I understand as including all evil caused deliberately by humans doing what they ought not to do (or allowed to occur by humans negligently failing to do what they ought to do) *and* also the evil constituted by such deliberate actions or negligent failure . . .

MORAL EVIL

The central core of any theodicy must, I believe, be the 'free-will defence', which deals—to start with—with moral evil, but can be extended to deal with much natural evil as well. **The free-will defence** claims that it is a great good that humans have a certain sort of free will which I shall call free and responsible choice, but that, if they do, then necessarily there will be the natural possibility of moral evil. (By the 'natural possibility' I mean that it will not be determined in advance whether or not the evil will occur.) A God who gives humans such free will necessarily bring about the possibility, and puts outside his own control whether or not that evil occurs. It is not logically possible— that is, it would be self-contradictory to suppose—that God could give us such free will and yet ensure that we always use it in the right way . . . I have urged . . . that humans do have such free will. But humans could have that kind of free will merely in virtue of being able to choose freely between two equally good and unimportant alternatives. [87] Free and responsible choice is rather free will . . . to make significant choices between good and evil, which make a big difference to the agent, to others, and to the world . . .

[H]umans are so made that they can form their characters. Aristotle famously remarked: 'we become just by doing just acts, prudent by doing prudent acts, brave by doing brave acts'. That is, by doing a just act when it is difficult—when it goes against our natural inclinations (which is what I understand by desires)—we make it easier to do a just act next time . . . Thereby we can free ourselves from the power of the less good desires to which we are subject. And, by choosing to acquire knowledge and to use it to build machines of various sorts, humans can extend the range of the differences they can make to the world—they can build universities to last for centuries, or save energy for the next generation; and by co-operative effort over many decades they can eliminate poverty. The possibilities for free and responsible choice are enormous.

It is **good that the free choices of humans should include genuine responsibility for other humans, and that involves the opportunity to benefit or harm them**. God has the power to benefit or to harm humans. If other agents are to be given a share in his creative work, it is good that they have that power too (although perhaps to a lesser degree). A world in which agents can benefit each other but not do each other harm is one where they have only very limited responsibility for each other. If my responsibility for you is limited to whether or not to give you a camcorder, but I cannot cause you pain, stunt your growth, or limit your education, then I do not have a great deal of responsibility [88] for you. A God who gave agents only such limited responsibilities for their fellows would not have given much. God would have reserved for himself the all-important choice of the kind of world it was to be, while simply allowing humans the minor choice of filling in the details . . . A good God, like a good father, will delegate responsibility. In order to allow creatures a share in creation, he will allow them the choice of hurting and maiming, of frustrating the divine plan. Our world is one where creatures have just such deep responsibility for each other. I cannot only benefit my children, but harm them. One way in which I can harm them is that I can inflict physical pain on them. But there are much more damaging things which I can do to them. Above all I can stop them growing into creatures with significant knowledge, power, and freedom; I can determine whether they come to have the kind of free and responsible choice which I have. The possibility of humans bringing about significant evil is a logical consequence of their having this free and responsible choice. Not even God could give us this choice without the possibility of resulting evil.

Now . . . an action would not be intentional unless it was done for a reason—that is, seen as in some way a good thing (either in itself or because of its consequences). And, if reasons alone influence actions, that regarded by the subject as most important will determine what is done . . . If an agent does not do the action which he regards as overall the best, he must have allowed factors other than reason to exert an influence on him. In other words, he must have allowed desires for what he regards as good only in a certain respect, but not overall, to influence his conduct. So, **in order to have a choice between good and evil, agents** [89] **need already a certain depravity**, in the sense of a system of desires for what they correctly believe to be evil. I need to *want* to overeat, get more than my fair share of money or power, indulge my sexual appetites even by deceiving my spouse or partner, want to see you hurt, if I am to have choice between good and evil. This depravity is itself an evil which is a necessary condition of the greater good. It makes possible a choice made seriously and deliberately, because made in the face of a genuine alternative. I stress that, according to the free-will defence, it is the natural possibility of moral evil which is the necessary condition of the great good, not the actual evil itself. Whether that occurs is (through God's choice) outside God's control and up to us.

Note further and crucially that, if I suffer in consequence of your freely chosen bad action, that is not by any means pure loss for me. In a certain respect it is a good for *me*. My suffering would be pure loss for me if the only good thing in life was sensory pleasure, and the only bad thing sensory pain . . . If these were the only good and bad things, the occurrence of suffering would indeed be a conclusive objection to the existence of God. But we have already noted the great good of freely choosing and influencing our future, that of our fellows, and that of the world. And now note another great good—the good of our life serving a purpose, of being of use to ourselves and others. Recall the words of Christ, 'it is more blessed to give than to receive' (as quoted by St Paul (Acts 20: 35)). We tend to think, when the beggar appears on our doorstep and we feel obliged to give and do give, that that was lucky for him but not for us who happened to be at home. That is not what Christ's words say. They say that *we* are the lucky ones, not just because we have a lot, out of which we can give a little, but because we are privileged to contribute to the beggar's happiness—and that privilege is worth a lot more than money. And, just as it is a great good freely to choose to do good, so it is also a good to be used by someone else for a worthy purpose (so long, that is, that he or she has the right, the authority, to use us in this way). **Being allowed to suffer to make possible a great good is a privilege**, even [90] if the privilege is forced upon you. Those who are allowed to die for their country and thereby save their country from foreign oppression are privileged. Cultures less obsessed than our own by the evil of purely physical pain have always recognized that. And they have recognized that it is still a blessing, even if the one who died had been conscripted to fight . . .

It follows from that fact that being of use is a benefit for him who is of use, that those who suffer at the hands of others and thereby make possible the good of those others who have free and responsible choice, are themselves benefited in this respect. I am fortunate if the natural possibility of my suffering if you choose to hurt me is the vehicle which makes your choice really matter. My vulnerability, my openness to suffering (which necessarily involves my actually suffering if you make the wrong choice), means that you are not just like a pilot in a simulator, where it does not matter if mistakes are made. That our choices matter tremendously, that we can make great differences to things for good or ill, is one of the greatest gifts a creator can give us. And if my suffering [91] is the means by which he can give you that choice, I too am in this respect fortunate. Though of course suffering is in itself a bad thing, my good fortune is that the suffering is not random, pointless suffering. It is suffering which is a consequence of my vulnerability which makes me of such use.

Someone may object that the only good thing is not *being* of use (dying for one's country or being vulnerable to suffering at your hands), but *believing* that one is of use—believing that one is dying for one's country and that this is of use; the 'feel-good' experience. But that cannot be correct. Having comforting beliefs is only a good thing if they are true beliefs . . . [T]he belief that I am vulnerable to suffering at your hands, and that that is a good thing, can only be a good thing if **being vulnerable to suffering at your hands is itself a good thing (independently of whether I believe it or not)**. Certainly, when my life is of use and that is a good for me, it is even better if I believe it and get comfort therefrom; but it can only be even better if it is already a good for me whether I believe it or not.

But though suffering may in these ways serve good purposes, **does God have the right to allow me to suffer for your benefit**, without asking my permission? For surely, an objector will say, no one has the right to allow one person A to suffer for the benefit of another one B without A's consent. We judge that doctors who use patients as involuntary objects of experimentation in medical experiments, which they hope will produce results that can be used to benefit others are doing something wrong. After all, if my arguments about the utility of suffering are sound, ought we not all to be causing suffering to others [92] in order that those others may have the opportunity to react in the right way?

There are, however, crucial differences between God and the doctors. The first is that **God as the author of our being has certain rights**, a certain authority **over us, which we do not have over our fellow humans**. He is the cause of our existence at each moment of our existence and sustains the laws of nature which give us everything we are and have. To allow someone to suffer for his own good or that of others, one has to stand in some kind of parental relationship towards him. I do not have the right to let some stranger suffer for the sake of some good, when I could easily prevent this, but I do have *some* right of this kind in respect of my own children. I may let the younger son suffer *somewhat* for his own good or that of his brother. I have this right because in small part I am responsible for the younger son's existence, his beginning and continuance. If I have begotten him, nourished, and educated him, I have some limited rights over him in return; to a *very limited* extent I can use him for some worthy purpose. If this is correct, then a God who is so much more the author of our being than are our parents has so much more right in this respect. But doctors do not have over their patients even the limited rights that parents have over their children.

But secondly and all-importantly, the doctors *could* have asked the patients for permission; and the patients, being free agents of some power and knowledge, could have made an informed choice of whether or not to allow themselves to be used. By contrast, **God's choice is** not about how to use already existing agents, but **about the sort of agents to make and the sort of world into which to put them**. In God's situation there are no agents to be asked. I am arguing that it is good that one agent A should have deep responsibility for another B (who in turn could have deep responsibility for another C). It is not logically possible for God to have asked B if he wanted things thus, for, if A is to be responsible for B's growth in freedom, knowledge, and power, there will not be a B with enough freedom and knowledge to make any choice, before God has to choose whether or not to give A responsibility for [93] him. One cannot ask a baby into which sort of world he or she wishes to be born. The creator has to make the choice independently of his creatures. He will seek on balance to benefit them— all of them. And, in giving them the gift of life—whatever suffering goes with it—that is a substantial benefit. But when one suffers at the hands of another, often perhaps it is not enough of a benefit to outweigh the suffering. Here is the point to recall that it is an additional benefit to the sufferer that his suffering is the means whereby the one who hurt him had the opportunity to make a significant choice between good and evil which otherwise he would not have had.

Although for these reasons, as I have been urging, God has the right to allow humans to cause each other to suffer, **there must be** . . . limits even to the moral right of God, our creator and sustainer, to use free sentient beings as pawns in a greater game. Yet, if these limits were too narrow, God would be unable to give humans much real responsibility; he would be able to allow them only to play a toy game. Still, limits there must be to God's rights to allow humans to hurt each other; and limits there are in the world to the extent to which they can hurt each other, provided above all by the short finite life enjoyed by humans and other creatures—one human can hurt another for no more than eighty years or so. And there are a number of other safety-devices in-built into our physiology and psychology, limiting the amount of pain we can suffer. But the primary safety limit is that provided by the shortness of our finite life. Unending unchosen suffering would indeed to my mind provide a very strong argument against the existence of God. But that is not the human situation.

So then God, without asking humans, has to choose for them between the kinds of world in which they can live—basically either a world in which there is very little opportunity for humans to benefit or harm each other, or a world in which there is considerable opportunity. How [94] shall he choose? There are clearly reasons for both choices. But it seems to me (just, on balance) that his choosing to create the world in which we have considerable opportunity to benefit or harm each other is to bring about a good at least as great as the evil which he thereby allows to occur. *Of course* the suffering he allows is a bad thing; and, other things being equal, to be avoided. But having the natural possibility of causing suffering makes possible a greater good. God, in creating humans who (of logical necessity) cannot choose for themselves the kind of world into which they are to come, plausibly exhibits his goodness in making for them the heroic choice that they come into a risky world where they may have to suffer for the good of others.

NATURAL EVIL

Natural evil is not to be accounted for along the same lines as moral evil. Its main role rather, I suggest, is to make it possible for humans to have the kind of choice which the free-will defence extols, and to make available to humans specially worthwhile kinds of choice.

There are two ways in which natural evil operates to give humans those choices. First, **the operation of natural laws producing evils gives humans knowledge** (if they choose to seek it) of how to bring about such evils themselves. Observing you catch some disease by the operation of natural processes gives me the power either to use those processes to give that disease to other people, or through negligence to allow others to catch it, or to take measures to prevent others from catching the disease. Study of the mechanisms of nature producing various evils (and goods) opens up for humans a wide range of choice. This is the way in which in fact we learn how to bring about (good and) evil. But could not God give us the requisite knowledge (of how to bring about good or evil) which we need in order to have free and responsible choice by a less costly means? Could he not just whisper in our ears from time to time what are the different consequences of different actions of ours? Yes. But anyone who believed that an action of his would have some effect because he believed that God had told him so would see all his actions [95] as done under the all-watchful eye of God. He would not merely believe strongly that there was a God, but would know it with real certainty. That knowledge would greatly inhibit his freedom of choice, would make it very difficult for him to choose to do evil. This is because we all have a natural inclination to wish to be thought well of by everyone, and above all by an all-good God . . . Natural processes alone give humans knowledge of the effects of their actions without inhibiting their freedom, and if evil is to be a possibility for them they must know how to allow it to occur.

The other way in which **natural** evil operates to give humans their freedom is that it **makes possible certain kinds of action towards it between which agents can choose**. It increases the range of significant choice. A particular natural evil, such as physical pain, gives to the sufferer a choice—whether to endure it with patience, or to bemoan his lot. His friend can choose whether to show compassion towards the sufferer, or to be callous. The pain makes possible these choices, which would not otherwise exist. There is no guarantee that our actions in response to the pain will be good ones, but the pain gives us the opportunity to perform good actions. The good or bad actions which we perform in the face of natural evil themselves provide opportunities for further choice—of good or evil stances towards the former actions . . . The actions which natural evil makes [96] possible are ones which allow us to perform at our best and interact with our fellows at the deepest level.

It may, however, be suggested that adequate opportunity for these great good actions would be provided by the occurrence of moral evil without any need for suffering to be caused by natural processes. You can show courage when threatened by a gunman, as well as when threatened by cancer; and show sympathy to those likely to be killed by gunmen as well as to those likely to die of cancer. But just imagine all the suffering of mind and body caused by disease, earthquake, and accident unpreventable by humans removed at a stroke from our society. No sickness, no bereavement in consequence of the untimely death of the young. Many of us would then have such an easy life that we simply would not have much opportunity to show courage or, indeed, manifest much in the way of great goodness at all. We need those insidious processes of decay and dissolution which money and strength cannot ward off for long to give us the opportunities, so easy otherwise to avoid, to become heroes.

God has the right to allow natural evils to occur (for the same reason as he has the right to allow moral evils to occur)—up to a limit. It would, of course, be crazy for God to multiply evils more and more in order to give endless opportunity for heroism, but to have *some* significant opportunity for real heroism and consequent character formation is a benefit for the person to whom it is given. Natural evils give to us the knowledge to make a range of choices between good and evil, and the opportunity to perform actions of especially valuable kinds.

There is, however, no reason to suppose that **animals** have free will. So **what about their suffering?** Animals had been suffering for a long time before humans appeared on this planet—just how long depends on which animals are conscious beings. The first thing to take into account here is that, while the higher animals, at any rate the vertebrates, suffer, it is most unlikely that they suffer nearly as much as humans do. Given that suffering depends directly on brain events (in turn caused by events in other parts of the body), then, since the lower animals do not suffer at all and humans suffer a lot, animals of intermediate complexity (it is [97] reasonable to suppose) suffer only a moderate amount. So, while one does need a theodicy to account for why God allows animals to suffer, one does not need as powerful a theodicy as one does in respect of humans. One only needs reasons adequate to account for God allowing an amount of suffering much less than that of humans. That said, there is, I believe, available for animals parts of the theodicy which I have outlined above for humans.

The good of animals, like that of humans, does not consist solely in thrills of pleasure. For animals, too, there are more worthwhile things, and in particular intentional actions, and among them serious significant intentional actions. The life of animals involves many serious significant intentional actions. Animals look for a mate, despite being tired and failing to find one. They take great trouble to build nests and feed their young, to decoy predators and explore. But all this inevitably involves pain (going on despite being tired) and danger. An animal cannot intentionally avoid forest fires, or take trouble to rescue its offspring from forest fires, unless there exists a serious danger of getting caught in a forest fire. The action of rescuing despite danger simply cannot be done unless the danger exists—and the danger will not exist unless there is a significant natural probability of being caught in the fire. Animals do not choose freely to do such actions, but the actions are nevertheless worthwhile. It is great that animals feed their young, not just themselves; that animals explore when they know it to be dangerous; that animals save each other from predators, and so on. These are the things that give the lives of animals their value. But they do often involve some suffering to some creatures.

To return to the central case of humans—the reader will agree with me to the extent to which he or she values responsibility, free choice, and being of use very much more than thrills of pleasure or absence of pain. There is no other way to get the evils of this world into the right perspective, except to reflect at length on innumerable, very detailed thought experiments (in addition to actual experiences of life) in which we postulate very different sorts of worlds from our own, and then ask ourselves whether the perfect goodness of God would require him to [98] create one of these (or no world at all) rather than our own. But **I conclude with a very small thought experiment**, which may help to begin this process. Suppose that you exist in another world before your birth in this one, and are given a choice as to the sort of life you are to have in this one. You are told that you are to have only a short life, maybe of only a few minutes, although it will be an adult life in the sense that you will have the richness of sensation and belief characteristic of adults. You have a choice as to the sort of life you will have. You can have either a few minutes of very considerable pleasure, of the kind produced by some drug such as heroin, which you will experience by yourself and which will have no effects at all in the world (for example, no one else will know about it); or you can have a few minutes of considerable pain, such as the pain of childbirth, which will have (unknown to you at the time of pain) considerable good effects on others over a few years. You are told that, if you do not make the second choice, those others will never exist—and so you are under no moral obligation to make the second choice. But you seek to make the choice which will make *your* own life the best life for *you* to have led. How will you choose? The choice is, I hope, obvious. You should choose the second alternative.

For someone who remains unconvinced by my claims about the relative strengths of the good and evils involved—holding that, great though the goods are, they do not justify the evils which they involve—there is a fall-back position. My arguments may have convinced you of the greatness of the goods involved sufficiently for you to allow that a perfectly good God would be justified in bringing about the evils for the sake of the good which they make possible, if and only if God also provided **compensation in the form of happiness after death to the victims whose sufferings make possible the goods** . . . While believing that God does provide at any rate for many humans such life after death, I have expounded a theodicy without relying on this assumption. But I can [99] understand someone thinking that the assumption is needed, especially when we are considering the worst evils. (This compensatory after-life need not necessarily be the everlasting life of Heaven.)

It remains the case, however, that evil is evil, and there is a substantial price to pay for the goods of our world which it makes possible. God would not be less than perfectly good if he created instead a world without pain and suffering, and so without the particular goods which those evils make possible. Christian, Islamic, and much Jewish tradition claims that God has created worlds of both kinds—our world, and the **Heaven** of the blessed. The latter is a marvelous world with a vast range of possible deep goods, but it lacks a few goods which our world contains, including the good of being able to reject the good. A generous God might well choose to give some of us the choice of rejecting the good in a world like ours before giving to those who embrace it a wonderful world in which the former possibility no longer exists.

HUMAN NATURE AND
PERSONAL IDENTITY

THE RING OF GYGES
(390?–370? BC)

Plato

Plato—see p. 23.

What to look for: Socrates has held that it is always better to be just than unjust. Thrasymachus has argued to the contrary that "justice is the advantage of the stronger" [338c]. In this selection from Book II, Glaucon (Plato's brother) revisits the matter. What are three classes of goods and how are they ranked? In which class is justice? What three steps does Glaucon propose to revive Thrasymachus' argument? How does each step go? What is the popular view as to the origin of justice? Would you want Gyges ring? Why (not)? If you were given it, what would you do? What can we conclude from all this as to the nature of man?

[Stephanus 357] WITH these words I [Socrates] was thinking that I had made an end of the discussion; but the end, in truth, proved to be only a beginning. For Glaucon, who is always the most pugnacious of men, was dissatisfied at Thrasymachus' retirement; he wanted to have the battle out. So he said to me: Socrates, do you wish really to persuade us, or only to seem to have persuaded us, that to be just is always better than to be unjust?

I should wish really to persuade you, I replied, if I could. Then you certainly have not succeeded. Let me ask you now: —How would you arrange goods—are there not some which we welcome for their own sakes, and independently of their consequences, as, for example, harmless pleasures and enjoyments, which delight us at the time, although nothing follows from them?

I agree in thinking that there is such a class, I replied.

Is there not also a second class of goods, such as knowledge, sight, health, which are desirable not only in themselves, but also for their results?

Certainly, I said.

"Apology," by Plato, from *The Republic of Plato: Translated into English with Introduction, Analysis, Marginal Analysis, and Index.* Trans. B. Jowett. 3rd ed. (Oxford: Clarendon Press, 1888).

And would you not recognize a third class, such as gymnastic, and the care of the sick, and the physician's art; also the various ways of money-making — these do us good but we regard them as disagreeable; and no one would choose them for their own sakes, but only for the sake of some reward or result which flows from them?

There is, I said, this third class also. But why do you ask?

Because I want to know in which of the three classes you would place justice?

In the highest class, I replied, —among those goods which [358] he who would be happy desires both for their own sake and for the sake of their results.

Then the many are of another mind; they think that justice is to be reckoned in the troublesome class, among goods which are to be pursued for the sake of rewards and of reputation, but in, themselves are disagreeable and rather to be avoided.

I know, I said, that this is their manner of thinking, and that this was the thesis which Thrasymachus was maintaining just now, when he censured justice and praised injustice. But I am too stupid to be convinced by him.

I wish, he said, that you would hear me as well as him, and then I shall see whether you and I agree. For Thrasymachus seems to me, like a snake, to have been charmed by your voice sooner than he ought to have been; but to my mind the nature of justice and injustice have not yet been made clear. Setting aside their rewards and results, I want to know what they are in themselves, and how they inwardly work in the soul. If you please, then, I will revive the argument of Thrasymachus. And first I will speak of the nature and origin of justice according to the common view of them. Secondly, I will show that all men who practise justice do so against their will, of necessity, but not as a good. And thirdly, I will argue that there is reason in this view, for the life of the unjust is after all better far than the life of the just —if what they say is true, Socrates, since I myself am not of their opinion. But still I acknowledge that I am perplexed when I hear the voices of Thrasymachus and myriads of others dinning in my ears; and, on the other hand, I have never yet heard the superiority of justice to injustice maintained by any one in a satisfactory way. I want to hear justice praised in respect of itself; then I shall be satisfied, and you are the person from whom I think that I am most likely to hear this; and therefore I will praise the unjust life to the utmost of my power, and my manner of speaking will indicate the manner in which I desire to hear you too praising justice and censuring injustice. Will you say whether you approve of my proposal?

Indeed I do; nor can I imagine any theme about which a man of sense would oftener wish to Converse.

I am delighted, he replied, to hear you say so, and shall begin by speaking, as I proposed, of the nature and origin of justice.

They say that to do injustice is, by nature, good; to suffer injustice, evil; but that the evil is greater than the good. And so when men have both done and suffered injustice and have had experience of both, not being able to avoid the one [359] and obtain the other, they think that they had better agree among themselves to have neither; hence there arise laws and mutual covenants; and that which is ordained by law is termed by them lawful and just. This they affirm to be the origin and nature of justice; —it is a mean or compromise, between the best of all, which is to do injustice and not be punished, and the worst of all, which is to suffer injustice without the power of retaliation; and justice, being at a middle point between the two, is tolerated not as a good, but as the lesser evil, and honoured by reason of the inability of men to do injustice. For no man who is worthy to be called a man would ever submit to such an agreement if he were able to resist; he would be mad if he did. Such is the received account, Socrates, of the nature and origin of justice.

Now that those who practise justice do so involuntarily and because they have not the power to be unjust will best appear if we imagine something of this kind: having given both to the just and the unjust power to do what they will, let us watch and see whither desire will lead them; then we shall discover in the very act the just and unjust man to be proceeding along the same road, following their interest, which all natures deem to be their good, and are only diverted into the path of justice by the force of law. The liberty which we are supposing, may be most completely given to them in the form of such a power as is said to have been possessed by Gyges, the ancestor of Croesus the Lydian. According to the tradition, Gyges was a shepherd in the service of the king of Lydia; there was a great storm, and an earthquake made an opening in the earth at the place where he was feeding his flock. Amazed at the sight, he descended into the opening, where, among other marvels, he beheld a hollow brazen horse, having doors, at which he stooping and looking in saw a dead body of stature, as appeared to him, more than human, and having nothing on but a gold ring; this he took from the finger of the dead and reascended. Now the shepherds met together, according to custom, that they might send their monthly report about the flocks to the king; into their assembly he came having the ring on his finger, and as he was sitting among them he chanced to turn the collet of the ring inside his hand, when instantly he became invisible to the rest of the company and they began to speak of him as if he were no longer present. [360] He was astonished at this, and again touching the ring he turned the collet outwards and reappeared; he made several trials of the ring, and always with the same result —when he turned the collet inwards he became invisible, when outwards he reappeared. Whereupon he contrived to be chosen one of the messengers who were sent to the court; where as soon as he arrived he seduced the queen, and with her help conspired against the king and slew him, and took the kingdom. Suppose now that there were two such magic rings, and the just put on one of them and the unjust the other; no man can be imagined to be of such an iron nature that he would stand fast in justice. No man would keep his hands off what was not his own when he could safely take what he liked out of the market, or go into houses and lie with any one at his pleasure, or kill or release from prison whom he would, and in all respects be like a God among men. Then the actions of the just would be as the actions of the unjust; they would both come at last to the same point. And this we may truly affirm to be a great proof that a man is just, not willingly or because he thinks that justice is any good to him individually, but of necessity, for wherever any one thinks that he can safely be unjust, there he is unjust. For all men believe in their hearts that injustice is far more profitable to the individual than justice, and he who argues as I have been supposing, will say that they are right. If you could imagine any one obtaining this power of becoming invisible, and never doing any wrong or touching what was another's, he would be thought by the lookers-on to be a most wretched idiot, although they would praise him to one another's faces, and keep up appearances with one another from a fear that they too might suffer injustice. Enough of this.

Now, if we are to form a real judgment of the life of the just and unjust, we must isolate them; there is no other way; and how is the isolation to be effected? I answer: Let the unjust man be entirely unjust, and the just man entirely just; nothing is to be taken away from either of them, and both are to be perfectly furnished for the work of their respective lives. First, let the unjust be like other distinguished masters of craft; like the skilful pilot or physician, who knows intuitively his own powers and keeps [361] within their limits, and who, if he fails at any point, is able to recover himself. So let the unjust make his unjust attempts in the right way, and lie hidden if he means to be great in his injustice: (he who is found out is nobody:) for the highest reach of injustice is, to be deemed just when you are not. Therefore I say that in the perfectly unjust man we must assume the most perfect injustice; there is to be no deduction, but we must allow him, while doing the most unjust acts, to have acquired the greatest reputation for justice. If he have taken a false step he must be able to recover himself; he must be one who can speak with effect, if any of his deeds come to light, and who can force his way where force is required by his courage and strength, and command of money and friends. And at his side let us place the just man in his nobleness and simplicity, wishing, as Aeschylus says, to be and not to seem good. There must be no seeming, for if he seem to be just he will be honoured and rewarded, and then we shall not know whether he is just for the sake of justice or for the sake of honours and rewards; therefore, let him be clothed in justice only, and have no other covering; and he must be imagined in a state of life the opposite of the former. Let him be the best of men, and let him be thought the worst; then he will have been put to the proof; and we shall see whether he will be affected by the fear of infamy and its consequences. And let him continue thus to the hour of death; being just and seeming to be unjust. When both have reached the uttermost extreme, the one of justice and the other of injustice, let judgment be given which of them is the happier of the two.

Heavens! my dear Glaucon, I said, how energetically you polish them up for the decision, first one and then the other, as if they were two statues.

I do my best, he said. And now that we know what they are like there is no difficulty in tracing out the sort of life which awaits either of them. This I will proceed to describe; but as you may think the description a little too coarse, I ask you to suppose, Socrates, that the words which follow are not mine. —Let me put them into the mouths of the eulogists of injustice: They will tell you that the just man who is thought unjust will be scourged, racked, bound —will have his eyes burnt out; and, at last, after suffering every kind of evil, he will be impaled: Then he will understand that he [362] ought to seem only, and not to be, just; the words of Aeschylus may be more truly spoken of the unjust than of the just. For the unjust is pursuing a reality; he does not live with a view to appearances —he wants to be really unjust and not to seem only: —

'His mind has a soil deep and fertile,
Out of which spring his prudent counsels.'[1]

In the first place, he is thought just, and therefore bears rule in the city; he can marry whom he will, and give in marriage to whom he will; also he can trade and deal where he likes, and always to his own advantage, because he has no misgivings about injustice; and at every contest, whether in public or private, he gets the better of his antagonists, and gains at their expense, and is rich, and out of his gains he can benefit his friends, and harm his enemies; moreover, he can offer sacrifices, and dedicate gifts to the gods abundantly and magnificently, and can honour the gods or any man whom he wants to honour in a far better style than the just, and therefore he is likely to be dearer than they are to the gods. And thus, Socrates, gods and men are said to unite in making the life of the unjust better than the life of the just.

---

[1] Seven against Thebes, 574.

THE MADMAN (1882)

Friedrich Nietzsche

Friedrich Wilhelm Nietzsche [NEE-cha] (1844–1900) was born in Röcken, a village near Leipzig in the Prussian province of Saxony. When he was 5, both his father (a Lutheran pastor) and toddler brother died and the family moved to Naumburg to live with his paternal grand-mother and two unmarried aunts. At 10, he enrolled in the Domgym-nasium, where he excelled in music, language, and religious studies. At 14, he was admitted to the internationally known Schulpforta prepara-tory school, where he was introduced to Greek and Roman literature and to a life beyond his early small-town Christian upbringing. At 20, he entered the University of Bonn to study theology. After his first semester, however, Nietzsche announced that he had lost his faith and turned to classical philology (the study of the history and development of classical languages). The next year (1865), he followed his philology professor to the University of Leipzig and soon was publishing in the field. In Leip-zig, Nietzsche expanded his interests into philosophy, especially that of Arthur Schopenhauer (1788–1860). At 24, he announced that he was giv-ing up philology and joined the Prussian Army. A serious riding accident cut that service short, however, and he accepted the chair of classical philology at the University of Basel (in Switzerland). He renounced his Prussian citizenship, but still took leave to serve as a medical orderly in the Franco-Prussian war (1870–1871), where he witnessed the horrors of war (and contracted diphtheria and dysentery). Back in Basel, Nietzsche became close friends with Richard Wagner. Wagner, who subscribed to Schopenhauer's view that only art can overcome human misery, became something of a surrogate father. In 1872, Nietzsche published Birth of Tragedy out of the Spirit of Music, pessimistically asserting that it is best not to have been born, but failing that, it is best to die young. Using his rising celebrity, Nietzsche promoted construction of the Festival The-atre in Bayreuth (Germany), built solely for the performance of Wag-ner's operas. The Ring of the Nibelung had its first performance there in 1786, and Nietzsche hated it. He started questioning Prussian culture in general (and particularly the rising anti-Semitism) and discovered the French Enlightenment. Rising tensions between Wagner and Nietzsche ended their friendship in 1878, the same year that Nietzsche portrayed his developing individualistic philosophy in Human, All Too Human. In 1879, Nietzsche's failing health forced him to retire from teaching. He became a stateless tourist-scholar, living in boarding houses in Italy, France, and Switzerland. Between 1881 and 1888, he returned repeatedly to a sparsely furnished room in Sils Maria in the Swiss Alps, where he wrote each morning and produced much of his most important work. A rejection when he proposed marriage, a falling out with his mother, and poor health led him to contemplate suicide, but he kept working. In just four days, he wrote the first part of Thus Spoke Zarathustra (published in four parts, 1883–1885). The book did not sell well. Its alienating style and atheistic content brought Nietzsche further isolation. He broke with his anti-Semitic German editor and, though he had little money, printed Beyond Good and Evil (1886) at his own expense. His declining health made it more and more difficult to work. Still, in 1887, he published what may be his most important work, On the Genealogy of Morals. The following year, he wrote Twilight of the Idols, The Antichrist, and the autobiographical Ecce Homo. Between 1872 and 1888, he published nine works and completed four others. In 1889, in Turin, Nietzsche began to write crazy letters in which he claimed to be Jesus, Napoleon, Dionysus, Buddha, or Alexander the Great. Psychiatric treatment in an asylum brought only further decline. His mother and sister cared for him during his final, uncommunicative years (during which his work gained significant recognition and respect). He is buried beside his father at the church in Röcken.

What to look for: *Who is the madman? What does the madman mean by his claim that we have killed God? In what sense is God dead and what brought about this death? What does the absence of God (or even the absence of the idea of God) mean for man? What does "Whither are we moving now?" mean? If there is no ultimate reference point, what are the implications for ethics, for meaning or purpose, for human nature, and for truth?*

"The Madman," by Frederich Nietzsche, from *The Complete Works of Friedrich Nietzsche*. Ed. Oscar Levy. Trans. Thomas Common, Paul Victor Cohn, Maude Dominica, and Mary Petre. Vol. 10, *The Joyful Wisdom* (*La Gaya Scienza*). (New York: Macmillin, 1910).

APHORISM 125

Have you ever heard of the madman who on a bright morning lighted a lantern and ran to the market-place calling out unceasingly: "I seek God! I seek God! "—As there were many people standing about who did not believe in God, he caused a great deal of amusement. Why! is he lost? said one. Has he strayed away like a child? said another. Or does he keep himself hidden? Is he afraid of us? Has he taken a sea-voyage? Has he emigrated? —the people cried out laughingly, all in a hubbub. The insane man jumped into their midst and transfixed them with his glances. "Where is God gone?" he called out. "I mean to tell you! *We have killed him*,—you and I! We are all his murderers! But how have we done it? How were we able to drink up the [168] sea? Who gave us the sponge to wipe away the whole horizon? What did we do when we loosened this earth from its sun? Whither does it now move? Whither do we move? Away from all suns? Do we not dash on unceasingly? Backwards, sideways, forewards, in all directions? Is there still an above and below? Do we not stray, as through infinite nothingness? Does not empty space breathe upon us? Has it not become colder? Does not night come on continually, darker and darker? Shall we not have to light lanterns in the morning? Do we not hear the noise of the grave-diggers who are burying God? Do we not smell the divine putrefaction? —for even Gods putrefy! God is dead! God remains dead! And we have killed him! How shall we console ourselves, the most murderous of all murderers? The holiest and the mightiest that the world has hitherto possessed, has bled to death under our knife,—who will wipe the blood from us? With what water could we cleanse ourselves? What lustrums, what sacred games shall we have to devise? Is not the magnitude of this deed too great for us? Shall we not ourselves have to become Gods, merely to seem worthy of it? There never was a greater event, — and on account of it, all who are born after us belong to a higher history than any history hitherto!" — Here the madman was silent and looked again at his hearers; they also were silent and looked at him in surprise. At last he threw his lantern on the ground, so that it broke in pieces and was extinguished. "I come too early," he then said, " I am not yet at the right time. This [169] prodigious event is still on its way, and is travelling, —it has not yet reached men's ears. Lightning and thunder need time, the light of the stars needs time, deeds need time, even after they are done, to be seen and heard. This deed is as yet further from them than the furthest star, — *and yet they have done it!*"—It is further stated that the madman made his way into different churches on the same day, and there intoned his *Requiem aeternam deo*. When led out and called to account, he always gave the reply: "What are these churches now, if they are not the tombs and monuments of God?"

EXISTENTIALISM IS A HUMANISM (1946)

Jean-Paul Sartre

Jean-Paul Charles Aymard Sartre (1905–1980) was born in Paris, France. Upon his father's death, the 15-month-old and his mother moved in with her father (Albert Schweitzer's brother), a teacher of German in Paris who introduced the small, cross-eyed, socially awkward child to classical literature and mathematics. When Sartre was 12, his mother remarried and moved to La Rochelle. As a teenager, he was attracted to philosophy through reading Essay on the Immediate Data of Conscious-ness by Henri Bergson (1859–1941). At 19, Sartre entered Paris's elite École Normale Supérieure, where he studied Kant, Hegel, Husserl, and Heidegger (among others) and met Maurice Merleau-Ponty, Claude Lévi-Strauss, and Simone de Beauvoir (who became his lifelong companion). He graduated with a doctorate in philosophy in 1929. After two years of conscription in the French Army, he taught philosophy in Le Havre. In 1933, a study grant took him to Berlin, where he formed the core of his own existential philosophy. In 1936, he published Transcendence of the Ego, followed in 1938 by Sketch for a Theory of the Emotions and the groundbreaking novel, Nausea. In 1939 (the start of WWII), Sartre was drafted into the French Army, captured by the Germans, and shipped to Stalag 12D at Trier, Germany (where poor health got him released (in 1941) after only nine months). He returned to teach in Paris, settled near Montparnasse, and met with other intellectuals in cafés (especially Café de Flore) on the Left Bank. During the occupation, he, de Beauvoir, Merleau-Ponty, and others formed the underground group, "Socialisme et Liberté," which dissolved after André Gide and André Malraux chose not to join. Sartre then concentrated on writing. His contributions to clandestine resistance newspapers led to a close friendship with Albert Camus. The scholarly Being and Nothingness and a play, The Flies, came out in 1943. No Exit followed in 1944. After the war, he and de Beauvoir founded a monthly literary/political review, Les Temps Mod-erne. He portrayed his wartime experiences in The Roads to Freedom trilogy (1945–1949). The Roman Catholic Church placed his complete works on its Index of Prohibited Books in 1948. He lived openly and could easily be found chatting in cafés on the Left Bank. His relationship with de Beauvoir did not stop him from having a number of mistresses, and when the press began to hound him for moral corruption and spreading hopelessness among the young, he abandoned his café lifestyle and retreated to his mother's house in the rue Bonaparte, where he could work in peace. He long embraced Communism, but never joined the party. He condemned the Soviet invasion of Budapest in 1956. He struggled to reconcile individualistic existentialism with collectivist communism in his Critique of Dialectical Reason (1960). He met Fidel Castro in Cuba and spent time with Ernesto "Che" Guevara. He supported the socialist National Liberation Front in the Algerian War (1954–1962) and was one of the signatories of the Manifeste des 121. In 1964 (in Words), Sartre renounced literature as a bourgeois substitute for real commitment, and, on that ground, declined the Nobel Prize for Literature. He opposed the Vietnam war and supported the Parisian student strikes of 1968. He slowly became more anarchist than communist. His attempt to justify the 1972 massacre at the Munich Olympics (in which Palestinian terrorists killed 11 Israeli athletes) caused considerable scandal. In declining health, he started to write a biography of Gustave Flaubert and a second volume of the Critique of Dialectical Reason, but finished neither. Fifty-thousand attended his funeral. He is buried in the Cimetière de Montparnasse.

What to look for*: The essence of a thing is the intrinsic nature or indispensable quality (or qualities) that determine what it is. What is human nature? What does "existence precedes essence" mean? To what does it apply? What does "subjectivity" mean? How is value given? What is anguish? What does "abandonment" mean? Whom can we turn to for advice? How are values created? Why does Sartre say that we are condemned to be free? What does Sartre say about despair? Is existentialism a doctrine of quietism? How is life like a painting? Are there excuses?*

What is meant by the term *existentialism*?

Most people who use the word would be rather embarrassed if they had to explain it, since, now that the word is all the rage, even the work of a musician or painter is being called existentialist. A gossip columnist in *Clartes* signs himself *The Existentialist*, so that by this time the word has been so stretched and has taken on so broad a meaning, that it no longer means anything at all.

"Existentialism is a Humanism," by Jean Paul Sartre, from *Existentialism and Human Emotions*. Selection trans. Bernard Frechtmann. (New York: Citadel Press. Kensington Publishing Company. Copyright © 1957, 1985, Philosophical Library Inc.). Used by permission of Philosophical Library.

It seems that for want of an advance-guard doctrine analogous to surrealism, the kind of people who are eager for scandal and flurry turn to this philosophy which in other respects does not at all serve their purposes in this sphere.

Actually, it is the least scandalous, the most austere of doctrines. It is intended strictly for specialists and philosophers. Yet it can be defined easily. What complicates matters is that [13] there are two kinds of existentialist; first, those who are Christian, among whom I would include Jaspers and Gabriel Marcel, both Catholic; and on the other hand the atheistic existentialists, among whom I class Heidegger, and then the French existentialists and myself. What they have in common is that they think that existence precedes essence, or, if you prefer, that subjectivity must be the starting point.

Just what does that mean? Let us consider some object that is manufactured, for example, a book or a paper-cutter: here is an object which has been made by an artisan whose inspiration came from a concept. He referred to the concept of what a paper-cutter is and likewise to a known method of production, which is part of the concept, something which is, by and large, a routine. Thus, the paper-cutter is at once an object produced in a certain way and, on the other hand, one having a specific use; and one can not postulate a man who produces a paper-cutter but does not know what it is used for. Therefore, let us say that, for the paper-cutter, essence—that is, the ensemble of both the production routines and the properties which enable it to be both produced and defined—precedes existence. Thus, the presence of the paper-cutter or book in front of me [14] is determined. Therefore, we have here a technical view of the world whereby it can be said that production precedes existence.

When we conceive God as the Creator, He is generally thought of as a superior sort of artisan. Whatever doctrine we may be considering, whether one like that of Descartes or that of Leibnitz, we always grant that will more or less follows understanding or, at the very least, accompanies it, and that when God creates He knows exactly what He is creating. Thus, the concept of man in the mind of God is comparable to the concept of paper-cutter in the mind of the manufacturer, and, following certain techniques and a conception, God produces man, just as the artisan, following a definition and a technique, makes a paper-cutter. Thus, the individual man is the realization of a certain concept in the divine intelligence.

In the eighteenth century, the atheism of the *philosophes* discarded the idea of God, but not so much for the notion that essence precedes existence. To a certain extent, this idea is found everywhere; we find it in Diderot, in Voltaire, and even in Kant. Man has a human nature; this human nature, which is the concept of the human, is found in all men, which means that each man is a particular example of a universal concept, man. In Kant, the [15] result of this universality is that the wild-man, the natural man, as well as the bourgeois, are circumscribed by the same definition and have the same basic qualities. Thus, here too the essence of man precedes the historical existence that we find in nature.

Atheistic existentialism, which I represent, is more coherent. It states that if God does not exist, there is at least one being in whom existence precedes essence, a being who exists before he can be defined by any concept, and that this being is man, or, as Heidegger says, human reality. What is meant here by saying that existence precedes essence? It means that, first of all, man exists, turns up, appears on the scene, and, only afterwards, defines himself. If man, as the existentialist conceives him, is indefinable, it is because at first he is nothing. Only afterward will he be something, and he himself will have made what he will be. Thus, there is no human nature, since there is no God to conceive it. Not only is man what he conceives himself to be, but he is also only what he wills himself to be after this thrust toward existence.

Man is nothing else but what he makes of himself. Such is the first principle of existentialism. It is also what is called subjectivity, the name we are labeled with when charges are brought against us. But what do we mean [16] by this, if not that man has a greater dignity than a stone or table? For we mean that man first exists, that is, that man first of all is the being who hurls himself toward a future and who is conscious of imagining himself as being in the future. Man is at the start a plan which is aware of itself, rather than a patch of moss, a piece of garbage, or a cauliflower; nothing exists prior to this plan; there is nothing in heaven; man will be what he will have planned to be. Not what he will want to be. Because by the word "will" we generally mean a conscious decision, which is subsequent to what we have already made of ourselves. I may want to belong to a political party, write a book, get married; but all that is only a manifestation of an earlier, more spontaneous choice that is called "will" But if existence really does precede essence, man is responsible for what he is. Thus, existentialism's first move is to make every man aware of what he is and to make the full responsibility of his existence rest on him. And when we say that a man is responsible for himself, we do not only mean that he is responsible for his own individuality, but that he is responsible for all men.

The word subjectivism has two meanings, and our opponents play on the two. Subjectivism means, on the one hand, that an individual chooses and makes himself; and, on the other, [17] that it is impossible for man to transcend human subjectivity. The second of these is the essential meaning of existentialism. When we say that man chooses his own self, we mean that every one of us does likewise; but we also mean by that that in making this choice he also chooses all men. In fact, in creating the man that we want to be, there is not a single one of our acts which does not at the same time create an image of man as we think he ought to be. To choose to be this or that is to affirm at the same time the value of what we choose, because we can never choose evil. We always choose the good, and nothing can be good for us without being good for all.

If, on the other hand, existence precedes essence, and if we grant that we exist and fashion our image at one and the same time, the image is valid for everybody and for our whole age. Thus, our responsibility is much greater than we might have supposed, because it involves all mankind. If I am a working-man and choose to join a Christian trade-union rather than be a communist, and if by being a member I want to show that the best thing for man is resignation, that the kingdom of man is not of this world, I am not only involving my own case—I want to be resigned for everyone. As a result, my action has involved all humanity. To take a more individual matter, if I [18] want to marry, to have children; even if this marriage depends solely on my own circumstances or passion or wish, I am involving all humanity in monogamy and not merely myself. Therefore, I am responsible for myself and for everyone else. I am creating a certain image of man of my own choosing. In choosing myself, I choose man.

This helps us understand what the actual content is of such rather grandiloquent words as anguish, forlornness and despair. As you will see, it's all quite simple.

First, what is meant by anguish? The existentialists say at once that man is anguish. What that means is this: the man who involves himself and who realizes that he is not only the person he chooses to be, but also a law maker who is, at the same time, choosing all mankind as well as himself, can not help escape the feeling of his total and deep responsibility. Of course, there are many people who are not anxious; but we claim that they are hiding their anxiety, that they are fleeing from it. Certainly, many people believe that when they do something, they themselves are the only ones involved, and when someone says to them, "What if everyone acted that way?" They shrug their shoulders and answer, "Everyone doesn't act that way." But really, one should always ask himself, "What would [19] happen if everybody looked at things that way?" There is no escaping this disturbing thought except by a kind of double-dealing. A man who lies and makes excuses for himself by saying "not everybody does that," is someone with an uneasy conscience, because the act of lying implies that a universal value is conferred upon the lie.

Anguish is evident even when it conceals itself. This is the anguish that Kierkegaard called the anguish of Abraham. You know the story: an angel has ordered Abraham to sacrifice his son; if it really were an angel who has come and said, "You are Abraham, you shall sacrifice your son," everything would be all right. But everyone might first wonder, "Is it really an angel, and am I really Abraham? What proof do I have?"

There was a madwoman who had hallucinations; someone used to speak to her on the telephone and give her orders. Her doctor asked her, "Who is it who talks to you?" She answered, "He says it's God." What proof did she really have that it was God? If an angel comes to me, what proof is there that it's an angel? And if I hear voices, what proof is there that they come from heaven and not from hell, or from the subconscious, or a pathological condition? What proves that they are addressed to me? What proof is there that I have been [20] appointed to impose my choice and my conception of man on humanity?

I'll never find any proof or sign to convince me of that. If a voice addresses me, it is always for me to decide that this is the angel's voice; if I consider that such an act is a good one, it is I who will choose to say that it is good rather than bad.

Now, I'm not being singled out as an Abraham, and yet at every moment I'm obliged to perform exemplary acts. For every man, everything happens as if all mankind had its eyes fixed on him and were guiding itself by what he does. And every man ought to say to himself, "Am I really the kind of man who has the right to act in such a way that humanity might guide itself by my actions?" And if he does not say that to himself, he is masking his anguish.

There is no question here of the kind of anguish which would lead to quietism, to inaction. It is a matter of a simple sort of anguish that anybody who has had responsibilities is familiar with. For example, when a military officer takes the responsibility for an attack and sends a certain number of men to death, he chooses to do so, and in the main he alone makes the choice. Doubtless, orders come from above, but they are too broad; he interprets them, and on this interpretation depend the lives of ten or fourteen or twenty men. In [21] making a decision he can not help having a certain anguish. All leaders know this anguish. That doesn't keep them from acting; on the contrary, it is the very condition of their action. For it implies that they envisage a number of possibilities, and when they choose one, they realize that it has value only because it is chosen. We shall see that this kind of anguish, which is the kind that existentialism describes, is explained, in addition, by a direct responsibility to the other men whom it involves. It is not a curtain separating us from action, but is part of action itself.

When we speak of forlornness, a term Heidegger was fond of, we mean only that God does not exist and that we have to face all the consequences of this. The existentialist is strongly opposed to a certain kind of secular ethics which would like to abolish God with the least possible expense. About 1880, some French teachers tried to set up a secular ethics which went something like this: God is a useless and costly hypothesis; we are discarding it; but, meanwhile, in order for there to be an ethics, a society, a civilization, it is essential that certain values be taken seriously and that they be considered as having an *a priori* existence. It must be obligatory, *a priori*, to be honest, not to lie, not to beat your wife, to have children, etc., etc. So we're going [22] to try a little device which will make it possible to show that values exist all the same, inscribed in a heaven of ideas, though otherwise God does not exist. In other words—and this, I believe, is the tendency of everything called reformism in France—nothing will be changed if God does not exist. We shall find ourselves with the same norms of honesty, progress, and humanism, and we shall have made of God an outdated hypothesis which will peacefully die off by itself.

The existentialist, on the contrary, thinks it very distressing that God does not exist, because all possibility of finding values in a heaven of ideas disappears along with Him; there can no longer be an *a priori* Good, since there is no infinite and perfect consciousness to think it. Nowhere is it written that the Good exists, that we must be honest, that we must not lie; because the fact is we are on a plane where there are only men. Dostoyevsky said, "If God didn't exist, everything would be possible." That is the very starting point of existentialism. Indeed, everything is permissible if God does not exist, and as a result man is forlorn, because neither within him nor without does he find anything to cling to. He can't start making excuses for himself.

If existence really does precede essence, there is no explaining things away by [23] reference to a fixed and given human nature. In other words, there is no determinism, man is free, man is freedom. On the other hand, if God does not exist, we find no values or commands to turn to which legitimize our conduct. So, in the bright realm of values, we have no excuse behind us, nor justification before us. We are alone, with no excuses.

That is the idea I shall try to convey when I say that man is condemned to be free. Condemned, because he did not create himself, yet, in other respects is free; because, once thrown into the world, he is responsible for everything he does. The existentialist does not believe in the power of passion. He will never agree that a sweeping passion is a ravaging torrent which fatally leads a man to certain acts and is therefore an excuse. He thinks that man is responsible for his passion.

The existentialist does not think that man is going to help himself by finding in the world some omen by which to orient himself. Because he thinks that man will interpret the omen to suit himself. Therefore, he thinks that man, with no support and no aid, is condemned every moment to invent man. Ponge, in a very fine article, has said, "Man is the future of man." That's exactly it. But if it is taken to mean that this future is recorded in heaven, that God sees it, then it is false, because it [24] would really no longer be a future. If it is taken to mean that, whatever a man may be, there is a future to be forged, a virgin future before him, then this remark is sound. But then we are forlorn.

To give you an example which will enable you to understand forlornness better, I shall cite the case of one of my students who came to see me under the following circumstances: his father was on bad terms with his mother, and, moreover, was inclined to be a collaborationist; his older brother had been killed in the German offensive of 1940, and the young man, with somewhat immature but generous feelings, wanted to avenge him. His mother lived alone with him, very much upset by the half-treason of her husband and the death of her older son; the boy was her only consolation.

The boy was faced with the choice of leaving for England and joining the Free French Forces—that is, leaving his mother—behind or remaining with his mother and helping her to carry on. He was fully aware that the woman lived only for him and that his going-off—and perhaps his death—would plunge her into despair. He was also aware that every act that he did for his mother's sake was a sure thing, in the sense that it was helping her to carry on, whereas every effort he made toward [25] going off and fighting was an uncertain move which might run aground and prove completely useless; for example, on his way to England he might, while passing through Spain, be detained indefinitely in a Spanish camp; he might reach England or Algiers and be stuck in an office at a desk job. As a result, he was faced with two very different kinds of action: one, concrete, immediate, but concerning only one individual; the other concerned an incomparably vaster group, a national collectivity, but for that very reason was dubious, and might be interrupted en route. And, at the same time, he was wavering between two kinds of ethics. On the one hand, an ethics of sympathy, of personal devotion; on the other, a broader ethics, but one whose efficacy was more dubious. He had to choose between the two.

Who could help him choose? Christian doctrine? No. Christian doctrine says, "Be charitable, love your neighbor, take the more rugged path, etc., etc." But which is the more rugged path? Whom should he love as a brother? The fighting man or his mother? Which does the greater good, the vague act of fighting in a group, or the concrete one of helping a particular human being to go on living? Who can decide *a priori*? Nobody. No book of ethics can tell him. The Kantian ethics [26] says, "Never treat any person as a means, but as an end." Very well, if I stay with my mother, I'll treat her as an end and not as a means; but by virtue of this very fact, I'm running the risk of treating the people around me who are fighting, as means; and, conversely, if I go to join those who are fighting, I'll be treating them as an end, and, by doing that, I run the risk of treating my mother as a means.

If values are vague, and if they are always too broad for the concrete and specific case that we are considering, the only thing left for us is to trust our instincts. That's what this young man tried to do; and when I saw him, he said, "In the end, feeling is what counts. I ought to choose whichever pushes me in one direction. If I feel that I love my mother enough to sacrifice everything else for her—my desire for vengeance, for action, for adventure—then I'll stay with her. If, on the contrary, I feel that my love for my mother isn't enough, I'll leave."

But how is the value of a feeling determined? What gives his feeling for his mother value? Precisely the fact that he remained with her. I may say that I like so-and-so well enough to sacrifice a certain amount of money for him, but I may say so only if I've done it. I may say "I love my mother well enough to remain with her" if I have remained with her. [27] The only way to determine the value of this affection is, precisely, to perform an act which confirms and defines it. But, since I require this affection to justify my act, I find myself caught in a vicious circle.

On the other hand, Gide has well said that a mock feeling and a true feeling are almost indistinguishable; to decide that I love my mother and will remain with her, or to remain with her by putting on an act, amount somewhat to the same thing; In other words, the feeling is formed by the acts one performs; so, I can not refer to it in order to act upon it. Which means that I can neither seek within myself the true condition which will impel me to act, nor apply to a system of ethics for concepts which will permit me to act. You will say, "At least, he did go to a teacher for advice." But if you seek advice from a priest, for example, you have chosen this priest; you already knew, more or less, just about what advice he was going to give you. In other words, choosing your adviser is involving yourself. The proof of this is that if you are a Christian, you will say, "Consult a priest." But some priests are collaborating, some are just marking time, some are resisting. Which to choose? If the young man chooses a priest who is resisting or collaborating, he has already decided on the kind of advice he's going to get. Therefore, [28] in coming to see me he knew the answer I was going to give him, and I had only one answer to give: "You're free, choose, that is, invent." No general ethics can show you what is to be done; there are no omens in the world. The Catholics will reply, "But there are." Granted—but, in any case, I myself choose the meaning they have.

When I was a prisoner, I knew a rather remarkable young man who was a Jesuit. He had entered the Jesuit order in the following way: he had had a number of very bad breaks; in childhood, his father died, leaving him in poverty, and he was a scholarship student at a religious institution where he was constantly made to feel that he was being kept out of charity; then, he failed to get any of the honors and distinctions that children like; later on, at about eighteen, he bungled a love affair; finally, at twenty-two, he failed in military training, a childish enough matter, but it was the last straw.

This young fellow might well have felt that he had botched everything. It was a sign of something, but of what? He might have taken refuge in bitterness or despair. But he very wisely looked upon all this as a sign that he was not made for secular triumphs, and that only the triumphs of religion, holiness, and faith were open to him. He saw the hand of [29] God in all this, and so he entered the order. Who can help seeing that he alone decided what the sign meant?

Some other interpretation might have been drawn from this series of setbacks; for example, that he might have done better to turn carpenter or revolutionist. Therefore, he is fully responsible for the interpretation. Forlornness implies that we ourselves choose our being. Forlornness and anguish go together.

As for despair, the term has a very simple meaning. It means that we shall confine ourselves to reckoning only with what depends upon our will, or on the ensemble of probabilities which make our action possible. When we want something, we always have to reckon with probabilities. I may be counting on the arrival of a friend. The friend is coming by rail or street-car; this supposes that the train will arrive on schedule, or that the street-car will not jump the track. I am left in the realm of possibility; but possibilities are to be reckoned with only to the point where my action comports with the ensemble of these possibilities, and no further. The moment the possibilities I am considering are not rigorously involved by my action, I ought to disengage myself from them, because no God, no scheme, can adapt the world and its possibilities to my will. When Descartes said, "Conquer yourself [30] rather than the world," he meant essentially the same thing.

The Marxists to whom I have spoken reply "You can rely on the support of others in your action, which obviously has certain limits because you're not going to live forever. That means: rely on both what others are doing elsewhere to help you, in China, in Russia, and what they will do later on, after your death, to carryon the action and lead it to its fulfillment, which will be the revolution. You even have to rely upon that, otherwise you're immoral" I reply at once that I will always rely on fellow-fighters insofar as these comrades are involved with me in a common struggle, in the unity of a party or a group in which I can more or less make my weight felt; that is, one whose ranks I am in as a fighter and whose movements I am aware of at every moment. In such a situation, relying on the unity and will of the party is exactly like counting on the fact that the train will arrive on time or that the car won't jump the track. But, given that man is free and that there is no human nature for me to depend on, I can not count on men whom I do not know by relying on human goodness or man's concern for the good of society. I don't know what will become of the Russian revolution; I may make an example of it to the extent that at the present [31] time it is apparent that the proletariat plays a part in Russia that it plays in no other nation. But I can't swear that this will inevitably lead to a triumph of the proletariat. I've got to limit myself to what I see.

Given that men are free and that tomorrow they will freely decide what man will be, I can not be sure that, after my death, fellow-fighters will carry on my work to bring it to its maximum perfection. Tomorrow, after my death, some men may decide to set up Fascism, and the others may be cowardly and muddled enough to let them do it. Fascism will then be the human reality, so much the worse for us.

Actually, things will be as man will have decided they are to be. Does that mean that I should abandon myself to quietism? No. First, I should involve myself; then, act on the old saw, "Nothing ventured, nothing gained." Nor does it mean that I shouldn't belong to a party, but rather that I shall have no illusions and shall do what I can. For example, suppose I ask myself, "Will socialization, as such, ever come about?" I know nothing about it. All I know is that I'm going to do everything in my power to bring it about. Beyond that, I can't count on anything. Quietism is the attitude of people who say, "Let others do what I can't do." The doctrine I am presenting is the very [32] opposite of quietism, since it declares, "There is no reality except in action." Moreover, it goes further, since it adds, "Man is nothing else than his plan; he exists only to the extent that he fulfills himself; he is therefore nothing else than the ensemble of his acts, nothing else than his life."

According to this, we can understand why our doctrine horrifies certain people. Because often the only way they can bear their wretchedness is to think, "Circumstances have been against me. What I've been and done doesn't show my true worth. To be sure, I've had no great love, no great friendship, but that's because I haven't met a man or woman who was worthy. The books I've written haven't been very good because I haven't had the proper leisure. I haven't had children to devote myself to because I didn't find a man with whom I could have spent my life. So there remains within me, unused and quite viable, a host of propensities, inclinations, possibilities, that one wouldn't guess from the mere series of things I've done."

Now, for the existentialist there is really no love other than one which manifests itself in a person's being in love. There is no genius other than one which is expressed in works of an; the genius of Proust is the sum of Proust's [33] works; the genius of Racine is his series of tragedies. Outside of that, there is nothing. Why say that Racine could have written another tragedy, when he didn't write it? A man is involved in life, leaves his impress on it, and outside of that there is nothing. To be sure, this may seem a harsh thought to someone whose life hasn't been a success. But, on the other hand, it prompts people to understand that reality alone is what counts, that dreams, expectations, and hopes warrant no more than to define a man as a disappointed dream, as mis-carried hopes, as vain expectations. In other words, to define him negatively and not positively. However, when we say, "You are nothing else than your life," that does not imply that the artist will be judged solely on the basis of his works of art; a thousand other things will contribute toward summing him up. What we mean is that a man is nothing else than a series of undertakings, that he is the sum, the organization, the ensemble of the relationships which make up these undertakings.

When all is said and done, what we are accused of, at bottom, is not our pessimism, but an optimistic toughness. If people throw up to us our works of fiction in which we write about people who are soft, weak, cowardly, and [34] sometimes even downright bad, it's not because these people are soft, weak, cowardly, or bad; because if we were to say, as Zola did, that they are that way because of heredity, the workings of environment, society, because of biologi-cal or psychological determinism, people would be reassured. They would say, "Well, that's what we're like, no one can do anything about it." But when the existentialist writes about a coward, he says that this coward is responsible for his cowardice. He's not like that because he has a cowardly heart or lung or brain; he's not like that on account of his physiological make-up; but he's like that because he has made himself a coward by his acts. There's no such thing as a cowardly constitution; there are nervous constitutions; there is poor blood, as the common people say, or strong constitutions. But the man whose blood is poor is not a coward on that account, for what makes cowardice is the act of renouncing or yielding. A constitution is not an act; the coward is defined on the basis of the acts he performs. People feel, in a vague sort of way, that this coward we're talking about is guilty of being a coward, and the thought frightens them, What people would like is that a coward or a hero be born that way.

One of the complaints most frequently [35] made about *The Ways of Freedom* can be summed up as follows: "After all, these people are so spineless, how are you going to make heroes out of them?" This objection almost makes me laugh, for it assumes that people are born heroes. That's what people really want to think. If you're born cowardly, you may set your mind perfectly at rest; there's nothing you can do about it; you'll be cowardly all your life, whatever you may do. If you're born a hero, you may set your mind just as much at rest; you'll be a hero all your life; you'll drink like a hero and eat like a hero. What the existentialist says is that the coward makes himself cowardly, that the hero makes himself heroic. There's always a possibility for the coward not to be cowardly any more and for the hero to stop being heroic. What counts is total involvement; some one particular action or set of circumstances is not total involvement.

THE MYTH OF SISYPHUS (1942)

Albert Camus

Albert Camus (1913–1960) was born in Mondovi, Algeria. He was just a year old when his father died. His mother, half-deaf and penniless, moved into the grandmother's apartment near the Arab Quarter of Algiers. As a youth, Camus excelled in both school and sports. At age 10, he passed the lycée entrance exams and was accepted to the school of philosophy at the University of Algiers, but a bout with tuberculosis delayed his education until he was 17. Camus worked odd jobs to pay for school. He joined the Communist Party in 1937 but remained somewhat ambivalent about communism throughout his life. He and a group of left-wing intellectuals founded the "Worker's Theater" and presented plays by Malraux, Synge, Gide, and Dostoevsky as well as collectively written original works. At age 23 (1936), he received the <u>diplôme d'études supérieures</u>, ended a two-year marriage, and first visited Europe. In 1937, he published Betwixt and Between, *a collection of essays. In 1938, he turned to journalism, writing for the anticolonialist newspaper,* Alger-Republican, *reporting on the condition of Muslims in the Kabylie region. These reports attracted much public notice and brought the Algerian government to take action. In 1940, Camus sought to find work as a reporter for the leftist press in Paris, but ended up returning to North Africa, where he found a teaching position in Oran and married the math teacher. His short stay in Oran ended when he exiled himself to Paris after the growing political right declared him a "threat to national security." He arrived just before the Germans took Paris from the demoralized French army. In 1943, Camus joined "Combat," a clandestine resistance cell engaged in underground intelligence and sabotage. He traveled behind enemy lines using fake documents under the name "Beauchard" and smuggled war news into Paris. For four years beginning in 1943, he edited the Combat paper. During the war, he wrote his main works on alienation and the absurd:* The Stranger *(1942),* The Myth of Sisyphus *(1942),* Cross Purpose *(1944), and* Caligula *(1944). In 1944, he became the father of twins. He had become an important voice for the French working class. He tried unsuccessfully to start a socialist party but finally rejected Marxism, earning the criticism of numerous communist factions. In 1949, with a tuberculosis relapse, he* *went into seclusion to write. In 1951, he published* The Rebel, *drawing a distinction between revolution and revolt, criticizing Hegel for emphasizing power over social morality and Marx for using Hegel to justify any means to reach an end. The left saw this as treasonous and it led to the end of Camus' friendship with Sartre. Even so, Camus continued to advocate for human rights throughout the 1950s. In 1955, he covered the Algerian war for* l'Express. *He pleaded for rebels and soldiers to spare the civilian population from violence. He regained favor among intellectuals with* The Fall *(1956), and received the Nobel Prize for Literature in 1957. He died in an automobile accident near Sens, France.*

What to look for: *Who is Sisyphus? How is the myth an allegory for the human condition? What does Camus mean by "the absurd"? How are happiness and absurdity related? How (does Camus think) can one keep going in the face of the absurdity, or ultimate meaninglessness, of existence? How can Sisyphus be happy? Where does meaning in life come from?*

---

[119] The gods had condemned Sisyphus to ceaselessly rolling a rock to the top of a mountain, whence the stone would fall back of its own weight. They had thought with some reason that there is no more dreadful punishment than futile and hopeless labor.

If one believes Homer, Sisyphus was the wisest and most prudent of mortals. According to another tradition, however, he was disposed to practice the profession of highwayman. I see no contradiction in this. Opinions differ as to the reasons why he became the futile laborer of the underworld. To begin with, he is accused of a certain levity in regard to the gods. He stole their secrets. Ægina, the daughter of Æsopus, was carried off by Jupiter. The father was shocked by that disappearance and complained to Sisyphus. He, who knew of the abduction, offered to tell about it on condition that Æsopus would give water to the citadel of Corinth. To the celestial thunderbolts he preferred the benediction of water. He was punished for this in the underworld. Homer tells us also that Sisyphus had put Death in chains. Pluto could not endure the sight of his deserted, silent empire. He dispatched the god of war, who liberated Death from the hands of her conqueror.

It is said that Sisyphus, being near to death, rashly wanted to test his wife's love. He ordered her to [120] cast his unburied body into the middle of the public square. Sisyphus woke up in the underworld. And there, annoyed by an obedience so contrary to human love, he obtained from Pluto permission to return to earth in order to chastise his wife. But when he had seen again the face of this world, enjoyed water and sun, warm stones and the sea, he no longer wanted to go back to the infernal darkness. Recalls, signs of anger, warnings were of no avail. Many years more he lived facing the curve of the gulf, the sparkling sea, and the smiles of earth. A decree of the gods was necessary. Mercury came and seized the impudent man by the collar and, snatching him from his joys, lead him forcibly back to the underworld, where his rock was ready for him.

You have already grasped that Sisyphus is the absurd hero. He is, as much through his passions as through his torture. His scorn of the gods, his hatred of death, and his passion for life won him that unspeakable penalty in which the whole being is exerted toward accomplishing nothing. This is the price that must be paid for the passions of this earth. Nothing is told to us about Sisyphus in the underworld. Myths are made for the imagination to breathe life into them. As for this myth, one sees merely the whole effort of a body straining to raise the huge stone, to roll it, and push it up a slope a hundred times over; one sees the face screwed up, the cheek tight against the stone, the shoulder bracing the clay-covered mass, the foot wedging it, the fresh start with arms outstretched, the wholly human security of two earthclotted hands. At the very end of his long effort [121] measured by skyless space and time without depth, the purpose is achieved. Then Sisyphus watches the stone rush down in a few moments toward that lower world whence he will have to push it up again toward the summit. He goes back down to the plain.

It is during that return, that pause, that Sisyphus interests me. A face that toils so close to stones is already stone itself! I see that man going back down with a heavy yet measured step toward the torment of which he will never know the end. That hour like a breathing-space which returns as surely as his suffering, that is the hour of consciousness. At each of those moments when he leaves the heights and gradually sinks toward the lairs of the gods, he is superior to his fate. He is stronger than his rock.

If this myth is tragic, that is because its hero is conscious. Where would his torture be, indeed, if at every step the hope of succeeding upheld him? The workman of today works everyday in his life at the same tasks, and his fate is no less absurd. But it is tragic only at the rare moments when it becomes conscious. Sisyphus, proletarian of the gods, powerless and rebellious, knows the whole extent of his wretched condition: it is what he thinks of during his descent. The lucidity that was to constitute his torture at the same time crowns his victory. There is no fate that cannot be surmounted by scorn.

* * *

If the descent is thus sometimes performed in sorrow, it can also take place in joy. This word is not too much. Again I fancy Sisyphus returning toward his rock, [122] and the sorrow was in the beginning. When the images of earth cling too tightly to memory, when the call of happiness becomes too insistent, it happens that melancholy rises in man's heart: this is the rock's victory, this is the rock itself. The boundless grief is too heavy to bear. These are our nights of Gethsemane. But crushing truths perish from being acknowledged. Thus, Œdipus at the outset obeys fate without knowing it. But from the moment he knows, his tragedy begins. Yet at the same moment, blind and desperate, he realizes that the only bond linking him to the world is the cool hand of a girl. Then a tremendous remark rings out: "Despite so many ordeals, my advanced age and the nobility of my soul make me conclude that all is well." Sophocles' Œdipus, like Dostoevsky's Kirilov, thus gives the recipe for the absurd victory. Ancient wisdom confirms modern heroism.

One does not discover the absurd without being tempted to write a manual of happiness. "What! by such narrow ways—?" There is but one world, however. Happiness and the absurd are two sons of the same earth. They are inseparable. It would be a mistake to say that happiness necessarily springs from the absurd discovery. It happens as well that the feeling of the absurd springs from happiness. "I conclude that all is well," says Œdipus, and that remark is sacred. It echoes in the wild and limited universe of man. It teaches that all is not, has not been, exhausted. It drives out of this world a god who had come into it with dissatisfaction and a reference for futile sufferings. It makes of fate a human matter, which must be settled among men. [123]

All Sisyphus' silent joy is contained therein. His fate belongs to him. His rock is his thing. Likewise, the absurd man, when he contemplates his torment, silences all the idols. In the universe suddenly restored to its silence, the myriad wondering little voices of the earth rise up. Unconscious, secret calls, invitations from all the faces, they are the necessary reverse and price of victory. There is no sun without shadow, and it is essential to know the night. The absurd man says yes and his effort will henceforth be unceasing. If there is a personal fate, there is no higher destiny, or at least there is but one which he concludes is inevitable and despicable. For the rest, he knows himself to be the master of his days. At that subtle moment when man glances backward over his life, Sisyphus returning toward his rock, in that slight pivoting he contemplates that series of unrelated actions which becomes his fate, created by him, combined under his memory's eye and soon sealed by his death. Thus, convinced of the wholly human origin of all that is human, a blind man eager to see who knows that the night has no end, he is still on the go. The rock is still rolling.

I leave Sisyphus at the foot of the mountain! One always finds one's burden again. But Sisyphus teaches the higher fidelity that negates the gods and raises rocks. He too concludes that all is well. This universe henceforth without a master seems to him neither sterile nor futile. Each atom of that stone, each mineral flake of that night-filled mountain, in itself forms a world. The struggle itself toward the heights is enough to fill a man's heart. One must imagine Sisyphus happy.

WHERE AM I? (1978/1981)

Daniel Dennett

Daniel C. Dennett (1942–) was born in Boston, MA. Early on, the family moved to Lebanon, where his father worked as a counterintelligence agent undercover as a cultural attaché at the American Embassy in Beirut. His father was killed in a plane crash when Daniel was 5, and the family returned to Massachusetts. He graduated from the Phillips Exeter Academy at 17, spent one year at Connecticut Wesleyan University, and then transferred to Harvard (where he studied under W. V. Quine). Following graduation in 1963, Dennett then went to Christ Church, Oxford, where he completed the D.Phil degree in 1965 under the supervision of Gilbert Ryle. He then taught at the University of California Irvine until 1971 when he moved permanently to Tufts University (except for occasional visiting posts at Harvard, Pittsburgh, Oxford, the Parisian École Normale Supérieure, The London School of Economics, and the American University of Beirut). His books include Content and Consciousness (1969), Brainstorms (1978), The Mind's I (coedited with Douglas Hofstadter, 1981), Elbow Room (1984), The Intentional Stance (1987), Consciousness Explained (1991), Darwin's Dangerous Idea (1995), Kinds of Minds (1996), Brainchildren: A Collection of Essays 1984-1996 (1998), Freedom Evolves (2003), Sweet Dreams: Philosophical Obstacles to a Science of Consciousness (2005), Breaking the Spell (2006), Intuition Pumps and Other Tools for Thinking (2013), and Caught in the Pulpit: Leaving Belief Behind (cowritten with Linda LaScola, 2013). He has published more than four hundred scholarly articles on various aspects on the mind, writing for journals such as Artificial Intelligence, Behavioral and Brain Sciences, Poetics Today, and The Journal of Aesthetics and Art Criticism. He has delivered the prestigious John Locke Lectures (Oxford, 1983), the Gavin David Young Lectures (Adelaide, Australia, 1985), and the Tanner Lecture (Michigan, 1986). He has received two Guggenheim Fellowships, a Fulbright Fellowship, and a Fellowship at the Center for Advanced Studies in Behavioral Science. In 1985, he cofounded the Curricular Software Studio at Tufts. He was elected to the American Academy of Arts and Sciences (in 1987), is a Fellow of the Committee for Skeptical Inquiry, and a Humanist Laureate of the International Academy of Humanism. In 2012, he was awarded the Erasmus Prize for exceptional contribution to European culture, society, or social science "for his ability to translate the cultural significance of science and technology to a broad audience." He has helped design computer exhibits for the Smithsonian Institution, the Museum of Science in Boston, and the Computer Museum in Boston. He acknowledges that hundreds of hours of informal tutoring by some of the world's best scientists were crucial to the development of his thought. His present post is Co-Director of the Center for Cognitive Studies, University Professor, and Austin B. Fletcher Professor of Philosophy at Tufts. He has for many summers hobby farmed in Maine, but plans to sell the farm, move to an island, do some sailing, and maybe sculpt.

What to look for: *What happened to Dennett's brain? Where is "here?" Who/what are Yorick and Hamlet? What are the possibilities as to where Dennett is and what "issues" does each raise? What is an illusory shift? What happened under Tulsa? What "demonstrated" the immateriality of a soul? Who/what are Fortinbras and Hubert? What are Dennett's fears upon learning about Hubert? What happens at the end of Dennett's lecture? Where is Dennett? Who is Dennett? Why?*

Now that I've won my suit under the Freedom of Information Act, I am at liberty to reveal for the first time a curious episode in my life that may be of interest not only to those engaged in research in the philosophy of mind, artificial intelligence, and neuroscience but also to the general public.

Several years ago I was approached by Pentagon officials who asked me to volunteer for a highly dangerous and secret mission. In collaboration with NASA and Howard Hughes, the Department of Defense was spending billions to develop a Supersonic Tunneling Underground Device, or STUD. It was supposed to tunnel through the earth's core at great speed and deliver a specially designed atomic warhead "right up the Red's missile silos," as one of the Pentagon brass put it.

The problem was that in an early test they had succeeded in lodging a warhead about a mile deep under Tulsa, Oklahoma, and they wanted me to retrieve it for them. "Why me?" I asked. Well, the mission involved some pioneering applications of current brain research, and they had heard of my interest in brains and of course my Faustian curiosity and great courage and so forth . . . . Well, how could I refuse? The difficulty that brought the Pentagon to my door was that the device I'd been asked to recover was fiercely radioactive, in a new

"Where Am I," by Daniel C. Dennett, from *Brainstorms: Philosophical Essays on Mind and Psychology*. (Cambridge, MA: Bradford Books, The MIT Press, 1981). Used by permission of MIT Press.

way. According to monitoring instruments, something about the nature of the device and its complex interactions with pockets of material deep in the earth had produced radiation that could cause severe abnormalities in certain tissues of the brain. No way had been found to shield the brain from these deadly rays, which were apparently [311] harmless to other tissues and organs of the body. So it had been decided that the person sent to recover the device should *leave his brain behind*. It would be kept in a safe place as there it could execute its normal control functions by elaborate radio links. Would I submit to a surgical procedure that would completely remove my brain, which would then be placed in a life-support system at the Manned Spacecraft Center in Houston? Each input and output pathway, as it was severed, would be restored by a pair of microminiaturized radio transceivers, one attached precisely to the brain, the other to the nerve stumps in the empty cranium. No information would be lost, all the connectivity would be preserved. At first I was a bit reluctant. Would it really work? The Houston brain surgeons encouraged me. "Think of it," they said, "as a mere *stretching* of the nerves. If your brain were just moved over an *inch* in your skull, that would not alter or impair your mind. We're simply going to make the nerves indefinitely elastic by splicing radio links into them."

I was shown around the life-support lab in Houston and saw the sparkling new vat in which my brain would be placed, were I to agree. I met the large and brilliant support team of neurologists, hematologists, biophysicists, and electrical engineers, and after several days of discussions and demonstrations I agreed to give it a try. I was subjected to an enormous array of blood tests, brain scans, experiments, interviews, and the like. They took down my autobiography at great length, recorded tedious lists of my beliefs, hopes, fears, and tastes. They even listed my favorite stereo recordings and gave me a crash session of psychoanalysis.

The day for surgery arrived at last and of course I was anesthetized and remember nothing of the operation itself. When I came out of anesthesia, I opened my eyes, looked around, and asked the inevitable, the traditional, the lamentably hackneyed postoperative question: "Where am I?" The nurse smiled down at me. "You're in Houston," she said, and I reflected that this still had a good chance of being the truth one way or another. She handed me a mirror. Sure enough, there were the tiny antennae poling up through their titanium ports cemented into my skull.

"I gather the operation was a success," I said. "I want to go see my brain." They led me (I was a bit dizzy and unsteady) down a long corridor and into the life-support lab. A cheer went up from the assembled support team, and I responded with what I hoped was a jaunty salute. Still feeling lightheaded, I was helped over to the life-support [312] vat. I peered through the glass. There, floating in what looked like ginger ale, was undeniably a human brain, though it was almost covered with printed circuit chips, plastic tubules, electrodes, and other paraphernalia. "Is that mine?" I asked. "Hit the output transmitter switch there on the side of the vat and see for yourself," the project director replied. I moved the switch to OFF, and immediately slumped, groggy and nauseated, into the arms of the technicians, one of whom kindly restored the switch to its ON position. While I recovered my equilibrium and composure, I thought to myself: "Well, here I am sitting on a folding chair, staring through a piece of plate glass at my own brain.... But wait," I said to myself, "shouldn't I have thought, 'Here I am, suspended in a bubbling fluid, being stared at by my own eyes'?" I tried to think this latter thought. I tried to project it into the tank, offering it hopefully to my brain, but I failed to carry off the exercise with any conviction. I tried again. "Here am *I*, Daniel Dennett, suspended in a bubbling fluid, being stared at by my own eyes." No, it just didn't work. Most puzzling and confusing. Being a philosopher of firm physicalist conviction, I believed unswervingly that the tokening of my thoughts was occurring somewhere in my brain: yet, when I thought "Here I am," where the thought occurred to me was *here*, outside the vat, where I, Dennett, was standing staring at my brain.

I tried and tried to think myself into the vat, but to no avail. I tried to build up to the task by doing mental exercises. I thought to myself, "The sun is shining *over there*," five times in rapid succession, each time mentally ostending a different place: in order, the sunlit corner of the lab, the visible front lawn of the hospital, Houston, Mars, and Jupiter. I found I had little difficulty in getting my "there's" to hop all over the celestial map with their proper references. I could loft a "there" in an instant through the farthest reaches of space, and then aim the next "there" with pinpoint accuracy at the upper left quadrant of a freckle on my arm. Why was I having such trouble with "here"? "Here in Houston" worked well enough, and so did "here in the lab," and even "here in this part of the lab," but "here in the vat" always seemed merely an unmeant mental mouthing. I tried closing my eyes while thinking it. This seemed to help, but still I couldn't manage to pull it off, except perhaps for a fleeting instant. I couldn't be sure. The discovery that I couldn't be sure was also unsettling. How did I know *where* I meant by "here" when I thought "here"? Could I *think* I meant one place when in fact I meant another? I didn't see [313] how that could be admitted without untying the few bonds of intimacy between a person and his own mental life that had survived the onslaught of the brain scientists and philosophers, the physicalists and behaviorists. Perhaps I was incorrigible about where I *meant* when I said "here." But in my present circumstances it seemed that either I was doomed by sheer force of mental habit to thinking systematically false indexical thoughts, or where a person is (and hence where his thoughts are tokened for purposes of semantic analysis) is not necessarily where his brain, the physical seat of his soul, resides. Nagged by confusion, I attempted to orient myself by falling back on a favorite philosopher's ploy. I began naming things.

"Yorick," I said aloud to my brain, "you are my brain. The rest of my body, seated in this chair, I dub 'Hamlet.'" So here we all are: Yorick's my brain, Hamlet's my body, and I am Dennett. *Now,* where am I? And when I think "where am I?", where's that thought tokened? Is it tokened in my brain, lounging about in the vat, or right here between my ears where it *seems* to be tokened? Or nowhere? Its *temporal* coordinates give me no trouble; must it not have spatial coordinates as well? I began making a list of the alternatives.

(1) *Where Hamlet goes there goes Dennett.* This principle was easily refuted by appeal to the familiar brain-transplant thought experiments so enjoyed by philosophers. If Tom and Dick switch brains, Tom is the fellow with Dick's former body—just ask him; he'll claim to be Tom and tell you the most intimate details of Tom's autobiography. It was clear enough, then, that my current body and I could part company, but not likely that I could be separated from my brain. The rule of thumb that emerged so plainly from the thought experiments was that in a brain-transplant operation, one wanted to be the *donor* not the recipient. Better to call such an operation a *body* transplant, in fact. So perhaps the truth was,

(2) *Where Yorick goes there goes Dennett.* This was not at all appealing, however. How could I be in the vat and not about to go anywhere, when I was so obviously outside the vat looking in and beginning to make guilty plans to return to my room for a substantial lunch? This begged the question I realized, but it still seemed to be getting at something important. Casting about for some support for my intuition, I hit upon a legalistic sort of argument that might have appealed to Locke.

Suppose, I argued to myself, I were now to fly to California, rob a bank, and be apprehended. In which state would I be tried: In [314] California, where the robbery took place, or in Texas, where the brains of the outfit were located? Would I be a California felon with an out-of-state brain, or a Texas felon remotely controlling an accomplice of sorts in California? It seemed possible that I might beat such a rap just on the undecidability of that jurisdictional question, though perhaps it would be deemed an interstate, and hence Federal, offense. In any event, suppose I were convicted. Was it likely that California would be satisfied to throw Hamlet into the brig, knowing that Yorick was living the good life and luxuriously taking the waters in Texas? Would Texas incarcerate Yorick, leaving Hamlet free to take the next boat to Rio? This alternative appealed to me. Barring capital punishment or other cruel and unusual punishment, the state would be obliged to maintain the life-support system for Yorick though they might move him from Houston to Leavenworth, and aside from the unpleasantness of the opprobrium, I, for one, would not mind at all and would consider myself a free man under those circumstances. If the state has an interest in forcibly relocating persons in institutions, it would fail to relocate *me* in any institution by locating Yorick there. If this were true, it suggested a third alternative.

(3) *Dennett is wherever he thinks he is.* Generalized, the claim was as follows: At any given time a person has a *point of view* and the location of the point of view (which is determined internally by the content of the point of view) is also the location of the person.

Such a proposition is not without its perplexities, but to me it seemed a step in the right direction. The only trouble was that it seemed to place one in a heads-I-win/tails-you-lose situation of unlikely infallibility as regards location. Hadn't I myself often been wrong about where I was, and at least as often uncertain? Couldn't one get lost? Of course, but getting lost *geographically* is not the only way one might get lost. If one were lost in the woods one could attempt to reassure oneself with the consolation that at least one knew where one was: one was right *here* in the familiar surroundings of one's own body. Perhaps in this case one would not have drawn one's attention to much to be thankful for. Still, there were worse plights imaginable, and I wasn't sure I wasn't in such a plight right now.

Point of view clearly had something to do with personal location, but it was itself an unclear notion. It was obvious that the content of one's point of view was not the same as or determined by the content of one's beliefs or thoughts. For example, what should we say about the point of view of the Cinerama viewer who shrieks and twists in [315] his seat as the roller-coaster footage overcomes his psychic distancing? Has he forgotten that he is safely seated in the theater? Here I was inclined to say that the person is experiencing an illusory shift in point of view. In other cases, my inclination to call such shifts illusory was less strong. The workers in laboratories and plants who handle dangerous materials by operating feedback-controlled mechanical arms and hands undergo a shift in point of view that is crisper and more pronounced than anything Cinerama can provoke. They can feel the heft and slipperiness of the containers they manipulate with their metal fingers. They know perfectly well where they are and are not fooled into false beliefs by the experience, yet it is as if they were inside the isolation chamber they are peering into. With mental effort, they can manage to shift their point of view back and forth, rather like making a transparent Necker cube or an Escher drawing change orientation before one's eyes. It does seem extravagant to suppose that in performing this bit of mental gymnastics, they are transporting *themselves* back and forth.

Still their example gave me hope. If I was in fact in the vat in spite of my intuitions, I might be able to train myself to adopt that point of view even as a matter of habit. I should dwell on images of myself comfortably floating in my vat, beaming volitions to that familiar body *out there*. I reflected that the ease or difficulty of this task was presumably independent of the truth about the location of one's brain. Had I been practicing before the operation, I might now be finding it second nature. You might now yourself try such a *trompe l'oeil*. Imagine you have written an inflammatory letter which has been published in the *Times*, the result of which is that the government has chosen to impound your brain for a probationary period of three years in its Dangerous Brain Clinic in Bethesda, Maryland. Your body of course is allowed freedom to earn a salary and thus to continue its function of laying up income to be taxed. At this moment, however, your body is seated in an auditorium listening to a peculiar account by Daniel Dennett of his own similar experience. Try it. Think yourself to Bethesda, and then hark back longingly to your body, far away, and yet *seeming* so near. It is only with long-distance restraint (yours? the government's?) that you can control your impulse to get those hands clapping in polite applause before navigating the old body to the rest room and a well-deserved glass of evening sherry in the lounge. The task of imagination is certainly difficult, but if you achieve your goal the results might be consoling.

Anyway, there I was in Houston, lost in thought as one might say, but not for long. My speculations were soon interrupted by the [316] Houston doctors, who wished to test out my new prosthetic nervous system before sending me off on my hazardous mission. As I mentioned before, I was a bit dizzy at first, and not surprisingly, although I soon habituated myself to my new circumstances (which were, after all, well nigh indistinguishable from my old circumstances). My accommodation was not perfect, however, and to this day I continue to be plagued by minor coordination difficulties. The speed of light is fast, but finite, and as my brain and body move farther and farther apart, the delicate interaction of my feedback systems is thrown into disarray by the time lags. Just as one is rendered close to speechless by a delayed or echoic hearing of one's speaking voice so, for instance, I am virtually unable to track a moving object with my eyes whenever my brain and my body are more than a few miles apart. In most matters my impairment is scarcely detectable, though I can no longer hit a slow curve ball with the authority of yore. There are some compensations of course. Though liquor tastes as good as ever, and warms my gullet while corroding my liver, I can drink it in any quantity I please, without becoming the slightest bit inebriated, a curiosity some of my close friends may have noticed (though I occasionally have *feigned* inebriation, so as not to draw attention to my unusual circumstances). For similar reasons, I take aspirin orally for a sprained wrist, but if the pain persists I ask Houston to administer codeine to me *in vitro*. In times of illness the phone bill can be staggering.

But to return to my adventure. At length, both the doctors and I were satisfied that I was ready to undertake my subterranean mission. And so I left my brain in Houston and headed by helicopter for Tulsa. Well, in any case, that's the way it seemed to me. That's how I would put it, just off the top of my head as it were. On the trip I reflected further about my earlier anxieties and decided that my first postoperative speculations had been tinged with panic. The matter was not nearly as strange or metaphysical as I had been supposing. Where was I? In two places, clearly: both inside the vat and outside it. Just as one can stand with one foot in Connecticut and the other in Rhode Island, I was in two places at once. I had become one of those scattered individuals we used to hear so much about. The more I considered this answer, the more obviously true it appeared. But, strange to say, the more true it appeared, the less important the question to which it could be the true answer seemed. A sad, but not unprecedented, fate for a philosophical question to suffer. This answer did not completely satisfy me, of course. There lingered some question to which I should have liked an answer, which was neither "Where are all my various and sundry parts?" nor "What is my current point of view?" Or at least [317] there seemed to be such a question. For it did seem undeniable that in some sense *I* and not merely *most of me* was descending into the earth under Tulsa in search of an atomic warhead.

When I found the warhead, I was certainly glad I had left my brain behind, for the pointer on the specially built Geiger counter I had brought with me was off the dial. I called Houston on my ordinary radio and told the operation control center of my position and my progress. In return, they gave me instructions for dismantling the vehicle, based upon my on-site observations. I had set to work with my cutting torch when all of a sudden a terrible thing happened. I went stone deaf. At first I thought it was only my radio earphones that had broken, but when I tapped on my helmet, I heard nothing. Apparently the auditory transceivers had gone on the fritz. I could no longer hear Houston or my own voice, but I could speak, so I started telling them what had happened. In midsentence, I knew something else had gone wrong. My vocal apparatus had become paralyzed. Then my right hand went limp—another transceiver had gone. I was truly in deep trouble. But worse was to follow. After a few more minutes, I went blind. I cursed my luck, and then I cursed the scientists who had led me into this grave peril. There I was, deaf, dumb, and blind, in a radioactive hole more than a mile under Tulsa. Then the last of my cerebral radio links broke, and suddenly I was faced with a new and even more shocking problem: whereas an instant before I had been buried alive in Oklahoma, now I was disembodied in Houston. My recognition of my new status was not immediate. It took me several very anxious minutes before it dawned on me that my poor body lay several hundred miles away, with heart pulsing and lungs respirating, but otherwise as dead as the body of any heart-transplant donor, its skull packed with useless, broken electronic gear. The shift in perspective I had earlier found well nigh impossible now seemed quite natural. Though I could think myself back into my body in the tunnel under Tulsa, it took some effort to sustain the illusion. For surely it was an illusion to suppose I was still in Oklahoma: I had lost all contact with that body.

It occurred to me then, with one of those rushes of revelation of which we should be suspicious, that I had stumbled upon an impressive demonstration of the immateriality of the soul based upon physicalist principles and premises. For as the last radio signal between Tulsa and Houston died away, had I not changed location from Tulsa to Houston at the speed of light? And had I not accomplished this without any increase in mass? What moved from A to B at such speed was surely myself, or at any rate my soul or mind—the massless center [318] of my being and home of my consciousness. My *point of view* had lagged somewhat behind, but I had already noted the indirect bearing of point of view on personal location. I could not see how a physicalist philosopher could quarrel with this except by taking the dire and counterintuitive route of banishing all talk of persons. Yet the notion of personhood was so well entrenched in everyone's world view, or so it seemed to me, that any denial would be as curiously unconvincing, as systematically disingenuous, as the Cartesian negation, "non sum."

The joy of philosophic discovery thus tided me over some very bad minutes or perhaps hours as the helplessness and hopelessness or my situation became more apparent to me. Waves of panic and even nausea swept over me, made all the more horrible by the absence of their normal body-dependent phenomenology. No adrenaline rush of tingles in the arms, no pounding heart, no premonitory salivation. I did feel a dread sinking feeling in my bowels at one point, and this tricked me momentarily into the false hope that I was undergoing a reversal of the process that landed me in this fix—a gradual undisembodiment. But the isolation and uniqueness of that twinge soon convinced me that it was simply the first of a plague of phantom body hallucinations that I, like any other amputee, would be all too likely to suffer.

My mood then was chaotic. On the one hand, I was fired up with elation of my philosophic discovery and was wracking my brain (one of the few familiar things I could still do), trying to figure out how to communicate my discovery to the journals; while on the other, I was bitter, lonely, and filled with dread and uncertainty. Fortunately, this did not last long, for my technical support team sedated me into a dreamless sleep from which I awoke, hearing with magnificent fidelity the familiar opening strains of my favorite Brahms piano trio. So that was why they had wanted a list of my favorite recordings! It did not take me long to realize that I was hearing the music without ears. The output from the stereo stylus was being fed through some fancy rectification circuitry directly into my auditory nerve. I was mainlining Brahms, an unforgettable experience for any stereo buff. At the end of the record it did not surprise me to hear the reassuring voice of the project director speaking into a microphone that was now my prosthetic ear. He confirmed my analysis of what had gone wrong and assured me that steps were being taken to re-embody me. He did not elaborate, and after a few more recordings, I found myself drifting off to sleep. My sleep lasted, I later learned, for the better part of a year, and when I awoke, it was to find myself fully restored to my senses. When I looked into the mirror, though, I was a bit startled to see an unfamiliar face. Bearded and a bit heavier, bearing no doubt a family [319] resemblance to my former face, and with the same look of spritely intelligence and resolute character, but definitely a new face. Further self-explorations of an intimate nature left me no doubt that this was a new body, and the project director confirmed my conclusions. He did not volunteer any information on the past history of my new body and I decided (wisely, I think in retrospect) not to pry. As many philosophers unfamiliar with my ordeal have more recently speculated, the acquisition of a new body leaves one's *person* intact. And after a period of adjustment to a new voice, new muscular strengths and weaknesses, and so forth, one's *personality* is by and large also preserved. More dramatic changes in personality have been routinely observed in people who have undergone extensive plastic surgery, to say nothing of sex-change operations, and I think no one contests the survival of the person in such cases. In any event I soon accommodated to my new body, to the point of being unable to recover any of its novelties to my consciousness or even memory. The view in the mirror soon became utterly familiar. That view, by the way, still revealed antennae, and so I was not surprised to learn that my brain had not been moved from its haven in the life-support lab.

I decided that good old Yorick deserved a visit. I and my new body, whom we might as well call Fortinbras, strode into the familiar lab to another round of applause from the technicians, who were of course congratulating themselves, not me. Once more I stood before the vat and contemplated poor Yorick, and on a whim I once again cavalierly flicked off the output transmitter switch. Imagine my surprise when nothing unusual happened. No fainting spell, no nausea, no noticeable change. A technician hurried to restore the switch to ON, but still I felt nothing. I demanded an explanation, which the project director hastened to provide. It seems that before they had even operated on the first occasion, they had constructed a computer duplicate of my brain, reproducing both the complete information-processing structure and the computational speed of my brain in a giant computer program. After the operation, but before they had dared to send me off on my mission to Oklahoma, they had run this computer system and Yorick side by side. The incoming signals from Hamlet were sent simultaneously to Yorick's transceivers and to the computer's array of inputs. And the outputs from Yorick were not only beamed back to Hamlet, my body; they were recorded and checked against the simultaneous output of the computer program, which was called "Hubert" for reasons obscure to me. Over days and even weeks, the outputs were identical and synchronous, which of course did not *prove* that they [320] had succeeded in copying the brain's functional structure, but the empirical support was greatly encouraging.

Hubert's input, and hence activity, had been kept parallel with Yorick's during my disembodied days. And now, to demonstrate this, they had actually thrown the master switch that put Hubert for the first time in on-line control of my body—not Hamlet, of course, but Fortinbras. (Hamlet, I learned, had never been recovered from its underground tomb and could be assumed by this time to have largely returned to the dust. At the head of my grave still lay the magnificent bulk of the abandoned device, with the word STUD emblazoned on its side in large letters—a circumstance which may provide archeologists of the next century with a curious insight into the burial rites of their ancestors.)

The laboratory technicians now showed me the master switch, which had two positions, labeled *B*, for Brain (they didn't know my brain's name was Yorick), and *H*, for Hubert. The switch did indeed point to *H*, and they explained to me that if I wished, I could switch it back to *B*. With my heart in my mouth (and my brain in its vat), I did this. Nothing happened. A click, that was all. To test their claim, and with the master switch now set at *B*, I hit Yorick's output transmitter switch on the vat and sure enough, I began to faint. Once the output switch was turned back on and I had recovered my wits, so to speak, I continued to play with the master switch, flipping it back and forth. I found that with the exception of the transitional click, I could detect no trace of a difference. I could switch in mid-utterance, and the sentence I had begun speaking under the control of Yorick was finished without a pause or hitch of any kind under the control of Hubert. I had a spare brain, a prosthetic device which might some day stand me in very good stead, were some mishap to befall Yorick. Or alternatively, I could keep Yorick as a spare and use Hubert. It didn't seem to make any difference which I chose, for the wear and tear and fatigue on my body did not have any debilitating effect on either brain, whether or not it was actually causing the motions of my body, or merely spilling its output into thin air.

The one truly unsettling aspect of this new development was the prospect, which was not long in dawning on me, of someone detaching the spare— Hubert or Yorick, as the case might be—from Fortinbras and hitching it to yet another body—some Johnny-come-lately Rosencrantz or Guildenstern. Then (if not before) there would be *two* people, that much was clear. One would be me, and the other would be a sort of super-twin brother. If there were two bodies, one under the control of Hubert and the other being controlled by Yorick, then [321] which would the world recognize as the true Dennett? And whatever the rest of the world decided, which one would be *me*? Would I be the Yorick- brained one, in virtue of Yorick's causal priority and former intimate relationship with the original Dennett body, Hamlet? That seemed a bit legalistic, a bit too redolent of the arbitrariness of consanguinity and legal possession, to be convincing at the metaphysical level. For suppose that before the arrival of the second body on the scene, I had been keeping Yorick as the spare for years, and letting Hubert's output drive my body—that is, Fortinbras—all that time. The Hubert- Fortinbras couple would seem then by squatter's rights (to combat one legal intuition with another) to be the true Dennett and the lawful inheritor of everything that was Dennett's. This was an interesting question, certainly, but not nearly so pressing as another question that bothered me. My strongest intuition was that in such an eventuality *I* would survive so long as *either* brain-body couple remained intact, but I had mixed emotions about whether I should want both to survive.

I discussed my worries with the technicians and the project director. The prospect of two Dennetts was abhorrent to me, I explained, largely for social reasons. I didn't want to be my own rival for the affections of my wife, nor did I like the prospect of the two Dennetts sharing my modest professor's salary. Still more vertiginous and distasteful, though, was the idea of knowing *that much* about another person, while he had the very same goods on me. How could we ever face each other? My colleagues in the lab argued that I was ignoring the bright side of the matter. Weren't there many things I wanted to do but, being only one person, had been unable to do? Now one Dennett could stay at home and be the professor and family man while the other could strike out on a life of travel and adventure—missing the family of course, but happy in the knowledge that the other Dennett was keeping the home fires burning. I could be faithful and adulterous at the same time. I could even cuckold myself—to say nothing of other more lurid possibilities my colleagues were all too ready to force upon my overtaxed imagination. But my ordeal in Oklahoma (or was it Houston?) had made me less adventurous, and I shrank from this opportunity that was being offered (though of course I was never quite sure it was being offered to *me* in the first place).

There was another prospect even more disagreeable—that the spare, Hubert or Yorick as the case might be, would be detached from any input from Fortinbras and just left detached. Then, as in the other case, there would be two Dennetts, or at least two claimants to my name and possessions, one embodied in Fortinbras, and the other [322] sadly, miserably disembodied. Both selfishness and altruism bade me take steps to prevent this from happening. So I asked that measures be taken to ensure that no one could ever tamper with the transceiver connections or the master switch without my (our? no, *my*) knowledge and consent. Since I had no desire to spend my life guarding the equipment in Houston, it was mutually decided that all the electronic connections in the lab would be carefully locked. Both those that controlled the life-support system for Yorick and those that controlled the power supply for Hubert would be guarded with fail-safe devices, and I would take the only master switch, outfitted for radio remote control, with me wherever I went. I carry it strapped around my waist and—wait a moment—here it is. Every few months I reconnoiter the situation by switching channels. I do this only in the presence of friends, of course, for if the other channel were, heaven forbid, either dead or otherwise occupied, there would have to be somebody who had my interests at heart to switch it back, to bring me back from the void. For while I could feel, see, hear, and otherwise sense whatever befell my body, subsequent to such a switch, I'd be unable to control it. By the way, the two positions on the switch are intentionally unmarked, so I never have the faintest idea whether I am switching from Hubert to Yorick or vice versa. (Some of you may think that in this case I really don't know *who* I am, let alone where I am. But such reflections no longer make much of a dent on my essential Dennettness, on my own sense of who I am. If it is true that in one sense I don't know who I am then that's another one of your philosophical truths of underwhelming significance.)

In any case, every time I've flipped the switch so far, nothing has happened. *So let's give it a try* . . .

"THANK GOD! I THOUGHT YOU'D NEVER FLIP THAT SWITCH! You can't imagine how horrible it's been these last two weeks—but now you know; it's your turn in purgatory. How I've longed for this moment! You see, about two weeks ago—excuse me, ladies and gentlemen, but I've got to explain this to my ... um, brother, I guess you could say, but he's just told you the facts, so you'll understand—about two weeks ago our two brains drifted just a bit out of synch. I don't know whether *my* brain is now Hubert or Yorick, any more than you do, but in any case, the two brains drifted apart, and of course once the process started, it snowballed, for I was in a slightly different receptive state for the input we both received, a difference that was soon magnified. In no time at all the illusion that I was in control of my body—our body—was completely dissipated. There was nothing I could do—no way to call you. YOU DIDN'T EVEN KNOW [323] I EXISTED! It's been like being carried around in a cage, or better, like being possessed—hearing my own voice say things I didn't mean to say, watching in frustration as my own hands performed deeds I hadn't intended. You'd scratch our itches, but not the way I would have, and you kept me awake, with your tossing and turning. I've been totally exhausted, on the verge of a nervous breakdown, carried around helplessly by your frantic round of activities, sustained only by the knowledge that some day you'd throw the switch.

"Now it's your turn, but at least you'll have the comfort of knowing *I* know you're in there. Like an expectant mother, I'm eating—or at any rate tasting, smelling, seeing—for *two* now, and I'll try to make it easy for you. Don't worry. Just as soon as this colloquium is over, you and I will fly to Houston, and we'll see what can be done to get one of us another body. You can have a female body—your body could be any color you like. But let's think it over. I tell you what—to be fair, if we both want this body, I promise I'll let the project director flip a coin to settle which of us gets to keep it and which then gets to choose a new body. That should guarantee justice, shouldn't it? In any case, I'll take care of you, I promise. These people are my witnesses.

"Ladies and gentlemen, this talk we have just heard is not exactly the talk *I* would have given, but I assure you that everything he said was perfectly true. And now if you'll excuse me, I think I'd— we'd—better sit down."

DO WE SURVIVE DEATH? (1936)

Bertrand Russell

Bertrand Russell—see p. 9.

What to look for: What makes a body <u>the same</u>? What makes a mind or soul <u>the same</u>? Does Russell think that belief in life after death is based on rational argument? What are the two main reasons given for survival after death? Does nature care about human values? What do we learn from Aesop's fable and the popular song about flies? What does Russell think of the "excellence of man" argument?

Before we can profitably discuss whether we shall continue to exist after death, it is well to be clear as to the sense in which a man is the same person as he was yesterday. Philosophers used to think that there were definite substances, the soul and the body, that each lasted on from day to day, that a soul, once created, continued to exist throughout all future time, whereas a body ceased temporarily from death till the resurrection of the body.

The part of this doctrine which concerns the present life is pretty certainly false. The matter of the body is continually changing by processes of nutriment and wastage. Even if it were not, atoms in physics are no longer supposed to have continuous existence; there is no sense in saying: this is the same atom as the one that existed a few minutes [89] ago. The continuity of a human body is a matter of appearance and behavior, not of substance.

The same thing applies to the mind. We think and feel and act, but there is not, in addition to thoughts and feelings and actions, a bare entity, the mind or the soul, which does or suffers these occurrences. The mental continuity of a person is a continuity of habit and memory: there was yesterday one person whose feelings I can remember, and that person I regard as myself of yesterday; but, in fact, myself of yesterday was only certain mental occurrences which are now remembered and are regarded as a part of the person who now recollects them. All that constitutes a person is a series of experiences connected by memory and by certain similarities of the sort we call habit.

If, therefore, we are to believe that a person survives death, we must believe that the memories and habits which constitute the person will continue to be exhibited in a new set of occurrences.

No one can prove that this will not happen. But it is easy to see that it is very unlikely. Our memories and habits are bound up with the structure of the brain, in much the same way in which a river is connected with the riverbed. The water in the river is always changing, but it keeps to the same course because previous rains have worn a channel. In like manner, previous events have worn a channel in the brain, and our thoughts flow along this channel. This is the cause of memory and mental habits. But the brain, as a structure, is dissolved at death, and memory therefore may be expected to be also dissolved. There is no more reason to think otherwise than to expect a river to persist in its old course after an earthquake has raised a mountain where a valley used to be.

All memory, and therefore (one may say) all minds, [90] depend upon a property which is very noticeable in certain kinds of material structures but exists little if at all in other kinds. This is the property of forming habits as a result of frequent similar occurrences. For example: a bright light makes the pupils of the eyes contract; and if you repeatedly flash a light in a man's eyes and beat a gong at the same time, the gong alone will, in the end, cause his pupils to contract. This is a fact about the brain and nervous system—that is to say, about a certain material structure. It will be found that exactly similar facts explain our response to language and our use of it, our memories and the emotions they arouse, our moral or immoral habits of behavior, and indeed everything that constitutes our mental personality, except the part determined by heredity. The part determined by heredity is handed on to our posterity but cannot, in the individual, survive the disintegration of the body. Thus both heredity and the acquired parts of a personality are, so far as our experience goes, bound up with the characteristics of certain bodily structures. We all know that memory may be obliterated by an injury to the brain, that a virtuous person may be rendered vicious by encephalitis lethargica, and that a clever child can be turned into an idiot by lack of iodine. In view of such familiar facts, it seems scarcely probable that the mind survives the total destruction of brain structure which occurs at death.

It is not rational arguments but emotions that cause belief in a future life.

The most important of these emotions is fear of death, which is instinctive and biologically useful. If we genuinely and wholeheartedly believed in the future life, we should cease completely to fear death. The effects would be curious, and probably such as most of us would deplore. But our human and subhuman ancestors have fought and ex-[91] terminated their enemies throughout many geological ages and have profited by courage; it is therefore an advantage to the victors in the struggle for life to be able, on occasion, to overcome the natural fear of death. Among animals and savages, instinctive pugnacity suffices for this purpose; but at a certain stage of development, as the Mohammedeans first proved, belief in Paradise has considerable military value as reinforcing natural pugnacity. We should therefore admit that militarists are wise in encouraging the belief in immortality, always supposing that this belief does not become so profound as to produce indifference to the affairs of the world.

Another emotion which encourages the belief in survival is admiration of the excellence of man. As the Bishop of Birmingham says, "His mind is a far finer instrument than anything that had appeared earlier—he knows right and wrong. He can build Westminster Abbey. He can make an airplane. He can calculate the distance of the sun. . . . Shall, then, man at death perish utterly? Does that incomparable instrument, his mind, vanish when life ceases?"

The Bishop proceeds to argue that "the universe has been shaped and is governed by an intelligent purpose," and that it would have been unintelligent, having made man, to let him perish.

To this argument there are many answers. In the first place, it has been found, in the scientific investigation of nature, that the intrusion of moral or aesthetic values has always been an obstacle to discovery. It used to be thought that the heavenly bodies must move in circles because the circle is the most perfect curve, that species must be immutable because God would only create what was perfect and what therefore stood in no need of improvement, that [92] it was useless to combat epidemics except by repentance because they were sent as a punishment for sin, and so on. It has been found, however, that, so far as we can discover, nature is indifferent to our values and can only be understood by ignoring our notions of good and bad. The Universe may have a purpose, but nothing that we know suggests that, if so, this purpose has any similarity to ours.

Nor is there in this anything surprising. Dr. Barnes tells us that man "knows right and wrong." But, in fact, as anthropology shows, men's view of right and wrong have varied to such an extent that no single item has been permanent. We cannot say, therefore, that man knows right and wrong, but only that some men do. Which men? Nietzsche argued in favor of an ethic profoundly different from Christ's, and some powerful governments have accepted his teaching. If knowledge of right and wrong is to be an argument for immortality, we must first settle whether to believe Christ or Nietzsche, and then argue that Christians are immortal, but Hitler and Mussolini are not, or vice versa. The decision will obviously be made on the battlefield, not in the study. Those who have the best poison gas will have the ethic of the future and will therefore be the immortal ones.

Our feelings and beliefs on the subject of good and evil are, like everything else about us, natural facts, developed in the struggle for existence and not having any divine or supernatural origin. In one of Aesop's fables, a lion is shown pictures of huntsmen catching lions and remarks that, if he had painted them, they would have shown lions catching huntsmen. Man, says Dr. Barnes, is a fine fellow because he can make airplanes. A little while ago there was a popular song about the cleverness of flies in walking upside down on the ceiling, with the chorus: "Could Lloyd [93] George do it? Could Mr. Baldwin do it? Could Ramsey Mac do it? Why, NO." On this basis a very telling argument could be constructed by a theologically-minded fly, which no doubt the other flies would find most convincing.

Moreover, it is only when we think abstractly that we have such a high opinion of man. Of men in the concrete, most of us think the vast majority very bad. Civilized states spend more than half their revenue on killing each other's citizens. Consider the long history of the activities inspired by moral fervor: human sacrifices, persecutions of heretics, witch-hunts, pogroms leading up to wholesale extermination by poison gases, which one at least of Dr. Barnes's episcopal colleagues must be supposed to favor, since he holds pacifism to be un-Christian. Are these abominations, and the ethical doctrines by which they are prompted, really evidence of an intelligent creator? And can we really wish that the men who practiced them should live forever? The world in which we live can be understood as a result of muddle and accident; but if it is the outcome of deliberate purpose, the purpose must have been that of a fiend. For my part, I find accident a less painful and more plausible hypothesis.

A DEFENSE OF LIFE AFTER DEATH (1963/1973)

John Hick

John Hick (1922–2012) was born in Scarborough, England, to a work-ing middle-class family. As his early schooling at a local preparatory school did not go well, he was briefly tutored at home and then spent two good years at Bootham, a Quaker boarding school in York. By age 17, he was reading Western philosophy, particularly Kant. After graduat-ing, he began work at his father's small law firm and commuted twice a week to University College, Hull, to study law. His was not a particu-larly religious family, and he leaned toward the anti-Christian views of writers like George Bernard Shaw, H. G. Wells, and Bertrand Russell until, while riding a bus at Hull, he had a religious experience/conver-sion and decided to study for the ministry at the University of Edinburgh, Scotland. His philosophy professor there was Norman Kemp Smith. After an interruption for conscientious-objector service with a Friends Ambu-lance Unit in Egypt, Italy, and Greece in WWII, he graduated in 1948. He completed the D. Phil degree at Oriel College, Oxford, in 1950, where-upon he attended Westminster College, Cambridge, to study for the Pres-byterian ministry. Upon graduation, he took a small church in Belford, Northumberland, but soon left to join Max Black, Norman Malcolm, and John Rawls (among others) on the faculty at Cornell (Ithaca, NY). There, he published an elaborated version of his doctoral thesis under the title Faith and Knowledge (1957). Hick stayed at Cornell for three and a half years. He left to take the Stuart chair of Christian philosophy at Princeton Theological Seminary. While at Princeton, he caused quite a stir when he suggested that several points in the Westminster Confession of 1647 were open to question and declined to affirm the virgin birth. In 1961, Hick received fellowships, which took him to Caius College, Cambridge, where he wrote his second book, Evil and the God of Love (1966). After another semester at Princeton, Hick accepted a position at Cambridge. Three years later, he was appointed to the H. G. Wood chair of philosophy of religion at Birmingham. In Birmingham, he worked with groups from multiple faiths to improve race relations in the city. This experience led him toward a pluralistic perspective on religion. Visits to India to study Hinduism and Sikhism (and to Sri Lanka to study Buddhism) led to publication of Death and Eternal Life (1976). An edited work, The Myth of God Incarnate (1977), sparked much controversy. In 1978, Hick became Danforth Professor of Philosophy of Religion at the Claremont Graduate University in California. His 1986–1987 Gifford lectures (published in 1989 as An Interpretation of Religion) led to the Grawemeyer Award in 1991 from the University of Louisville and the Louisville Presbyterian Theological Seminary for Religion (1991). At age 70, Hick returned to Birmingham as a Fellow of its Institute for Advanced Research in Arts and Social Sciences. In retirement, he published a number of books, including The New Frontier of Religion and Science: Religion, Neuroscience and the Transcendent (2006), Who or What Is God? And Other Investigations (2008), and Beyond Faith and Doubt: Dialogues on Religion and Reason (2010). His books have between them been translated into seventeen languages. He received honorary doctorates from Uppsala University and the University of Glasgow. In 2011, the University of Birmingham established the John Hick Centre for Philosophy of Religion and awarded him an honorary doctorate of divinity. He gave his last public speech at the award ceremony.

What to look for: *Where do we get our ideas of body and soul? What issues does this duality raise in the modern mind? How is man seen in the Old Testament? Why is death something fearful? Is Hick correct that we would properly say in each of the three "Smith" cases that the replica is in fact Smith? Is hell compatible with God's existence?*

Some kind of distinction between physical body and immaterial or semi-material soul seems to be as old as human culture; the existence of such a distinction has been indicated by the manner of burial of the earliest human skeletons yet discovered. Anthropologists offer various conjectures about the origin of the distinction: perhaps it was first suggested by memories of dead persons; by dreams of them; by the sight of reflections of oneself in water and on other bright surfaces; or by meditation upon the significance of religious rites which grew up spontaneously in face of the fact of death.

It was Plato, the philosopher who has most deeply and lastingly influenced Western culture, who systematically developed the body-mind dichotomy and first attempted to prove the immortality of the soul.[1]

---

[1]*Phaedo*

"A Defense of Life After Death," by John Hick, from *Philosophy of Religion*. 3rd ed. (Englewood Cliffs, New Jersey: Prentice-Hall, Inc., 1983), 122-132. Used by permission of Pearson Education Inc., New York, New York.

Plato argues that although the body belongs to the sensible world,[2] and shares its changing and impermanent nature, the intellect is related to the unchanging realities of which we are aware when we think not of particular [98] good things but of Goodness itself, not of specific just acts but of Justice itself, and of the other "universals" or eternal Ideas in virtue of which physical things and events have their own specific characteristics. Being related to this higher and abiding realm, rather than to the evanescent world of sense, reason or the soul is immortal. Hence, one who devotes his life to the contemplation of eternal realities rather than to the gratification of the fleeting desires of the body will find at death that whereas his body turns to dust, his soul gravitates to the realm of the unchanging, there to live forever. Plato painted an awe-inspiring picture, of haunting beauty and persuasiveness, which has moved and elevated the minds of men in many different centuries and lands. Nevertheless, it is not today (as it was during the first centuries of the Christian era) the common philosophy of the West; and a demonstration of immortality which presupposes Plato's metaphysical system cannot claim to constitute a proof for the twentieth-century disbeliever.

Plato used the further argument that the only things that can suffer destruction are those that are composite, since to destroy something means to disintegrate it into its constituent parts. All material bodies are composite; the soul, however, is simple and therefore imperishable. This argument was adopted by Aquinas and has become standard in Roman Catholic theology, as in the following passage from the modern Catholic philosopher, Jacques Maritain:

A spiritual soul cannot be corrupted, since it possesses no matter; it cannot be disintegrated, since it has no substantial parts; it cannot lose its individual unity, since it is self-subsisting, nor its internal energy, since it contains within itself all the sources of its energies. The human soul cannot die. Once it exists, it cannot disappear; it will necessarily exist for ever, endure without end. Thus, philosophic reason, put to work by a great metaphysician like Thomas Aquinas, is able to prove the immortality of the human soul in a demonstrative manner.[3]

This type of reasoning has been criticized on several grounds. Kant pointed out that although it is true that a simple substance cannot disintegrate, consciousness may nevertheless cease to exist through the diminution of its intensity to zero.[4] Modern psychology has also questioned the basic premise that the mind is a simple entity. It seems instead to be a structure of only relative

---

[2]The world known to us through our physical senses

[3]Jacques Maritain, *The Range of Reason* (London: Geoffrey Bles Ltd. and New York: Charles Scribner's Sons, 1953), p. 60.

[4]Kant, *Critique of Pure Reason, Transcendental Dialectic,* "Refutation of Mendelessohn's Proof of the Permanence of the Soul."

unity, normally fairly stable and tightly integrated but capable under stress of various degrees of division and dissolution. This comment from psychology makes it clear that the assumption that the soul is a simple substance is not an empirical observation but a metaphysical theory. As such, it cannot provide the basis for a general proof of immortality. [99]

The body-soul distinction, first formulated as a philosophical doctrine in ancient Greece, was baptized into Christianity, ran through the medieval period, and entered the modern world with the public status of a self-evident truth when it was redefined in the seventeenth century by Descartes. Since World War II, however, the Cartesian mind-matter dualism, having been taken for granted for many centuries, has been strongly criticized by philosophers of the contemporary analytical school.[5] It is argued that the words that describe mental characteristics and operations—such as "intelligent," "thoughtful," "carefree," "happy," "calculating" and the like—apply in practice to types of human behavior and to behavioral dispositions. They refer to the empirical individual, the observable human being who is born and grows and acts and feels and dies, and not to the shadowy proceedings of a mysterious "ghost in the machine." Man is thus very much what he appears to be—a creature of flesh and blood, who behaves and is capable of behaving in a characteristic range of ways—rather than a non-physical soul incomprehensibly interacting with a physical body.

As a result of this development much mid-twentieth-century philosophy has come to see man in the way he is seen in the biblical writings, not as an eternal soul temporarily attached to a mortal body, but as a form of finite, mortal, Psychophysical life. Thus, the Old Testament scholar, J. Pedersen, says of the Hebrews that for them "... the body is the soul in its outward form."[6] This way of thinking has led to quite a different conception of death from that found in Plato and the neo-Platonic strand in European thought.

THE RE-CREATION OF THE PSYCHO-PHYSICAL PERSON

Only toward the end of the Old Testament period did after-life beliefs come to have any real importance in Judaism. Previously, Hebrew religious insight had focused so fully upon God's covenant with the nation, as an organism that continued through the centuries while successive generations lived and died, that the thought of a divine purpose for the individual, a purpose that transcended this present life, developed only when the breakdown of the nation as a political entity threw into prominence the individual and the problem of his personal destiny.

---

[5]Gilbert Ryle's *The Concept of Mind* (London: Hutchinson & Co., Ltd, 1949) is a classic statement of this critique.

[6]*Israel* (London: Oxford University Press, 1926), I, 170.

When a positive conviction arose of God's purpose holding the individual in being beyond the crisis of death, this conviction took the non-Platonic form of belief in the resurrection of the body. By the turn of the eras, this had become an article of faith for one Jewish sect, the Pharisees, although it was still rejected as an innovation by the more conservative Sadducees. [100]

The religious difference between the Platonic belief in the immortality of the soul, and the JudaicChristian belief in the resurrection of the body is that the latter postulates a special divine act of recreation. This produces a sense of utter dependence upon God in the hour of death, a feeling that is in accordance with the biblical understanding of man as having been formed out of "the dust of the earth,"[7] a product (as we say today) of the slow evolution of life from its lowly beginnings in the primeval slime. Hence, in the Jewish and Christian conception, death is something real and fearful. It is not thought to be like walking from one room to another, or taking off an old coat and putting on a new one. It means sheer unqualified extinction—passing out from the lighted circle of life into "death's dateless night." Only through the sovereign creative love of God can there be a new existence beyond the grave.

What does "the resurrection of the dead" mean? Saint Paul's discussion provides the basic Christian answer to this question.[8] His conception of the general resurrection (distinguished from the unique resurrection of Jesus) has nothing to do with the resuscitation of corpses in a cemetery. It concerns God's re-creation or reconstitution of the human Psychophysical individual, not as the organism that has died but as a soma pneumatikon, a "spiritual body," inhabiting a spiritual world as the physical body inhabits our present physical world.

A major problem confronting any such doctrine is that of providing criteria of personal identity to link the earthly life and the resurrection life. Paul does not specifically consider this question, but one may, perhaps, develop his thought along lines such as the following.[9]

Suppose, first, that someone—John Smith—living in the USA were suddenly and inexplicably to disappear from before the eyes of his friends, and that at the same moment an exact replica of him were inexplicably to appear in India. The person who appears in India is exactly similar in both physical and mental characteristics to the person who disappeared in America. There is continuity of memory, complete similarity of bodily features including fingerprints, hair and eye coloration, and stomach contents, and also of beliefs, habits, emotions, and mental dispositions. Further, the "John Smith" replica thinks

[7]Genesis, 2:7; Psalm 103:14

[8]I Corinthians 15.

[9]The following paragraphs are adapted, with permission, from a section of my article, "Theology and Verification," published in *Theology Today* (April, 1960) and reprinted in *The Existence of God* (New York: The Macmillan Company, 1964).

of himself as being the John Smith who disappeared in the USA. After all possible tests have been made and have proved positive, the factors leading his friends to accept "John Smith" as John Smith would surely prevail and would cause them to overlook even his mysterious transference from one continent to another, rather than [101] treat "John Smith," with all John Smith's memories and other characteristics, as someone other than John Smith.

Suppose, second, that our John Smith, instead of inexplicably disappearing, dies, but that at the moment of his death a "John Smith" replica, again complete with memories and all other characteristics, appears in India. Even with the corpse on our hands we would, I think, still have to accept this "John Smith" as the John Smith who died. We would have to say that he had been miraculously re-created in another place.

Now suppose, third, that on John Smith's death the "John Smith" replica appears, not in India, but as a resurrection replica in a different world altogether, a resurrection world inhabited only by resurrected persons. This world occupies its own space distinct from that with which we are now familiar. That is to say, an object in the resurrection world is not situated at any distance or in any direction from the objects in our present world, although each object in either world is spatially related to every other object in the same world.

This supposition provides a model by which one may conceive of the divine recreation of the embodied human personality. In this model, the element of the strange and the mysterious has been reduced to a minimum by following the view of some of the early Church Fathers that the resurrection body has the same shape as the physical body,[10] and ignoring Paul's own hint that it may be as unlike the physical body as a full grain of wheat differs from the wheat seed.[11]

What is the basis for this Judaic-Christian belief in the divine re-creation or reconstitution of the human personality after death? There is, of course, an argument from authority, in that life after death is taught throughout the New Testament (although very rarely in the Old Testament). But, more basically, belief in the resurrection arises as a corollary of faith in the sovereign purpose of God, which is not restricted by death and which holds man in being beyond his natural mortality. In the words of Martin Luther, "Anyone with whom God speaks, whether in wrath or in mercy, the same is certainly immortal. The Person of God who speaks, and the Word, show that we are creatures with whom God wills to speak, right into eternity, and in an immortal manner."[12] In a similar vein it is argued that if it be God's plan to create finite persons to exist in fellowship with himself, then it contradicts both his own intention and his love for the creatures made in his image if he allows men to pass out of existence when his purpose for them remains largely unfulfilled.

[10]For example, Irenaeus, *Against Heresies*, Book II, Chap. 34, para. 1.
[11]I Corinthians, 15:37.
[12]Quoted by Emil Brunner, *Dogmatics*, II, 69.

It is this promised fulfillment of God's purpose for man, in which the full possibilities of human nature will be realized, that constitutes the [102] "heaven" symbolized in the New Testament as a joyous banquet in which all and sundry rejoice together.

As we saw when discussing the problem of evil, no theodicy can succeed without drawing into itself this eschatological[13] faith in an eternal, and therefore infinite, good which thus outweighs all the pains and sorrows that have been endured on the way to it. Balancing the idea of heaven in Christian tradition is the idea of hell. This, too, is relevant to the problem of theodicy. For just as the reconciling of God's goodness and power with the fact of evil requires that out of the travail of history there shall come in the end an eternal good for man, so likewise it would seem to preclude man's eternal misery. The only kind of evil that is finally incompatible with God's unlimited power and love would be utterly pointless and wasted suffering, pain which is never redeemed and worked into the fulfilling of God's good purpose. Unending torment would constitute precisely such suffering; for being eternal, it could never lead to a good end beyond itself. Thus, hell as conceived by its enthusiasts, such as Augustine or Calvin, is a major part of the problem of evil! If hell is construed as eternal torment, the theological motive behind the idea is directly at variance with the urge to seek a theodicy. However, it is by no means clear that the doctrine of eternal punishment can claim a secure New Testament basis.[14] If, on the other hand, "hell" means a continuation of the purgatorial suffering often experienced in this life, and leading eventually to the high good of heaven, it no longer stands in conflict with the needs of theodicy. Again, the idea of hell may be deliteralized and valued as a mythos, as a powerful and pregnant symbol of the grave responsibility inherent in man's freedom in relation to his Maker.

---

[13]From the Greek *eschaton*, end.

[14]The Greek word *aionios*, which is used in the New Testament and which is usually translated as "eternal" or "everlasting," can bear either this meaning or the more limited meaning of "for the aeon, or age."

FREE WILL AND DETERMINISM (1952)

W. T. Stace

W(alter) T(erence) Stace, (1886-1967) was born in London, England, into a military family whose service traced back to his great-grandfather at the Battle of Waterloo. When he was a teenager, a religious conversion set him toward a career with the Anglican Church. He attended college in Bath and Edinburgh before settling at Trinity College, Dublin, where he developed an interest in Hegel and systematic philosophy and, in 1908, graduated with a degree in philosophy. Under pressure from his family, he entered the British Civil Service and served in Ceylon (now Sri Lanka) from 1910 to 1932. There, he served as magistrate and judge, became mayor of the capital city, Colombo—Stace Street is named after him— and acquired an interest in Hinduism and Buddhism. He routinely took tea at 6 and read and wrote for a couple of hours before breakfast. This yielded A Critical History of Greek Philosophy (1920), The Philosophy of Hegel (1924), and The Meaning of Beauty. (1929). After 22 years of service, he accepted an offer of early retirement and was appointed to Princeton where, after three years (in 1935), he became Stuart Professor of Philosophy. While at Princeton, he published The Theory of Knowledge and Existence *(1932),* The Concept of Morals *(1937),* Time and Eternity *(1952),* Mysticism and Philosophy *(1960), and a number of scholarly articles. His writing earned him an American Council of Learned Societies award as well as the Reynal and Hitchcock prize. He served as President of the Eastern Division of the American Philosophical Association in 1949-1950. He retired in 1955 and lived in Laguna Beach, California, until his death.*

What to look for: *Why is scientific determinism thought to be a problem for free will? How does one find a correct definition? Are the examples that Stace uses all "correct" usages of the term "free?" What definition* *of "free acts" does Stace arrive at? Does predictability challenge Stace's view? What justifies punishment? How, from Stace's perspective, does freedom actually require determinism?*

[A] GREAT PROBLEM WHICH THE RISE OF SCIENTIFIC naturalism has created for the modern mind concerns the foundations of morality. The old religious foundations have largely crumbled away, and it may well be thought that the edifice built upon them by generations of men is in danger of collapse. A total collapse of moral behavior is, as I pointed out before, very unlikely. For a society in which this occurred could not survive. Nevertheless the danger to moral standards inherent in the virtual disappearance of their old religious foundations is not illusory.

I shall first discuss the problem of free will, for it is certain that if there is no free will there can be no morality. Morality is concerned with what men ought and ought not to do. But if a man has no freedom to choose what he will do, if whatever he does is done under compulsion, then it does not make sense to tell him that he ought not to have done what he did and that he ought to do something different. All moral precepts would in such case be meaningless. Also if he acts always under compulsion, how can he be held morally responsible for his actions? How can he, for example, be punished for what he could not help doing?

It is to be observed that those learned professors of philosophy or psychology who deny the existence of free will do so only in [249] their professional moments and in their studies and lecture rooms. For when it comes to doing anything practical, even of the most trivial kind, they invariably behave as if they and others were free. They inquire from you at dinner whether you will choose this dish or that dish. They will ask a child why he told a lie, and will punish him for not having chosen the way of truthfulness. All of which is inconsistent with a disbelief in free will. This should cause us to suspect that the problem is not a real one; and this, I believe, is the case. The dispute is merely verbal, and is due to nothing but a confusion about the meanings of words. It is what is now fashionably called a semantic problem.

How does a verbal dispute arise? Let us consider a case which, although it is absurd in the sense that no one would ever make the mistake which is involved in it, yet illustrates the principle which we shall have to use in the solution of the problem. Suppose that someone believed that the word "man" means a certain sort of five-legged animal; in short that "five-legged animal" is the correct definition of man. He might then look around the world, and rightly observing that there are no five-legged animals in it, he might proceed

"Free Will and Determinism," by W. T. Stace, from *Religion and the Modern Mind*. (Philadelphia: J. B. Lippincott Co., 1952; renewed 1980 by Blanche Stace). Used by permission of Harper Collins Publishers and Jennifer Stace.

to deny the existence of men. This preposterous conclusion would have been reached because he was using an incorrect definition of "man." All you would have to do to show him his mistake would be to give him the correct definition; or at least to show him that his definition was wrong. Both the problem and its solution would, of course, be entirely verbal. The problem of free will, and its solution, I shall maintain, is verbal in exactly the same way. The problem has been created by the fact that learned men, especially philosophers, have assumed an incorrect definition of free will, and then finding that there is nothing in the world which answers to their definition, have denied its existence. As far as logic is concerned, their conclusion is just as absurd as that of the man who denies the existence of men. The only difference is that the mistake in the latter case is obvious and crude, while the mistake which the deniers of free will have made is rather subtle and difficult to detect.

Throughout the modern period, until quite recently, it was [250] assumed, both by the philosophers who denied free will and by those who defended it, that *determinism is inconsistent with free will*. If a man's actions were wholly determined by chains of causes stretching back into the remote past, so that they could be predicted beforehand by a mind which knew all the causes, it was assumed that they could not in that case be free. This implies that a certain definition of actions done from free will was assumed, namely that they are actions *not* wholly determined by causes or predictable beforehand. Let us shorten this by saying that free will was defined as meaning indeterminism. This is the incorrect definition which has led to the denial of free will. As soon as we see what the true definition is we shall find that the question whether the world is deterministic, as Newtonian science implied, or in a measure indeterministic, as current physics teaches, is wholly irrelevant to the problem.

Of course there is a sense in which one can define a word arbitrarily in any way one pleases. But a definition may nevertheless be called correct or incorrect. It is correct if it accords with a *common usage* of the word defined. It is incorrect if it does not. And if you give an incorrect definition, absurd and untrue results are likely to follow. For instance, there is nothing to prevent you from arbitrarily defining a man as a five-legged animal, but this is incorrect in the sense that it does not accord with the ordinary meaning of the word. Also it has the absurd result of leading to a denial of the existence of men. This shows that *common usage is the criterion for deciding whether a definition is correct or not*. And this is the principle which I shall apply to free will. I shall show that indeterminism is not what is meant by the phrase "free will" *as it is commonly used*. And I shall attempt to discover the correct definition by inquiring how the phrase is used in ordinary conversation.

Here are a few samples of how the phrase might be used in ordinary conversation. It will be noticed that they include cases in which the question whether a man acted with free will is asked in order to determine whether he was morally and legally responsible for his acts. [251]

Jones: I once went without food for a week.
Smith: Did you do that of your own free will?
Jones: No. I did it because I was lost in a desert and could find no food.

But suppose that the man who had fasted was Mahatma Gandhi. The conversation might then have gone:

Gandhi: I once fasted for a week.
Smith: Did you do that of your own free will?
Gandhi: Yes. I did it because I wanted to compel the British Government to give India its independence.

Take another case. Suppose that I had stolen some bread, but that I was as truthful as George Washington: Then, if I were charged with the crime in court, some exchange of the following sort might take place:

Judge: Did you steal the bread of your own free will?
Stace: Yes. I stole it because I was hungry.

Or in different circumstances the conversation might run:

Judge: Did you steal of your own free will?
Stace: No. I stole because my employer threatened to beat me if I did not.

At a recent murder trial in Trenton some of the accused had signed confessions, but afterwards asserted that they had done so under police duress. The following exchange might have occurred:

Judge: Did you sign this confession of your own free will?
Prisoner: No. I signed it because the police beat me up.

Now suppose that a philosopher had been a member of the jury. We could imagine this conversation taking place in the jury room.

Foreman of the Jury: The prisoner says he signed the confession because he was beaten, and not of his own free will. [252]
Philosopher: This is quite irrelevant to the case. There is no such thing as free will.
Foreman: Do you mean to say that it makes no difference whether he signed because his conscience made him want to tell the truth or because he was beaten?
Philosopher: None at all. Whether he was caused to sign by a beating or by some desire of his own—the desire to tell the truth, for example—in either case his signing was causally determined, and therefore in neither case did he act of his own free will. Since there is no such thing as free will, the question whether he signed of his own free will ought not to be discussed by us.

The foreman and the rest of the jury would rightly conclude that the philosopher must be making some mistake. What sort of a mistake could it be? There is only one possible answer. The philosopher must be using the phrase "free will" in some peculiar way of his own which is not the way in which men usually use it when they wish to determine a question of moral responsibility. That is, he must be using an incorrect definition of it as, implying action not determined by causes.

Suppose a man left his office at noon, and were questioned about it. Then we might hear this:

Jones: Did you go out of your own free will?
Smith: Yes. I went out to get my lunch.

But we might hear:

Jones: Did you leave your office of your own free will?
Smith: No. I was forcibly removed by the police.

We have now collected a number of cases of actions which, in the ordinary usage of the English language, would be called cases in which people have acted of their own free will. We should also say in all these cases that they chose to act as they did. We should also say that they could have acted otherwise, if they had chosen. For instance, Mahatma Gandhi was not compelled to fast; he *chose* to do so. He could have eaten if he had wanted to. [253]

When Smith went out to get his lunch, he chose to do so. He could have stayed and done some more work, if he had wanted to. We have also collected a number of cases of the opposite kind. They are cases in which men were not able to exercise their free will. They had no choice. They were compelled to do as they did. The man in the desert did not fast of his own free will. He had no choice in the matter. He was compelled to fast because there was nothing for him to eat. And so with the other cases. It ought to be quite easy, by an inspection of these cases, to tell what we ordinarily mean when we say that a man did or did not exercise free will. We ought therefore to be able to extract from them the proper definition of the term. Let us put the cases in a table:

Free Acts	Unfree Acts
Gandhi fasting because he wanted to free India.	The man fasting in the desert because there was no food.
Stealing bread because one is hungry.	Stealing because one's employer threatened to beat one.
Signing a confession because one wanted to tell the truth.	Signing because the police beat one.
Leaving the office because one wanted one's lunch.	Leaving because forcibly removed.

It is obvious that to find the correct definition of free acts we must discover what characteristic is common to all the acts in the left-hand column, and is, at the same time, absent from all the acts in the right-hand column. This characteristic which all free acts have, and which no unfree acts have, will be the defining characteristic of free will.

Is being uncaused, or not being determined by causes, the characteristic of which we are in search? It cannot be, because although it is true that all the acts in the right-hand column have causes, such as the beating by the police or the absence of food in the desert, so also do the acts in the left-hand column. Mr. Gandhi's fasting was caused by his desire to free India, the man's [254] leaving his office by his hunger, and so on. Moreover there is no reason to doubt that these causes of the free acts were in turn caused by prior conditions, and that these were again the results of causes, and so on back indefinitely into the past. Any physiologist can tell us the causes of hunger. What caused Mr. Gandhi's tremendously powerful desire to free India is no doubt more difficult to discover. But it must have had causes. Some of them may have lain in peculiarities of his glands or brain, others in his past experiences, others in his heredity, others in his education. Defenders of free will have usually tended to deny such facts. But to do so is plainly a case of special pleading, which is unsupported by any scrap of evidence. The only reasonable view is that all human actions, both those which are freely done and those which are not, are either wholly determined by causes, or at least as much determined as other events in nature. It may be true, as the physicists tell us, that nature is not as deterministic as was once thought. But whatever degree of determinism prevails in the world, human actions appear to be as much determined as anything else. And if this is so, it cannot be the case that what distinguishes actions freely chosen from those which are not free is that the latter are determined by causes while the former are not. Therefore, being uncaused or being undetermined by causes, must be an incorrect definition of free will.

What, then, is the difference between acts which are freely done and those which are not? What is the characteristic which is present to all the acts in the left-hand column and absent from all those in the right-hand column? Is it not obvious that, although both sets of actions have causes, the causes of those in the left-hand column are *of a different kind* from the causes of those in the right-hand column? The free acts are all caused by desires, or motives, or by some sort of internal psychological states of the agent's mind. The unfree acts, on the other hand, are all caused by physical forces or physical conditions, outside the agent. Police arrest means physical force exerted from the outside; the absence of food in the desert is a physical condition of the outside world. We may therefore frame the following rough definitions. *Acts* [255] *freely done are those whose immediate causes are psychological states in the agent. Acts not freely done are those whose immediate causes are states of affairs external to the agent.*

It is plain that if we define free will in this way, then free will certainly exists, and the philosopher's denial of its existence is seen to be what it is—nonsense. For it is obvious that all those actions of men which we should ordinarily attribute to the exercise of their free will, or of which we should say that they freely chose to do them, are in fact actions which have been caused by their own desires, wishes, thoughts, emotions, impulses, or other psychological states.

In applying our definition we shall find that it usually works well, but that there are some puzzling cases which it does not seem exactly to fit. These puzzles can always be solved by paying careful attention to the ways in which words are used, and remembering that they are not always used consistently. I have space for only one example. Suppose that a thug threatens to shoot you unless you give him your wallet, and suppose that you do so. Do you, in giving him your wallet, do so of your own free will or not? If we apply our definition, we find that you acted freely, since the immediate cause of the action was not an actual outside force but the fear of death, which is a psychological cause. Most people, however, would say that you did not act of your own free will but under compulsion. Does this show that our definition is wrong? I do not think so. Aristotle, who gave a solution of the problem of free will substantially the same as ours (though he did not use the term "free will") admitted that there are what he called "mixed" or borderline cases in which it is difficult to know whether we ought to call the acts free or compelled. In the case under discussion, though no actual force was used, the gun at your forehead so nearly approximated to actual force that we tend to say the case was one of compulsion. It is a borderline case.

Here is what may seem like another kind of puzzle. According to our view an action may be free though it could have been predicted beforehand with certainty. But suppose you told a lie, and it was certain beforehand that you would tell it. How could [256] one then say, "You could have told the truth"? The answer is that it is perfectly true that you could have told the truth if you had wanted to. In fact you would have done so, for in that case the causes producing your action, namely your desires, would have been different, and would therefore have produced different effects. It is a delusion that predictability and free will are incompatible. This agrees with common sense. For if, knowing your character, I predict that you will act honorably, no one would say when you do act honorably, that this shows you did not do so of your own free will.

Since free will is a condition of moral responsibility, we must be sure that our theory of free will gives a sufficient basis for it. To be held morally responsible for one's actions means that one may be justly punished or rewarded, blamed or praised, for them. But it is not just to punish a man for what he cannot help doing. How can it be just to punish him for an action which it was certain beforehand that he would do? We have not attempted to decide whether, as a matter of fact, all events, including human actions, are completely determined. For that question is irrelevant to the problem of free will. But if we assume for the purposes of argument that complete determinism is true, but that we are nevertheless free, it may then be asked whether such a deterministic free will is compatible with moral responsibility. For it may seem unjust to punish a man for an action which it could have been predicted with certainty beforehand that he would do.

But that determinism is incompatible with moral responsibility is as much a delusion as that it is incompatible with free will. You do not excuse a man for doing a wrong act because, knowing his character, you felt certain beforehand that he would do it. Nor do you deprive a man of a reward or prize because, knowing his goodness or his capabilities, you felt certain beforehand that he would win it.

Volumes have been written on the justification of punishment.

But so far as it affects the question of free will, the essential principles involved are quite simple. The punishment of a man for doing a wrong act is justified, either on the ground that it will [257] correct his own character, or that it will deter other people from doing similar acts. The instrument of punishment has been in the past, and no doubt still is, often unwisely used; so that it may often have done more harm than good. But that is not relevant to our present problem. Punishment, if and when it is justified, is justified only on one or both of the grounds just mentioned. The question then is how, if we assume determinism, punishment can correct character or deter people from evil actions.

Suppose that your child develops a habit of telling lies. You give him a mild beating. Why? Because you believe that his personality is such that the usual motives for telling the truth do not cause him to do so. You therefore supply the missing cause, or motive, in the shape of pain and the fear of future pain if he repeats his untruthful behavior. And you hope that a few treatments of this kind will condition him to the habit of truth-telling, so that he will come to tell the truth without the infliction of pain. You assume that his actions are determined by causes, but that the usual causes of truth-telling do not in him produce their usual effects. You therefore supply him with an artificially injected motive, pain and fear, which you think will in the future cause him to speak truthfully.

The principle is exactly the same where you hope, by punishing one man, to deter others from wrong actions. You believe that the fear of punishment will cause those who might otherwise do evil to do well.

We act on the same principle with non-human, and even with inanimate, things, if they do not behave in the way we think they ought to behave. The rose bushes in the garden produce only small and poor blooms, whereas we want large and rich ones. We supply a cause which will produce large blooms, namely fertilizer. Our automobile does not go properly. We supply a cause which will make it go better, namely oil in the works. The punishment for the man, the fertilizer for the plant, and the oil for the car, are all justified by the same principle and in the same way. The only difference is that different kinds of things require different kinds of causes to make them do what they should. Pain may be the [258] appropriate remedy to apply, in certain cases, to human beings, and oil to the machine. It is, of course, of no use to inject motor oil into the boy or to beat the machine.

Thus we see that moral responsibility is not only consistent with determinism, but requires it. The assumption on which punishment is based is that human behavior is causally determined. If pain could not be a cause of truth-telling there would be no justification at all for punishing lies. If human actions and volitions were uncaused, it would be useless either to punish or reward, or indeed to do anything else to correct people's bad behavior. For nothing that you could do would in any way influence them. Thus moral responsibility would entirely disappear. If there were no determinism of human beings at all, their actions would be completely unpredictable and capricious, and therefore irresponsible. And this is in itself a strong argument against the common view of philosophers that free will means being undetermined by causes.

ARE WE REALLY FREE? (1950)

John Hospers

John Hospers (1918–2011) was born in Pella, Iowa, into a family that held to its Dutch-speaking heritage at home. He attended public schools and graduated from Central College in 1939. As a freshman at Central, he took an astronomy class taught by the college dean who soon realized that Hospers knew more about the subject than he did and had Hospers take over the class. The thrill of teaching stayed with him the rest of his life. Hospers earned a masters in literature at the University of Iowa in 1941 and a doctorate in philosophy at Columbia in 1944. Early in his career, he taught philosophy at Columbia, the University of North Carolina, the University of Minnesota, Cal State Los Angeles, and Brooklyn College. At Brooklyn, in 1960, he met Ayn Rand, and they became close friends. In 1968, Hospers was appointed chair of the philosophy department at the University of Southern California, a position he held until retirement. Hospers was editor of The Personalist (1968–1982) and The Monist (1982–1992) and was a senior editor at Liberty magazine. He published roughly 150 articles and several books, including Meaning and Truth in the Arts (1946), Introductory Readings in Aesthetics (1969), Artistic Expression (1971), Libertarianism—A Political Philosophy for Tomorrow (1971), Understanding the Arts (1982), Law and the Market (1985), Human Conduct (3rd edition, 1995), and An Introduction to Philosophical Analysis (4th edition, 1996). Libertarianism, the first full-length study of the modern libertarian philosophy, was influential in the founding of the Libertarian Party and led to his nomination in 1972 as its first presidential candidate. The ticket made the ballot in only two states and received just 3,674 popular votes, but it made history when a Nixon elector switched his vote to Hospers and vice-presidential candidate, Tonie Nathan, making Nathan the first woman to receive an electoral vote in a US presidential election. In 1974, Hospers ran (unsuccessfully) as the Libertarian candidate for governor of California. Hospers was always an extremely popular teacher, but he was forced to give that up when he reached compulsory retirement age at USC in 1988. Of course, USC could not force him to give up reading and writing philosophy, which he continued to do throughout his remaining 23 years.

What to look for: Hospers' opening discussion should remind us of Stace. As you work through the article, notice where the two would agree and where they differ. Why is identifying a voluntary act with a free act problematic? What are some cases where most people would agree that they are not "masters of their fate?" At what age is one's personality-structure inelastic? How does Hospers explain the male attitude toward women? If Hospers were to use Stace's terminology, would he say that the unconscious mind is an internal or an external cause? Can a term be used significantly if it has no significant opposite? To what degree, according to Hospers, are we free?

It has become customary in philosophy to treat the free-will issue as "simply a matter of words," as "a mere verbal dispute." . . . If we say, "It all depends on what you mean by the word 'free,'" "we might first proceed to inquire of various persons what they meant by the word. But if we did this, we would soon find. . . that they had no clear idea in mind at all, that they could not say what they did mean by it. Most people, confronted by the question "What do you mean by 'free' when you say that we are free?" could only sputter, "I mean— well, I mean that we're free, that's all!"

This brings us at once to a problem of a general nature which we may well pause over before coming to our specific issue. It is a commonplace of semantics that meanings are not intrinsic to words or sentences, but that they are *given* meaning by the users of language. Meanings, that is to say, are not inherent but conferred. . . Thus, we come to say in some specific dispute, it's not quite accurate to say that it's a question of what the words mean, rather it's a question of what we mean by the words. . . However, one thing is surely evident: if we are interested not in conferring some arbitrary meaning on the word "free," but want to get at some analysis which, as we say, "really tells us what people in ordinary life mean when they use the word," then it is a genuine obstacle to discover that people as a whole cannot explicate their meaning because they have no "clear and distinct idea" in their minds at all in employing words such as this . . . A good motto is, "If you want to know what a person means by a word or sentence, don't ask him watch him use it for a while; see when he applies the word and when he doesn't." . . . If we know in what situations people are willing to use the word and in what situations they are not, shall we not have a much better idea what they "mean" by it?

But the moment we have embarked on this enterprise we shall find that not all persons are in agreement in the criteria thus revealed. There are certain

"Free Will and Psychoanalysis," by John Hospers, from "Meaning and Free Will." *Philosophy and Phenomenological Research*, 10.3 (March 1950), 307-330. Used by permission of Blackwell Publishing, Ltd.

fundamental similarities in the way people use the word, but certainly no identity. . . . Hence, philosophers who want to use the term "free" precisely without doing any great violence to "the sort of thing that most people most of the time mean when they use the word"—or perhaps what they could be interpreted to mean, judging by their verbal behavior—have suggested varying but overlapping criteria . . .

Perhaps the most obvious conception of freedom is this: an act is free if and only if it is a voluntary act. A response that occurs spontaneously, not as a result of your willing it, such as a reflex action, is not a free act . . . As it stands, of course, it is ambiguous: does "voluntary" entail "premeditated?" are acts we perform semi-automatically through habit to be called free acts? To what extent is a conscious decision to act required for the act to be classified as voluntary? What of sudden outbursts of feeling? They are hardly premeditated or decided upon, yet they may have their origin in the presence or absence of habit-patterns due to self-discipline which may have been consciously decided upon. Clearly the view needs to be refined.

Now, however we may come to define "voluntary," it is perfectly possible to maintain that all voluntary acts are free acts and vice versa. . . But it soon becomes apparent [314] that this is not the meaning which most of us want to give it: for there are classes of actions which we want to refrain from calling "free" even though they are voluntary. . .

When a man tells a state secret under torture, he does choose voluntarily between telling and enduring more torture; and when he submits to a bandit's command at the point of a gun, he voluntarily chooses to submit rather than to be shot. And still such actions would not generally be called free; it is clear that they are performed under compulsion. Voluntary acts performed under compulsion would not be called free; and the cruder view is to this extent amended.

For some persons, this is as far as we need to go. Schlick, for example, says that the free-will issue is the scandal of philosophy and nothing but so much wasted ink and paper, because the whole controversy is nothing but an inexcusable confusion between compulsion and universal causality.[1] . . . The free act is the uncompelled act, says Schlick, and controversies about causality and determinism have nothing to do with the case. When one asks whether an act done of necessity is free, the question is ambiguous: if "of necessity" means "by compulsion," then the answer is no; if, on the other hand, "of necessity" is a way of referring to "causal uniformity" in nature—the sense in which we may misleadingly speak of the laws of nature as "necessary" simply because there are no exceptions to them then the answer is clearly yes; every act is an instance of some causal law (uniformity) or other, but this has nothing to do with its being free in the sense of uncompelled.

---

[1] Moritz Schlick, *The Problems of Ethics*, Chapter VII.

For Schlick, this is the end of the matter. Any attempt to discuss the matter further simply betrays a failure to perceive the clarifying distinctions that Schlick has made.

> Freedom means the opposite of compulsion; a man is *free* if he does not act under *compulsion*, and he is compelled or unfree when he is hindered from without in the realization of his natural desires. Hence he is unfree when he is locked up, or chained, or when someone forces him at the point of a gun to do what otherwise he would not do. This is quite clear, and everyone will admit that the everyday or legal notion of the lack of freedom is thus correctly interpreted, and that a man will be considered quite free if no such external compulsion is exerted upon him.[2]

This all seems clear enough. And yet if we ask whether it ends the matter, whether it states what we "really mean" by "free," many of us will [315] feel qualms. We remember statements about human beings being pawns of their environment, victims of conditions beyond their control, the result of causal influences stemming from parents, etc., and we think, "Still, are we really free?" We do not want to say that the uniformity of nature itself binds us or renders us unfree; yet is there not something in what generations of wise men have said about man being fettered? Is there not something too facile, too sleight-of-hand, in Schlick's cutting of the Gordian knot?

It will be noticed that we have slipped from talking about acts as being free into talking about human beings as free . . . If it is we and not our acts that are to be called free, the most obvious reflection to make is that we are free to do some things and not free to do other things; we are free to lift our hands but not free to lift the moon. We cannot simply call ourselves free or unfree *in toto*; we must say at best that we are free in respect of certain actions only. G. E. Moore states the criterion as follows: we are free to do an act if we can do it if we want to; that which we can do if we want to is what we are free to do.[3] Some things certain people are free to do while others are not: most of us are free to move our legs, but paralytics are not; some of us are free to concentrate on philosophical reading matter for three hours at a stretch while others are not. In general, we could relate the two approaches by saying that a *person* is free *in respect of* a given action if he can do it if he wants to, and in this case his act is free.

Moore himself, however, has reservations that Schlick has not. He adds that there is a sense of "free" which fulfills the criterion he has just set forth;

---

[2] *Ibid.*, p. 150.
[3] G. E. Moore, *Ethics*, p. 205.

but that there may be *another* sense in which man cannot be said to be free in all the situations in which he could rightly be said to be so in the first sense . . .

In practice most of us would not call free many persons who behave voluntarily and even with calculation aforethought, and under no compulsion either of any obvious sort. A metropolitan newspaper headlines an article with the words "Boy Killer Is Doomed Long before He Is Born,"[4] and then goes on to describe how a twelve-year-old boy has just been sentenced to thirty years in Sing Sing for the murder of a girl; his [316] family background includes records of drunkenness, divorce, social maladjustment, epilepsy, and paresis. He early displays a tendency to sadistic activity to hide an underlying masochism and "prove that he's a man"; being coddled by his mother only worsens this tendency, until, spurned by a girl in his attempt on her, he kills her not simply in a fit of anger, but calculatingly, deliberately. Is he free in respect of his criminal act, or for that matter in most of the acts of his life? Surely to ask this question is to answer it in the negative. Perhaps I have taken an extreme case; but it is only to show the superficiality of the Schlick analysis the more clearly. Though not everyone has criminotic tendencies, everyone has been molded by influences which in large measure at least determine his present behavior; he is literally the product of these influences, stemming from periods prior to his "years of discretion," giving him a host of character traits that he cannot change now even if he would. So obviously does what a man is depend upon how a man comes to be, that it is small wonder that philosophers and sages have considered man far indeed from being the master of his fate. It is not as if man's will were standing high and serene above the flux of events that have molded him; it is itself caught up in this flux, itself carried along on the current. An act is free when it is determined by the man's character, say moralists; but when there was nothing the man could do to shape his character, and even the degree of will power available to him in shaping his habits and disciplining himself to overcome the influence of his early environment is a factor over which he has no control, what are we to say of this kind of "freedom?" Is it not rather like the freedom of the machine to stamp labels on cans when it has been devised for just that purpose? Some machines can do so more efficiently than others, but only because they have been better constructed.

It is not my purpose here to establish this thesis in general, but only in one specific respect which has received comparatively little attention, namely, the field referred to by psychiatrists as that of unconscious motivation. In what follows I shall restrict my attention to it because it illustrates as clearly as anything the points I wish to make.

---

[4] *New York Post*, Tuesday, May 18, 1948, p. 4.

Let me try to summarize very briefly the psychoanalytic doctrine on this point.[5] The conscious life of the human being, including the conscious [317] decisions and volitions, is merely a mouthpiece for the unconscious not directly for the enactment of unconscious drives, but of the compromise between unconscious drives and unconscious reproaches. There is a Big Three behind the scenes which the automaton called the conscious personality carries out: the id, an "eternal gimme," presents its wish and demands its immediate satisfaction; the super-ego says no to the wish immediately upon presentation, and the unconscious ego, the mediator between the two, tries to keep peace by means of compromise.[6]

To go into examples of the functioning of these three "bosses" would be endless; psychoanalytic case books supply hundreds of them. The important point for us to see in the present context is that it is the unconscious that determines what the conscious impulse and the conscious action shall be.[7] . . .

We have always been conscious of the fact that we are not masters of our fate in every respect—that there are many things which we cannot do, that nature is more powerful than we are, that we cannot disobey laws without danger of reprisals, etc. Lately we have become more conscious, too, though novelists and dramatists have always been fairly conscious of it, that we are not free with respect to the emotions that we feel—whom we love or hate, what types we admire, and the like. More lately still we have been reminded that there are unconscious motivations for our basic attractions and repulsions, our compulsive actions or inabilities to act. But what is not welcome news is that our very acts of volition, and the [318] entire train of deliberations leading up to them, are but facades for the expression of unconscious wishes, or rather, unconscious compromises and defenses.

A man is faced by a choice: shall he kill another person or not? Moralists would say, here is a free choice—the result of deliberation, an action consciously entered into. And yet, though the agent himself does not know it, and has no awareness of the forces that are at work within him, his choice is already determined for him: his conscious will is only an instrument, a slave,

---

[5] I am aware that the theory presented below is not accepted by all practicing psychoanalysts. Many non-Freudians would disagree with the conclusions presented below. But I do not believe that this fact affects my argument, as long as the concept of unconscious motivation is accepted. I am aware, too, that much of the language employed in the following descriptions is animistic and metaphorical; but as long as I am presenting a view I would prefer to "go the whole hog" and present it in its strongest possible light. The theory can in any case be made clearest by the use of such language, just as atomic theory can often be made clearest to students with the use of models.

[6] This view is very clearly developed in Edmund Bergler, *Divorce Won't Help*, especially Chapter I.

[7] See *The Basic Writings of Sigmund Freud*, Modern Library Edition, p. 310. (In *The Interpretation of Dreams*.) Cf. also the essay by Ernest Jones, "A Psycho-analytical Study of Hamlet."

in the hands of a deep unconscious motivation which determines his action. If he has a great deal of what the analyst calls "free-floating guilt," he will not; but if the guilt is such as to demand immediate absorption in the form of self-damaging behavior, this accumulated guilt will have to be discharged in some criminal action. The man himself does not know what the inner clockwork is; he is like the hands on the clock, thinking they move freely over the face of the clock.

A woman has married and divorced several husbands. Now she is faced with a choice for the next marriage: shall she marry Mr. A, or Mr. B, or nobody at all? She may take considerable time to "decide" this question, and her decision may appear as a final triumph of her free will. Let us assume that A is a normal, well-adjusted, kind, and generous man, while B is a leech, an impostor, one who will become entangled constantly in quarrels with her. If she belongs to a certain classifiable psychological type, she will inevitably choose B, and she will do so even if her previous husbands have resembled B, so that, one would think that she "had learned from experience." Consciously, she will of course "give the matter due consideration," etc., etc. To the psychoanalyst all this is irrelevant chaff in the wind only a camouflage for the inner workings about which she knows nothing consciously. If she is of a certain kind of masochistic strain, as exhibited in her previous set of symptoms, she *must* choose B: her super-ego, always out to maximize the torment in the situation, seeing what dazzling possibilities for self-damaging behavior are promised by the choice of B, compels her to make the choice she does, and even to conceal the real basis of the choice behind an elaborate facade of rationalizations .... [319]

A man has wash-compulsion. He must be constantly washing his hands he uses up perhaps 400 towels a day. Asked why he does this, he says, "I need to, my hands are dirty"; and if it is pointed out to him that they are not really dirty, he says "They feel dirty anyway, I feel better when I wash them." So once again he washes them. He "freely decides" every time; he feels that he must wash them, he deliberates for a moment perhaps, but always ends by washing them. What he does not see, of course, is the invisible wires inside him pulling him inevitably to do the thing he does: the infantile id-wish concerns preoccupation with dirt, the super-ego charges him with this, and the terrified ego must respond, "No, I don't like dirt, see how clean I like to be, look how I wash my hands!" Let us see what further "free acts" the same patient engages in (this is an actual case history): he is taken to a concentration camp, and given the worst of treatment by the Nazi guards. In the camp he no longer chooses to be clean, does not even try to be—on the contrary, his choice is now to wallow in filth as much as he can. All he is aware of now is a disinclination to be clean, and every time he must choose he chooses not to be. Behind the scenes, however, another drama is being enacted: the super-ego, perceiving that enough torment is being administered from the outside, can afford to cease pressing its charges in this quarter—the outside world is doing the torturing now, so the super-ego is relieved of the responsibility. Thus the ego is relieved of the agony of constantly making terrified replies [320] in the form of washing to prove that the super-ego is wrong. The defense no longer being needed, the person slides back into what is his natural predilection anyway, for filth. This becomes too much even for the Nazi guards: they take hold of him one day, saying "We'll teach you how to be clean!" drag him into the snow, and pour bucket after bucket of icy water over him until he freezes to death. Such is the end-result of an original id-wish, caught in the machinations of a destroying super-ego.

Let us take, finally, a less colorful, more everyday example. A student at a university, possessing wealth, charm, and all that is usually considered essential to popularity, begins to develop the following personality-pattern: although well taught in the graces of social conversation, he always makes a faux pas somewhere, and always in the worst possible situation; to his friends he makes cutting remarks which hurt deeply—and always apparently aimed in such a way as to hurt the most: a remark that would not hurt A but would hurt B he invariably makes to B rather than to A, and so on. None of this is conscious. Ordinarily he is considerate of people, but he contrives always (unconsciously) to impose on just those friends who would resent it most, and at just the times when he should know that he should not impose: at 3 o'clock in the morning, without forewarning, he phones a friend in a near-by city demanding to stay at his apartment for the weekend; naturally the friend is offended, but the person himself is not aware that he has provoked the grievance ("common sense" suffers a temporary eclipse when the neurotic pattern sets in, and one's intelligence, far from being of help in such a situation, is used in the interest of the neurosis), and when the friend is cool to him the next time they meet, he wonders why and feels unjustly treated. Aggressive behavior on his part invites resentment and aggression in turn, but all that he consciously sees is other's behavior toward him—and he considers himself the innocent victim of an unjustified "persecution."

Each of these choices is, from the moralist's point of view, free: he chose to phone his friend at 3 a.m., he chose to make the cutting remark that he did, etc. What he does not know is that an ineradicable masochistic pattern has set in. His unconscious is far more shrewd and clever than is his conscious intellect; it sees with uncanny accuracy just what kind of behavior will damage him most, and unerringly forces him into that behavior. Consciously, the student "doesn't know why he did it"—he gives different "reasons" at different times, but they are all, once again, rationalizations cloaking the unconscious mechanism which propels him willy-nilly into actions that his "common sense" eschews.

The more of this sort of thing you see, the more you can see what the psychoanalyst means when he talks about "the illusion of free-will." And the more of a psychiatrist you become, the more you are overcome with a [321] sense of what an illusion this precious free-will really is. In some kinds of cases most of us can see it already: it takes no psychiatrist to look at the epileptic and sigh with sadness at the thought that soon this person before you will be as one possessed, not the same thoughtful intelligent person you knew. But people are not aware of this in other contexts, for example when they express surprise at how a person whom they have been so good to could treat them so badly. Let us suppose that you help a person financially or morally or in some other way, so that he is in your debt; suppose further that he is one of the many neurotics who unconsciously identify kindness with weakness and aggression with strength, then he will unconsciously take your kindness to him as weakness and use it as the occasion for enacting some aggression against you. He can't help it, he may regret it himself later; still, he will be driven to do it. If we gain a little knowledge of psychiatry, we can look at him with pity, that a person otherwise so worthy should be so unreliable—but we will exercise realism too and be aware that there are some types of people that you cannot be good to in "free" acts of their conscious volition, they will use your own goodness against you . . .

We talk about free will, and we say, yes, the person is free to do so-and-so if he can do so *if* he wants to—and we forget that his wanting to is itself caught up in the stream of determinism, that unconscious forces drive him into the wanting or not wanting to do the thing in question. The idea of the puppet whose motions are manipulated from behind by invisible wires, or better still, by springs inside, is no mere figure of speech. The analogy is a telling one at almost every point.

And the pity of it is that it all started so early, before we knew what was happening. The personality-structure is inelastic after the age of five, and comparatively so in most cases after the age of three. Whether one acquires a neurosis or not is determined by that age—and just as involuntarily as if it had been a curse of God. If, for example, a masochistic pattern was set up, under pressure of hyper-narcissism combined with real or fancied infantile deprivation, then the masochistic snowball was on its course downhill long before we or anybody else know what was happening, and long before anyone could do anything about it. To speak of human beings as "puppets" in such a context is no mere metaphor, but a stark rendering of a literal fact: only the psychiatrist knows what puppets people [322] really are; and it is no wonder that the protestations of philosophers that "the act which is the result of a volition, a deliberation, a conscious decision, is free" leave these persons, to speak mildly, somewhat cold.

But, one may object, all the states thus far described have been abnormal, neurotic ones. The well-adjusted (normal) person at least is free.

Leaving aside the question of now clearly and on what grounds one can distinguish the neurotic from the normal, let me use an illustration of a proclivity that everyone would call normal, namely, the decision of a man to support his wife and possibly a family, and consider briefly its genesis."[8]

Every baby comes into the world with a full-fledged case of megalomania— interested only in himself, naively assuming that he is the center of the universe and that others are present only to fulfill his wishes, and furious when his own wants are not satisfied immediately no matter for what reason. Gratitude, even for all the time and worry and care expended on him by the mother, is an emotion entirely foreign to the infant, and as he grows older it is inculcated in him only with the greatest difficulty; his natural tendency is to assume that everything that happens to him is due to himself, except for denials and frustrations, which are due to the "cruel, denying" outer world, in particular the mother; and that he owes nothing to anyone, is dependent on no one. This omnipotence-complex, or illusion of non-dependence, has been called the "autarchic fiction." Such a conception of the world is actually fostered in the child by the conduct of adults, who automatically attempt to fulfill the infant's every wish concerning nourishment, sleep, and attention. The child misconceives causality and sees in these wish-fulfillments not the results of maternal kindness and love, but simply the result of his own omnipotence.

This fiction of omnipotence is gradually destroyed by experience, and its destruction is probably the deepest disappointment of the early years of life. First of all, the infant discovers that he is the victim of organic urges and necessities: hunger, defecation, urination. More important, he discovers that the maternal breast, which he has not previously distinguished from his own body (he has not needed to, since it was available when he wanted it), is not a part of himself after all, but of another creature upon whom he is dependent. He is forced to recognize this, e.g., when he wants nourishment and it is at the moment not present; even a small delay is most damaging to the "autarchic fiction." Most painful of all is the experience of weaning, probably the greatest tragedy in every baby's life, when his dependence is most cruelly emphasized; it is a frustrating experience because what he wants is no longer there at all; and if he has been able to some extent to preserve the illusion of non-dependence heretofore, [323] he is not able to do so now—it is plain that the source of his nourishment is not dependent on him, but he on it. The shattering of the autarchic fiction is a great disillusionment to every child, a tremendous blow to his ego which he will, in one way or another, spend the rest of his life trying to repair. How does he do this?

First of all, his reaction to frustration is anger and fury; and he responds by kicking, biting, etc., the only ways he knows. But he is motorically helpless, and these measures are ineffective, and only serve to emphasize his dependence the more. Moreover, against such responses of the child the parental reaction is one of prohibition, generally accompanied by physical force of

---

[8] Edmund Bergler, *The Battle of the Conscience*, Chapter I.

some kind. Generally the child soon learns that this form of rebellion is profit-less, and brings him more harm than good. He wants to respond to frustration with violent aggression, and at the same time learns that he will be punished for such aggression, and that in any case the latter is ineffectual. What face-saving solution does he find? Since he must "face facts," since he must in any case "conform" if he is to have any peace at all, he tries to make it seem as if he himself is the source of the commands and prohibitions: the *external* pro-hibitive force is *internalized*—and here we have the origin of conscience. By making the prohibitive agency seem to come from within himself, the child can "save face"—as if saying, "The prohibition comes from within me, not from outside, so I'm not subservient to external rule, I'm only obeying rules I've set up myself," thus to some extent saving the autarchic fiction, and at the same time avoiding unpleasant consequences directed against himself by complying with parental commands.

Moreover, the boy[9] has unconsciously never forgiven the mother for his dependence on her in early life, for nourishment and all other things. It has upset his illusion of non-dependence. These feelings have been repressed and are not remembered; but they are acted out in later life in many ways—e.g., in the constant deprecation man has for woman's duties such as cooking and housework of all sorts ("All she does is stay home and get together a few meals, and she calls that work"), and especially in the man's identification with the mother in his sex experiences with women. By identifying with someone one cancels out in effect the person with whom he identifies—replacing that person, unconsciously denying his existence, and the man, identifying with his early mother, playing the active role in "giving" to his wife as his mother has "given" to him, is in effect the denial of his mother's existence, a fact which is narcissistically embarrassing to [324] his ego because it is chiefly responsible for shattering his autarchic fiction. . In supporting his wife, he can unconsciously deny that his mother gave to him, and that he was dependent on her giving. Why is it that the husband plays the provider, and wants his wife to be dependent on no one else, although twenty years before he was nothing but a parasitic baby? This is a face-saving device on his part: he can act out the reasoning "See, I'm not the parasitic baby, on the contrary I'm the provider, the giver." His playing the provider is a constant face-saving device, to deny his early dependence which is so embarrassing to his ego. It is no wonder that men generally dislike to be reminded of their babyhood, when they were dependent on woman.

Thus we have here a perfectly normal adult reaction which is uncon-sciously motivated. The man "chooses" to support a family—and his choice is

---

[9]The girl's development after this point is somewhat different. Society demands more aggres-siveness of the adult male, hence there are more super-ego strictures on tendencies toward pas-sivity in the male; accordingly his defenses must be stronger.

as unconsciously motivated as anything could be. (I have described here only the "normal" state of affairs, uncomplicated by the well-nigh infinite number of variations that occur in actual practice.)

Now, what of the notion of responsibility? What happens to it on our analysis?

Let us begin with an example, not a fictitious one. A woman and her two-year-old baby are riding on a train to Montreal in mid-winter. The child is ill. The woman wants badly to get to her destination. She is, unknown to herself, the victim of a neurotic conflict whose nature is irrelevant here except for the fact that it forces her to behave aggressively toward the child, partly to spite her husband whom she despises and who loves the child, but chiefly to ward off super-ego charges of masochistic attachment. Consciously she loves the child, and when she says this she says it, sincerely, but she most behave aggressively toward it nevertheless, just as many children love their mothers but are nasty to them most of the time in neurotic pseudo-aggression. The child becomes more ill as the train approaches Montreal; the heating system of the train is not working, and the conductor advises the woman to get off the train at the next town and get the child to a hospital at once. The woman says no, she must get to Montreal. Shortly afterward, as the child's condition worsens, and the mother does all she can to keep it alive, without, however, leaving the train, for she declares that it is absolutely necessary that she reach her destination. But before she gets there the child is dead. After that, of course, the mother grieves, blames herself, weeps hysterically, and joins the church to gain surcease from the guilt that constantly overwhelms her when she thinks of how her aggressive behavior has killed her child.

Was she responsible for her deed? In ordinary life, after making a mistake, we say, "Chalk it up to experience." Here we say, "Chalk it up to the neurosis." No, she is not responsible. She could not help it if her neurosis forced her to act this way she didn't even know what was going on behind [325] the scenes, she merely acted out the part assigned to her. This is far more true than is generally realized: criminal actions in general are not actions for which their agents are responsible; the agents are passive, not active—they are victims of a neurotic conflict. Their very hyper-activity is unconsciously determined.

To say this is, of course, not to say that we should not punish criminals. Clearly, for our own protection, we must remove them from our midst so that they can no longer molest and endanger organized society. And, of course, if we use the word "responsible" in such a way that justly to hold someone responsible for a deed is by definition identical with being justified in punishing him, then we can and do hold people responsible. But this is like the sense of "free" in which free acts are voluntary ones. It does not go deep enough. In a deeper sense we cannot hold the person responsible: we may hold his neurosis responsible, but he is not responsible for his neurosis, particularly since the age at which its onset was inevitable was an age before he could even speak.

The neurosis is responsible—but isn't the neurosis a part of him? We have been speaking all the time as if the person and his unconscious were two separate beings; but isn't he one personality, including conscious and unconscious departments together?

I do not wish to deny this. But it hardly helps us here; for what people want when they talk about freedom, and what they hold to when they champion it, is the idea that the *conscious* will is the master of their destiny." I am the master of my fate, I am the captain of my soul"—and they surely mean their conscious selves, the self that they can recognize and search and introspect. Between an unconscious that willy-nilly determines your actions, and an external force which pushes you, there is little if anything to choose. The unconscious is just *as if* it were an outside force; and indeed, psychiatrists will assert that the inner Hitler can torment you far more than any external Hitler can. Thus the kind of freedom that people want, the only kind they will settle for, is precisely the kind that psychiatry says that they cannot have.

Heretofore it was pretty generally thought that, while we could not rightly blame a person for the color of his eyes or the morality of his parents, or even for what he did at the age of three, or to a large extent what impulses he had and whom he fell in love with, one *could* do so for other of his adult activities, particularly the acts he performed voluntarily and with premeditation. Later this attitude was shaken. Many voluntary acts came to be recognized, at least in some circles, as compelled by the unconscious. Some philosophers recognized this too—Ayer"[10] talks about the kleptomaniac [326] being unfree, and about a person being unfree when another person exerts a habitual ascendancy over his personality. But this is as far as he goes. The usual examples, such as the kleptomaniac and the schizophrenic, apparently satisfy most philosophers, and with these exceptions removed, the rest of mankind is permitted to wander in the vast and alluring fields of freedom and responsibility. So far, the inroads upon freedom left the vast majority of humanity untouched; they began to hit home when psychiatrists began to realize, though philosophers did not, that the domination of the conscious by the unconscious extended, not merely to a few exceptional individuals, but to all human beings, that the "big three behind the scenes" are not respecters of persons, and dominate us all, even including that *sanctum sanctorum* of freedom, our conscious will. To be sure, the domination in the case of "normal" individuals is somewhat more benevolent than the tyranny and despotism exercised in neurotic cases, and therefore the former have evoked less comment; but the principle remains in all cases the same: the unconscious is the master of every fate and the captain of every soul.

We speak of a machine turning out good products most of the time but every once in a while it turns out a "lemon." We do not, of course, hold the product responsible for this, but the machine, and via the machine, its maker.

---

[10] A. J. Ayer, "Freedom and Necessity," *Polemic* (September-October 1946), pp. 40-43.

Is it silly to extend to inanimate objects the idea of responsibility? Of course. But is it any less silly to employ the notion in speaking of human creatures? Are not the two kinds of cases analogous in countless important ways? Occasionally a child turns out badly too, even when his environment and training are the same as that of his brothers and sisters who turn out "all right." He is the "bad penny." His acts of rebellion against parental discipline in adult life (such as the case of the gambler, already cited) are traceable to early experiences of real or fancied denial of infantile wishes. Sometimes the denial has been real, though many denials are absolutely necessary if the child is to grow up to observe the common decencies of civilized life; sometimes, if the child has an unusual quantity of narcissism, every event that occurs is interpreted by him as a denial of his wishes, and nothing a parent could do, even granting every humanly possible wish, would help. In any event, the later neurosis can be attributed to this. Can the person himself be held responsible? Hardly. If he engages in activities which are a menace to society, he must be put into prison, of course, but responsibility is another matter. The time when the events occurred which rendered his neurotic behavior inevitable was a time long before he was capable of thought and decision. As an adult, he is a victim of a world he never made—only this world is inside him.

What about the children who turn out "all right"? All we can say is that "it's just lucky for them" that what happened to their unfortunate [327] brother didn't happen to them; *through no virtue of their own* they are not doomed to the life of unconscious guilt, expiation, conscious depression, terrified ego-gestures for the appeasement of a tyrannical super-ego that he is. The machine turned them out with a minimum of damage. But if the brother cannot be blamed for his evils, neither can they be praised for their good. It will take society a long time to come round to this attitude. We do not blame people for the color of their eyes, but we have not attained the same attitude toward their socially significant activities.

We all agree that machines turn out "lemons", we all agree that nature turns out misfits in the realm of biology—the blind, the crippled, the diseased; but we hesitate to include the realm of the personality, for here, it seems, is the last retreat of our dignity as human beings. Our ego can endure anything but this; this island at least must remain above the encroaching flood. But may not precisely the same analysis be made here also? Nature turns out psychological "lemons" too, in far greater quantities than any other kind; and indeed all of us are "lemons" in some respect or other, the difference being one of degree. Some of us are lucky enough not to have a gambling-neurosis or criminotic tendencies or masochistic mother-attachment or overdimensional repetition-compulsion to make our lives miserable, but most of our actions, those usually considered the most important, are unconsciously dominated just the same. And, if a neurosis may he likened to a curse of God, let those of us, the elect, who are enabled to enjoy a measure of life's happiness without the hell-fire of neurotic guilt, take this, not as our own achievement, but simply for what it is—a gift of God.

Let us, however, quit metaphysics and put the situation schematically in the form of a deductive argument.

1. An occurrence over which we had no control is something we cannot be held responsible for.

2. Events E, occurring during our babyhood, were events over which we had no control.

3. Therefore events E were events which we cannot be held responsible for.

4. But if there is something we cannot be held responsible for, neither can we be held responsible for something that inevitably results from it.

5. Events E have as inevitable consequence Neurosis N, which in turn has as inevitable consequence Behavior B.

6. Since N is the inevitable consequence of E and B is the inevitable consequence of N, B is the inevitable consequence of E.

7. Hence, not being responsible for E, we cannot be responsible for B. . . . [328]

Our discussion thus far has developed into a kind of double-headed monster. We started to talk about analysis of meaning, and we have ended by taking a journey into the realm of the unconscious. Can we unite the two heads into one, or at least make them look at each other?

I think the second possibility is not a remote one. Surely we have shown that the "meaning of a word" is not the same as "what we had in mind in using the word," and the word "free" is a concrete illustration of this. The psychoanalytic examples we have adduced have (if one was not acquainted with them before) added, so to speak, a new dimension to the term "free." In our ordinary use of this word we probably had nothing in mind as concrete as the sort of thing brought to light in our examples; but now that we have, we hesitate to label many actions as free which previously we had so labeled without hesitation. And we would, I think, call people "free" in far fewer respects than we would have previously.

Can human beings, in the light of psychiatric knowledge, be called "free" in any respect at all? [329]

We must remember that every term that can be significantly used must have a significant opposite. If the opposite cannot significantly be asserted, neither can its original. If the term "unfree" can be significantly used, so can the term "free." Even though there may be no actual denotation of a term naming an opposite, one must know what it would be like—what it would mean to speak of it; even though there are no white crows, it must be significant, as indeed it is, to speak of them. Now is the case of freedom like that of the white crows that don't exist but can be significantly spoken of, or like the black crows that do exist and can be significantly spoken of as well?

Unless "freedom" is taken to mean the same as "lack of cause" and a principle of universal causality is taken for granted, I think the latter must be the case.

If we asked the psychoanalysts for their opinion on this, they would doubtless reply somewhat as follows. They would say that they were not accustomed to using the term "free" at all, but that if they had to suggest a criterion for distinguishing the free from the unfree, they would say that a person's freedom occurs in inverse proportion to his neuroticism; the more he is compelled in his behavior by a *malevolent* unconscious, the less free he is. We speak of degrees of freedom—and the psychologically normal and well-adjusted individual is comparatively the freest, even though most of his behavior is determined by his unconscious.

But suppose it is the determination of his behavior by his unconscious, no matter what kind, that we balk at? We may then say that a man is free only to the extent that his behavior is *not* unconsciously motivated at all. If this be our criterion, most of our behavior could not be called free: everything, including both impulses and volitions, having to do with our basic attitudes toward life, the general tenor of our tastes, whether we become philosophers or artists or business men, our whole affective life including our preferences for blondes or brunettes, active or passive, older or younger, has its inevitable basis in the unconscious. Only those comparatively vanilla-flavored aspects of life—such as our behavior toward people who don't really matter to us—are exempted from this rule.

These, I think, are the two principal criteria for distinguishing freedom from the lack of it which we might set up on the basis of psychoanalytic knowledge. Conceivably we might set up others. In every case, of course, it remains trivially true that "it all depends on how we choose to use the word." The facts are what they are, regardless of how we choose to label them. But if we choose to label facts in a way which is out of accordance with people's deep-seated and traditional methods of labeling them, as we would be doing if we labeled "free" human actions which we know as much [330] about as we now do through modern psychiatry, then we shall only be manipulating words to mislead our fellow creatures.

John Hospers
University of Minnesota

CPSIA information can be obtained
at www.ICGtesting.com
Printed in the USA
LVHW042117290719
625774LV00003B/3